Faith in God Through Jesus Christ

Foundational Theology II

M. John Farrelly, O.S.B.

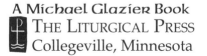

A Michael Glazier Book
THE LITURGICAL PRESS
Collegeville, Minnesota

THEOLOGY AND LIFE SERIES
Volume 38

BX
1753
.F37Ø
1997

A Michael Glazier Book published by The Liturgical Press

Cover design by David Manahan, O.S.B. Head of Christ, detail; Rembrandt (1609–1669)

1   2   3   4   5   6   7   8

Library of Congress Cataloging-in-Publication Data

Farrelly, John, 1927–
      Faith in God through Jesus Christ / M. John Farrelly.
            p.   cm. — (Foundational theology ; 2) Theology and life
      series ; 38)
      Includes bibliographical references and indexes.
      ISBN 0-8146-5859-8
      1. Jesus Christ—Person and offices. 2. Catholic Church—
Doctrines.   3. Theology, Doctrinal.   4. Apologetics—History—20th
century.   I. Title.   II. Series.   III. Series: Farrelly, John,
1927–   Foundational theology ; 2.
      BX1752.F375   1997
      [BX1753]
      230'.2 s—dc21
      [232]   96-36929
                                                                CIP

To
my colleagues and students
at De Sales School of Theology,
past and present, in friendship

Contents

Preface

The present book is a theological study of the meaning and grounds of our Christian faith in God through Jesus Christ. It critically evaluates the Christian Churches'—particularly Vatican II's but also the World Council of Churches'—understanding of faith in God through Jesus Christ, and ways in which they interpret the meaning, value, and foundations of such belief.

This study follows my earlier work *Belief in God in Our Time: Foundational Theology I* and depends on it, though I try to make the present volume stand on its own by the occasional use of summaries from findings mentioned in the first volume, without, however, offering the evidence here for those conclusions.

Many of the disagreements among Christians and, more specifically, theologians on issues raised in this volume depend on their answers to issues addressed in the earlier volume. In that volume we were engaged in a critical evaluation of the Christian Churches' belief in God, that is, of the meaning, importance, and foundations of such belief. We first presented an interpretation of the problem many people have with such belief in the culture of the North Atlantic countries, particularly the United States. With many others, I propose that a central problem with such belief is a widespread modern historical consciousness that is, in practice, largely naturalistic. Modern historical consciousness is the awareness that we live more in the flow of history than in the cycle of nature's seasons, that we are within one culture as distinct from others, and that our future is both of enormous importance and that its outcome is largely dependent on our decisions, individual and communal. Moreover, many people in practice consider that the goals, agents, and resources of history are only those within the human and natural order. This of course erodes faith in God for many Christians.

There are many other Christians who do preserve a strong faith but do so while erecting a previous culture's understanding of this into an absolute, without integrating much of modern science or modern historical consciousness. Many Christian believers find themselves between the siren calls of fundamentalisms and liberalisms. And there are a significant number who have designed their own religions from some syncretism between Christian and Asian or Native American beliefs.

We addressed this problem by first showing that the scriptural understanding of God and belief in God had a very positive relation to people's legitimate concern for their historical future; in fact, this future depended on their faith in God, and faith in God entailed people's responsibility to act for the future of their communities as well as their own. But history has a larger context than simply what is within it because of human transcendence and the God who transcends history.

We also evaluated this human transcendence from the context of modern historical consciousness. We used developmental psychology, for example, that of Erik Erikson and others, to evaluate a classical and specifically Thomistic assertion that to be human is to be oriented toward an infinite good. This reflection, which starts from a contemporary experience, integrates intermediate human goods and history, individual and social, with human transcendence, perhaps better than Thomas' philosophy did. Being comes to human beings in particular historical contexts, and human transcendence to Ultimate Being is similarly through history. We also evaluated a classical affirmation of human cognitive transcendence, the possibility of metaphysics, by the use of contemporary cognitive developmental psychology; we both concurred with classical philosophy and integrated with it dimensions of a later epistemology.

With this background we evaluated intimations of divinity that people of our time have through their experiences of the evolving physical world and of conscience, showing that there are reasons to see these as testimonies God gives to himself and therefore that belief in God is justified. From this, we also defended some characteristics of the Judeo-Christian God, namely, that God is transcendent personal being who is profoundly involved in love with human beings in time. Specifically, a brief dialogue with Hinduism underlines the dynamic immanence of God; this has a great deal to contribute to

correct a Western traditional understanding of God so that it can better answer some very legitimate contemporary concerns of feminism
and ecology without relapsing into a primordialism.

This understanding of the human person and of God has implications for what faith is and should be in our time. We believe God has
made the world and human beings so that they would change through
time in a way related to culture and freedom, has called human beings to be co-creators with him of a historical future that is more humane for all, and does not always intercept the evils that nature or
humans inflict on people but uses even these experiences to call us to
a deeper conversion of living faith, though there is no adequate answer to the mystery of evil outside the death and resurrection of
Jesus. Thus in volume one we sought to evaluate critically and positively belief in God in our period of modern historical consciousness.

In the present volume we seek to evaluate the Churches' understanding of faith in God through Jesus Christ—its meaning, value,
and foundations. In our first chapter we will show what we propose
this task involves. In this preface we simply show some major conclusions we arrive at in this study.

God offers us salvation now through a way he has lovingly and
freely determined. This is through Jesus Christ, who has gone,
through his ministry, death, and resurrection, into the fullness of the
kingdom and who sends his Holy Spirit from that future. The apocalyptic understanding of the kingdom, or salvation, has been hidden
by an excessive influence of Neoplatonism on traditional Catholic
theology; God's economy, or dispensation of salvation, has been interpreted too much on the model of the economy of creation. The
apocalyptic kingdom integrates and subsumes the messianic and
does not discount it; thus faith in God through Jesus Christ entails
our efforts as his disciples to instantiate values of the kingdom here
and now in our individual and social lives. The place of the Spirit in
the salvation offered us has similarly been hidden in the West by a
theology more centered on Christ than on the Trinity, a theology too
enamored by claims to objectivity in the Western scientific and
philosophical tradition.

The revelation God has offered us and continues to offer us
through Jesus Christ and the Spirit does not discount God's earlier
revelations; by a dialogical process it calls us more deeply into his
and our mystery, and by a dialectical moment it liberates us from an
all too constricted view of God and God's loving and free plan of sal-

vation for us. This revelation comes to us now from the future—from Christ who has gone into the fullness of the kingdom. Christ speaks to his bride the Church from there through the gift of the Spirit, who recalls to us what Christ did and said as he walked upon this earth and gives an inner testimony to God's revelation.

True freedom and liberation today is found only in accepting God as the Other he is, who in love freely shows himself to his friends through Jesus Christ and the Holy Spirit. It is only those who are, through God's grace, open to this Other who will find God's way and their way in the midst of the confusion engendered by many who claim to speak for God today. These conclusions depend upon a study of the Gospels that makes use of both historical and literary criticism. We seek to present the Christian message in a way that is appropriately inculturated for our age of historical consciousness, without being controlled by its presuppositions.

This volume—the second part of *Foundational Theology*—is preceded by a volume that treats the meaning and foundations of belief in God. It is to be followed by a concluding volume that evaluates the Christian norm of faith and the nature of theology. This present volume uses the Churches' assertion that Scripture is the norm of faith in that it evaluates how Vatican II's interpretation of the character of the Gospels—and of the nature of salvation and revelation—accords with the New Testament. But we must also face the historical question of Jesus' life, death, and resurrection as we look at objections posed by our culture's interpretations of reason and human good against Scripture's witness. As foundational theology this study does not treat the full Christian perspective on salvation and revelation because it does not treat these themes, except in a passing way, within the context of Christology and trinitarian theology. It seeks simply to fulfill the injunction of Scripture "to give an explanation *[apologia]* to anyone who asks you for a reason for your hope" (1 Pet 3:15).

This is a task very relevant to the faith and identity of the contemporary Christian believer and is undertaken in an ecumenical spirit. I would venture to say that the main issues between Christians and the world that surrounds us, as well as among Christians, are those treated in these first two volumes of *Foundational Theology*. How one interprets the salvation we look for through Jesus Christ depends in large part on what one thinks it means to be human and who one thinks God is. And how one interprets both God and what it means to be human depends on how open one is to the revelation mediated through Jesus and the Spirit. A degree of resolution of these differences is extremely important so that we Christians may present a united witness to God's message of salvation for our world and achieve a greater degree of that unity for which Christ prayed. This resolution depends more on the questions addressed in these volumes than on questions such as that of the authority of the Church. If a number of these issues are resolved, other issues that divide Christians can be addressed more easily.

This study is an introductory one such as would be given—and I have frequently given it—to first-year students in theology. Therefore many themes are treated in a way not as developed as their importance merits, though I refer the reader to books and articles where they are treated more adequately. As will be apparent, I depend on many Scripture scholars, students of the history of Christian theology, and contemporary theologians, without whose work this present volume would not be possible. This dependence makes the present volume a cooperative work, though one for which I must take responsibility.

As in the previous volume, I have sought to write in a way that recognizes that women constitute half of the human race and half of the Church. Because the main symbols for the Holy Spirit are feminine, I use the feminine personal pronoun in reference to the Spirit. The main symbol for the Second Person of the Trinity is masculine, for we believe that the Word became flesh in Jesus Christ. And I have chosen, in accord with Christian tradition, to speak of God generally by way of the masculine pronoun, understanding this to mean grammatical rather than sexual gender. I ask the forbearance of those readers who think this is an inadequate solution today.

My greatest debt of gratitude for what is of worth in this study is to the many scholars and theologians whose works I cite in the pages of this book. I wish also to express my gratitude to Evelyn Thibeaux, member of the Rhetoric and New Testament Section of the Society of Biblical Literature, for reading and critiquing chapters 2 and 3 of this work, and to Mark Whitters, M.A., a doctoral student in biblical studies at The Catholic University of America, for reading and critiquing chapters 2 through 5. They saved me from a number of errors. Those that remain are mine. I also thank Sheila Garcia, Elizabeth Montgomery, my editor at The Liturgical Press, and Paul McKane, O.S.B., who read the complete manuscript and proposed many improvements. I thank my students of many years, from whom I have learned much, and my colleagues at De Sales School of Theology for many favors. And finally, I thank Abbot Aidan Shea, O.S.B., of St. Anselm's Abbey and my brethren for the time I have been allowed to write this book.

I am grateful for permissions received to quote rather extensively from the following works: G. R. Beasley-Murray, *Jesus and the Kingdom of God* (Grand Rapids: Eerdmans, 1986); Peter Gay, *The Enlightenment: The Rise of Modern Paganism* (New York: Norton, 1977); and Bernard McGinn, *The Calabrian Abbot: Joachim of Fiore in the History of Western Thought* (New York: Macmillan, 1985).

M. John Farrelly, O.S.B.
St. Anselm's Abbey
Washington, D.C.
August 28, 1995

Abbreviations

AA	*Apostolicam actuositatem*
ABD	*The Anchor Bible Dictionary*
AG	*Ad gentes*
CBQ	*Catholic Biblical Quarterly*
DFT	*Dictionary of Fundamental Theology*
DS	Denzinger-Schönmetzer, *Enchiridion symbolorum,* 35th edition
DV	*Dei verbum*
GS	*Gaudium et spes*
ITC	International Theological Commission
JAAR	*Journal of the American Academy of Religion*
JBC	*Jerome Biblical Commentary*
JBL	*Journal of Biblical Literature*
LG	*Lumen gentium*
NA	*Nostra aetate*
NDT	*The New Dictionary of Theology*
NJBC	*New Jerome Biblical Commentary*
NRT	*La nouvelle revue théologique*
SC	*Sacrosanctum concilium*
ST	Thomas Aquinas, *Summa theologiae*
TS	*Theological Studies*
UR	*Unitatis redintegratio*
WCC	World Council of Churches

1

Faith in Jesus Christ: The Problematic

What are some central problems people of our time and place have with belief in Jesus Christ as *the* mediator between God and humanity? Here we are concerned with those problems that reflect the tension between Christianity and our contemporary culture rather than those due simply to an individual's experience. We ask this because it is these problems we should address theologically in this work. In the earlier volume I did articulate these problems, though more in relation to belief in God than specifically in reference to belief in Jesus Christ. Presupposing that volume's explanation and defense of belief in God, here we ask for problems that even one who believes in God may have with Christian belief in Jesus Christ, as this is appropriate for foundational theology.

We shall try to identify the problems we treat and the approach we take by (I) sketching a conflict of identities between what the Churches propose for the Christian believer and what many modern people oppose in this, and then identifying some major problems a book such as ours should address, and (II) recalling some diverse twentieth-century theological approaches to mediating Christian belief in our culture, and Vatican II's approach to the question, which we will defend as more integral and accept as our method.

I. A Conflict of Identities and Major Issues

The Christian Churches proclaim their belief in Jesus Christ as our Savior, God's ultimate revelation to us, and as God.[1] Thus they

---

[1] The World Council of Churches (WCC) was formed in 1948, and its member Churches professed their acceptance of Jesus as Savior and as God. See, for example, a statement accepted by

proclaim that human beings are in their deepest identity and dignity oriented toward God; their ultimate and only fulfillment consists in communion with God and with other men and women in God. But human beings are also divided beings, within themselves and from one another, because of the impact of sin upon them—personal, social, and original sin. And they cannot free themselves from sin, the internal and external divisions that afflict them, and the alienation from God and religious ignorance this involves. They need God's loving forgiveness and God's enablement to turn themselves to put God first in their lives.

God freely gives us the gift to liberate us from domination by sin, division, and alienation from God and to enable us to live by our deepest dignity through communion with God and others. He chose to offer us this gift through Jesus Christ living and active in the world today by his word and Spirit—the same Jesus Christ who lived, died, and rose in Palestine some two thousand years ago. Jesus is the way God lovingly and freely chose to give us salvation, and it is through a living belief in him that we gain this salvation. This living belief in him means becoming his disciples through surrendering to him in heart and mind and accepting God's message of salvation through him. God has revealed to us through Jesus Christ that he is the Way God offers us to himself and to a genuine and lasting human community. God has given us both the Spirit to enable us to respond in faith and sufficient reason to believe that Jesus is the one the Churches proclaim. The Gospels proclaim Jesus and do so in genuine honesty to his life, ministry, death, and resurrection; thus we can have access to what God reveals through him. It is only through God's grace that we can respond by faith to God's gift.

This primacy of Jesus Christ and his Spirit is not contradictory to God's using other mediators, as he used Moses, for example, but it

---

the WCC at its first general assembly in Amsterdam in 1948: "We speak, as Christians from many lands and many traditions. . . . God's redeeming activity in the world has been carried out through His calling a People to be His own chosen People. The old covenant was fulfilled in the new when Jesus Christ, the Son of God incarnate, died and was raised from the dead, ascended into heaven and gave the Holy Ghost to dwell in His Body, the Church. It is our common concern for that Church which draws us together, and in that concern we discover our unity in relation to her Lord and Head" (David Gaines, *The World Council of Churches: A Study of Its Background and History* [Peterborough, N.H.: Richard R. Smith, 1966] 277–8). See also P. C. Roger and Lukas Vischer, eds., *The Fourth Conference on Faith and Order: The Report from Montreal* (New York: Association Press, 1964); George H. Tavard, "The Ecumenical Search for Tradition: Thirty Years After the Montreal Statement," *Journal of Ecumenical Studies* 30 (1993) 315–30.

does mean that God's greatest gift of revelation and salvation comes through Jesus Christ, and that other mediators insofar as they come from God lead us to him. Jesus is God's revelation of his way, of his disposition toward us, of himself, and also of the sons and daughters of God we are called to be and can be through the gift of the Spirit.

There are many people in our society who never had this belief in Jesus Christ in their background—Jews and Muslims, for example. These find such belief in Jesus Christ excluded by their own belief in God and his mediators. But there are many more people in our culture who previously accepted such discipleship to Jesus Christ or whose parents or grandparents did and who no longer feel able to do so. Many of these who do not believe in Jesus in the way the Churches call for still acknowledge that they believe in God and that a relation to God is of great importance to their lives; they admire Jesus as a human being of a particular time and place whose message and example still have much to teach us. However, these people feel it is appropriate for them to take what they think true and of value wherever they find it, and the result is in many cases a certain fragmentation of any traditional Christian belief. The faith of many today is a certain pastiche derived from many sources, in which specifically Christian faith as the Churches understand it is not dominant and integrating. We may perhaps give three basic reasons for which people who come from the Christian tradition now build their identities on other foundations—reasons, however, that overlap. In chapter 6 we shall see something of the historical development of these reasons in the modern West.

First, many people as children of the *Enlightenment* hold that we should live by our own knowledge and experience rather than by that which is proposed to us as authoritative because it is a "supernatural revelation." Moreover, they cannot take at face value the miracles and resurrection ascribed to Jesus in the Gospels. The picture of Jesus Christ the Gospels give us does not fit into our current understanding of the world as it did in the world of that time. Many people cannot think that our preeminent knowledge comes to us by way of a supernatural revelation mediated by a man of Palestine two thousand years ago; they hold that we should live not by the norms of tradition but by present experience and knowledge. There is a "scandal of particularity" in Christianity's identification with one person of a particular age of the past. Also, the application of the historical-critical method to the Gospels has shown that there is little we can know of Jesus' life and teaching. There are other ways to interpret the language of the Gospels rather than taking them to be historical documents; they can be understood as a kind of myth, as Rudolf Bultmann has shown.

Second, we are practical people concerned for our future in history; with our *modern historical consciousness* we tend to look more to the future than to the past for answers to our human perplexities and problems. Some people consider this the second stage of modernity and one that poses another difficulty with Christian belief, added to that of the Enlightenment. We should use creatively all the human resources at our disposal to improve life or to bring us forward; but Christianity frequently undervalued human creativity to deal with real human problems and the demands of justice that would shake the social order, as liberation theologians and feminist theologians have documented. The way the modern world has coped gives us some promise, and the way the Churches have at times seriously obstructed modern science and social change makes us wary of their claims for themselves or for Jesus Christ. *Ideology critique,* which was practiced by such philosophers as Feuerbach, Marx, Dewey, Freud, and Nietzsche and which now is widespread in our culture, must be directed at the Churches' view of Jesus Christ and belief. Our problems are human, and we should look for solutions to them that are human rather than to expect revelation and salvation from elsewhere.

Third, our current awareness of the great religions of the world makes the Christian claim to being *the* medium of God's salvation and revelation less plausible; rather, this shows us that Christianity is a specifically Western form of premodern religion. Both a certain cultural relativism that respects the "other" and a pluralism mark contemporary consciousness that some people designate as *postmodernism.* This pluralism is present within Christianity itself, ranging between fundamentalisms in reaction to Modernism and liberalisms in acceptance of it. There are such varied interpretations of who Jesus Christ was and what Christianity is that the specific proclamation of the Churches noted above loses credibility for many Christians. There are forms of Christian belief that have become modern enough for many people to accept without rejecting what they hold to be central criteria for human values and truth widely accepted today.

For many today, priority over what the Churches proclaim as what it means to be Christian should be given to the ways in which we can be in touch with ourselves, our cosmos, and/or the Ultimate; recognition of the New Testament as largely metaphorical is not contradictory to this but rather has much to contribute to it and its healing effect in our lives and world.[2] Giving primacy to Christian revelation seems to these people narrow; this would make us unable to integrate knowledge and practice to which we should be open and which we can discover by personal experience, science, and awareness of different cultures. We can and should borrow selectively from many peoples of the past, but this borrowing should be subsumed into our experience of what deeply fulfills us today. Related to this, Harold Bloom finds that both early American experiential Christianity, for example, at Cane Ridge in 1801, and Ralph Waldo Emerson's trust in his inner experience as coming from the divine within him, to be foundational for a specifically American gnosticism that now affects members of all denominations. He finds this present in many forms, such as in Mormonism and in the most important theologian of the Southern Baptist confession, E. Y. Mullins (d. 1928), who gave "soul competency" as the basis for the legitimacy of each individual's interpretation of Scripture. Bloom recognizes a marked difference between these religious forms and historical Christianity.[3]

What, in view of these difficulties with such belief, are some major issues we should address in our effort to critically evaluate the meaning and grounds of our belief in Jesus Christ as *the* mediator of God's salvation and revelation? These difficulties we mention are not simply

[2]See John Hick and Paul Knitter, eds., *The Myth of Christian Uniqueness* (Maryknoll, N.Y.: Orbis Books, 1987); Gavin D'Costa, ed., *Christian Uniqueness Reconsidered: The Myth of a Pluralistic Theology of Religions* (Maryknoll, N.Y.: Orbis Books, 1990); Peter Phan, ed., *Christianity and the Wider Ecumenism* (New York: Paragon, 1990); Robert Berkey and Sarah Edwards, eds., *Christology in Dialogue,* pt. 3, "Christology in Dialogue with Other Faiths" (Cleveland: The Pilgrim Press, 1993), 183–266. Also see, for example, Charles Davis, *What Is Living, What Is Dead in Christianity: Breaking the Liberal-Conservative Deadlock* (San Francisco: Harper & Row, 1986); James Lewis and J. Gordon Melton, *Perspectives on the New Age* (Albany, N.Y.: SUNY Press, 1992); Michael Fuss, "New Age," René Latourelle and Rino Fisichella, eds., *Dictionary of Fundamental Theology* (New York: Crossroad, 1994) 738–40 (hereafter cited as *DFT*). One recent analysis of the origin of a widespread religious consciousness we are describing is offered by Louis Duprè, *Passage to Modernity: An Essay in the Hermeneutics of Nature and Culture* (New Haven: Yale University Press, 1994).

[3]See Harold Bloom, *The American Religion: The Emergence of the Post-Christian Nation* (New York: Simon & Schuster, 1992) 102–3, 114, passim. For example, see 176–7, where Bloom writes of Pentecostals: "To know that one's own spirit is part of the Holy Spirit, existent before the foundation of the world, is an exhilarating experience. . . . Pentecostalism['s] . . . extreme supernaturalism had to be a reaction against a triumphant naturalism, against a society where power was enshrined in an abundant materialism." For a more balanced evaluation of Pentecostalism and the state of current Catholic-Pentecostal dialogue, see Kilian McDonnell, "The Death of Mythologies: The Classical Pentecostal/Roman Catholic Dialogue," *America* (March 25, 1995). On page 259 Bloom writes: "The God of the American Religion is an experiential God, so radically *within* our

present in those who are not Christian; they affect many of us Christian believers. And in foundational theology we are addressing more the ground and meaning of our own Christian faith in view of present-day difficulties and resources than we are seeking to convert others.

What we offer in reference to our theme in this volume depends on what we offered in our earlier volume. We gave examples of conversion to belief in God and Jesus Christ in twentieth-century people such as Thomas Merton. We sought to critically validate grounds and meaning for the openness of human beings of the twentieth century to God as transcendent personal being who is immanently active in history and nature. We showed, with the help of developmental psychology, that human persons are indeed in search of a value that transcends history and opens to a knowledge beyond the scientific, and specifically a metaphysical knowledge. Further, we gave evidence that there are intimations of God present to human beings through conscience and the evolving physical world that we can validly appropriate; that these prereligious experiences support parts of Scripture's proclamation of God; and that it is reasonable, fulfilling, and liberating for us to respond to God, who manifests himself to us, and to do so by a faith that is a surrender of ourselves to this larger horizon, environment, and self thereby revealed.

There are positive and negative experiences in our lives that corroborate a religious interpretation of ourselves and the world. People of our time are not necessarily locked into an understanding of themselves, their lives, and their world that is restricted to history interpreted naturalistically. When they are so locked in, they are blind to or resisting signals of transcendence within themselves and outside themselves. They are alienated from themselves because they are building up superficial dimensions of the self at the cost of undermining their deeper human identity. We sought to show that there is both a desperate human need and a legitimation for our interpreting and living our individual and social lives within the context of our relation to God and God's relation to us—a relationship that is experientially grounded and symbolically mediated.

own being as to become a virtual identity with what is most authentic (oldest and best) in the self. Much of early Emerson hovers near this vision of God: 'It is by yourself without ambassador that God speaks to you. . . . It is God in you that responds to God without, or affirms his own words trembling on the lips of another.'" See Martin Marty's review of Bloom's book, *The Christian Century* (May 20–7, 1992). Also see Hans Waldenfels, "Christianity in Today's Pluralism," *Theology Digest* 26 (1989) 237–41.

In our earlier volume, then, we systematically and critically validated, in view of modern attacks on this, the centrality of God in our lives and our need for God's help to live in accord with who we most truly are. We are genuinely *encountered* by God. We defended grounds and meaning for our belief in God given that vast numbers of people in our modern world as well as in the past claim in faith that God has encountered them. We sought to defend such belief not simply on objective bases but in the context of our search for value and of the symbols that gave intimations of God, the creative imagination these evoke in those coming to believe, and a critical evaluation of evidence on which their discernment was based. Now we critically and systematically reflect on the meaning and grounds of our acceptance of Jesus in faith as God's definitive salvation and revelation. We ask whether people who claim they are *encountered* by Jesus and the Spirit in essential continuity with Christians of the first century have critical grounds for claiming this, and we do this in view of major current difficulties with such belief.

In this context, then, what are some major issues we should raise in this book? The major questions we should raise are whether we can critically justify this view. That is, can we critically validate the view of many that Jesus Christ, understood as the Churches proclaim him, can encounter them in a way similar to that mediated by the witness of the apostles and, indeed, the witness of Jesus during his ministry? From our position in the late twentieth-century West, from what we know and need, do we need the salvation he offers and can we find sufficient critical reason to believe in him and become his disciples? Or, counter to this, can we of ourselves, without Christ and his Spirit, find meaning in life and put God—and the community our very humanity shows that God asks us to build—first in our lives? What, in the midst of current mutually opposed interpretations, does Christian belief mean?

We should ask, for example, whether the modern critiques of Christianity interpret both Christianity and the human condition correctly. Does the Christian claim that God gave us through Christ a revelation further and more definitive than that mediated by conscience and the cosmos or earlier religions have some historical basis, and is it constrictive or liberating for human beings individually and as a community to accept this tradition? How is the salvation promised us by Christ related to our concerns for our future in history, and do we need such salvation from some source outside ourselves? Is Christian revelation mediated by authority alone or by a kind of experience, and if so should we and how do we allow for the "otherness" of God and his way, and how does this relate to other revelations with which God has graced us?

These questions involve a critical evaluation of the kind of documents the Gospels are and of whether, in proclaiming the good news, they are substantially faithful to what Jesus said and did. Similarly, it calls for a critical evaluation of what Jesus and the early Church meant by the kingdom of God, which is promised to those who believe, and what revelation, the basis on which it is presented to us, is. Also, can the modern person and postmodern person who views the world with modern historical consciousness accept such an offer and such a message while being faithful to himself or herself, the needs of our society, and the best knowledge available to us in our time and place? In fact, can we be faithful to ourselves if we refuse to accept God's offer to us through Jesus Christ when this is presented in a manner both faithful to Scripture and appropriately inculturated in our world? We ask this without prejudice to those who do not believe as we do. As Scripture says, "There is an appointed time for everything, and a time for every affair under the heavens" (Eccl 3:1).

II. Some Twentieth-Century Theological Models for Mediating Belief in Jesus Christ

To identify the theological task of mediating belief in Jesus Christ we should also recall in an ecumenical context varied representative models that have been used for this purpose in our century. We have much to learn from our theological colleagues, and we should give reasons when we differ from them in our methodology. We need not develop this material at length, since we have already outlined and evaluated representative models in our earlier volume; we did so there (in ch. 2) as an introduction to both the first and the second volumes of *Foundational Theology,* and we depend here on that treatment of the issues. We will simply recall some central elements of these models as they are appropriate to the theme of the present volume to show some issues we must face. We will treat pre-Vatican II models, Vatican II's model, and some post-Vatican II models, concluding by indicating what we understand our task to be in this volume of *Foundational Theology.* We do not present our models as adequate interpretations of the theologians we mention but as some *possible basic theological approaches* to disbelief in our time.

1. Pre-Vatican II Models

Before Vatican II the Catholic models for mediating faith in Jesus Christ differed clearly from Protestant models. The Catholic models were more dialogical, while the dominant Protestant model, that of Karl Barth, was dialectical. We can recall something of how these theologians saw the problem and the issues between them by looking briefly at representative Catholic theologians and then at Barth and Bultmann.

The dominant Catholic model at that time was that of Neoscholasticism. In strict continuity with Vatican I and the antimodernist teaching of the Church, the primary thrust of this approach was to show that there are *objective* bases for believing that God revealed himself and his way through Jesus Christ. Dominant modern philosophies held that one cannot prove the existence of God by reason and one cannot know that God revealed through Jesus Christ. In reference to this latter issue, Neoscholastic theologians sought to show that the Gospels were historically credible documents because they were written by witnesses to the life of Jesus Christ or in dependence on such witnesses and were written by men of integrity who did not deceive. Jesus' miracles witnessed to God's testimony to him as God's authorized mediator. Revelation here was primarily understood to be given through the words of Jesus; consequently, at times it is called "propositional revelation." The resurrection is the ultimate miracle that testifies to Jesus. What we receive through belief in Jesus is God's justification and salvation, interpreted in continuity with the Council of Trent's decree on justification, that is, as an intrinsic change in the believer—from being unjust to being just—by sanctifying grace and the theological virtues that make one a child of God and an heir to eternal happiness with him.[4]

Karl Rahner can be taken as a representative of a growing reaction to the Neoscholastic approach to this issue before Vatican II. He reacted against the inadequacy of the intellectualist, extrinsicist, and

---

[4]See René Latourelle, "A New Image of Fundamental Theology," *Problems and Perspectives of Fundamental Theology,* ed. R. Latourelle and Gerald O'Collins (New York: Paulist Press, 1982) 37–41; Francis Schüssler Fiorenza, "Fundamental Theology and the Resurrection of Jesus" (ch. 1), *Foundational Theology* (New York: Crossroad, 1984), where he treats Neoscholastics', Rahner's, and Schillebeeckx's approach to the resurrection of Jesus.

objectivist approach to belief that the Neoscholastic or manualist method manifested. Starting with a revised anthropology, he understood the human person as "Spirit in the World," that is, as a dynamic thrust toward the Absolute, one who knows Being not primarily through the cosmos but through the mediation of the self. God, who wants all to be saved, gives all humans a transcendental revelation of himself through a way correlated with the person's thrust toward and knowledge of Being—a revelation of himself that is nonconceptual, nonobjective, and apophatic.

When one presents to a potential Christian believer what God has revealed historically through Jesus Christ, one needs to present it in relation to the human person's subjectivity, to show him or her its meaning in relation to the person's orientation to the Absolute. The primary way to elicit belief in the resurrection of Jesus is to show that this categorical revelation expresses objectively what the individual already accepts in accepting transcendental revelation, that is, God's offer of a communion with himself not ruptured by death. Belief is available to people who are not able to follow all the technical exegetical problems that beset the issue of the resurrection of Jesus. Jesus and his resurrection are God's revelation of himself as the ultimate *symbol* of God and God's love; revelation does not primarily occur through the words that Jesus speaks. And what we receive through belief is not primarily the created gift of sanctifying grace but God's own self-communication and presence, which in part can be experienced.[5]

One difficulty with the Neoscholastic approach is that it addresses the human being not as a whole person but rather as an intellectual. Rahner corrects this by his emphasis on subjectivity, but he does this somewhat on an existentialist model rather than with a full acknowledgment of modern historical consciousness. His method is liable, in lesser hands, to the danger of making human subjectivity a criterion of God's revelation.

Both of these Catholic models for mediating belief in Jesus Christ are, in spite of their differences, dialogical; that is, they begin by engaging the human person on a human level and seek to induce him or her from common ground to acknowledge positive grounds to come to belief in Jesus Christ. Karl Barth's approach is dialectical.

---

[5]See Fiorenza, *Foundational Theology;* on the contrast between the Neoscholastics' and Rahner's view of grace, see Roger Haight, "Sin and Grace," *Systematic Theology: Roman Catholic Perspectives,* ed. Francis Schüssler Fiorenza and John Galvin (Minneapolis: Fortress Press, 1991), especially his section entitled "Catholic Theology of Grace Today," 2:108ff.

He begins with the revelation God makes through Jesus Christ and rejects the search for some human point of contact by which we first know and thereby see the credibility of God's call to faith. He rejects Protestant liberalism's way of apologetic and Catholic ways, both of which he thinks result in a reductionism that does not allow God to be totally Other. Revelation is, for Barth, God's action through Jesus Christ; other claims to knowledge of God are "religion," or efforts to make God in our human image. God's revelation occurs through the death and resurrection of Jesus Christ, whereby God declares that we are sinners and that through our belief he accepts or justifies us. What is needed is not an apologetic but our acknowledgment that we are sinners and that we are accepted by God. Revelation is through God's Word, to be distinguished from, though mediated by, the human word of Scripture that is fallible. Belief is not dependent upon the changing fashions of Scripture study or the historical-critical method; it is dependent upon the reality of God's revelation through the death and resurrection of Jesus Christ. Barth interprets God's acceptance of us, which we receive through faith, in continuity with the Reformers' interpretation in the sixteenth century; thus his view is also called neo-orthodoxy.[6]

Rudolf Bultmann basically agrees with Barth that revelation is God's action, but he counters that we cannot expect people's acceptance in faith of Christian revelation if we do not relate this proclamation to some *preunderstanding* in the human person in virtue of which it is significant. This preunderstanding is found in the human person's appropriation of his or her search for authenticity and acknowledgment of the obstacles that obstruct this search; this anthropology is articulated, in a way the twentieth-century person can accept, in Heidegger's *Being and Time.* God's revelation is presented to us through the Christian kerygma, or proclamation of God's love for us. It is not mediated by the words and deeds of Jesus himself, which in any case are scarcely accessible to us due to the way the Gospels are modified by the faith and needs of the early Christian Church. Rather, it is mediated by the Christian proclamation itself. Through this we are told of God's love for us and his invitation to us, and through acceptance of this we are enabled truly to live authentically.

[6]See Bruce Marshall, *Christology in Conflict: The Identity of a Saviour in Rahner and Barth* (Oxford: Blackwell, 1987); see also a series of articles evoked by this book in *Toronto Journal of Theology* 10 (1994) 7–52; on Bultmann, see Wm. Thompson, *The Jesus Debate: A Survey and Synthesis* (New York: Paulist Press, 1985) 97f.

This proclamation is made through the use of the story of Jesus; but this story, particularly the account of miracles and the resurrection, must be interpreted as myth. That is, our Christian faith is not dependent upon our acceptance of a historical resurrection from the dead, something we cannot accept today. As Greek myths, for example, that of Prometheus, are to be taken not literally but as objectifications of religious experience, so too the resurrection story is to be taken as a mythical way of expressing the experience of a new life that those who believe in God's love receive. Barth's approach has seemed to many authoritarian and too disconnected from the human, while Bultmann's has appeared reductionistic.

These are major ways in which theologians mediated Christian faith in the first half of this century. One can see in them different suppositions about what modern men and women can accept, how the Gospels are related to the Christian message, what this message is, and what Christian revelation and faith are. We propose that the way of mediating Christian belief implicit in Vatican II is superior to those we have just recalled.

2. A Model for Mediating Christian Faith Implicit in Vatican II

How does the Church give meaning and grounds for our belief in God through Jesus Christ? It is this particularly that we should critically evaluate. Vatican II shows us how the Church proclaims Christ in our time of historical consciousness, and we can find implicit in that proclamation what it proposes as constitutive of this belief and a method for evaluating it. In this it is united to major Christian denominations.

It is central to the Church's belief in Jesus Christ that in our day God *is* offering us salvation and revelation in a definitive way that completes what earlier mediators of salvation and revelation offered and is doing so through Jesus Christ and the Spirit whom he sent. The Church affirms that God communicates to human beings through other means such as world religions, the testimony of the physical world and of conscience, and the signs of the times, but it asserts that God *is now* offering forgiveness of sins, communion with himself, and revelation through a mediator who subsumes all other agencies, namely Jesus Christ and the Spirit he sends. Thus the council fathers make their own in our time what John wrote in the first century: "We proclaim to you the eternal life which was with the Father and was made manifest to us—that which we have seen and heard we proclaim also to you, so that you may have fellowship with us; and our fellowship is with the Father and his Son Jesus Christ" (1 John 1:2-3).[7]

For example, the Church holds that "Christ is always present in his Church, especially in her liturgical celebrations" (The Constitution on the Sacred Liturgy, *SC* 7), to effect the salvation he won for us. This is the Christ who has gone through death and resurrection to his ascension. Thus the council states: "In the earthly liturgy we take part in a foretaste of that heavenly liturgy which is celebrated in the Holy City of Jerusalem toward which we journey as pilgrims, where Christ is sitting at the right hand of God, Minister of the holies and of the true tabernacle" (*SC* 8). This Christ is also acting in the Church's proclamation of his message so that people can believe and share in its works of mercy, and through the Holy Spirit whom he pours out upon human beings to give them faith, hope, and charity: "The Holy Spirit sanctifies the People of God through the ministry and the sacraments. However, for the exercise of the apostolate he gives the faithful special gifts besides (cf. 1 Cor 12:7), 'allotting them to each one as he wills' (1 Cor 12:11)" (Decree on the Apostolate of Lay People, *AA* 3).

Thus the Church proclaims that God *is now* offering us salvation through Jesus Christ and the Spirit and *is now* speaking to us through Jesus Christ and the Spirit. This emphasis could be shown by many texts (see, e.g., Dogmatic Constitution on Divine Revelation, *DV* 21: "In the sacred books the Father who is in heaven comes lovingly to meet his children, and talks with them. . . . 'The Word of God is living and active'" [Heb 4:12]). But what grounds does Vatican II give for the Church's belief to this effect and for the Church's interpretation of what it means to claim that God saves us and reveals to us through Jesus Christ and the Holy Spirit? It is making these assertions through awareness of its identity with that group of followers of Jesus who proclaimed him at Pentecost or after Jesus' death and resurrection, and the fidelity of this group's mission, message, and life to the mission, message, and life of Jesus. So we will briefly recall Vatican II's teaching that through Jesus Christ and the Spirit

---

[7]Vatican II, Dogmatic Constitution on Divine Revelation, prologue *(DV)*. I am using the translation of Vatican II documents in Austin Flannery, ed., *Vatican II: The Conciliar and Post Conciliar Documents* (Collegeville: The Liturgical Press, 1975). I will cite the Vatican documents in the text through abbreviation and "paragraph" number. For commentaries on Vatican II documents see H. Vorgrimler, ed., *Commentary on the Documents of Vatican II*, 5 vols. (New York: Herder & Herder, 1969); on *Dei verbum* see R. Fisichella and R. Latourelle, "Dei Verbum," *DFT,* 214–24.

God has offered and continues to offer us salvation and revelation, and its teaching on the character of the Gospels that give us access to what Jesus said and did in his ministry, and to its deeper meaning.

The Church's way of giving grounds for belief in God through Jesus Christ and its interpretation of this belief differ in part from a number of twentieth-century theologians. We are proposing it as more appropriate to this task today than approaches that bypass these issues, and we will later critically evaluate faith in God through Jesus Christ through critically evaluating what Vatican II claims as the grounds and meaning of Christian faith.

First, we should believe in Jesus Christ because God has freely and lovingly chosen to *save* us through him, and we are all in need of this salvation, even though we may by God's help come to some knowledge of God by other mediations. God has a universal plan for the salvation of humankind, and it

> is not carried out solely in a secret manner, as it were in the minds of men, nor by the efforts, even religious, through which they in many ways seek God in an attempt to touch him and find him, although God is not far from any of us (cf. Acts 17:27); their efforts need to be enlightened and corrected, although in the loving providence of God they may lead one to the true God and be a preparation for the Gospel. However, in order to establish a relationship of peace and communion with himself, and in order to bring about fraternal union among men, and they sinners, God decided to enter into the history of humanity in a new and definitive manner, by sending his Son in human flesh, so that through him he might snatch men from the power of darkness and of Satan (cf. Col 1:13; Acts 10:38) and in him reconcile the world to himself. . . . Jesus Christ was sent into the world as the true Mediator between God and men. (Decree on the Church's Missionary Activity, *AG* 3).

This asserts something about human beings:

> No one is freed from sin by himself or by his own efforts, no one is raised above himself or completely delivered from his own weakness, solitude or slavery; all have need of Christ who is the model, master, liberator, saviour, and giver of life. Even in the secular history of humanity the Gospel has acted as a leaven in the interests of liberty and progress, and it always offers itself as a

leaven with regard to brotherhood, unity and peace. So it is not without reason that Christ is hailed by the faithful as "the hope of nations and their saviour" (*AG* 8).

To effect their deliverance the risen and exalted Christ sent the Holy Spirit "to exercise inwardly his saving influence . . . [although] without doubt, the Holy Spirit was at work in the world before Christ was glorified" (*AG* 4). "Everyone, therefore, ought to be converted to Christ, who is known through the preaching of the Church, and they ought, by baptism, [to] become incorporated into him, and into the Church which is his body" (*AG* 7).

Since Vatican II the Church has insisted in a special way that the redemption wrought by Christ has implications for the transformation of the temporal order for individuals and for societies. In a much quoted statement, the Synod of Bishops in 1971 asserted: "Action on behalf of justice and participation in the transformation of the world fully appear to us as a constitutive dimension of the preaching of the Gospel, or, in other words, of the Church's mission for the redemption of the human race and its liberation from every oppressive situation."[8] Salvation is not simply a matter of the individual's relation to God or Jesus; rather the acceptance of salvation entails a commitment to seek here and now to free people from oppression. The first reason, then, for faith in Jesus Christ is that God has freely chosen to offer us salvation specifically through him.

Second, why should we believe this? Because God has freely and lovingly revealed, and this is what he has revealed: "It has pleased God, in his goodness and wisdom, to reveal himself and to make known the mystery of his will (cf. Eph 1:19). His will was that men should have access to the Father through Christ, the Word made flesh, in the Holy Spirit, and thus become sharers in the divine nature (cf. Eph 2:18; 2 Pet 1:4)" (*DV* 2). What does it mean that God reveals? "The invisible God . . . from the fullness of his love addresses men as his friends . . . and moves among them . . . in order to invite and receive them into his own company" (*DV* 2).

God prepared us in history for his revelation through Jesus Christ by his testimony to himself through creation itself; by his care for all peoples, and thus in part by the religions of the world that "often

---

[8]Synod of Bishops, Second General Assembly (1971), *Justice in the World,* 8. Also see *AA* 5; and the International Theological Commission (hereafter cited as ITC), "Human Development and Christian Salvation," *Origins* 7 (November 3, 1977).

reflect a ray of that truth which enlightens all men" (Declaration of the Relation of the Church to Non-Christian Religions, *NA* 2); and by his special providence for the people of Israel. It is Jesus who "completed and perfected revelation and confirmed it with divine guarantees." He did this by his presence, "by words and works, signs and miracles, but above all by his death and glorious resurrection from the dead, and finally by sending the Spirit of truth. He revealed that God was with us, to deliver us from the darkness of sin and death, and to raise us up to eternal life" (*DV* 4). Jesus Christ is also the perfect revelation of who we are called to be and "the goal of human history." Animated by his Spirit we press on in our journey "toward the consummation of history which fully corresponds to the plan of his [God's] love: 'to unite all things in him. . . ' (Eph 1:10)" (Pastoral Constitution on the Church in the Modern World, *GS* 45).

It is the responsibility of human beings to give "'the obedience of faith' . . . to God as he reveals himself." By faith "man freely commits his entire self to God, making 'the full submission of our intellect and will to God who reveals,' and willingly assenting to the revelation given by him" (*DV* 5). We are not able to respond to God and his revelation by faith save through the grace of God, or the "interior helps of the Holy Spirit, who moves the heart and converts it to God" (*DV* 5). Thus the basis for the Church's call for us to have faith in God through Jesus Christ is God's own revelation. We could of course go further and show the Church's teaching on the relation of this revelation to other truths to which we have access, but we will have occasion to treat this question later.

A *third* basis for the Church's call that we have faith in God through Jesus Christ is its understanding of Scripture and how the Gospels give us access to Jesus Christ. We are not here relying systematically on the belief that Scripture is inspired, but we may note that the Church does not interpret the inerrancy of Scripture in a way that excludes every factual error in science and history (see *DV* 11). Nor are we relying on the Church's belief that there is divine authorship in Scripture as well as human and thus that there may be more meaning in a passage than the human author understood (e.g., in some Old Testament prophecies about the Messiah). What is most relevant to our topic is the council's teaching about the Gospels. It affirms the "historicity" of the Gospels in the sense that they "faithfully hand on what Jesus, the Son of God, while he lived among men, really did and taught for their salvation until the day when he was taken up (cf. Acts 1:1-2)" (*DV* 19). The council recognizes that the apostles preached and the sacred authors wrote of what Jesus said and did "with the fuller understanding which they, instructed by the glorious events of Christ and enlightened by the Spirit of truth," enjoyed after the resurrection and ascension of Christ. It also acknowledges that the authors of the Gospels wrote what had been handed on in the primitive Church (tradition), that they selected some things from this tradition, that they synthesized what they received or explained it "with an eye on the situation of the churches," and presented it in the form of a preaching. But the council affirms that they did this "always in such a fashion that they have told us the honest truth about Jesus" (*DV* 19).

The Gospels give us access, then, not only to what Jesus said and did but to the deeper meaning these words and deeds had. This shows us how, in its presentation of the meaning and grounds for belief in Jesus Christ, the Church relies upon and interprets the Gospels. This is markedly different both from a fundamentalist position, which would not accept modern historical criticism of the Gospels, and from a liberal position, which would present bases for belief in Jesus Christ that do not rely on a genuine historicity of the Gospels or the validity of the evangelists' interpretations of Jesus' acts and words.

By this recall of Vatican II's teaching we can see that its method of giving grounds and meaning for faith in God through Jesus Christ differs in part from the theological methods we earlier indicated. For example, against the Neoscholastics the Church teaches that God reveals through deed as well as word, and it accepts much that modern historical criticism has to offer. It appears also that it makes much more use of Scripture than Rahner does in interpreting Christian salvation and revelation and has an interpretation of salvation more appropriate to our modern historical consciousness than at least the early and rather existentialist Rahner. It does not seek a way of vindicating belief in Jesus Christ, as Barth and Bultmann did, that is safe from the critical-historical method, though it does not restrict what Scripture can affirm to a naturalistic historical consciousness. And against Bultmann, it sees Christian revelation as mediated by Jesus and not simply by the early Christian community. It makes the resurrection of Jesus central to our belief and the grounds of our belief.

In this volume we will critically evaluate the grounds and meaning of faith in God through Jesus Christ through critically evaluating whether the Gospels are the kind of documents Vatican II claims, and whether its interpretation of Christian salvation and revelation accords with these documents and the reality to which they testify. We will evaluate whether its view of the Gospels is correct and, on that basis, whether its interpretation of salvation and revelation is genuinely Christian, taking the New Testament as normative of what is Christian. This will still leave the question of whether we can accept this in our time—a question we will address in later chapters. Can we accept that God encounters us through Jesus Christ and his Spirit as the Churches proclaim? Is there anything central to our modern or postmodern identity counter to our acceptance of such an encounter, or on the contrary, can we acknowledge such an encounter to be a supreme gift, a desperate need, and sufficiently vindicated?

3. Some Post-Vatican II Models for Mediating Faith in Christ

What are *some* post-Vatican II theological models for mediating faith in God through Jesus Christ, and how do they compare to the approach of Vatican II? We reflect on some major issues among these varied models just for the purpose of identifying and giving reasons for the approach we propose in accord with Vatican II. Further analyses of these options can be found elsewhere.

It is very difficult to systematize post-Vatican II models of theological mediations of belief in Jesus Christ. The pluralism of approaches is so great that it almost verges on chaos. But we propose that differences on the following issues are central to this pluralism. There are great differences on how to relate human experience to revelation through Jesus Christ that is claimed to be definitive. Some dispense with much modern experience that initially seems opposed to Christian revelation so they may remain faithful to Christian revelation, though this is interpreted according to some premodern paradigm. Some seem to interpret Christian revelation's understanding of God within a broader view gained from modern science or religious experience. Some interpret God's salvation offered us through Jesus Christ in a very traditional way, seeking to keep it clearly distinguished from what many people today claim they experience—a need to be saved here and now in history—and thus to preserve its transcendence. Others seek to emphasize the implications of Christian salvation for present liberation from evils that oppress people such as poverty, a patriarchal oppression of women, ecological threats, and racism—sometimes to the extent of subordinating their interpretation of Christian salvation to such inner-historical liberations. And in their interpretation of Scriptures, particularly the Gospels, some reject the historical-critical method or literary-critical method for the purpose of keeping faith with the Christian message, while others use these methods but with the result that the Christian message seems to be eroded. Thus the basic conflict of models seems to be between forms of fundamentalism or conservatism and forms of liberalism or Modernism.

In our earlier volume we sought to integrate what some major modern experiences of the world, the human, and God have to contribute to our belief in and understanding of God. We thus sought to respond to both some conservative and some liberal resistances to such integration. We found that implications of these major modern experiences contribute to rather than undercut our Christian understanding of God. In the present work, supposing the earlier volume as our "preunderstanding," we seek to go further and critically evaluate our distinctively Christian faith in Jesus Christ. We will simply note here fundamentalism, certain developments of pre-Vatican II models, and exegetical studies of the Gospels that largely concur with Vatican II's use of them. Then we will examine, though still briefly, some *theoria* and praxis based models and contrasting postmodern and postliberal models.

The fundamentalist option, on which many Christians base their belief in Jesus, is not so much defended theologically as preached and affirmed.[9] It must be taken more seriously today than earlier in the century because very conservative Christian denominations are growing while liberal denominations have suffered erosion. We will take it seriously by being faithful to the constitutive Christian message, though not by discounting modern approaches to exegesis and experiences of the world that affect our belief in God. With Vatican II we hold that Christian faith can integrate all truth. There are certain analogies between Christian fundamentalist reactions to perceived Modernisms and reactions to modernity among some Jews, Muslims, Hindus, and others.[10]

---

[9]See William Dinges, "Fundamentalism," *The New Dictionary of Theology* (hereafter cited as *NDT*), ed. Joseph Komonchak and others (Wilmington, Del.: Michael Glazier, 1987); Hans Küng and Jürgen Moltmann, eds., *Fundamentalism as an Ecumenical Challenge,* Concilium (London: SCM Press, 1992/3).

[10]See, for example, Küng and Moltmann, *Fundamentalism;* Bruce Lawrence, *Defenders of God: The Fundamentalist Revolt Against the Modern Age* (San Francisco: Harper & Row, 1989); Martin Marty and R. Scott Appleby, *The Power and the Glory: The Fundamentalist Challenge to*

We note that there are strong reaffirmations, with some adjustments, of major pre-Vatican II options continuing after Vatican II. For example, Karl Rahner made substantial additions and modifications to his earlier theological work, as did Bernard Lonergan. Eberhard Jüngel continued the basic approach of Karl Barth; Schubert Ogden brought forward the approach of Rudolf Bultmann, as did others.[11]

We note too that there has been an enormous amount of work by New Testament scholars, Protestant and Catholic alike, that manifests an approach to the Gospels with which Vatican II's evaluation of the Gospels coheres, with similar confidence in the unity of the Christ of faith and the Jesus of history. We will use many of these works in our own study of the Gospels. Much of the best in recent research on the Gospels has been made accessible to one who is not a scholar in that field in *The New Jerome Biblical Commentary* and *Harper's Bible Commentary.*[12] Also, many theologians have sought to integrate recent scriptural studies into their Christologies and theologies of Christian revelation while supporting interpretations similar to those of Vatican II. It will be apparent in the course of this work that I have found many of these theologians helpful in my own efforts. Where the present work differs from a number of them is particularly in its effort to integrate within foundational theology a critical evaluation both of our belief in God and in Jesus Christ as *the* mediator between God and us, and in some particular interpretations we make along the way (e.g., the integration of the apocalyptic). It is in the tension between what we understand as the first and second parts of foundational theology that many theological divisions and problems of faith now lie.

In continuity with and dependence on our first volume, though even more briefly than there, we will recall some different methodologies among Christian theologians for theologically mediating be-

---

the Modern World (Boston: Beacon Press, 1992); Gilles Kepel, *The Revenge of God: The Resurgence of Islam, Christianity, and Judaism in the Modern World* (Philadelphia: Pennsylvania State University Press, 1994).

[11]See Karl Rahner, *Foundations of Christian Faith* (New York: Crossroad, 1978); Bernard Lonergan, *Method in Theology* (New York: Herder & Herder, 1972); Eberhard Jüngel, *God as the Mystery of the World* (Grand Rapids: Eerdmans, 1983); Schubert Ogden, *The Point of Christology* (San Francisco: Harper & Row, 1982).

[12]See Raymond Brown, Joseph Fitzmyer, and Roland Murphy, eds., *The New Jerome Biblical Commentary* (Englewood Cliffs, N.J.: Prentice Hall, 1990) (hereafter cited as *NJBC*); James Mays and others, eds., *Harper's Bible Commentary* (San Francisco: Harper & Row, 1988).

lief in God specifically through Jesus Christ—methodologies related
to issues between *theoria* approaches and praxis approaches—and to
some differences among postmodern and postliberal approaches.
Some of these methods are used as ways of addressing questions
such as those raised by economic injustice, feminism, ecology, and
world religions to the adequacy of belief in God through Jesus
Christ. There is overlap among some of these approaches. We suggest that while some of these methods have much to offer, Vatican
II's approach is more integral and thus superior, though it is just the
beginning of addressing some of these issues.

Some theological methods of mediating belief in Jesus Christ depend on objective intellectual grounds, while others depend on the
impact of such belief to transform social, economic, and political
life, and thus liberate people of our time. We can find quite differing
examples for the first of these, the *theoria* approach, in process theologian John Cobb and Wolfhart Pannenberg. In his work on
Christology, Cobb begins with Whitehead's process philosophy. He
understands the Greek notion of "logos" as a principle of order and
then states that in the Christian tradition "'Christ' is therefore a name
for the Logos."[13] He confesses that the Logos is uniquely present in
Jesus, though not in the way Chalcedon stated, and adds that whether
others have participated in the same structure is an open question. He
affirms that "[i]t is my conviction that Jesus brought into being for
those who responded to him a final and unsurpassable structure of
existence. This structure was the solution of the problem posed in the
Jewish structure of existence and in that sense was salvation."[14]

Thus Cobb begins with a philosophy and interprets Jesus more as
a principle within this philosophy than as a historical person; his philosophy controls his view of Jesus. In our earlier volume we differed
in part from process thought in our interpretation of the human person and of God as transcendent personal being. Cobb's approach
does not reflect the Christian view of Jesus Christ expressed by
Vatican II and the World Council of Churches.

Counter to Cobb, Pannenberg begins with Scripture, accepts the
resurrection of Jesus as a historical fact, and accepts revelation as

[13]John Cobb, *Christ in a Pluralistic Age* (Philadelphia: Westminster Press, 1975) 76; see also
Leslie Muray, "Christology in Dialogue with Process Theology," in Berkey and Edwards,
Christology, 282–91.

[14]John Cobb, "A Whiteheadian Christology," *Process Philosophy and Christian Thought,* ed.
Delwin Brown, Ralph James, and Jene Reeves (New York: Bobbs-Merrill, 1971) 398.

conveyed by it. He argues on these grounds that one can reasonably believe in Jesus in the sense of trusting that God will bring about the future proleptically anticipated by the resurrection of Jesus, and that this future is shared even now by us partially through the Spirit and justification, sanctification, and salvation. Pannenberg is more fully in accord with the Christian belief concerning Jesus Christ than Cobb. There is much of value in his theology; for example, his use of apocalyptic to interpret the resurrection of Jesus helps to relate the Christian mystery to modern historical consciousness. However, he does not make a distinction between foundational theology and systematic theology, as I think Vatican II does implicitly, and his analysis of the relation between our natural human knowledge and our knowledge of Christian revelation differs in part from the one I presented in my earlier volume. Also, while I think Pannenberg agrees with Vatican II's methodology in that both make faith in Jesus Christ dependent on one's acceptance of the resurrection as a revelatory and confirmatory act in history, the Church stresses more than Pannenberg that this acceptance depends on one's openness through grace to conversion rather than on a neutral historical search.[15]

Differing examples of a praxis approach can be found in a way parallel to the differences between Cobb and Pannenberg if we compare some American theologians who seem to give pragmatism a precedence over Scripture, and Jürgen Moltmann and some liberation theologians who give Scripture precedence, even to the point of calling into question the reality of human nature or its importance as a Christian ethical norm.

An example of the former is offered by Sallie McFague. She starts from the position that our human "world" has been shown by the Enlightenment and movements like liberation theology to be a constructed world, and hence a relative one. The essential core of Christianity is not an absolute deposit of sacred writings or a particular model or paradigm of the God-human relationship. Rather it is "the

---

[15]See Wolfhart Pannenberg, *Jesus—God and Man* (Philadelphia: Westminster Press, 1968); *Systematic Theology,* vol. 2 (Grand Rapids: Eerdmans, 1994) ch. 11, "The Reconciliation of the World." Also see Stanley Grenz, *Reason for Hope: The Systematic Theology of Wolfhart Pannenberg* (New York: Oxford, 1990) 40–2, where Pannenberg's critics and his responses on this issue are discussed. Also see Grenz, *Reason for Hope,* 17–8, 28–30, on Pannenberg's rejection of fundamental (or foundational) theology and his somewhat related view that faith in the Christian God is "provisional" until confirmed, particularly at the eschaton. I write briefly of Cobb's and Pannenberg's methodologies; see M. John Farrelly, *Belief in God in Our Time* (Collegeville: The Liturgical Press, 1992) 58–62.

transformative *event* of new life, a new way of being in the world that is grounded in the life and death of Jesus of Nazareth."[16] Christianity is one paradigm among others of the God-human relationship. How then judge its truth? The truth of a model of reality, and this is what Christianity is, is judged by "its internal consistency, its capacity to comprehend the various dimensions of existence, its 'fit' with life as lived, its ability to deal with personal and public evil, and its fruitfulness for understanding the depths and heights of existence."[17]

Historical criticism has shown that Scripture is like any other human text, but we can rightly see it as a classic because it has won its authority by its ability to speak to all sorts of people in very different circumstances. The traditional Christian hierarchical, patriarchal model for the divine-human relationship is experienced today as oppressive, for example, in its lack of sufficient female imagery for God, but that model is not a central constituent of Christianity. What is central in the transforming event associated with the life and death of Jesus is "a dynamic process between a responsive, loving deity redeeming the suffering and supporting the growth of humanity."[18]

All of this shows that in our construction of a Christian model, or preferably of a variety of Christian models of the God-human relationship, we should be open to the future rather than absolutize the past. In my view this approach to mediating belief in Jesus is dominated by pragmatism; it represents a radically different view of what constitutes Christianity than that which the Christian Churches confess. This sense of freedom from Scripture is in part due to McFague's neoliberalist interpretation of religious and scriptural language as metaphor. We have differed from her interpretation of the human person and of God in our earlier volume, and we propose that the issues she is concerned about can be addressed adequately without denying Vatican II's view of what is constitutive in the revelation God has offered through Jesus Christ and the Spirit.

---

[16]Sallie McFague, "An Epilogue: The Christian Paradigm," *Christian Theology: An Introduction to Its Traditions and Tasks,* rev. ed., ed. Peter Hodgson and Robert King (Philadelphia: Fortress Press, 1985) 378; also see David Burrell, "Sallie McFague's 'Metaphorical Theology,'" *Journal of the American Academy of Religion* 61 (1993) 485–504 (hereafter cited as *JAAR*).

[17]McFague, "Epilogue: The Christian Paradigm," 382. See also Sallie McFague, *Models of God: Theology for an Ecological, Nuclear Age* (Philadelphia: Fortress Press, 1987) 192: "I do not *know* who God is, but I find some models better than others for constructing an image of God commensurate with my trust in a God as on the side of life. God is and remains a mystery."

[18]McFague, "Epilogue," 387.

Jürgen Moltmann's and liberation theology's dependence on praxis for mediating faith in God through Jesus Christ seeks to take Scripture as the norm of Christian belief. They do not start with a critical evaluation of the grounds and meaning of belief in God but with the specifically Christian mystery. In their mediation of faith they offer the resurrection of Jesus as promise and in its transforming impact upon us to make us agents to bring justice to the world, particularly in the socioeconomic fields, rather than adopt Pannenberg's use of historical evidence for the resurrection of Jesus as a historical fact.[19] In continuity with Barth, Moltmann dialectically dispenses with philosophical problems at times; this reflects the discontinuity he stresses between the order of creation and the new possibilities introduced by Jesus Christ. For example, he holds that to say that human beings have a nature that perdures through times of change denies history; human beings have not a nature but a history.[20] His norm for the human community is the perichoretic relation of Father, Son, and Holy Spirit. He makes a dichotomy between eschatology and nature. This is a different view of the relation between humanity and the order of grace or the order of creation and the order of redemption from that of Vatican II. Recently, however, he seems to be redressing this imbalance by seeking to integrate an ecological doctrine of creation into his theology.[21]

The starting point for liberation theologians is their position as chaplains, as it were, for base communities facing, with the poor of Latin America, what the liberation Jesus offers is and what action it should evoke. Their knowledge of Jesus, then, comes in worship, through the poor with whom Jesus identified himself, and in the signs of the times; and they look to Scripture from this perspective. Their Christologies emphasize Jesus' concern for the poor and the

---

[19]See John Sobrino, *Christology at the Crossroads* (Maryknoll: Orbis Books, 1978) 244: "Basic discussion of Jesus' resurrection . . . has to do with the triumph of justice. Who will be victorious, the oppressor or the oppressed?" And (255): "It is possible to verify the truth of what happened in the resurrection only through a transforming praxis based on the ideals of the resurrection. . . . The resurrection can be understood only through a praxis that seeks to transform the world." For Moltmann, see his *Way of Jesus Christ* (Minneapolis: Fortress Press, 1990) 214ff.; Farrelly, *Belief in God*, 63–4.

[20]See Douglas Schuurman, *Creation, Eschaton, and Ethics* (New York: Peter Lang, 1991) 125 and passim.

[21]See Jürgen Moltmann, *God in Creation: A New Theology of Creation and the Spirit of God* (New York: Harper & Row, 1985); Paul Molnar, "The Function of the Trinity in Moltmann's Ecological Doctrine of Creation," *Theological Studies* 51 (1990) 673ff. (Hereafter cited as *TS*).

socially transformative character of the salvation he offered. Though they use the scholarship of exegetes, they do not accept academic biblical scholarship as adequate for the understanding of the historical Jesus.[22] In their response to the specificity of the circumstances of poverty that they are combatting some of them are hesitant to accept the dignity of the human person as their ethical norm, because they suspect the Church's use of this norm in its social teaching to be a way of claiming a position above the fray rather than identifying with those unjustly oppressed. Liberation theologians have done a great service not only for the poor but for the Church and theology in their insistence on a faith that does justice as the only faith that justifies. But as understandable as this is, it, as in the case of Moltmann, raises the question of how one forms common ground with non-Christians and preserves some objective norm for the practical implications of Christian transformative praxis. Also, does this position presuppose a dichotomy between *theoria* and praxis? Vatican II integrates *theoria* and praxis, and its way of relating the God of creation and the God of redemption gives a basis for a retention of a natural law, at least one that recognizes its prescriptions as historically conditioned.

We now recall very briefly two stances by Christian theologians who seek to present the Christian message responsibly in a world that many call "postmodern"—one where the gap between traditional Christianity and contemporary culture seems to have enlarged enormously. In one of these responses the concern is primarily for communication even in these circumstances; in the other the concern is primarily for the retention of the uniqueness of the Christian story. We are referring particularly to the works of David Tracy and George Lindbeck. Though I have read their major works, here I wish simply to show in a rough way their basic orientations and give my reason for preferring the orientation we find in Vatican II, and so I will depend on a sympathetic summary of these tendencies given by William Placher in his book, *Unapologetic Theology: A Christian Voice in a Pluralistic Conversation*. The presentation we give is sufficient for

---

[22]See John P. Meier's critique of John Sobrino's *Christology at the Crossroads* (Maryknoll, N.Y.: Orbis Books, 1978) and *Jesus in Latin America* (Maryknoll, N.Y.: Orbis Books, 1987), and of Juan Segundo's *The Historical Jesus of the Synoptics* (Maryknoll, N.Y.: Orbis Books, 1985) in "The Bible as Source for Theology," *Proceedings of the Catholic Theological Society of America,* 43 (1988) 1–14, and Jon Nilson's response, 15–8. Also see Peter Phan, "Peacemaking in Latin American Liberation Theology," *Eglise et Théologie* 24 (1993) 25–41. I comment briefly on Moltmann's and liberation theologians' methodologies; see Farrelly, *Belief in God,* 63–6.

our purpose of showing mutually opposed theological approaches to vindicating belief in Jesus Christ but it is not an adequate expression of the views of these theologians.

In his first elaboration of his theological approach, Tracy claimed that "contemporary Christian theology is best understood as philosophical reflection upon the meanings present in common human experience and the meanings present in the Christian tradition."[23] Tracy wrote that "the fundamental loyalty of the theologian *qua* theologian is to that morality of scientific knowledge which he shares with his colleagues, the philosophers, historians, and social scientists. No more than they, can he allow his own—or his tradition's—beliefs to serve as warrants for his arguments."[24] If Christian theology is to be taken seriously by the intellectual community, it must commend itself by criteria that are generally accepted.

In his next book Tracy continues his advocacy of a "public theology" but with greater acknowledgment, counter to the presuppositions of the Enlightenment, that everyone stands in a particular tradition. For Christians this means that their "trust in and loyalty to the reality of the God disclosed in Jesus Christ finally determine and judge all other loyalties."[25] In his earlier book Tracy dealt with fundamental theology, whereas here, in *The Analogical Imagination,* he deals primarily with systematic theology. He distinguishes these as follows:

> *Fundamental* theologies will be concerned principally to provide arguments that all reasonable persons, whether "religiously involved" or not, can recognize as reasonable. . . . *Systematic* theologies will ordinarily show less concern with such obviously public modes of argument. They will have as their major concern the re-presentation, the reinterpretation of what is assumed to be the ever-present disclosive and transformative power of the particular religious tradition to which the theologian belongs.[26]

---

[23]David Tracy, *Blessed Rage for Order: The New Pluralism in Theology* (New York: Seabury, 1975) 34. See William Placher, "Revisionist and Postliberal Theologies Revisited," *Unapologetic Theology: A Christian Voice in a Pluralistic Conversation* (Louisville: Westminster/John Knox Press, 1989) 154–74. Also see Richard Lints, "The Postpositivist Choice: Tracy or Lindbeck?" *JAAR* 61 (1993) 655–77; Stephen Stell, "Hermeneutics in Theology and the Theology of Hermeneutics: Beyond Lindbeck and Tracy," ibid., 679–703.

[24]Tracy, *Blessed Rage for Order,* 7.

[25]David Tracy, *The Analogical Imagination* (New York: Crossroad, 1981) 132.

[26]Ibid., 57.

This does not mean that systematic theology is not public theology. This theology is the interpretation of a religious classic, the Bible, and "any classic . . . is always public, never private."[27] A classic is a text that addresses the human condition in a way that transcends the limits of a particular time and place because of its depth; it can be appreciated by people of very differing times and places. The hermeneutical task is to interpret the Bible in a way that shows its power to an age as different as ours is from the time when it was written. This allows interreligious dialogue, where each person speaks from his or her tradition.

George Lindbeck's postliberal theology began with Hans Frei's interpretation of biblical hermeneutics. Frei found that modern biblical criticism interpreted the "truth" of the Bible as either in accord with what historically happened or, when this could not be affirmed, as illustrating some general message about human life. Frei notes, however, that we interpret the statements of a historical novel differently. For example, in the sentence "'Mr. Trench went out to look for his ether cylinder'—the *meaning* of this sentence does not involve reference to historical characters or events, but neither can it be reduced to some moral lesson or general claim about human nature."[28] Frei proposes that we start with the "biblical world, and let those narratives define what is real, so that *our* lives have meaning to the extent that we fit them into *that* framework. . . . A theology based on that way of reading scripture would operate . . . [by] narratively describing how the world looks from a Christian perspective, making connections with other perspectives only unsystematically."[29]

Lindbeck's book, *The Nature of Doctrine: Religion and Theology in a Postliberal Age,* proposes that religious doctrine is presently interpreted in three different ways. Some see it as informative propositions about objective realities (the propositionalist position); some see it as secondary to some core religious experience accessible to all human beings and expressive of it (the experiential-expressive position). Counter to these, Lindbeck proposes a cultural-linguistic interpretation. Here, religious doctrines operate primarily "as communally

[27]Ibid., 14.

[28]Placher, *Unapologetic Theology,* 161. See Hans Frei, *The Eclipse of Biblical Narrative* (New Haven, Conn.: Yale University Press, 1974) and *The Identity of Jesus Christ* (Philadelphia: Fortress Press, 1975).

[29]Placher, *Unapologetic Theology,* 161–2.

authoritative rules of discourse, attitude, and action."[30] To understand what the word "God" means in a religion, one examines the way it shapes reality and experience rather than the ways the first two interpretations of doctrine suggest. Lindbeck then sees religions "as comprehensive interpretive schemes, usually embodied in myths or narratives and heavily ritualized, which structure human experience and understanding of self and world. . . . Stated more technically, a religion can be viewed as a kind of cultural and/or linguistic framework or medium that shapes the entirety of life and thought."[31] Doctrines then do not primarily have reference; they are not statements about ontological reality. If one keeps to the language rules of a religion, one is orthodox. Secondarily, one may speculate on the relation of such rules to ontological reality and make truth-claims, for example, about the Trinity.

Richard Lints claims that both Tracy and Lindbeck start with the collapse of positivism. We no longer have the assurance this epistemology had that we can make absolute affirmations about reality; we are in a postfoundationalism period. But Tracy reacts to this in one way, Lindbeck in another. Tracy keeps faith with the Enlightenment conviction of a universal human norm for truth-claims but opts for a looser one than earlier philosophers, namely "genuine conversation." This is necessary to make theology public. We can give as an instance of this Tracy's statement that "the theologian has no more right than any other thinker (that is, no right at all) to violate the canons of history, hermeneutics, social science, literary criticism, philosophy or any other mode of disciplined reflection in making one's case."[32] Lindbeck, seemingly convinced that there is no universal epistemological structure of human knowledge, and not wanting to subordinate the Christian uniqueness to such norms, opts for Christian doctrine as setting the rules for Christian identity, though in a way that does not bind Christian identity with the ontological reference of its doctrines.

---

[30]George Lindbeck, *The Nature of Doctrine: Religion and Theology in a Postliberal Age* (Philadelphia: Westminster Press, 1984).

[31]Lindbeck, *Nature of Doctrine,* 32–3.

[32]Tracy, *Analogical Imagination,* 81. One way this works itself out is that Tracy uses the word "historical" within the limits of the historical-critical method and its principle of analogy. He is hesitant then to call the resurrection of Jesus "historical," though he later distances himself from conclusions others draw from this. See ibid., 300–1; Elizabeth Johnson, "The Theological Relevance of the Historical Jesus: A Debate and a Thesis," *The Thomist* 48 (1984) 1–43. Also see Lints, "The Postpositivist Choice."

It seems to me that Vatican II's implicit method for giving meaning and foundations for our belief in Jesus Christ addresses the issues of publicness and Christian uniqueness more adequately than these positions do. It claims that God has been revealing himself from the beginning of human history, for example, through the testimony of creation itself and the rays of the light that enlightens all and that are present in the religions of the world, but that he has completed his revelation through Jesus Christ and confirmed it. The resurrection of Jesus Christ is part both of this revelation and of this confirmation.

The council does not abandon a human epistemological structure, though it does not restrict what God offers us through the resurrection of Jesus to the limits of recent interpretations of history and epistemology. Similarly, its recognition of stages of God's revelation of himself and his saving design preserves the uniqueness of Christianity without abandoning dialogue responsible to all human truth. So, once more, we prefer its method of giving grounds and meaning for belief in Jesus Christ to those explicit or implicit in Tracy or Lindbeck. I think Vatican II does justice to their legitimate concerns. We have addressed epistemological issues central to their positions in our earlier volume.

What questions, then, should we address in our effort to theologically mediate belief in Jesus Christ as befits foundational theology to our world today? Since Jesus Christ and his Spirit are proposed to us as God's definitive encounter with us, I think that we should first examine the New Testament and particularly the Gospels to understand this encounter from the side of Jesus Christ, as we can learn from the New Testament. Later we will address this encounter from the perspective of men and women of our time, as we found them open to God in our first volume. But even as we treat Scripture, we do so from this hermeneutical perspective, that is, our preunderstanding of the human condition as presented in our earlier volume. So, we will (in ch. 2) ask what sort of documents the Gospels claim to be, thereby examining, on their terms, the relation between the Christ of faith and the Jesus of history contained within them and evaluating Vatican II's teaching on them in chapter 5 of *Dei verbum.*

Then, accepting the substantial historicity of the Gospels, we shall ask what Jesus meant by salvation (ch. 3) and revelation and faith (ch. 4), in view of the teaching on these issues taught by Vatican II and other Christian Churches and the mutually opposed interpretations of these matters by some Christian theologians. Then too, we must treat the central question of the resurrection of Jesus Christ as both revelation and confirmation of Jesus' message to ask whether the New Testament account deserves credence, and how it influenced some early Christian interpretations of salvation and revelation (ch. 5). We shall also take soundings in Christian (and some anti-Christian) reflections in history on these themes to show how the state of the question has changed through the ages and its present shape emerged (ch. 6).

Finally, we shall offer a contemporary constructive theology of the kingdom of God, or salvation (ch. 7), and revelation and faith (ch. 8) appropriate to foundational theology. Do we need the salvation offered by Jesus Christ, and how does Christian salvation address our human needs? How do Christian revelation and faith relate to our contemporary human knowledge? We treat these questions to articulate and vindicate theologically the meaning and grounds for our faith in God specifically through Jesus Christ, but we do so in only an introductory fashion. We shall refer the reader to many more developed studies of these themes as we proceed.

2

The Christ of Faith and
the Jesus of History

The Churches hold that the validity of their claims about Jesus Christ—that it is through him and his Spirit that God by his free choice offers us his ultimate revelation in history and the way by which we may be liberated and fulfilled as individuals and communities in what is deepest in our humanity—depends upon the New Testament writings and, in particular, on the Gospels. Vatican II and other Churches understand these texts to be proclamations of the good news God gives us through Jesus Christ; to present to us *substantively* what Jesus did and said in his ministry, passion and death, and resurrection; and to be valid in their interpretation of Jesus Christ. In this chapter we are going back to Scripture to evaluate the Christian Churches' claims about these texts.

If we are to ask whether the Church's view of the meaning and grounds for our faith in Jesus Christ is in accord with Scripture—and thus is fully Christian—and also whether it is worthy of acceptance by us in our time, there are several questions we should address in the context of this chapter. *First,* we should ask briefly how, from the perspective of our late twentieth-century life, we can find meaning in these texts from the first century. This is a question of hermeneutics.

Second, we should ask how the evangelists envisaged the relation between the Christ they proclaimed and the Jesus of history. We wish to evaluate critically the New Testament on its own terms as it witnesses to Jesus rather than to impose an interpretation on it that is alien to it or to judge it on terms other than its own. In this chapter we shall address this question primarily by analyzing the literary form of Luke's Gospel. Since the Gospels themselves derive from and reflect the early Christian preaching, what we offer later, in chapter 5, on the early Christian preaching of the resurrection is also relevant to the theme of this chapter, and so the reader may wish to look ahead to that.

Third, we expand this to ask how Mark's Gospel relates the Christ of faith and the Jesus of history, and we answer an objection to Vatican II's and our view that the narrative proclamation in the Gospels offers us substantially what Jesus said and did, which comes from a recent, somewhat naturalistic interpretation of history. On these basic questions we offer reflections that are introductory and dependent upon Scripture scholars while referring the reader to more adequate treatments of these themes.

I. A Hermeneutical Question

There is something modern in all of us that contests the plausibility of the ultimate answer to our deepest problems in life coming from events and texts of two thousand years ago. This is the problem of *tradition.* (1) Before looking at the New Testament texts themselves, we should ask how tradition is related to our being human and our understanding as human beings, and then how texts of the ancient past such as Scripture can have meaning for us in a later age. These are questions of hermeneutics. (2) It will also be helpful to recall briefly some conditions of the religious search present in the world at the time the texts of the New Testament were written.

1. Tradition, Human Identity, and Texts of Our Past

Many people of our time do not understand themselves in relation to their tradition. In fact, many think that tradition is a limit, a constraint, a bondage that, to be free, they must reject. This view comes in large part from the Enlightenment, which proposed that human beings should guide themselves by their own reason and experience. This viewpoint had antecedents even in Descartes' view of the human being as a lone thinker assaulted by doubts, yet able to gain a certain grounding in the self by reflection within these doubts. This viewpoint gained support from Kant's understanding of the human person as an autonomous human agent who is held to moral standards simply by his own sense of the categorical imperative. It was further strengthened by the ideology critique of masters of suspicion such as Marx, Freud, and Nietzsche. And it is still further ingrained by relativists among the postmoderns.

Hans-Georg Gadamer has, in partial reliance on Heidegger, contested this interpretation of the human person and human understanding.[1] Largely in accord with his view, we can recall that the human person does not create himself or herself epistemologically any more than he or she does it physically. We are born into a family from which we learn a language and, as our social environment expands, a particular culture with its tradition and heritage. This heritage is central to our identity, and it is from here that we gain what appear to us as ideals, goals, values. There are figures in our immediate environment or in our tradition (e.g., Abraham Lincoln) who are held up to us as instantiating these values, representing them somewhat as icons through which we are motivated and moved. We are oriented, then, to a horizon of values and life that we in large part gain from our particular tradition. Events and texts of this tradition are central for who we are, as the American Revolution and the Declaration of Independence and Constitution exemplify. It is not beneath our dignity as human beings to acknowledge the authority of this extended historical experience of our culture, as it is not beneath our dignity to acknowledge the authority a medical doctor has through his or her study and experience. In fact, to deny this authority is to deny the historical character of our being human and to impoverish and maim ourselves.

Tradition enables us to be creative, because the events and significant texts of our tradition are not simply facts of the past but have an effective history. That is, they have both a determinate meaning that is, however, subject to a limited pluralism of valid interpretations and an impact on later history, and their meaning changes and grows through that. For example, we read in the Declaration of Independence

---

[1]See Hans-Georg Gadamer, *Truth and Method* (New York: Seabury, 1975); Richard Palmer, *Hermeneutics: Interpretation Theory in Schleiermacher, Dilthey, Heidegger, and Gadamer* (Evanston, Ill.: Northwestern University Press, 1969); George McLean, "Hermeneutics and Heritage," *Man and Nature: The Chinese Tradition and the Future,* ed. Tang Yi-Jie, Li Zhen, and George McLean (Washington, D.C.: The Council for Research in Values and Philosophy, 1989) 57–70; Sandra Schneiders, *The Revelatory Text: Interpreting the New Testament as Sacred Scripture* (San Francisco: Harper, 1991). In my earlier volume, *Belief in God in Our Time* (Collegeville: The Liturgical Press, 1992), I underlined the centrality of cultural tradition for our human identity by my use of Erik Erikson and Clifford Geertz.

that "all men are created equal." There are interpretations of this that are invalid, contradictory to the initial meaning of this statement, and there is also a pluralism of more or less adequate interpretations. This statement has stimulated generations to find applications that the original writers did not envisage and the original audience did not hear in the statement. It has had a creative transforming impact in leading to the emancipation of slaves, the enfranchising of women, and the reforms of the civil rights movement; and it still evokes creativity in our time. Our identity and historical consciousness depend on such a tradition and its growing meaning. The goals at the base of our tradition are not realized sufficiently by actions of the past; they evoke still further self-understanding and action in accord with it.

Also, tradition itself is susceptible to and evokes critique. Jürgen Habermas has critiqued Gadamer's call on tradition as disallowing criticism of the past and his appeal simply to practical reason *(phronesis)* as providing inadequate criteria for public knowledge. Critique of the past, Habermas holds, is fostered by human science and occurs in the context of interests that establish a frame of meaning. There has to be communication on some basis deeper than technique if there is to be consensus, a communication that Habermas calls communicative action, or praxis. But we note that Habermas, like Gadamer, rejects metaphysics and that he gives the Enlightenment a primacy in our history that divorces it from our larger tradition. For us together to nourish and foster genuine emancipation, we must draw

> upon our heritage in the manner suggested by Heidegger. We need to retrieve or reach back into our heritage—now as never before—in order to find the radically new resources needed for emancipation in an increasingly dominated world. . . . [C]ritique, rather than being opposed to tradition or taking a questioning attitude thereto, is itself an appeal to tradition. Criticism appeals unabashedly to the heritage of emancipation it has received from the Enlightenment. But this tradition has longer roots which reach back to the liberating acts of the Exodus and the Resurrection. "Perhaps" writes Ricoeur "there would be no more interest in emancipation, no more anticipation of freedom, if the Exodus and Resurrection were effaced from the memory of mankind."[2]

---

[2]McLean, "Hermeneutics and Heritage," 68–9. The enclosed quotation is from Paul Ricoeur, "Hermeneutics and the Critique of Ideology," *Paul Ricoeur, Hermeneutics and the Human*

This is a theme we will return to later, but in a preliminary way this reflection should help us to accept more fully than many of our contemporaries the importance of a profound study of the formative events and documents of our tradition, among which those that surround the life, ministry, death, and resurrection of Jesus Christ hold primacy of place. Our human identity is rooted in our tradition, for we are cultural beings. We are not making a dichotomy between tradition and what we can learn about our humanity by philosophical reflection, in continuity with Plato, Aristotle, and many others. I sought to show in my previous volume that as human beings we are oriented toward the fullness of Being, God himself, through our cultural environment, our maturing potential, and our freedom. Not infrequently today a rejection of God and of self is manifested and expressed by a rejection of our tradition.[3]

Granted that our tradition is part of our identity, we ask now in a preliminary way how we can approach the texts of Scripture in a manner that evaluates critically our faith in Jesus Christ, or acceptance of discipleship toward him, and what this discipleship means. Vatican II and other Christian Churches of our time base the validity of their call in part on the New Testament. We will study this question in some detail, but here we treat it briefly as a question of hermeneutics. One way of posing this question is the following: "The problem of New Testament hermeneutics is precisely how later believers [or, we may add, searchers], who do not see and hear the earthly Jesus but encounter him only through the text, who are overfamiliar with the stories and know how they turn out, can experience

---

Sciences, ed. J. B. Thompson (New York: Cambridge University Press, 1981) 99–100. Also see Susan Shapiro, "Rhetoric as Ideology Critique: The Gadamer-Habermas Debate Reinvented," *JAAR* 62 (1994) 123–50. There is reason to interpret Habermas' own position as a rhetoric rather than totally neutral and disinterested. On Gadamer's and Habermas' "moderate postmodernism" and theologians influenced by them see Thomas Guarino, "Between Foundationalism and Nihilism: Is *Phronesis* the *Via Media* for Theology?" *TS* 54 (1993) 37–54. For example, Guarino points out that "Gadamer . . . argues that *phronesis* is the prime analogue for all rationality in the postmetaphysical age" (45). Guarino concludes, however, that "Moderate postmodernism . . . cannot sustain . . . the type of hermeneutics of doctrine which this [the Christian] notion of revelation demands" (53). Jack Bonsor, "History, Dogma, and Nature: Further Reflections on Postmodernism and Theology," *TS* 55 (1994) 295–313, gives a quite different assessment of the relation between postmodernism and theology.

[3]In "Person, Work, and Religious Tradition," *The Place of Person in Social Life,* ed. Paul Peachey, John Kromkowski, and George McLean (Washington, D.C.: The Council for Research in Values and Philosophy, 1991) 259–68, I show and evaluate how John Paul II uses both hermeneutics and a philosophy of the person in *Laborem exercens* to reflect creatively and critically on the world of work in our time.

the invitation into the world before the text that will be as truly transforming for them as it was for those who first heard the parables and
followed Jesus."[4] Can the Gospels bear the weight as foundation and
norm for our faith in God through Jesus Christ that Vatican II and
other Christian Churches ascribe to them? In answer to this question
here we indicate the claim and challenge of these texts, the historical
and literary questions they raise, and the basis on which they can
make their claim on us in spite of the gap between us.

The claim and challenge of these texts is evident to one who first
approaches them. Jesus calls out for belief through these texts, even
to the reader of our time. To express how this engages the reader, we
make use, in our own way, of a summary statement David Tracy gives
of the first three "steps" in the process of interpretation of a classic
text.[5] *First,* the interpreter has some preunderstanding of the subject
matter of which the text speaks, for example, the question of God,
human uncertainties and weaknesses, and a search for resolution. I
sought to show in my earlier volume how the religious question to
which the Gospels offer an answer does indeed engage the person of
our time. *Second,* the interpreter notes a "claim to serious understanding elicited by the classic text as some kind of realized experience of meaning and truth." We can point to the way these texts have
engaged and changed multitudes of hearers and readers through the
ages, to the boldness of their claims, to the urgency of their call for
a response of belief. They are "classics," like the writings of Homer,
the Greek philosophers, Virgil, Shakespeare, and the Bhagavad Gita;
but as we shall see and as the Churches claim, they are more than
classics because of the way they mediate God's revelation and offer
of salvation to us and are normative for Christian faith.[6]

---

[4]Schneiders, *Revelatory Text,* 168. She makes good use of Gadamer and Ricoeur in her study of
this question. See also Paul Ricoeur, *Interpretation Theory: Discourse and the Surplus of Meaning*
(Fort Worth, Texas: Texas Christian University, 1976); idem, *Essays on Biblical Interpretation*
(Philadelphia, Fortress Press, 1980); Donald McKim, ed., *A Guide to Contemporary Hermeneutics:
Major Trends in Biblical Interpretation* (Grand Rapids, Eerdmans, 1986); in particular in this last
book, see Anthony Thiselton, "The New Hermeneutic," 78–107. Werner Jeanrond, *Theological
Hermeneutics: Development and Significance* (New York: Crossroad, 1991) 76, critiques
Ricoeur's distinction of sense and reference and holds that the text's sense already involves refer-
ence to the world of the reader.

[5]See David Tracy, *The Analogical Imagination: Christian Theology and the Culture of
Pluralism* (New York: Crossroad, 1981) 152, n. 107. Jeanrond, *Theological Hermeneutics,* 114–5,
rightly, I believe, prefers to speak of "dimensions" of interpretation rather than "steps."

[6]See, for example, John Reumann and Joseph Fitzmyer, "Scripture as Norm for Our Common
Faith," *Journal of Ecumenical Studies* 30 (1993) 81–107. Francis Schüssler Fiorenza addresses a

Third, the interpreter enters into an interaction with the text concerning its subject matter. It is not primarily the experience of the author that is engaged but, as Gadamer insists, the subject matter that the text is about. The message conveyed is, as it were, in front of the text, rather than behind it. In Ricoeur's words, it is conveyed by a noetic act (the subjective pole in communication) of the author; but what is conveyed, or the noematic meaning (the objective pole of communication), is the content of the discourse. This content, which we will refer to below as the meaning of the text, involves both the meaning or significance or relevance it had for hearers or readers of the age in which it was written and the meaning it has for readers of a later age. This interaction has something of the character of a conversation in which the interpreter listens and asks questions of the text and responds to it; and the text, as it were, acts similarly in reference to the reader. This engagement between reader and message is a two-way street; the message questions the reader and the reader asks his or her own questions of the text. The reader's questions are stimulated and made possible by the different time and place from which he or she engages the text. This is part of and contributes to the text's "surplus of meaning" and a legitimate pluralism of interpretations.

The way the texts engage us and how we engage them depends also on what is behind the text and what is in the text. Or, as David Tracy, dependent on Ricoeur, expresses it, the *fourth* step of the hermeneutical process expands to one of "understanding-explanation-understanding." That is, from initial understanding the interpreter uses methods appropriate to a more adequate understanding of the text—that is, explanations that can be derived from the study of literary genres, the sources of the text, the social circumstances surrounding the text, and so forth. We will see that the evangelists claim there is a determinate meaning in these texts, and "explanations" can help us identify such initial meanings. Many differences among interpreters, such as those between the Neoscholastics, Harnack, Bultmann, some who use diverse forms of hermeneutics and current literary criticism, and Vatican II depend on these questions. Are the texts histories; are they mythologies and/or poetry; are they proclamations of the good news, and if so, what relation do they have to what Jesus actually did and said in his ministry? In a sense, these questions are about the world behind the text.

---

weakening of the authority of Scripture among Christians in "The Crisis of Scriptural Authority: Interpretation and Reception," *Interpretation* 44 (1990) 353–68.

But there is also the "world of the text," or the meaning and reference discerned in the text. In Ricoeur's usage this content of the text involves both the "what" of discourse, or the sense immanent to it as expressed, for example, in a sentence; and the "about what," or the reference that goes beyond the sentence to the world to which the speech is related. Reference also involves the significance or relevance that this has to the supposed reader. (Others include reference in the sense of the text. We shall return to this question later.) These depend on the intention of the author, but once the text is written it has a certain autonomy. It has a certain independence from the author now; while its meaning is not wholly independent from the author's intention, it is not limited to this nor is this intention fully accessible to us.

There are ways the text can convey its meaning other than on the condition of an access to the intention of the author, which is in some way independent of the text.[7] For example, in Scripture we frequently find testimonies to God's saving intervention for his people presented in the form of a narrative. The narrative account gives us something of the meaning of the event through showing the consequences of the event. Also, the meaning of a statement is known in part through supposing that it conforms to the rules of the language, as human behavior is in part understood through supposing that the agent performed it in accordance with the rules of behavior in a certain society. Both language and action can have a meaning in what they signify and in what they seek to bring about (commands, admonitions, healings, forgiving, etc.).

Moreover, we can have access to the meaning of a document, event, statement, and so on by how it was received or interpreted at the time and at later times. For example, the meaning of the Exodus is shown to us by how it was interpreted initially and then reinterpreted by later prophets to have implications for their own time, and these interpretations were sanctioned by being accepted into the canon of Scripture.

Interpretation depends on the question of language. The language of the text is a convention of a particular culture that is related to the shared world of that culture. Any language is an ordered system. But also language is related to being human, and we have access to the

---

[7]See Francis Schüssler Fiorenza, *Foundational Theology: Jesus and the Church* (New York: Crossroad, 1984) 29–33, 108–22. Also see Jeanrond, *Theological Hermeneutics,* 110–9, who holds that Ricoeur did not give enough attention to the reader and who proposes an ethics of assessment of the text.

message of another age through a language that differs from our own.[8] It reflects the shared world of human beings, not simply that of a particular culture, as other human artifacts do, and more than most others because language is less subject to ambiguity than many human artifacts are.

We can place as the *fifth* step or dimension in the hermeneutical process the more critical understanding that comes through this earlier explanation. The point of this understanding is not primarily what is behind the text but rather, as Tracy writes, "a referent as the world-in-front-of-the-text awaiting understanding." This is the subject matter that is communicated. This refers to the way-of-being that the text invites us into, such as the world constituted by the love of God for us mediated through Jesus Christ and the Spirit. The meaning, for both Vatican II and the evangelists, is dependent upon what the text originally meant and its reference, but it is not restricted to that. It is its significance for the reader or hearer of another age that Ricoeur called its "ultimate reference." There is a gap between the text and such an interpreter due to the time and cultures that separate them, but this gap can contribute to a legitimate pluralism of meanings of the text, as we find in later interpretations of the Declaration of Independence, if some fusion of horizons comes about between the questions of human existence the text is dealing with and the questions of human existence interpreters are dealing with. In classics and specifically in Scripture the author's text is not restricted to his or her own culture but is significant for men and women of other cultures because of the depth of the questions posed and answers offered for the human condition.

There is, as we said, a legitimate pluralism that is found in, and is consequent upon, the conversation between text and interpreter. This depends upon such things as the time and place of the interpreter, which influence his or her preunderstanding both in theory and praxis; the richness of the text, which allows a pluralism of meaning; and the methods used to explain the text. The text can be critiqued on grounds of whether it contributes to, or detracts from, our human fulfillment, but this assessment is an ethical question. A resolution of contradictory interpretations depends at times on philosophical issues

---

[8]On the question of language as relevant to interpretation see Thomas Gillespie, "Biblical Authority and Interpretation: The Current Debate on Hermeneutics," *Guide to Contemporary Hermeneutics,* ed. McKim, 192–219.

among interpreters such as their understanding of the human person. I referred to this in my earlier volume by citing Jesus' words to Nicodemus in John 3:12: "If I tell you about earthly things and you do not believe, how will you believe if I tell you about heavenly things?" Pluralism in legitimate readings of Scripture is limited because the text has, as we will see, a definite initial meaning that excludes some interpretations.

2. An Overview of Religious Searches at the Time of the Writing of the New Testament

There is, it seems to me, an interesting parallel between the first century and the present century in reference to the context for coming to belief or to a more critical belief as Christians. A new culture has emerged in the Western world and, indeed, in the whole world in the last century or so with the Enlightenment, science, historical consciousness, and awareness of the worlds of many peoples. Many who were previously Christian have embraced this larger culture to the point of a near total erosion of their Christian belief, while many from this larger culture are now experiencing an emptiness in it and are examining Christianity anew. But many from a strong Christian background resist a great deal in this culture and keep to an earlier cultural expression of their Christian belief. All of us face the question of the interface of our Christian belief with our contemporary culture.

The Gospels (and books of the New Testament more generally), we will show in the next section, present themselves as an experientially based witness to God's symbolically mediated offer of revelation and salvation through Jesus Christ and the Spirit to a people concerned for themselves and their societies in a period when many people were searching, disappointed by the emptiness of the dominant culture of their time. Still others were being uprooted from a past into confrontation with a world empire and culture that challenged their traditional symbolic worlds and were adjusting their traditions in varied ways to these changed circumstances.

The texts of the New Testament are religious texts in the sense that they proclaim to people a religious world or God's relation to them that is symbolically mediated, and they address Christians who have accepted the Christian message in the midst of the pluralism of that time. They are addressed to Christians who came from this first-century world, and so it is helpful to say a word about some aspects of the world in which these texts were written. The interpretation of the texts is aided by some reference to the search of people at that time as a religious search, so different from, and yet analogous to, our own period of change. We will recall aspects of that time from the perspective of people's religious search—a search related to or inclusive of their economic, political, or social concerns but one that cannot be reduced to these concerns. The data relevant to this question can be found in the texts themselves (e.g., in the implied reader, or the kind of reader the text supposes is open to its message) and also in what other texts of the period witness.

We direct readers to other books where they can find analyses of the world of the New Testament.[9] Here we simply recall schematically that it was a world in transition. This was true for the Jewish world but also for the larger Mediterranean world of Roman power and Hellenistic culture. In fact, these two worlds were profoundly interconnected, because a central factor in Judaism's experience at the time was how to face this larger world that impacted them so severely and how to face it in a way faithful to their past. We shall first recall something of the larger Mediterranean world and then of Judaism's situation in the first century.

Hellenism had spread through the Mediterranean world from the time Alexander the Great had conquered so much of it and sought to spread Greek culture. This culture was initially centered in the city-states of Greece; after Alexander, the cities became too large for citizen participation, and they were not free but were included in empire, eventually that of Rome. This Roman rule was preoccupied with power and its efficient use to ensure a peace of sorts; along with the benefits it brought to many peoples, it also imposed heavy taxes and caused a sense of deracination. Inclusion within empire gave people opportunity for a new identity, but it also led to a breakdown of local roots and, not infrequently, to alienation and despair.

Religious syncretisms developed from this enlarged political context, some of which led toward monotheism. But many people sensed

---

[9]In this I am largely following Luke T. Johnson, *The Writings of the New Testament: An Interpretation* (Philadelphia: Fortress Press, 1986). See also, for example, Sean Freyne, *The World of the New Testament* (Wilmington, Del.: Michael Glazier, 1980); Hans J. Schultz, ed., *Jesus in His Time* (Philadelphia: Fortress Press, 1971); Bruce Malina, *The New Testament World: Insights from Cultural Anthropology* (Atlanta: John Knox Press, 1981); M. Hengel, *Judaism and Hellenism,* 2 vols. (Philadelphia: Fortress Press, 1974); Richard Horsley and John Hanson, *Bandits, Prophets, and Messiahs: Popular Movements at the Time of Jesus* (San Francisco: Harper & Row, 1988). The citations in the text at this point are to Johnson's book.

that their lives were ruled by an alternation of chance and fate. Since individuals sensed so often that they did not have control over their lives, both religion and philosophy gave increased attention to the individual. Popular Hellenistic religion tended to emphasize personal religious experience and to feed a hunger for revelation, for transformation, and for personal allegiance that would give a sense of identity in an alienating world (e.g., through the mystery religions). Hellenistic philosophy was now dedicated more to the art of living than to metaphysics. The Stoics taught that the universe was rational and that events were governed by divine providence. Cynics were individualistic and stressed freedom. Pythagoreans stressed community. Much philosophy called people to the virtuous life as the good life and fostered a religious view of the calling human beings had.

Thus Hellenism was characterized by a reinterpretation of its earlier symbols to make them suitable for a new age in which the acts of gods in Homeric stories did not accord with the ideals of virtue, and the virtues needed were no longer those of the archaic nobleman. The witness of the lives and words of the Hellenistic Jews of the Diaspora was not without its impact in this confused world. There were Gentiles who attached themselves to the synagogues and accepted monotheism and the moral code of the Torah, though they did not accept circumcision. It was among these that Christian missionaries first gained Gentile converts.

Judaism too was in a period of transition. It offered a consistent framework for self-definition but was not uniform. The Torah and the Temple were central for the Jews. The synagogue services were one central place of reinterpretation of the Torah. Both Torah and Temple implied that they were one with the people of old. God had made a covenant with them, had made them his people, was faithful to his covenant, and called them to be holy. But what did being holy mean? On this there was diversity. The Jews, and in a special way those in Palestine, were divided among themselves over the issue of Hellenism and Rome. The presence to them of Hellenistic culture and Roman power challenged them to interpret anew their inherited tradition concerning the relation between religious and sociopolitical-economic realities. The tax collectors and the Zealots had radically different reactions to Roman hegemony. Between these extremes there were also very marked differences among the Sadducees, the Pharisees, the Essenes, and the people of the land *(am-ha-aretz)*. They had different interpretations concerning what it was to be God's people, and they transformed their traditional religious symbols in different ways through their experiences and convictions. This had been in process for a long time.

We will return to a further analysis of some traditional Jewish symbols in the next chapter when we treat the question of salvation, but here we recall a few only to the point of showing diversity in the Judaism of the first century. Messianism, the expectation of God's promise of a Son of David to liberate them and fulfill God's promises, was one of these symbols central to many Jews' hope in their conflicted world. Another was strongly developed during the time of the persecution of the Jews about 165 B.C. at the time of Antiochus Epiphanes IV in his attempt to assimilate the Jews into Greek culture. Apocalyptic literature, in this instance the book of Daniel, was a specifically religious response to the persecution experienced by those faithful to Torah and their need for a deep conviction that God was faithful. In symbolic language this literature (e.g., Daniel 7) assured the people that God would soon come and liberate them; that in the age to come as distinct from the present age dominated by forces of evil, God's reign would be given to the people of God symbolized by "one like a Son of Man"; and that the just would experience a resurrection from the dead. Thus it led to a new interpretation of history.

The Rabbinic tradition, in contrast, did not give an analysis of history but rather of the Torah to apply what had earlier been written in a simpler society to a people in such changed circumstances. The Torah "is God's eternal blueprint for creation and for righteous human behavior," and the Pharisees sought to "put a hedge around the Torah" for the people (56). While these emphasized the development of the Torah and separatism, the Sadducees restricted the Torah to the Pentateuch, sought accommodation with the Romans, and contributed to the economic exploitation of the people. The Essenes, made known to us particularly through the manuscripts discovered at Qumran, had reacted to the imposition of a high priest not of the Zadokite line (ca. 152 B.C.) and other factors by a separatism more severe than that of the Pharisees, and so they interpreted the Torah and its prophecies as applying specifically to their group and its future. All these groups were interpreting the Torah, its promises, and the meaning of holiness for the new circumstances posed by Hellenistic culture and Roman power and the Jewish factions these changed conditions occasioned.

The Jews of the Diaspora, over twice as numerous as those within Palestine, also faced the issue of assimilation or separatism, but they did so "in a setting less colored by religious persecution and political oppression" (67). Rome gave the Jews certain rights and privileges to abide by their religious traditions. The Jews were admired by some Gentiles for their monotheism, the high moral code of the Torah, and their attractive claim to be God's people; but they were also under suspicion by others for their separatism. Though as attached to the Torah as the Palestinian Jews, they interpreted the Jewish tradition differently because they were in a different cultural setting.

Thus the Hellenistic Jews of the Diaspora—as distinct, for example, from those in Mesopotamia—read the Torah in the Septuagint translation and had done so for generations, since their native language was Greek. And in the efforts of many of them, particularly those in Alexandria, to make themselves understood favorably by outsiders, they reflected on their history and its main figures (e.g., Moses) by some use of Hellenistic categories. For example, Philo of Alexandria used allegory to interpret the Torah and wrote of Moses as the ideal philosopher-king. The book of Wisdom reflected on Wisdom, an emanation from God, as guiding his people, on the virtues that came from Wisdom, on immortality that was its reward, on God's philanthropy, and on the way God makes himself known by his works in creation that manifest him analogically.

We have reflected on the problem of hermeneutics and the gap between texts of the first century and interpreters of our century. We have also reflected on initial ways of bridging this gap. The texts of the New Testament were addressed to Christians—those who had responded to the Christ-event with faith and who had come from Palestinian and Diaspora Jews seeking fidelity to their tradition while facing the larger world of Hellenistic culture and Roman hegemony—and to Gentiles living in a world culture and empire marked by deracination and by religious and philosophical pluralism. That world bears some resemblance to our own. Some of us come from a strong Christian tradition and yet face a larger cultural world with its categories and its questions—a world that evokes assimilation or separatism from many Christians. Many come from this larger world and, while acclaiming its accomplishments, no longer find its presuppositions and symbols sufficient to give meaning to their lives.

II. Kerygma and History as Reflected in Luke's Gospel

A central problem standing in the way of our use of the New Testament in reference to the meaning and foundations for belief in Jesus Christ is the question of how the meaning contained in the text and the extratextual reality are related, or in terms more specific to the New Testament, how kerygma and history are related. Can we say confidently with Vatican II that the authors of the Gospels "selected certain of the many elements which had been handed on, either orally or already in written form, others they synthesized or explained with an eye to the situation of the churches, the while sustaining the form of preaching, but always in such a fashion that they have told us the honest truth about Jesus" (*DV* 19)? Is the Church correct when it claims that the Gospels, "whose historicity she unhesitatingly affirms, faithfully hand on what Jesus, the Son of God, while he lived among men, really did and taught for their eternal salvation," though they present this "with that fuller understanding which they [the evangelists], instructed by the glorious events of Christ and enlightened by the Spirit of truth, now enjoyed" (*DV* 19)?

Many non-Christians and many Christians, among them some Scripture scholars and theologians, would not accept Vatican II's interpretation of the relation in the Gospels between the early Christian proclamation, or kerygma, and the words and deeds of Jesus. For example, some hold that we cannot find in the Gospels *substantively* what Jesus actually said and did, and that this is not essential for the way Scripture grounds and is normative for Christian faith. Others hold that through the historical-critical method we can find some historical facts about Jesus' words and deeds, that these are the grounds and norms of Christian faith, but that the interpretations given them in the Gospels are not of themselves valid or normative. Because of their understanding of modern historical consciousness, some postmodernists hold that there is no determinate meaning in the Gospels but only interpretations of interpretations, that they do not have transhistorical reference, and that accounts of miracles cannot be credited as historical. Here we ask whether the authors of the Gospels are indeed claiming to do what Vatican II states they are doing and whether an examination of their procedures supports their claim. We do not wish to take them and evaluate them as some other form of literature, such as modern critical history, ancient myth, or some genres that contemporary literary criticism studies. We recognize that some modern interpreters find what the evangelists claim to be doing philosophically impossible. We have faced many of these difficulties in our earlier volume and will face some in this volume, partially in this chapter. We proceed by (1) showing major contexts in which this question is studied today, presenting a thesis, and offering initial support for it; and (2) examining how Luke articulates the relation between kerygma and the deeds and words of Jesus in his Gospel.

1. Contexts for This Question, a Thesis, and Its Initial Support

The question of the relation between the good news proclaimed and the words and deeds of Jesus in the Gospels is much disputed. Its answer has depended on many factors, and there have been changes in these factors in the twentieth century.[10] We shall recall two contexts for divisions on this question. One example of the context is offered by the work of Rudolf Bultmann. He was important both for a significant advance in the historical-critical method as applied to the Gospels and for a hermeneutical principle of interpretation of the gospel message. In the historical-critical method the interest is in discovering the sources of the text, and the goal is to reconstruct the historical development that occurred. That is, it normally takes a historical model as its perspective in approaching the text. As Luke Johnson writes:

> Despite many minor disaffections, the historical model remains dominant in NT scholarship. The historical model provides a distinctive imaginative construal of the writings and the task of studying them. First, the task: in answer to the question, What are these writings about? this model responds, They are about the history of the primitive Christian movement. The goal set by this model is the description, or possibly even the reconstruction, of that historical development. . . . The writings themselves, we see, play a secondary role: they are nothing more or less than sources for the reconstruction. The historian evaluates the writings as historical sources (are they first- or secondhand, authentic or inauthentic?), and asks of them questions that yield specifically historical infor-

---

[10]See Calvin Mercer, *Norman Perrin's Interpretation of the New Testament* (Macon, Ga.: Mercer University Press, 1986), for a study of the changing stages of Perrin's interpretation of the Gospels, representative of shifts in twentieth-century exegetical methods in Europe and the United States.

mation. Indeed, this model can use only such information. Whether the topic is ideas, rituals, literature, or institutions, the end result is the same: a picture of historical development. This model is neither unsophisticated nor without virtue.[11]

Bultmann contributed to the historical-critical method through his study of the oral tradition that lay behind the Gospels, the forms in which different aspects of Jesus' words and deeds were handed on in the primitive Church, and the way the needs and functions or institutional settings of the Church affected these traditions. In him this resulted in a greater skepticism about the historical value of the Gospels, though many of Bultmann's most prominent disciples (e.g., E. Käsemann, G. Bornkamm) eventually rejected his extreme skepticism because they reacted against the extent to which Bultmann ascribed free creativity of the tradition to the early Church. Also, many exegetes (e.g., J. Jeremias and V. Taylor) used form criticism but with more conservative results than Bultmann or his disciples.

Obviously Bultmann's view undercuts our ability to find in the Gospels the kind of meaning and foundations for belief in Jesus Christ that Vatican II asserted. Bultmann understood critical history largely as the first "historical questers" of the nineteenth century did, dependent upon a positivistic view of history such as that of Leopold von Ranke, who sought to construct the past "as it really happened," unaware of the influence on him of his own perspective. When the historical-critical method was transferred to the study of Scripture, many of its practitioners were unaware of their historical situatedness and did not question the philosophical presuppositions within which they were writing—namely, that they accepted as possible influences

---

[11]Johnson, *Writings of the New Testament,* 8. Two recent well-known historical-critical approaches to the life of Jesus are John Meier, *A Marginal Jew: Rethinking the Historical Jesus,* 2 vols. thus far (New York: Doubleday, 1992, 1994), and John Crossan, *The Historical Jesus: The Life of a Mediterranean Jewish Peasant* (San Francisco: Harper, 1992).

Johnson evaluates these from a perspective on the Gospels similar to that of Vatican II in *Commonweal* (April 24, 1992, and November 18, 1994). While he commends aspects of these books, he concludes that "I suspect that when the dust settles . . . we shall find that the 'historical Jesus' is just where he was all the time: in the fourfold testimony and interpretation of the Gospel narratives. For if what is essential to a person is not the facts of when and where or the facts of what was said and done, but rather the *meaning* of those facts for those whose experience and memory of the person was also part of their historical reality, then there is no place else for us to look" (*Commonweal* [November 18, 1994] 35). An exchange between Meier and Johnson is found in *Commonweal* (February 24, 1995). A somewhat similar evaluation of the two authors under consideration is offered by David Bartlett in *The Christian Century* (May 6, 1992).

in history only natural and human agency—and thus they antecedently excluded the possibility of miracles and resurrection of the dead. Many nineteenth-century questers for the historical Jesus thus confidently gave naturalistic explanations of the miracles of the Gospels and pictured Jesus as an enlightened nineteenth-century liberal. It was, as Albert Schweitzer said, as though they looked to the bottom of a well and saw a reflection of themselves.

Bultmann's understanding of the way religious language has meaning and his application of this to the New Testament gave him access to an interpretation of the New Testament's message, but one that did not depend on the historical reliability of the gospel accounts. "History" could refer to what actually happened in time or space *(Historie),* or it could refer to the significance people found in what happened *(Geschichte).* The latter, he held, does not depend on the former. For Bultmann religious language means an objectification of religious experience, and the Christian kerygma was an objectification of the Christian experience of a new life of authenticity gained through believing in God's love proclaimed in connection with Jesus' death. They expressed this in mythological language suitable for the time:

> The early Christian community thus regarded him [Jesus] as a mythological figure. It expected him to return as the Son of Man on the clouds of heaven to bring salvation and damnation as judge of the world. His person is viewed in the light of mythology when he is said to have been begotten of the Holy Spirit and born of a virgin, and this becomes clearer still in Hellenistic Christian communities where he is understood to be the Son of God in a metaphysical sense, a great, pre-existent heavenly being who became man for the sake of our redemption and took on himself suffering, even the suffering of the cross. It is evident that such conceptions are mythological, for they were widespread in the mythologies of Jews and Gentiles and then were transferred to the historical person of Jesus.[12]

Thus too, proclamation of the resurrection of Jesus Christ is to be taken as a myth; it signifies the new life people found through believing in the good news. It is clear that this approach, which is found

[12]Rudolf Bultmann, *Jesus Christ and Mythology* (New York: Scribners, 1958) 167.

in other exegetes and theologians also, contests the way of finding meaning and grounds for faith in Jesus Christ that Vatican II and the broader Christian tradition affirm.

Another context for this problem is posed by some who use in their interpretation of the Gospels contemporary hermeneutics and modern literary criticism. After the development of form criticism more attention came to be given to the authors of the Gospels and their theologies as these were present in their organization of the traditions common to them. This "redaction criticism" led gradually to a more pronounced use of modern literary-critical methods in interpreting the New Testament documents, that is, in seeing them as compositions and trying to understand them as such (e.g., as composition criticism, narrative criticism, and reader-response criticism).

To take one example here, we can refer to an article by William Vorster entitled "Meaning and Reference: The Parables of Jesus in Mark 4."[13] Vorster claims to depend largely on Ricoeur and states that the meaning of a word (e.g., *ophis* means "snake" in Revelation) and its reference (e.g., *ophis* refers to Satan in Revelation) are not the same. Furthermore, "reference" itself may be taken in two senses. It may refer to an event in history behind the text (in accord with the historical-critical method), or it may refer to the world-in-front-of-the-text (what Ricoeur calls "meaning or ultimate reference").

The parables in Mark's Gospel, for example, are set in the narrativity of this Gospel, and so their meaning and reference are those that this context indicates. The referent is the kingdom of God. Vorster suggests "that there is not a significant difference between the ways in which a parable and a gospel refer—both are 'made up' stories, even if not the same genre" (57). Mark's Gospel is indeed imbedded in first-century Palestine and thus a real world. But this does not answer the question of the reference of the text. For example, do the "disciples" of Jesus signify no more nor less than

---

[13]See Bernard Lategan and William Vorster, *Text and Reality: Aspects of Reference in Biblical Texts* (Philadelphia: Fortress Press, 1985) 27–65. Lategan contests Vorster's conclusions from literary criticism. We shall refer to his criticisms below. References in the text here are to Vorster's article. For more detailed analyses and evaluations of different forms of literary criticism recently applied to the Gospels, see Stephen Moore, *Literary Criticism and the Gospels: The Theoretical Challenge* (New Haven, Conn.: Yale University Press, 1989); W. Randolph Tate, *Biblical Interpretation: An Integrated Approach* (Peabody, Mass.: Hendrickson, 1991); Burton Mack, *Rhetoric and the New Testament* (Minneapolis: Fortress Press, 1990); The Pontifical Biblical Commission, *The Interpretation of the Bible in the Church* (Washington, D.C.: United States Catholic Conference, 1993).

Jesus' original disciples, or a group claiming to continue the position of the original disciples, or some other group contemporary to the writing of the Gospel; or do they occupy a purely informative role? Mark's Gospel is not a copy of reality; "it is reality remade"(58). Parables, too, are narratives. And written history is a "made up" story:

> The crux of the problem lies in the nature of narrative itself. Narrative is the remaking of reality (= creating a *narrative world*) through characterization, plot, and other narrative devices. The story-teller creates a world of his own making with its own time, space, characters, and plot, one which is called a "narrative world." Even if one were to be as true to the "real world" as possible in presenting part of it in narrative discourse, one will still be creating a "narrative world." . . . [T]heir significance is not the actuality of the events, but their logical structure. . . . Narratives are not merely windows, nor are they purely mirrors: they are both. . . . Mark's presentation of the disciples has to do with the narrative world he created. The answer as to how they refer is to be found in the way Mark created his narrative world. The same applies to parables (60–1).

Granted that the Gospels and the Acts of the Apostles are genuine literary creations of their authors and that they do not have a one-to-one correlation with what happened in time and space, does this mean that one is restricted to their "narrative world" in interpreting these texts and their reference? There are philosophical bases, at times those of a postmodernist antifoundationalism, in such literary criticism. That is, because of the limits of each cultural period, what we have in texts is simply the perspective of such a period, not a true and transhistorical reference and a determinate meaning accessible to a later age. This approach too is used by others than Vorster, and it contests Vatican II's approach.

We shall give our initial answer to these problems as a thesis and some preliminary support of it, and then show that this is supported by an analysis of Luke's literary composition. In the third section we shall show further support for this in a brief analysis of Mark's Gospel, and we shall answer an objection that comes from a somewhat naturalistic interpretation of history. The main point of our answer is that there is not, in the evangelists' intention or the resultant work, the dichotomy between the kerygma, or the good news—which is proclaimed by the mediation of Jesus' acts and words as both occurring in space and time and as historical symbols of this trans-historical good news of God's offer of salvation through Jesus—and what actually happened in space and time that Bultmann supposed; and there is not the dichotomy between the Gospels as literature, or composition, and their concern for mediating what God actually said and did through Jesus Christ that some who accept contemporary hermeneutics and the approach of literary criticism suppose.[14]

The proclamation of the good news—the Christian kerygma (from *kērusso,* I proclaim, herald, preach)—is the basic form of preaching in the primitive Church, and it is basic to such documents as the Gospels and the Acts of the Apostles.[15] The good news, or gospel, as we shall see more fully in the next chapter, is that God is offering his definitive salvation to the Jews and Gentiles through Jesus Christ and belief in him. This is a transhistorical event that enters history through Jesus Christ and his Spirit. It is expressed primarily through real symbols such as narratives of the acts of Jesus and his interpretative words of the kingdom and accounts of his death and resurrection—all of which point to what God is doing, because these are actions and words of God through Jesus Christ indicating God's dispositions, plans, and presence.

The accounts of Jesus' resurrection are symbolic in that they point to something else, namely what God is doing, that is, declarations of who Jesus is and offering those who believe in him salvation. These accounts—such as Peter's Pentecost sermon and the actions to which they give witness—are thus symbols of God's presence and action, and they are presented to the hearers of the proclamation (and later, readers) with something of a sacramental force. That is, God's salvific presence is mediated to the hearers through the proclamation itself of

---

[14]In this I see myself in agreement with James Dunn, *Unity and Diversity in the New Testament: An Inquiry into the Character of Earliest Christianity* (Philadelphia: Westminster Press, 1977); Luke Johnson; Avery Dulles (see his *Models of Revelation* [New York: Doubleday, 1983]); and many others. I have reflected on this in earlier writings: see Farrelly, *Belief in God,* chapter 3, pages 73–84; M. John Farrelly, "Christian Interpretation of History: A Dialogue," *God's Work in a Changing World* (1985; reprint, Washington, D.C.: The Council for Research in Values and Philosophy, 1994); and a review article on Louis Dupré, *The Other Dimension: A Search for the Meaning of Religious Attitudes* (New York: Doubleday, 1972), in *American Ecclesiastical Review* 167 (1973) 28–47. The understanding of the relation between God's symbolic mediation of his saving message and the grounds for and meaning of the faith response I offer in the text is analogous to what I offered in *Belief in God,* 216–20, 230–4.

[15]See, for example, Dunn, "Kerygma or Kerygmata?" *Unity and Diversity,* 11–32; Johnson, "Jesus in the Memory of the Church," *Writings of the New Testament,* 114–41, esp. 118–9.

his saving action through Jesus, so that it is available to them as both logos and life, offers them a kind of participative experience of God's action, and calls them to transformation through belief and conversion. This supposes Jesus' living presence in the early Church; what God had been doing through him as he walked the earth he is now doing through Jesus raised and exalted to God's right hand and through his ministers of the word, namely revealing and offering salvation. And it calls the hearers to a participation in God's new age of salvation as an all-inclusive horizon of life, somewhat as other religious symbols of that time—or myths—invited people to a relation to the Sacred.

The Christian proclamation was expressed primarily through symbols. But this is not to divorce these symbols from the order of events and words in history, or space and time. The primitive Christian kerygma is presented in the form of an apostolic *testimony,* or witness. That is, it is an announcement of the good news in virtue of events that happened in history, such as the resurrection appearances of Jesus and the words and deeds of his public ministry, and that revealed to the apostles, who claim to have witnessed them, what God was doing and revealing. These events were interpreted events, interpreted through the words of the Old Testament and of Jesus. Of themselves and divorced from such interpretation they were not a revelation (a theme we will develop particularly in chapters 4, 5, and 8), for they were still ambiguous. Indeed, only with the addition of the inner gift of the Holy Spirit, who opened human hearts to the life and logos they offered, were they the Christian revelation.

Thus the apostolic preaching was not primarily interested in history in the way modern historians are, namely as a developmental account of sequential events, but in deeds and words *as* symbolic acts of God among them. The experience on which they based their kerygma was not some private individual experience but rather experiences due to events and words that came to them from Jesus in his ministry, death, and appearances to them after his resurrection. For them the significance of history *(Geschichte)* was dependent upon what happened in history *(Historie)* in the sense of what happened in a particular time and space rather than in the sense of what can be reached by the specific tools of modern historical-critical methods.

Thus the "ministers of the word" (Luke 1:2) did not restrict what was possible historically to what could come from a restrictedly human agency, as distinct from a divine agency that could even raise the dead to life. Their belief was not within the limits of a modern naturalistic historical consciousness. Also, these ministers of the word presented this message within the context of their sense of mission to make available to others the salvation they had been offered; and thus they made it available rhetorically and with the possibility—and indeed, the Church's experience—of people's rejection of this message and differing interpretations of its implications for life. Thus there is the pluralism of the four Gospels.

We have spoken above of the real authors of the Christian message in early Christian preaching and documents such as the Gospels and the Acts of the Apostles and their real hearers or readers, seeking to overcome what we find to be a false dichotomy between symbolic proclamation and historical events and words in some twentieth-century interpretations of the New Testament. But what we have said supposes that the narrative and other compositions of the New Testament give us access to real authors, real hearers or readers, and real historical events of the first century. That is, this supposes that in the literary genre of the Gospels there is not a dichotomy between composition and concern for mediating what God actually said and did through Jesus Christ. Can we justify this supposition? We will first indicate a more general viewpoint on this question and then support it by reference to the prologue of Luke's Gospel.

The approach to the New Testament texts from the perspective of modern literary criticism has been fruitful, but it can be distorting if it divorces the "narrative world" of the text, the "implied author," and the "implied reader" (i.e., the one the author presupposes is capable of hearing his message and responding positively to it, as we can see from an examination of the text) from the real world, the real author, and the real reader of the text. Bernard Lategan makes this point when he argues that the reference of a gospel text cannot be taken to be restrictedly that which is within the "narrative world" of the text.[16] Until recently, under the influence of the historical-critical method, the interpretation of the text was sought primarily from its sources and tradition, whereas now many seek it largely in the reception of the text by the reader. The text is not simply an objective reality but an *intersubjective communication,* and so the receiver is important. There can

---

[16]See Bernard Lategan, "Reference: Reception, Redescription, and Reality," in Lategan and Vorster, *Text and Reality,* 67–93. References in the text at this point are to that article. With Jeanrond, Lategan contests Ricoeur's emphasis on text as text in a way that undervalues it as intersubjective communication.

be multiple meanings, but there *is* misinterpretation also, and therefore reception cannot be an ultimate norm for the meaning of a work.

Reference, then, counter to Vorster, cannot be analyzed merely in terms of the world of the text. We have to "give full recognition to the intersubjective nature of textual interpretation. . . . The world of the reader as presupposed by the text must also be taken into account. . . . The text constitutes the basis for analysing the anticipated reception of the reader" (68–9). It is through the "implied reader" that the author seeks to reach the real reader. "The implied reader becomes the route by which the author reaches the heart of the real reader" (70). And the author uses all rhetorical techniques for this purpose "to communicate with his reader, to entice him to get involved in the possibilities opened by the text" (73). He uses strategies "to provide the reader with a new perspective on the extratextual reality. In the case of the Lazarus story, the goal is to show Jesus for what he really is, the one who is coming into the world . . . , and to affirm the need for believing in him" (74). Thus attention to reception leads us to a larger understanding of reference than simply that of the "narrative world." Attention to the redescription of reality we find in the text leads us to the same conclusion. "Split reference" refers to the ability of the text to refer to two levels at the same time, for example, what Jesus was doing, and what God was doing through his actions. The gospel author seeks to help the reader see some event *as,* or in a particular perspective: "a shift takes place whereby a new perspective is opened on the second referential level" (80). This is a "redescription of reality" (Ricoeur). So too, although parables have their own internal integrity, "they only function as parables by virtue of an (indirect) outside reference" (82). Although the evangelists treat historical material rather freely in their narratives, this is for the purpose of redescription so that their readers could see the words and events of Jesus' life and death *as* the deeper understanding that was given the apostles through his resurrection called for and *as* it had implications for the needs of the Church of the time and place of the evangelists' writing. Thus it is not dissociated from the real world but rather gives access to the real world in this larger sense.

2. Kerygma and History in Luke's Gospel

We can turn to a study of the relation between text and reality that the evangelist Luke indicates is present in his Gospel and, implicitly, in Acts. This will exemplify and vindicate the above approach to the relation in the Gospels of text and extratextual reality, a vindication also supported by our brief study of Mark in this chapter and of the first missionary sermon in Acts in chapter 5. This study of the text's relation to reality, or its reference, is internal to the text, that is, based on the way it understands itself. Richard Dillon integrates the work of many exegetes as he studies this theme, and so we will follow his work. He takes his point of departure from the prologue to Luke's Gospel and measures its meaning by compositional trends in Luke's Gospel and its stratagems to relate the Gospel to Acts.[17] The prologue to Luke's Gospel reads as follows:

> Inasmuch as many have undertaken to compose a narrative concerning the events which have been brought to their fruition among us, as those handed them on to us who were eye-witnesses from the beginning and became servants of the word, it seemed opportune that I, too, having made an accurate investigation of all (the traditions) from the beginning, should write an orderly account for your Excellency, Theophilus, so that you might come to appreciate the certainty of the instruction *[asphalea logon]* you have received (Luke 1:1-4; Dillon's translation).

We shall ask four questions of this text. *First,* what is the *context* of Luke's endeavor? The fact that many have already given an account of events that he will treat (we may think of Mark and Q at least, if we adopt the two-source view) justifies his own efforts to

---

[17]Richard Dillon, "Previewing Luke's Project from His Prologue (Luke 1:1-4)," *Catholic Biblical Quarterly* 43 (1981) 205–27 (hereafter cited as *CBQ*). Also see idem, *From Eye-Witness to Ministers of the Word: Tradition and Composition in Luke 24* (Rome: Biblical Institute, 1978). Unless otherwise indicated our quotations from the Bible are from *The New American Bible.* References in the text here are to Dillon's article, where further documentation for our summary statements can be found. Also see Joseph Fitzmyer, *The Gospel According to Luke I–IX,* Anchor Bible (New York: Doubleday, 1981); Robert Tannehill, *The Narrative Unity of Luke-Acts: A Literary Interpretation,* vol. 1, *The Gospel According to Luke* (Philadelphia: Fortress Press, 1986); Luke T. Johnson, *The Gospel of Luke* (Collegeville: The Liturgical Press, 1991) 3–10; William Kurz, "Narrative Approaches to Luke-Acts," *Biblica* 68 (1987) 195–220; Joseph Plevnik, "The Eyewitnesses of the Risen Jesus in Luke 24," *CBQ* 49 (1987) 90–103; Evelyn Thibeaux, *The Narrative Rhetoric of Luke 7:36-53: A Study of Context, Text, and Interpretation* (Ph.D. diss., Graduate Theological Union, Berkeley, Calif., 1990). Thibeaux gives an extended analysis of Luke's Gospel in relation to genres of the ancient world and modern literary criticism, concluding that it is a "narrative-rhetorical sacred history" (61, passim). She writes that "Dillon's views are consonant with my own" (113).

compose a narrative of these events. We should note that we see in Luke's editing of Mark that he holds an equivalence between "narrating" and "proclaiming" (see Luke 8:39; Mark 5:19); so if "narrative" is taken as Luke's literary genre, "it should not be classified as some kind of non-kerygmatic historical reasoning which only modern theological debate could define" (209). The context of Luke's endeavor is clarified by his reference in the first clause to both his readers and himself by the word "us." The events are not contemporary with the author and his readers, so they were not personally witnessed by them.

Second, this leads us to ask what the *subject matter* of his Gospel is. It is not simply the events of the past but rather the effect of these events on Luke and people of a later generation that must be brought out if this "subject-matter is to be made pertinent to people like himself who did not participate in that formative past personally" (211). While Luke has many themes in his Gospel, he is centrally concerned with the saving events of the past as they have been brought to their fruition for a later generation. They came to their fruitfulness or fulfillment in this later generation, as Luke shows throughout his Gospel (particularly in the last chapter of his Gospel and the first chapters of Acts) through witnesses of these events who became "servants of the word."

Throughout his writing Luke is interested in events as fulfilling God's prophetic word; this shows God's actions in these events, and it is only by seeing these events in relation to God's word that they can be seen as God's actions. The last chapter of Luke's Gospel in particular shows the formation of the "servants of the word." After the death of Jesus, the women's experience of the empty tomb, and their report that Jesus was alive, two disciples were walking toward Emmaus talking about these things. A stranger began walking with them, asked them what they were discussing, and then began to explain to them the Scriptures showing that it was "necessary that the Messiah should suffer these things and enter into his glory" (Luke 24:26). It was only then and at the breaking of the bread that they recognized him as Jesus. "Only when he expounded the Scriptures, he who was their complete fulfillment as well as their master expounder, were the puzzled Easter *onlookers* made into prospective Easter *witnesses*" (213). Luke's subject matter is not only the original events but "how provision was made for their propagation through a mission modeled after Jesus' own, and how that mission begat the worldwide Christendom in which the Lucan generation was situated" (217).

Third, what is the *procedure* or *standard* of Luke's Gospel, as shown by the prologue? He writes that, having examined the traditions from the beginning, he is writing an "orderly account" *(kathexēs)* for Theophilus. This "order," as can be seen in the course of his Gospel, is not primarily chronological. As his use of this word "orderly" elsewhere (Acts 11:4) indicates, it can refer to a logical order or an order of ideas. And this fits his Gospel. He orders the traditions he has received (e.g., in his narrative of Jesus' journey to Jerusalem in Luke 9:51–18:14) to better express "the significance of the events and teachings they recorded" (222). So the word *kathexes,* or orderly, indicates a "modality of a literary presentation" to bring his readers to "the correct understanding of the events" (222–3), that is, in accord with their "directional thrust" or their contribution to the historical continuum or their place according to the logic of the divine plan. He places "his raw materials in relationship to the totality of sacred history, as it came to completion in the Easter Christ" (223).

Fourth, what is the *purpose* of Luke's orderly composition? It is, as the prologue states, that Theophilus may have "certainty" concerning the instruction he had received or the "words" he had been taught. By this use of "words" Luke is referring to the kerygma of salvation. For example, the risen Jesus' words explained how his death and resurrection were the fulfillment of God's saving plan (Luke 24:44). And the mission sermons of Acts are offered by Luke as key examples of this discourse of Jesus, now exercised through the disciples he had instructed, through whom "*he* came to 'proclaim light to the people and to the nations' (Acts 26:23)" (224). What "certainty" does Luke's way of ordering material give to Theophilus? "Obviously, a story which fully told how Jesus' own words of instruction were committed to appointed witnesses (Luke 24:44-48) could effectively instill a catechumen's *asphalea logon*" (225). This word "certainty" is used by Luke in Peter's Pentecost sermon at its conclusion after he had recounted the deeds of Jesus, his death and resurrection, and interpreted them by the prophetic texts of Scripture: "Let all Israel know with certainty *(asphalos)* that God has made both Lord and Christ this Jesus whom you have crucified! (Acts 2:36)." The certainty then is not simply about the occurrence of the events but about "the significance of the reported events as God's action in history . . . that God acted in the events recounted and

thereby fulfilled his documented promises of salvation for Israel"
(223, 225). Luke demonstrates a continuity between God's fulfillment of his promises of salvation and the present situation of
Christian proclamation of the good news and belief.

This study of Luke's composition, dependent both on the prologue
to his Gospel and on compositional trends in his Gospel, particularly
in Luke 24, shows us the relation between kerygma and history, narrative world, and reference to the extratextual world he intends in his
Gospel. I suggest it supports what we indicated toward the beginning
of this section. That is, the message (the-world-in-front-of-the-text)
is the kerygma, the good news that God is offering salvation to those
who believe in Jesus Christ, and what this salvation and its implications are. This message is conveyed by the acts and words of Jesus,
organized in the composition of the Gospel in a way to give us access to that significance. This does involve at times non-factual elements, for "ancient writers of history, including Luke, do sometimes
use the images and dramatic episodes of fiction to heighten the effect
and deepen the impact of the historical events upon their readers,"[18]
but this does not detract at all from Luke giving us *substantively* what
Jesus actually said and did.

These words and deeds have a split reference. They refer to what
Jesus said and did, but not out of a primary concern to write history
according to the historical model. They refer to this so that the
reader—and earlier, the hearer—could discern God's acts and words
offering salvation through Jesus and through this come to belief or
deeper belief. They refer symbolically to this larger reality through
referring to what Jesus said and did. Or, Jesus' actions and words are
presented as real symbols of what God was doing and revealing
through Jesus, and this from the deeper understanding the disciples
achieved by way of the death and resurrection and exaltation of
Jesus. Thus they point to what God is doing now through the exalted
Jesus and his ministers and to the need for faith to receive this salvation. This is counter to the dichotomy between kerygma and history
in the Gospels that a number of exegetes and theologians hold. And
it is corrective of some who use modern hermeneutics and literary

---

[18]Thibeaux, *Narrative Rhetoric of Luke,* 87. These non-factual accounts had to be plausible or
fit the character of the person to whom they were ascribed. Thibeaux cites (120) I. Howard
Marshall, *Gospel of Luke: A Commentary on the Greek Text* (Grand Rapids: Eerdmans, 1978) 40:
"It is clear from Lk. 7:21 and Acts 1:3 that Luke was concerned with the historical reliability of
his material."

criticism of the New Testament to make a dichotomy between composition, or narrative, and reference beyond this.

III. The Gospel Genre and the Jesus of History

Earlier in this chapter we indicated our thesis on the relation between the Christ of the kerygma and the Jesus of history. Briefly, this thesis, which is substantially in accord with chapter 5 of Vatican II's *Dei verbum,* can be stated in three parts. (1) The evangelists' composition of the Gospels is for the purpose of giving a deeper understanding of the mystery of Jesus and its implications for the Christian community—deeper, that is, than modern historical criticism in some of its major representatives seeks or allows. (2) They do this from the perspective of the postpaschal Christian community, which has, in the apostles and first disciples, experienced the appearances of the risen Jesus and the coming of the Holy Spirit; has experienced too the living presence of Jesus in the Eucharist, the proclamation of the word, and the community (Acts 2:42; 1 Cor 11:23f.); and has handed on the tradition amid problems of proclaiming the faith in different contexts. They write from faith engendered and matured by these experiences and the living of the Christian life. (3) Their fidelity to the task of strengthening and enlightening the faith of Christians through writing the Gospels depended on their being faithful to what Jesus actually said and did and who he was but also on their exercise of a hermeneutics—their arranging and explicating this—so that the deeper meaning and implications of Jesus and his words and deeds could be evident to their readers. It depended on their use of creative imagination, but one that shaped the tradition of the words and deeds of Jesus rather than substituted for this tradition. The Christ of faith and the Jesus of history are the same, though there is a pluralism of kerygmata according to diverse traditions and needs of different Christian communities.

We sought to show that this was supported specifically through an internal analysis of Luke's Gospel. Now we would like to illustrate and defend this by an internal analysis of a dominant theme or so in Mark's Gospel *(Sitz im Leben Evangelii)* and present and answer a recent interpretation of what history is that is opposed to our view. All this we do briefly, because it can be found more fully and adequately elsewhere. Before we do this, we would like to point to some further evidence confirming what we have so far supported mostly in reference to Luke's Gospel.

First, Scripture scholars generally put more historical credence now in the Gospel accounts of Jesus than they did a few decades ago.[19] Some even call this change "the third quest," to distinguish the present historical quest for Jesus from the nineteenth-century quest and from the post-Bultmannian quest. This is not to deny the great variety of interpretations of Jesus this present "quest" has given rise to. But this quest does involve a significant degree of consensus that Jesus performed healings and exorcisms. Jesus' miracles are so central to his ministry, the reason for his large following and the resulting opposition of Jewish leaders, that to excise them from the Gospel is to make much of Jesus' ministry meaningless. Within the present consensus, however, many would still disallow Jesus' raising the dead to life and the nature miracles. As Barry Blackburn writes: "It can hardly be denied that a major factor in this treatment of the nature miracles is the judgment that strictly miraculous events are simply impossible, or at least that they are so wildly improbable that human testimony would never be strong enough to render them otherwise."[20]

Second, the gospel writers did show a strong concern for being faithful to the tradition that goes back to the beginning of the Christian community, and criteria have been largely agreed on for use in discerning which of these traditions represent substantially the words and deeds of Jesus. Readers can find studies of these traditions (i.e., Mark, Q, special Matthew, special Luke, and John) elsewhere as well as analyses of the criteria mentioned (e.g., multiple attestation, dissimilarity, embarrassment, effect, coherence). But we should add that the care of Matthew and Luke to use Q, the written collection of sayings of Jesus inferred by Scripture scholars from the verbal agreements between Matthew and Luke, shows their interest in fidelity to

---

[19]See Bruce Chilton and Craig Evans, eds., *Studying the Historical Jesus: Evaluations of the State of Current Research* (New York: Brill, 1994); Ben Meyer, "Jesus Christ," *The Anchor Bible Dictionary* (New York: Doubleday, 1992) 3:773–96 (hereafter cited as *ABD*); Howard Kee, *Jesus in History: An Approach to the Study of the Gospels,* 2nd ed. (New York: Harcourt Brace Jovanovich, 1977).

[20]Barry Blackburn, "The Miracles of Jesus," *Studying the Historical Jesus,* ed. Chilton and Evans, 370. Also see Craig Evans, "Life-of-Jesus Research and the Eclipse of Mythology," *TS* 54 (1993) 3–36; Howard Kee, *Miracle in the Early Christian World: A Study in Sociohistorical Method* (New Haven, Conn.: Yale University Press, 1983).

the authentic tradition.[21] The historical value of the Gospels is also set off by their contrast to the greater freedom from tradition shown by the *Gospel of Thomas* as it reinterprets Jesus within its form of Hellenistic Judaism and early Gnosticism.[22]

Third, the evangelist John is explicit in what motivates his writing: "Jesus did many other signs in the presence of [his] disciples that are not written in this book. But these are written that you may [come to] believe that Jesus is the Messiah, the Son of God, and that through this belief you may have life in his name" (John 20:30-31). John tells us that he wrote only some of the things that Jesus did, his *semeia,* or symbolic acts, and did so that his readers may believe in Jesus. Thus his work is an artistic creation, but there is a close relation between the Johannine Jesus and the historical Jesus. Jesus and his works were a natural symbol or revelation, an icon, of God and his saving activity. As Sandra Schneiders points out, the artist liberates "the symbolized transcendent from its overparticularization in the natural symbol . . . by selecting only certain elements of the natural symbol, and modifying even these." Similarly, John "seizes upon certain details of the history of Jesus because of their remarkably revelatory, that is, symbolic potential. . . . What history revealed to John was the identity of Jesus as Son of God and it is that whole Christology which he pours back into the few historical events as artistic material."[23]

1. Mark's Gospel and the Jesus of History

We shall mention briefly a few internal characteristics of the Gospel of Mark that are widely accepted by Scripture scholars and that reflect the kind of reference it has to the Jesus of history and through him to God, as well as how this is integrated into Mark's overall rhetorical purpose. Mark's Gospel is widely accepted as being the first of the Gospels written. Thus he created the genre "gospel," at least in its written form, that is, the narrative form of the

---

[21]See Arland Hultgren, *The Rise of Normative Christianity* (Minneapolis: Fortress Press, 1994), and specifically "the Q Community," 31–41. On criteria, see Ben Meyer, "Jesus Christ"; John Meier, *A Marginal Jew;* and Craig Evans, "Life-of-Jesus Research."

[22]See Stevan Davies, "The Christology and Protology of the *Gospel of Thomas,*" *Journal of Biblical Literature* 111 (1992) 663–82 (hereafter cited as *JBL*).

[23]Sandra Schneiders, "History and Symbolism in the Fourth Gospel," *L'Evangile de Jean: Sources, rédaction, théologie,* ed. Marinus de Jonge (Leuven: University Press, 1977) 374, 375.

good news (or "kerygmatic narrative"), which covered the ministry, passion, death, and resurrection of Jesus as an integrated or coherent account. This is distinct from the form in which Paul proclaimed the good news and Q articulated the good news. Early Church tradition since Papias (ca. A.D. 120) attributed this Gospel to Mark, a companion of Peter in Rome (1 Pet 5:13) and the John Mark of Acts 12:12 and the Mark of several Pauline epistles (e.g., 2 Tim 4:1).

Though this has been attacked more recently, an internal analysis of aspects of the Gospel, which can be found elsewhere, show that "a Jewish-Christian community at Rome shortly after A.D. 70 would be an excellent candidate for the audience of the Gospel."[24] (According to others, a period shortly before the year 70 is thought more likely.) If these were the circumstances in which it was written, one of the main characteristics of the Marcan composition becomes quite understandable. That period in Rome was just after the persecution of Christians by Emperor Nero, and it was also just after (or before) the destruction of Jerusalem by Roman soldiers under Titus. It was a period in which Christians were subject to persecution if they were faithful to Jesus Christ. And Mark's Gospel is centered largely around who Jesus is and what belief and discipleship mean.

His Gospel states in the first verse: "The beginning of the gospel of Jesus Christ the Son of God" (Mark 1:1). The author writes from an acceptance of Jesus as Christ the Son of God, and his Gospel is structured about Jesus' proclamation in deed and word of the kingdom of God and repentance (Mark 1:15) and about outsiders' and insiders' reactions to him during his ministry, passion, and death. Mark is writing for Christians in his own time and place who face suffering, and he uses their tendency to identify themselves with Jesus' first disciples and the difficulties these had in acceptance of Jesus as suffering Messiah to instruct them about what true discipleship is. "Mark is an apocalyptic narrative in which the anticipated categories

---

[24]John Donahue, "Mark," *Harper's Bible Commentary,* ed. James L. Mays (San Francisco: Harper & Row, 1988) 984. Also see his comments on Mark 13:5-13 (p. 1002). Donahue has treated this question again in "Windows and Mirrors: The Setting of Mark's Gospel," *CBQ* 57 (1995) 1–26. Also see Frank Matera, *What Are They Saying About Mark?* (New York: Paulist Press, 1987); Augustine Stock, *Call to Discipleship: A Literary Study of Mark's Gospel* (Wilmington, Del.: Michael Glazier, 1982); *The Method and Message of Mark* (Wilmington, Del.: Michael Glazier, 1989); Howard Kee, *Jesus in History: An Approach to the Study of the Gospels,* 2nd ed. (New York: Harcourt Brace Jovanovich, 1977); Marinus de Jonge, *Jesus, the Servant-Messiah* (New Haven, Conn.: Yale University Press, 1991).

of insider and outsider are redefined in terms of response to the mystery of the kingdom who is Jesus."[25]

Mark presents acts and words of Jesus that show him *as* the bringer of eschatological salvation within God's plan of salvation as testified by the Jewish Scripture. He writes that Jesus' message was: "This is the time of fulfillment. The kingdom of God is at hand. Repent and believe in the gospel" (Mark 1:15). Howard Kee shows, for example, that

> Mark presents Jesus as one whose ministry among men was characterized by the work of interpreting anew God's Law, and doing so not in continuity with rabbinic methods of interpretation (1:22) but with his own unprecedented authority. Clearly, Mark wants his reader to see in Jesus of Nazareth the eschatological messenger who restores the true understanding of God's will in the End Time.[26]

Similarly, Mark presents many scenes in which Jesus fulfills the role of the bringer of salvation, for example, by his exorcisms, because wresting control of the world from Satan was central to what salvation was. Again, he shows that God anointed Jesus by the Spirit for this mission, and called him "my beloved Son" (Mark 1:10-11). Also, to Jesus is ascribed the messianic titles of "Son of God" (to be understood in a messianic, not metaphysical, sense) by the demons, who recognize him, and finally by the centurion at the foot of the cross, and "Messiah" by Peter (an issue we shall return to in the next chapter). He presents Jesus' words and saving actions to show that even during his ministry Jesus is Messiah. As Kee writes: "Jesus' message and ministry, as well as his passion and death, are set by Mark within a sequence of apocalyptic events, a schedule of eschatological actions by which God will establish his rule over creation."[27]

From his position in the early Church, which had the apostolic testimony to the resurrection of Jesus and the gift of the Spirit as well as the traditions of Jesus' ministry, Mark organizes a narration so that we may see Jesus *as* he was proclaimed to be. His creative imagination as author was in service of God's creative imagination, by which

---

[25]Johnson, "The Gospel of Mark," *Writings of the New Testament,* 158.

[26]Kee, *Jesus in History,* 148.

[27]Ibid., 155.

God showed who Jesus was through his words and deeds. Mark's words have reference to what Jesus did and through that to what God was doing through him. Jesus' rejection by leaders of his own people and his passion and death were a scandal for many, so Mark shows that Jesus' ministry with its concrete stages was in accord with God's plan of salvation.

Even in its beginning, Jesus' ministry results in a division between those who reject and those who accept him (Mark 1:16–3:34), a division between outsiders and insiders. To the former, Jesus teaches in parables, but to the Twelve he explains all things (4:1-34). But then, surprisingly, the Twelve too are slow to believe. As the outsiders had asked in effect, "Who is this man?" (1:27), the Twelve ask after Jesus stills the storm, "Who then is this whom even wind and sea obey?" (4:41). Mark shows the connection between faith, forgiveness of sins, and healing (e.g., 2:5; 5:21-43), and the lack of such healing when faith was absent (6:1-6). Even the Twelve remain dull and un-receptive. In recounting Jesus' healing of a blind man in stages, where his sight was still unclear after the first stage, Mark prepares for the incompleteness of Peter's and the Twelve's faith expressed on the way to Caesarea Philippi. Jesus asked, "Who do you say that I am?" and Peter responded, "You are the Messiah" (8:29).

This is a hinge point in Mark's Gospel. (We will treat Peter's confession and Jesus' proclamation of his coming death in reference to the question of revelation and faith in chapter 4.) Jesus received at least the beginnings of the faith he sought. And now he begins to teach the Twelve about the kind of Messiah he is: "He began to teach them that the Son of Man must suffer greatly and be rejected by the elders, the chief priests, and the scribes, and be killed, and rise after three days" (8:31). Peter immediately rebuked Jesus on hearing this, but Jesus in turn "rebuked Peter and said, 'Get behind me, Satan. You are thinking not as God does, but as human beings do'" (8:32-33). "Peter's vision is still blurred. A messiah could mean many things in that world, and the working definition of the disciples, we quickly learn, has to do with power and prestige."[28] The fact that Mark shows how imperfect the faith of the disciples was testifies to his concern for history.

The controversies between Jesus and the Jewish leaders become more intense when he enters Jerusalem. In the Marcan apocalypse

---

[28]Johnson, *Writings of the New Testament,* 164.

(Mark 13) the disciples of Jesus are warned of the sufferings in store for them and are warned to "watch" lest they too become outsiders. In his account of the Passion (14:1–15:47) Mark shows how the leaders of the Jews bring about Jesus' death and how Judas betrays Jesus, how Peter denies him and all the Twelve flee from him, while some women disciples remain with him. Jesus himself has a sense of God's absence (15:34). It is at the time of the deepest humiliation and defeat of Jesus that the greatest human witness to faith in him by a human in Mark's Gospel is offered, and this by an outsider, a Roman centurion who participated in his execution, who exclaimed, "Truly this man was the [or better, a] Son of God!" (15:39). There is great irony here that the disciples of Jesus fled and faith is offered by an executioner, and a warning to those who consider themselves insiders.

Mark's story shows that he is rhetorically communicating with the Christian disciples of his own time and place, but counter to some who use literary criticism on Mark's Gospel, it does not support the view that he is writing fiction for this purpose. His recall of the scandal of the cross and the embarrassing truth of the disciples' fleeing Jesus, as well as the way his account is supported by other early traditions, show he is using and organizing historical events and words for this purpose.[29]

2. An Objection to Viewing the Gospels as History and an Answer

The question many people in our time have is whether this gospel genre can be history. One of these questioners is Peter Hodgson, as we see in a book he wrote that exemplifies this difficulty. He notes that "the most difficult of modern theological questions [is] that of God's presence in history."[30]

---

[29]See Raymond Brown, *The Death of the Messiah: From Gethsemani to the Grave: A Commentary on the Passion Narratives in the Four Gospels,* 2 vols. (New York: Doubleday, 1994). On literary criticism of Mark's Gospel, see, for example, Mary Ann Tolbert, *Sowing the Gospel: Mark's World in Literary-Historical Perspective* (Minneapolis: Fortress Press, 1989), and a review of this book in *CBQ* 54 (1992) 382–4; Robert Fowler, *Let the Reader Understand: Reader-Response Criticism and the Gospel of Mark* (Minneapolis: Fortress Press, 1991). Literary criticism divorced from historical criticism is not sufficient. See de Jonge, *Jesus, the Servant-Messiah,* who holds from historical criticism that Mark probably interpreted Jesus aright, namely that "it is probable that he [Jesus] regarded himself as the Messiah and Son of David inspired and empowered by the Spirit" (75).

[30]Peter C. Hodgson, *God in History: Shapes of Freedom* (Nashville: Abingdon Press, 1989) 147. Numbered references in text below are to this book.

As a follower, with some significant modifications, of Hegel, he holds that God and history are correlative, that God should not be conceived as a personal agent, and that God's actual existence is increased and diminished in history: "God as absolute spirit is the dynamic, self-manifesting shape or figure that empowers the creative, synthesizing, emancipatory configurations of human life and culture, which are at the same time the self-shaping of God" (141). He analyzes what the writing of history is, particularly through narrativist constructions of history, which he finds very promising. And it is Hayden White and Paul Ricoeur who best articulate this position.

White's general thesis is that historical work is "a verbal structure in the form of a narrative prose discourse that purports to be a model, or icon, of past structures and processes in the interest of *explaining what they were by representing them.*"[31] There are different levels of historical writing; the emplotment found in narrative involves judgments concerning the meaning of a story; there is an ethical moment in historical writing when description implies a "should"; and the only basis for such a move is an ideology. Hodgson agrees with White that "there are no higher theoretical grounds, no 'extra-ideological grounds,' on the basis of which to choose among competing views of history and human existence. Just this is the 'crisis of historicism'" (158). But this impasse also "marks the 'turn to praxis,' for it is only by acting, by engaging in projects of emancipatory praxis, that we shall discover whether the vision is 'true'" (158).

There is a priority of "praxis," for it and not theoretical grounds allows us to interpret history and vindicate such an interpretation. This praxis involves a religious dimension, and Hodgson uses White's hermeneutic model to support a Christian theology of history as tragicomic and as a history of freedom, but he argues to this not "on the basis of appeals to authority or privileged experience, but only . . . in terms of its representational persuasiveness within a community of discourse. The same is true of any theological proposal" (159).

Hodgson also turns to Ricoeur's analysis of historical narrative. By metaphorical reference we redescribe reality that is not immediately accessible to us. For example, we redescribe human activity not present to us "by telling a story, inventing a narrative that imitates or 'mimics' the action. The narrative imitates by means of a plot"

[31]Hayden White, *Metahistory: The Historical Imagination in Nineteenth-Century Europe* (Baltimore: Johns Hopkins Press, 1973) 2, as quoted by Hodgson, page 153.

(89).[32] This is true of both history and fiction. Narrative emplotment presupposes and includes our familiar preunderstanding of action over time that has structure and symbolic meaning. Emplotment itself is an act of productive imagination and poetic composition that interrelates events, agents, goals, means, effects, and the like and synthesizes them temporally. The whole that is configured here is the story that can be followed and understood. Its "'end point' is the point from where the story can be seen as a whole, and once it is seen it permits a reading of time backward and as a coherent process" (91).

This configuration projects a world other than itself (it has reference and not only sense) for the reader: "What is interpreted in a text is the proposing of a world that I might inhabit and into which I might project my ownmost powers" (Ricoeur, quoted in Hodgson, 92). This means that the text moves toward praxis; the act of reading enables the text "to have a transforming effect on the world" (91), and we as readers have access to this world if there is a fusion between our horizon and that of the text. Both fiction and history propose such a world, but while fiction does this "primarily by metaphorical reference" history does so "primarily by reference to 'traces of the real'" found in writings and other monuments of the past, though both forms of reference are found interwoven in history as well as in fiction. "'Singular causal attribution' . . . is the characteristic mode of explanation in history" (160), and the objects of historical enquiry are larger and involve longer time spans than subjects of fiction.

After examining and critiquing some poststructuralist deconstructions of history, Hodgson builds particularly on White and Ricoeur to develop a "formal philosophy of history" (169). History leaves traces, and the historian must attend to the rules of evidence. But history is "an imaginative construct, made in accord with ideological convictions" (170). A variety of construals of historical process are possible. In history one must acknowledge defigurative elements, but in a way that allows not only for ambiguity but for an "open teleology"—not an overarching linear teleology that embraces the whole of history but one that gives us the responsibility to "shape new cultural syntheses, on both large and small scales, out of past resources, with an eye to present needs and possibilities, and on the basis of a commitment to universal ideals or values" (184).

---

[32]I am particularly following Hodgson's account of Ricoeur's thought here. Also see Paul Ricoeur, "Narrated Time," *Philosophy Today* 29 (1985) 259–72.

In his material theology of history Hodgson understands there to be an interaction between God and humans, but he understands God as a guiding gestalt: "This guiding gestalt is not a person or personal agent but a transpersonal structure of praxis that grounds personal existence and builds interpersonal relations since it itself is intrinsically relational, social, communicative in character" (208). For Christians "[t]he person of Jesus of Nazareth played and continues to play a normative role in mediating the shape of God in history, which is the shape of love in freedom" (209). However, "God takes shape in other religions as well, and their claims are as legitimate as ours" (214).

Hodgson develops criteria for praxis in continuity with Jürgen Habermas, but he thinks that humanity of itself cannot "overcome this self-concealing perversion of reason" (229). It must have deliverance, "but in the form of an empowerment from within, not of a supernatural rescue" (229). He criticizes another theologian who makes use of Habermas, Helmut Peukert,[33] for calling upon God's act of raising Jesus and others from the dead. For Hodgson these statements of Scripture are "elusive metaphors that require interpretative rigor on the part of each new generation of faith" (226). It is not that Hodgson thinks there is no transhistorical salvation, but he centers on a transformation within history and leaves the possibility of a transhistorical salvation undeveloped and perhaps uncertain—at least not tied to the resurrection of Jesus Christ, as we interpreted the New Testament in this chapter and will again when we treat the question of the resurrection of Jesus in chapter 5.

We are examining the relation between the Christ of the kerygma and the Jesus of history in the Gospels, and we have recalled some aspects of the Gospels of Luke and Mark, as literary criticism shows us these documents are composed so that we can evaluate them on their own terms rather than impose terms on them from outside. Part of what Hodgson offers us concerning the nature of historical writing is helpful in answering our question about the Gospels as history, and part implicitly denies that these Gospels can be history. We shall treat these questions in turn.

The fact that Mark and the other Gospels use creative imagination in their reconfiguration of the ministry, death, and resurrection of Jesus, and that they do so in virtue of a lived experience and a prac-

---

[33]See Helmut Peukert, *Science, Action, and Fundamental Theology: Toward a Theology of Communicative Action* (Cambridge, Mass.: M.I.T. Press, 1984).

tical desire to transform life in the sense of making possibilities of life known and commended, does not of itself mean they are not history, because this is what every history worthy of the name (as distinct from a chronicle) does. They are distinct from fiction, because the Gospels are responsible for the data of Jesus' ministry, death, and resurrection as we have in part seen and will also see in later chapters. The Gospels do this from differing perspectives and in view of differing transfigurations of existence they commend, and so they differ among themselves; but they all claim an identity between the Christ of faith and the Jesus of history, and there is substantial agreement in the kind of Christian life they commend and the data to which they are responsible. Perhaps John's Gospel can more appropriately be called a "theological elaboration of history," but it too reflects on data that the Synoptic Gospels show us to be based in the actions and words of Jesus.[34]

Of course, they do this from a perspective that is beyond a naturalistic historical consciousness that strongly influences the interpretation that Hodgson adopts. They write their accounts of the ministry, death, and resurrection of Jesus from the belief that God, as a personal transcendent being, has acted uniquely in the person, ministry, death, and resurrection of Jesus—a belief grounded, they and the early Church claim, in the appearances of the risen Jesus and the coming of the Holy Spirit upon the Church. And they seek to give an account of the ministry, passion, death, and resurrection of Jesus as a kerygma, that is, as a proclamation of the salvation that God is offering now through Jesus Christ. That is, they seek to give readers access to this deeper reality or mystery, namely, what *God* was doing through him and what the implications of this are for men and women for whom they are writing.[35] They recount all this to show not only what human beings are doing but what God is doing, that is, forgiving sins through Jesus, healing the sick, and offering other signs or symbols of his presence and his saving intention that should be understandable to those who had received the promises, and vindicating Jesus by raising him from the dead after he had been unjustly killed.

---

[34]See James D. Dunn, *The Evidence for Jesus* (Philadelphia: Westminster Press, 1985), chapter 2, "Did Jesus Claim to Be the Son of God?" 30–52.

[35]See Ignace de la Potterie, "Interpretation of Holy Scripture in the Spirit in Which It Was Written (*Dei Verbum* 12c)," *Vatican II: Assessment and Perspectives Twenty-Five Years After (1962–1987)*, René Latourelle, ed., (New York: Paulist Press, 1988) 1:220–66.

They see, from the perspective of their mature Christian faith, more in Jesus' ministry than the disciples initially perceived. And they transpose this later understanding to the way they recount the ministry of Jesus but do not impose it, since there are data they have from a tradition that took its origin in Jesus that give grounds for their interpretations. They witness, then, not only to what Jesus said and did but to what God did through Jesus, for they understand Jesus' words and deeds to be symbols of God's presence, words, and deeds with their saving and revealing significance. Accepting that this is what the evangelists were trying to do is called for even by the search critical historians undertake to understand the literal meaning of an author. As Roch Kereszty writes:

> For understanding what the authors intended to express it is not sufficient to study the sociological and cultural milieus in which they wrote and the literary forms which they used, but one needs to reconstruct their experience "from within." If all these are true, then the "reconstruction" of their faith experience becomes a necessary means to understanding the literal meaning. By doing so the historian does not leave the realm of history since the authors' faith that he tries to reconstruct is also a historical fact. The understanding through faith, then, as implied in BC[36] does not cause the intrusion of a foreign element that would distort the critical method but is required by its very logic if one applies it to analysing a confession of faith. Thus the critical method itself requires that it be surpassed or "transcended."[37]

This brings us to the supposition held by a number of those who use the critical-historical method (but not, apparently, by the majority of contemporary exegetes who use this method) that miracles and a resurrection from the dead are not possible and/or cannot be considered historical. Thus they reinterpret what the New Testament states about miracles and resurrection to bring it into accord with what is "possible." This is a large issue that has been addressed by many

---

[36]See Pontifical Biblical Commission, "Bible and Christology," (1984), translated and commented on in J. A. Fitzmyer, *Scripture and Christology: A Statement of the Biblical Commission with a Commentary* (New York: Paulist Press, 1986).

[37]Roch Kereszty, "The 'Bible and Christology' Document of the Biblical Commission," *Communio* 13 (1986) 354.

theologians and Scripture scholars. We will make two points here and return to this question when we treat the resurrection in chapter 5.

First, this supposition that miracles are impossible or that they are not history comes from the Enlightenment and is a presupposition that many students of the New Testament have brought and still bring to their study of the text. They bring this presupposition to the interpretation of Scripture, and we believers bring our faith, which they consider a distorting presupposition. We should agree that one cannot approach Scripture from a neutral position; but we should allow our presuppositions, whether they come from Christian faith or from Enlightenment philosophy, to be challenged by Scripture and the emergence of Christianity at a particular time and place. This is well expressed by I. Howard Marshall:

> Suppose that a person who disbelieves in the possibility of supernatural events comes up against some event for which every explanation except a supernatural explanation seems to be ruled out. What is he to do? He may resolve to hold on to his presuppositions and regard the alleged supernatural event as something which he cannot explain on these presuppositions, but he is not prepared to let it upset his presuppositions and therefore he suspends judgment upon it. . . . On the other hand, the person may realise that the fact which he cannot explain knocks a fair-sized dent in his presuppositions, and therefore he is prepared to revise them, and if necessary alter them. . . . A third possibility is that . . . the perplexed thinker may seek refuge in agnosticism, concluding that it is not possible for us to combine all phenomena in a satisfactory world view.
>
> There is perhaps no way of determining how a person's mind is going to work in such a situation. But what our argument is meant to show is that presuppositions and evidence stand in a dialectical relationship to one another. We interpret evidence in the light of our presuppositions, and we also form our presuppositions in the light of the evidence. It is only through a "dialogue" between presuppositions and evidence that we can gain both sound presuppositions and a correct interpretation of the evidence. The process is circular and unending. It demands openness on the part of the investigator. He must be prepared to revise his ideas in the light of the evidence, for ultimately it is the evidence which is decisive.[38]

---

[38]I. Howard Marshall, *I Believe in the Historical Jesus* (Grand Rapids: Eerdmans, 1977) 97–8.

Second, we have dealt with Hodgson's philosophical difficulties in our first volume, *Belief in God in our Time.* We proposed, for example, revisions of the classical understanding of the Christian God that take account of modern historical consciousness and that are faithful to the Christian understanding of God. And we reflected on the human person and human society in ways that offered evidence that there is a good or fulfillment proper to human beings as historical beings, that there is a transcendence in this and the human search, that there is a capacity in human beings for metaphysical knowledge, that through human praxis and the physical world around us there are testimonies to the existence of God that make belief in God reasonable, that these give basis for belief in God as a transcendent personal being who interrelates with the world and human beings in history.

There is a genuine immanence of God in history as well as transcendence, and immanence to such an extent that God is affected by what happens in history. We will not repeat this here, but we suggest that if God is a transcendent personal being as we defended in the earlier volume, it is plausible that he would act interpersonally with human beings as the New Testament indicates he did. Specifically, it is plausible that he has loving purposes with human beings in history to bring them into communion with himself and one another; that he uses, in part, the very nature that he has given to human beings to direct them to this purpose; and that he will at times act beyond the natural order if necessary according to his wisdom and love to achieve this purpose. If the order of nature comes from the personal and is directed ultimately to such a personal goal for the community of humankind and for the individual, then it should not be thought impossible that God will subordinate nature to such personal purposes. It is not counter, then, to nature and its purposes or history and its purposes if at times God acts within it by a power beyond the intrinsic capacities of human nature and human history. This means that miracles or a resurrection from the dead are not impossible for God as transcendent personal being nor counter to nature and history.

One may, it is true, define some sciences of nature and history in such a way that it is beyond their capacities, criteria, and methods to acknowledge the presence of a miracle or resurrection. But it is the part of wisdom and modesty to acknowledge that this comes from the exigencies of a particular discipline and does not impose stipulations on reality. As physics can fruitfully limit itself in such a way that it cannot discern testimonies in nature to the existence of God, much less the miraculous, so too critical history can limit itself in such a way that it cannot discern testimonies to God's action in human history, much less his action by way of the miraculous. But this simply shows us that such a form of historical study is only a partial study of factors present in history. This is a very legitimate and important enterprise; it is simply not the whole of what we are capable of discerning in the events of time and space that we call history or writing about in a narrative of these events that we also call history. We may add that even non-Christian historians such as Tacitus acknowledged that the historian could recognize an event in history that was beyond the powers of nature, for he accepted the story that the emperor Vespasian healed a cripple and a blind man in Alexandria.[39]

We conclude that Hodgson's strictures against the kind of history we find in the Gospels come from presuppositions about who God is and what is possible that we have contested in our earlier volume. These presuppositions also prevent his position from being fully Christian.

[39]See Hugo Staudinger, "The Resurrection of Jesus Christ as Saving Event and as 'Object' of Historical Research," *Scottish Journal of Theology* 36 (1983) 314.

3

The Salvation Jesus Proclaimed

After investigating in the preceding chapter what sort of documents the Gospels are, we here ask what the salvation offered by Jesus was. We have seen that Vatican II, in accord with Christian tradition, gives as a basis for faith the fact that through faith we receive salvation. And it analyzes the nature of this salvation to some extent. The grounds for believing and the nature of Christian faith are, then, dependent upon the fact that through Jesus Christ we receive salvation and what this salvation is.

Since in this volume we are examining the meaning and grounds for belief in Jesus Christ, it is necessary that we analyze Scripture's teaching on this matter. Here we are treating Scripture as having historical value, and we ask what we can know about how Jesus actually proclaimed God's offer of salvation. We also ask whether we can actually have a basis for trusting that we will receive such a salvation through him. The answer to the first of these questions depends on our having some understanding of the ministry of Jesus, while the answer to the second depends primarily on the basis and meaning of the early Church's proclamation of the resurrection of Jesus, an issue we shall treat in chapter 5.

We are not assuming that a historical analysis is sufficient for faith, but we hold that it is relevant to the meaning and grounding of our Christian faith. In fact, a study of the New Testament in relation to history is an essential component of our effort to give a reason for the hope we have. If Jesus historically proclaimed a salvation contradictory to that proclaimed by the Church at Vatican II, or if he did not proclaim it and confirm it by his resurrection from the dead, then

Vatican II's way of giving meaning and grounds for Christian faith—and the way of Christian Churches more generally—cannot be called Christian.

Part of the perspective from which we ask these questions comes from the main difficulties posed against the Church's current teaching. We have proposed that these difficulties can best be summed up, first, under the heading of a rather naturalistic modern historical consciousness, naturalistic more in practice than in theory but in both; and, second, under the heading of an interpretation of salvation in a way that is too identified with that of an earlier age. Because of the first of these, many people consider what the Church and, indeed, Jesus offer to be rather irrelevant to what they conceive their main purposes and problems to be, and also implausible in the extreme. Because of the second, some Christians interpret salvation in an individualistic way without, for example, accepting its entailing their acting to change the world so that it shows more of God's justice, particularly for those who are most in need. The present chapter will not answer all the problems these difficulties raise, but we will find that the Church's proclamation is faithful in this matter to what Jesus and the early Church proclaimed. We will return to this subject as it relates to some evils from which people need liberation and current views on anthropology in a later chapter. We study this within the limits of an introductory treatment of this matter.

In this effort our theological dialogue partners are those we mentioned in the second chapter of volume one of *Foundational Theology* and, more briefly, in the first chapter of this present volume. Before Vatican II the interpretation of the implications of faith for human existence offered by most theologians was more within an individualistic and/or existentialist interpretation of human life than within a holistic, and so in part political, interpretation. In part this was due to the continuing dominance of the sixteenth-century conflict on the justification of the sinner by grace. Of course, there were the further differences among Catholic theologians and among the Protestant theologians we pointed out earlier.

After Vatican II there was more agreement across the board on the historical or process character of human existence and on the historical-critical and literary-critical approaches to Scripture. In the interpretation of what salvation is, however, there are Christians who seek to be faithful to tradition but tend to equate tradition with an articulation of it too dependent on a premodern anthropology, and there are those who call for reinterpretations of Christian faith to meet the current situation but who tend at times to be too uncritical of current pragmatism and historicism.

We treated these issues as they relate to the meaning and foundations for belief in God in our earlier volume. And systematically, we presuppose that here. We presuppose, then, that we accept ourselves as human beings oriented through history to a good proper to human beings and even to an absolute good, and as believing in God as transcendent personal being who is related to history. We suppose that we accept *some* testimonies to God's offer of salvation to us but that we are desperately in need of a salvation these pre-Christian intimations of God and his offer of help do not meet. For example, what we have written in our first volume does not give an answer to our need of forgiveness or to the mystery of death. Neither does it give us an assurance that God's kingdom or salvation will prevail in history, nor does it show us the way of salvation and personal relation to him which God makes available to us. In reality, we look back as Christians on the foundations and meaning of our belief in Jesus Christ that we already live and accept, and we seek to evaluate these critically and in a way appropriate to our time and place.

After some introductory remarks, we shall treat (I) the context for the ministry of Jesus and (II) Jesus' proclamation of the kingdom of God in his ministry.

There have been radically differing interpretations of whether we can know what Jesus proclaimed in his ministry. The previous chapter concluded that we can know something significant about Jesus' ministry from the Gospels if we understand these texts on their own terms or as the kind of documents they claim to be. There seems to be a consensus among New Testament scholars in our time that Bultmann's skepticism was excessive and that we can know what kind of man Jesus was and what kinds of things he said and did, even if we cannot know exactly what he said and did.[1]

Broadly speaking, what are some major differences among New Testament scholars in their interpretation of Jesus' ministry and the

---

[1] See Marcus Borg, *Jesus. A New Vision: Spirit, Culture, and the Life of Discipleship* (San Francisco: Harper & Row, 1987) 15. Also see idem, *Conflict, Holiness, and Politics in the Teaching of Jesus* (New York: Edwin Mellen Press, 1984); John Meier, "Jesus," *NJBC* 1316–28; Ben Meyer, *The Aims of Jesus* (London: SCM Press, 1979); idem, "Jesus Christ," *ABD* 3:772–96; Bruce Chilton and Craig Evans, eds., *Studying the Historical Jesus: Evaluation of the State of Current Research* (New York: Brill, 1994).

kingdom he proclaimed?[2] We offer a rather foreshortened account of the many varied views for the purpose of identifying where the primary current differences of interpretation seem to be. A history of these differences over the past few centuries can be found elsewhere.[3] The first view we mention is not that of current Scripture scholars but rather the popular Christian view that depends largely on the Gospel of John. Jesus spoke of himself as God's Son, as equal to the Father, and offered eternal life to those who believe in him. What the early Christians articulated and what the Council of Chalcedon defined was explicit in the way Jesus spoke during his ministry. In reference to this view, those who accept the historical-critical method—even Catholics and other Christians who believe in Jesus in accord with John's Gospel—largely agree that most of the discourses John gives were not explicitly offered as such by Jesus. Otherwise it would be difficult to accept the three other Gospels, the Synoptics, in the substance of their account of Jesus' ministry, the focus of that ministry on the kingdom, and the kinds of controversies in which Jesus was involved.

While in the Synoptics the focus of Jesus' proclamation was the kingdom of God, in John it was more the identity of Jesus as God's Son and definitive revelation. The main controversies Jesus was involved in concerned, for the Synoptics, the Law, and for John, Jesus' claims about himself. John's discourses had, the Churches would hold, a basis in some things Jesus said and did as found even in the Synoptics; but they were "explications," or interpretative expansions,[4] arrived at by the Beloved Disciple after many years of Christian living and meditation on the implications of Christ's words and deeds and the experience of the living Christ in the Church, and in view of the differences among Christians prominent toward the end of the first century.[5]

Those who used (and who use) the historical-critical method in approaching the Gospels sought to get behind the Christ of faith to the Jesus of history and rejected the Johannine view as the most accurate historical representation of what Jesus explicitly said and did in his ministry. There are, of course, quite varied views of who Jesus was

[2]In this analysis I follow Borg substantially, though, as will be apparent, I do not wholly accept his view of what Jesus proclaimed. See Borg, *Jesus,* "Introduction. Clearing the Ground: Two Images of Jesus," 1–22.

[3]See, e.g., John Kselman and Ronald Witherup, "Modern New Testament Criticism" *NJBC* 1130–45.

[4]See Vatican II, *Dei verbum,* chapter 5, paragraph 19.

[5]See Pheme Perkins, "The Gospel According to John," *NJBC,* "Introduction," 942–50.

offered by those who use the historical-critical method. We can mention as an example of late nineteenth-century Protestant liberalism A. von Harnack, who considered that the essence of Christianity lay in certain ethical truths taught by Jesus—the fatherhood of God and the universal brotherhood of men. Albert Schweitzer in *The Quest of the Historical Jesus,* 1906, severely criticized liberal Protestantism's portrayal of Jesus as comparable to a man looking into a well and seeing an image of himself. Schweitzer found Jesus to be a figure radically different, namely a heroic figure who proclaimed the kingdom of God in an apocalyptic sense and thus expected the end of the world to occur during his generation, and who went to death to bring about the kingdom. He was mistaken, of course.

Except for some details, Schweitzer's view of Jesus as eschatological prophet became the view many exegetes accepted, particularly German exegetes, and it was these who had the most influence through the greater part of the twentieth century. Even Bultmann thought that Jesus did proclaim the kingdom with an apocalyptic meaning, though he built his theology not on Jesus but on the early Church kerygma as he interpreted it. A more recent representative of this view, an eminent exegete who differs radically from Bultmann on many issues, is James Dunn, who asserts that "[i]t is difficult to avoid the conclusion that Jesus' expectation of the future kingdom was apocalyptic in character," and that "[i]t . . . looks very much as though Jesus thought the End was *imminent* . . . , within the lifetime of his own generation . . . , before the disciples had completed the round of preaching to Israel."[6]

Counter to interpretations of Jesus as proclaiming an apocalyptic kingdom are views of Jesus as a leader of a renewal or reform movement among the poor and dispossessed in Palestine. This is found in varied ways, for example, in some liberation theologians[7] and some American Scripture scholars who incorporate the use of the social

[6]James Dunn, *Unity and Diversity in the New Testament* (Philadelphia: Westminster Press, 1977) 321, 320. See the entire chapter "Apocalyptic Christianity," 309–40. For an interpretation of eschatology in Jesus' preaching somewhat different from that of Dunn, see Oscar Cullmann, "Salvation History," in Kselman and Witherup, *NJBC* 1139–40.

[7]See Juan Segundo, *The Historical Jesus of the Scriptures* (Maryknoll, N.Y.: Orbis Books, 1985); Jon Sobrino, *Christology at the Crossroads* (Maryknoll, N.Y.: Orbis Books, 1978), especially chapters 3–5; Gustavo Gutierrez, *A Theology of Liberation: History, Politics, and Salvation* (Maryknoll, N.Y.: Orbis Books, 1973) 225ff. and passim; Arthur McGovern, *Liberation Theology and Its Critics: Toward an Assessment* (Maryknoll, N.Y.: Orbis Books, 1989) especially 72ff.; Pheme Perkins, "Theological Implications of New Testament Pluralism," *CBQ* 50 (1988) 11–13.

sciences to understand the setting in which Jesus' ministry was cast[8] and interpret Jesus as Spirit-filled, as holy man, as sage, as revitalization-movement founder and prophet.[9] Marcus Borg points out reasons for the emergence of this view. In the first place, most American exegetes now hold that Jesus did not expect the end of the world in his generation. The basis of their position is

> an emerging conviction that the "coming Son of man" sayings (which are the central foundation stones for saying that Jesus expected the imminent end of the world) are not authentic, that is, that they do not go back to Jesus but are the products of the early Church. Moreover, if Jesus did not expect the imminent end of the world, then it follows that "Kingdom of God" must be given a meaning other than its eschatological one.[10]

Use of the social sciences can help us put Jesus in the context of the challenges to the Judaism of his time and the divisions among the Jews in response to these challenges. Our renewed confidence that we can have access to the Jesus of history through the Gospels can help us give priority to those things the Gospels seem clearly to ascribe to him, for example, that he was a healer, Spirit-filled, concerned for the poor and for a change of the social attitudes and structures that kept them poor.

In our study of Jesus' ministry, we approach the question of what sort of salvation he was offering, particularly in the context of this dispute between those who interpret the kingdom proclaimed by Jesus as apocalyptic and those who interpret it as a revitalization or renewal or reform movement in Palestine.[11] We shall first recall the context in which Jesus proclaimed the kingdom and then his proclamation during his ministry.

[8]See Richard Horsley, *Sociology and the Jesus Movement* (New York: Crossroad, 1989).

[9]See Borg, *Jesus;* idem, *Conflict;* Daniel Harrington, "Jesus and Wisdom: Convergences and Challenges," *Proceedings of the Catholic Theological Society of America* 49 (1994) 100–4.

[10]Borg, *Jesus,* 14. See pages 197–9 for the way he interprets Jesus' use of "kingdom" language.

[11]An earlier essay of mine relevant to this theme is "The Peace of Christ in the Earthly City," *God's Work in a Changing World* (1985; now distributed by Washington, D.C.: The Council for Research in Values and Philosophy, 1994) 1–33.

I. Context for Jesus' Proclamation of the Kingdom

Mark summarizes Jesus' proclamation of the good news as follows: "This is the time of fulfillment. The kingdom of God is at hand.
Repent, and believe in the gospel" (Mark 1:15). In preaching thus he
used a term and concept familiar to those to whom he spoke. And he
spoke to them in the context of the troubles and hopes they were experiencing at the time. To understand this message, we have to
understand something of the Jews' beliefs in this matter and their
current situation.

1. The Old Testament and the Kingdom of God

The phrase "kingdom of God" is not used in the Old Testament,
but the theme is central, though God's rule is expressed as coming
about in a variety of ways that had not achieved synthesis for the
Jewish people by the time of Jesus.[12] God's coming in the Old
Testament was noted as being for revelation, in cultic events, and for
judgment and salvation. The most numerous group of texts refer to
the third. One of the oldest of the expressions of this is found in the
Canticle of Deborah:

> O Lord, when you went out from Seir, when you marched from the
> land of Edom, the earth quaked and the heavens were shaken,
> while the clouds sent down showers. Mountains trembled in the
> presence of the Lord, the One of Sinai, in the presence of the Lord,
> the God of Israel (Judg 5:4-5).

Deborah's canticle was sung after Israel's defeat of Sisera. The
coming of God it celebrated is his coming for the salvation of Israel
and his judgment on Israel's enemies in those circumstances. The re-

---

[12]In the following I depend particularly on G. R. Beasley-Murray, *Jesus and the Kingdom of
God* (Grand Rapids: Eerdmans, 1986). Also see G. Rochais, "Les Origines de l'Apocalyptic,"
Science et Esprit 25 (1973) 17–50; J. Coppens and others, "Règne de Dieu," *Supplément au
Dictionnaire de la Bible* (Paris: Letouzey & Ané, 1985) 10:1–199; J.D.G. Dunn, "Messianic Ideas
and Their Influence on the Jesus of History," *The Messiah: Developments in Earliest Judaism and
Christianity*, ed. James Charlesworth (Minneapolis: Fortress Press, 1992) 365–81. Page references
in the text here are to Beasley-Murray. Recently more attention is being given to the Spirit and
God's intervention for the salvation of his people. See Michael Welker, *God the Spirit*
(Minneapolis: Fortress Press, 1994); M. John Farrelly, "Holy Spirit," *The New Dictionary of
Catholic Spirituality*, ed. Michael Downey (Collegeville: The Liturgical Press, 1993) 492–503.

action of nature at the Lord's coming shows his power. His coming to save is described in a way that is reminiscent of surrounding peoples' myths of the battle of the god of heaven with the forces of primeval chaos (see Ps 77:16), but the central element comes from Israel's experience of the God of Sinai liberating them from slavery in Egypt, their Exodus, the covenant he made with them, and his leading them into the land of milk and honey.

Though early Israel did not use the phrase "kingdom of God," the Israelites thought of Yahweh as king. The leadership of Yahweh relates to his sovereign acts on behalf of his people. The covenant was modeled on the Hittite vassal-overlord relationship (Exod 19:5-6), and thus it was a theopolitical event. The purpose of God's action in his people's behalf was the establishment of them as committed to him and of what can be called "the kingdom of God"; the horizon was this-worldly and communal and included this people's commitment to be "a priestly kingdom and a holy nation" (Exod 19:6). Perhaps it was not until the period of the kings that Israel explicitly called God "king." Certainly, with Nathan's prophecy to David and his line, God's promise to Israel as a whole was expressed in a special way to David and his dynasty (2 Kgs 7:12-16). Their liturgy actualized God's kingship (e.g., Psalm 47) and encouraged hope.

The image of king is not fully adequate to express God's mediation of salvation at this time. The mediation of salvation was also ascribed to the Spirit. In the period of the judges, God's liberation of the people from the oppression their sins had caused was ascribed at times to the Spirit of God, which came upon finite individuals to empower them and to unite a fragmented society around them to throw off the yoke and restore some sense of community in fidelity to God. When David was anointed by Samuel, "the spirit of the Lord rushed upon David" (1 Sam 16:13).

The event in which God acts to overthrow his enemies, imaged in terms of battle, is frequently spoken of as "the Day of the Lord." Its first emergence is in Amos 5:18, where, to the consternation of those to whom he spoke, he prophesied calamity also for God's enemies in Israel. Isaiah (ca. 742–687 B.C.), in his ministry in the southern kingdom, calls for repentance and promises Yahweh's judgment on the nations (thus showing his universal dominion) and on Judah. There is something ultimate and complete in the horizon of his promises of God's destiny for Israel (Isa 2:2-5). Isaiah also reflected on Nathan's promises to the house of David and prophesied a future king who is described in idealized terms—the Immanuel prophecies (Isa 7:14; 9:1-6; 11:1-4). The Spirit of the Lord will rest upon this future anointed king or messianic figure, who as the bearer of the Spirit will establish justice, mercy, and knowledge of God. The messianic figure "is the representative of Yahweh in his kingdom, in whom Yahweh is present and through whom he acts" (22).

The Exile was a profound rift in the history of God's people. Before it were many threats of God's judgment; after it were many promises of his salvation. Salvation now more than before was expected from God alone, although there are human agents involved. For example, in his later period Jeremiah saw the evil in Judah as so great that the covenant God had made with it was no longer adequate. God would create a new covenant, putting his Law in their hearts (Jer 31:31ff.). And Ezekiel pictured the whole history of Israel as a rebellion. The new Israel could only come from a new creative act of God like restoring flesh and spirit to dry bones (Ezek 37:12-14), giving a new heart and a new spirit (Ezek 36:26-27): "I will give you a new heart and place a new spirit within you, taking from your bodies your stony hearts and giving you natural hearts. I will put my spirit within you and make you live by my statutes, careful to observe my decrees."

Toward the end of the Exile, Deutero-Isaiah manifested the break clearly. He proclaimed that Israel could expect a salvation from the Lord that is everlasting (Isa 45:17; 51:6, 8); God would conclude an everlasting alliance with his people (Isa 55:3); he would love them with an everlasting love (Isa 54:8); and he would liberate them for an everlasting happiness (Isa 51:11). A suffering servant of the Lord would have a role in bringing God's salvation and light to Israel and, indeed, to the nations: "I will make you a light to the nations, that my salvation may reach to the ends of the earth" (Isa 49:6); and his sufferings would have a part in achieving this (Isa 53:11-12). It does not seem that this is a substitute for the Messiah but rather "a reinterpretation of the messianic hope" (23). God is powerful enough to bring this about because of his creative power (Isa 40:21-23). Deutero-Isaiah uses myths at times to illustrate God's power (Isa 51:9f.) and describes the idyllic time of the future in terms of the beginning (Isa 51:3). Israel's hope of salvation reaches an eschatological dimension in these prophecies, but "when Yahweh comes to bring his kingdom, it is to this world that he comes and in this world that he establishes his reign" (25).

During the early postexilic period there began to be a transition from prophecy to apocalyptic. The small community of returned exiles did not experience the grandeur of Yahweh's salvific activity as Deutero-Isaiah had predicted. With time, some exegetes see a tension in the community between those who resigned themselves to be vassals of the Persians and centered their life around cult and others who still awaited the fulfillment of the promises of Deutero-Isaiah. Perhaps this conflict is reflected in Third Isaiah with its criticism of cult (Isa 66:1-4) and its description of the New Jerusalem (Isa 65: 17-25). Third Isaiah's eschatological vision, with the books of Ruth and Jonah, has a quite inclusive view of those, even among the nations, who would be saved. And Third Isaiah exults in the new creative act God would initiate: "Lo, I am about to create new heavens and a new earth; the things of the past shall not be remembered or come to mind" (Isa 65:17).

In the prophecy of Joel, perhaps between 450 and 350 B.C., the beginnings of apocalyptic are evident. He prophesies Yahweh's convocation of the nations in the valley of judgment (Joel 4:9-14), the exaltation of Jerusalem (4:7), the outpouring of the Spirit on earth and in the heavens: "Then afterward I will pour out my spirit upon all humankind. Your sons and daughters shall prophesy, your old men shall dream dreams, your young men shall see visions; Even upon the servants and the handmaids, in those days, I will pour out my spirit" (Joel 3:1-2). God's rule or kingdom or salvation will be effected through the Spirit as well as through figures such as the anointed King; and this Spirit will come upon all, even the humblest of people, changing them from within.

It is in the book of Daniel that we see the apocalyptic form and content most clearly. Since chapter 7 is particularly important for the New Testament designation of Jesus as the "Son of Man," we shall briefly reflect on it.

There is a rich use of symbols in this literature and this passage. Daniel is resistance literature, written about 167 to 164 B.C., when Antiochus IV was seeking to Hellenize the Jews and was persecuting those who were continuing the customs of their ancestors. It was written when the Jews felt powerless to overcome their oppressors, and its purpose was to encourage them to persevere in fidelity to God even though this fidelity might mean death. It presents itself as written many generations earlier and as foretelling the events of those last days. It prophesies that God will come very soon to liberate his people and reverse their fortunes, and to establish his kingdom, which will be everlasting, universal, and one of justice and peace. It thus makes a dichotomy between the present age dominated by evil and the age to come. This message is presented in the form of a succession of symbols: animals as symbols of four successive empires rising from the sea (itself a symbol of chaos), horns on the last of these animals as symbols of a succession of kings—all these symbols of the present age in opposition to God.

Then the prophet has a vision of the age to come, which is imminent and in which he sees an assembly in the heavens as "the Ancient One took his throne" (Dan 7:9) and "one like a son of man coming on the clouds of heaven," who receives from the Ancient One "dominion, glory, and kingship, nations and peoples of every language serve him. His dominion is an everlasting dominion" (7:13-14). This age to come includes a resurrection from the dead of those who have been faithful to God (12:1-3). Daniel's central message of hope is presented here in images taken from myths of surrounding peoples of the time: "In all these myths, the pattern of threat of the sea monster, assembly of the gods, deliverance by the storm god, and his consequent exercise of sovereignty is clear" (27). It is plausible that the "one like a son of man" is given sovereignty because he overcame the monster—here a symbol of Antiochus but including some continuation of preceding monsters. It is also possible that Yahweh overcomes the monster and then gives sovereignty to the man-like one.

There is disagreement concerning the identity of the "one like a son of man." In this we follow G. R. Beasley-Murray, where a detailed discussion of the issues can be found. One question is whether the man-like one is a symbol for the faithful people of God *or* a symbol that represents both the people and a representative of the people. It would seem the latter is the case, since in Daniel—as we see in the symbol for Antiochus and his kingdom—there is not a clear differentiation between king and kingdom.

Another issue is whether the "holy ones" (7:18) to whom the kingdom is to be given in the age to come denote angels or the people of God on earth. Some hold the former view, and hold that the man-like one represents the angel Michael, because elsewhere in Daniel "holy one" meant an angel (e.g., 8:13) and Michael is described as "the great prince, guardian of your people" (12:1). But counter to this is that in the interpretation of the vision given to Daniel, the "horn's" waging war against "the holy ones of the most High" (7:25) most probably refers directly to Antiochus' persecution of the people of God on earth, not his warring against angelic hosts. Thus the kingdom is given to the people of God and the "one like a son of man" (so Beasley-Murray and Dunn), not to the angels and Michael. The whole vision refers to an intervention of God for his people on earth.

Among the mediators of salvation we must include the figure of Wisdom in the Wisdom literature of the Old Testament. Roland Murphy interprets the teaching of Proverbs 1–9:

> The vision can be stated sharply: the book purports to offer "life" or "salvation" to the reader. When the psalmists pray to be "saved," they seek restoration to a full life in the here and now. Such is also the understanding in Proverbs. Personified Wisdom has a kerygma; she announces "security" (1:33) and "life" (8:35). The teaching of the wise is "a fountain of life" (13–14); this is also applied to "fear of the Lord" (14:27), which is also the beginning of wisdom. The symbols of fountain and tree of life are frequent . . . the concept of life is an ever expanding one (even within the Old Testament; cf. Wis 1:15; 2:23–3:3; etc.). But the perspective of Proverbs is life in the here and now.[13]

In the book of Wisdom, Wisdom, close to God and even immanent in human beings, is personified as a woman inviting people to know the way to God rather than the way of foolishness, and as associated with the Spirit of God. She gives a knowledge of God's ways that is not only intellectual but is transforming and saving. Solomon is presented as praying for wisdom: "Who ever knew your counsel, except you had given Wisdom, and sent your holy spirit from on high? And thus were the paths of those on earth made straight, and men learned what was your pleasure, and were saved by Wisdom" (Wis 9:18).

Of Wisdom it is said, "Passing into holy souls from age to age, she produces friends of God and prophets" (7:27). We will return to this theme as it relates to revelation in the next chapter. Here we simply note that this mediator of God's salvation is different from and not at that time integrated with the Messiah, the Son of Man and the Suffering Servant.

---

[13]Roland Murphy, *The Tree of Life: An Exploration of Biblical Wisdom Literature* (New York: Doubleday, 1990) 28–9.

2. The Situation of the Jews at the Time of Jesus

It is important for our interpretation of Jesus' message about the kingdom of God, or salvation, to have some understanding of the situation in Palestine at the time of his ministry. The Gospels are indeed compositions written by their authors in view of the needs of groups of Christians whom they were addressing, and in encouraging the faith of such groups the authors were substantially faithful to what Jesus said and did. Similarly, we are interpreting Jesus' message of the kingdom of God for people of our time and place, but in doing so we must be faithful to what Jesus said and did. The initial meaning of what he said and did depends in part on the situation he was addressing, the different expectations of God's promised salvation that his hearers had, the needs they felt were most urgent in their lives, and the divisions among them. As an understanding of what prophets of earlier centuries proclaimed depends in part on our understanding the age they addressed, so too with Jesus' message. It is not only the situation in the life of the Church at the time the Gospels were written but the situation in the time of Jesus' ministry that is important for a hermeneutics of the Gospels.

In recent years more use has been made on the part of exegetes of social description and social sciences to study this situation.[14] We assume that Jesus' proclamation of the kingdom of God had relevance to the historical situation of the Jews of Palestine during the time of his ministry, their situation as a people and not simply as individuals, and specifically to their sociopolitical-economic situation. This question is important in the hermeneutical context in which we are studying the meaning of the kingdom and in view of the diversity of current interpretations of Jesus' ministry. We will then briefly recall the external circumstances in which the Jews in Palestine were living, some diverse expectations of God's coming salvation among them, and some fragmentation among the Jews in their responses to the situation of their community.

The history of the Jews during this time can be read elsewhere.[15] Here we simply recall that after the success of the Maccabean revolt

---

[14]See, for example, Carolyn Osiek, "The New Handmaid: The Bible and Social Sciences," *TS* 50 (1989) 260–78; idem, *What Are They Saying About the Social Setting of the New Testament?* 2nd ed. (New York: Paulist Press, 1992).

[15]See, for example, Roland Murphy and Joseph Fitzmyer, "A History of Israel," *NJBC,* especially 1240–50; J. Andrew Overman and William Green, "Judaism in the Greco-Roman Period," *ABD* 3:1037–54; Steven Fraade, "Palestinian Judaism," *ABD* 3:1054–61.

against the Seleucids, a large degree of independence was gained under John Hyrcanus I (134–104 B.C.), who was both ruler and high priest, as his father, Simon Maccabee, had been before him. His son, Alexander Janneus (103–76 B.C.), had a reign marked by war and moral decline. After his death his widow ruled for a time, and then his son Aristobulus II (69–63 B.C.), from whom Pompey took power. Pompey made Aristobulus' brother, Hyrcanus II, high priest and ethnarch. Antipater, the father of Herod the Great, was a high official under Aristobulus.

In the shifting allegiances during the Roman civil wars and wars in Palestine among contenders for power, Herod the Great became governor of Galilee and later king of the Jews (37 B.C.–A.D. 4). On his death, his kingdom was divided among his three sons; but Judea in A.D. 6 became a Roman procuratorship, while Antipas continued as tetrarch of Galilee and Philip as tetrarch in northern Transjordan. Serious factions among the Jews developed at particular points during this long period, continued to exist during the ministry of Jesus, and were called the "four philosophies" of the Jews by Josephus. We recalled these in the preceding chapter and will say a word about them below. In this section we wish to recall briefly some intertestamental views among the Jews concerning their expectations of God's salvation and then factions among the Jews in Palestine that interpreted variously the relation of holiness to their sociopolitical situation.

Apocalyptic literature is well represented in Jewish apocrypha in the immediate pre-Christian era.[16] In this literature the coming of God is associated with disturbances of the physical world, the destruction of oppressive forces, and the restoration of righteousness. The day of the Lord is primarily a day of judgment. The kingdom of God, the central idea of apocalyptic literature, is envisioned as coming in the last times: "The simplest interpretation of the issue of the last times involves viewing it as being ushered in by *the coming of God and the Day of the Lord, which will entail the overthrow of evil powers and the establishment of the kingdom of God in this world*" (46). This is in continuity with Daniel 7. This also led both to a view that God's kingdom will exist in a transformed creation and to varied—and even confused—efforts to combine the kingdom of God in this world with

---

[16]Here I rely on Beasley-Murray, *Jesus and the Kingdom,* "The Coming of God in the Writings of Early Judaism," 39–68. Also see Raymond Brown, "Jewish Apocrypha" and "Dead Sea Scrolls," *NJBC* 1056–64, 1069–79.

that of the kingdom in the transformed creation, for example, a messianic kingdom in this world and a judgment and a kingdom in a new creation (see *1 Enoch,* 91–104; 2 Esdras).

It is disputed whether the Messiah is a necessary element in the expectation of the kingdom of God in this literature. Qumran spoke of a coming of a prophet and of two Messiahs, one priestly and one royal, and called upon three Old Testament texts to support this (Deut 18:18-19; Num 24:15f.; Deut 33:8f.). Also, some passages in the apocryphal literature imply that the Messiah is the "Son of God" (see *Testament of Levi* 18:16-17), and so there is a use of this title "in a non-Hellenistic context applied to an individual with a significant function among mankind" (57). What stands out is the variety of the formulations of the expectations of salvation. At times the Messiah is mentioned as having a mediating function in the kingdom; at times not.

In the preceding chapter we recalled very cursorily some divisions among the Jews of Palestine in their interpretations of holiness in their time and place. Here we will elaborate briefly on this and conclude by suggesting that part of the context of Jesus' ministry was this deep division concerning the implications of the Torah for the Jewish stance toward the sociopolitical-economic realities in which they lived. Many Jews who expected the Messiah thought that his ministry would be relevant to this central problem in their lives. We shall ask later how Jesus' proclamation of the kingdom was relevant to this.

Josephus mentions four "sects" or "philosophies" among the Jews.[17] The *Sadducees* are one of these. The New Testament associates these with the high priestly party (e.g., Acts 5:17). They accepted the Pentateuch, or Torah, but not the resurrection, angels, or providence. They were sympathizers with the occupying power and were their allies among the Jews; they had less influence with the people than the Pharisees, and they were more influenced by Hellenism than the Pharisees.

The *Pharisees,* so called because of their insistence on separation from all that was ritually impure, were primarily scribes and interpreters of Law. They accepted an oral as well as written tradition and so added their interpretations to the prescriptions of the Law. Their main emphasis was on how Jews could be faithful to the Torah and

---

[17]See Josephus, *The Jewish War,* 2, 119–66, and *Antiquities of the Jews,* 13, 171–3; 18, 11–22, *Flavius Josephus: Selections from His Works,* ed. Abraham Wasserstein (New York: Viking Press, 1974) 187–97. Also see Anthony Saldarini, *Pharisees, Scribes, and Sadducees in Palestinian Society: A Sociological Approach,* (Wilmington, Del.: Michael Glazier, 1988); Borg, *Jesus,* 87–93.

untainted by the surrounding culture and power even while being occupied. Thus they insisted on tithing, the laws of the Sabbath, pure and impure food, purifications of varied sorts, and so on. They imposed religious and social sanctions on those who did not keep these laws.

The *Essenes,* who are made known to us by the Qumran scrolls, were more separatist than the Pharisees. Initially, because of the appointment of a high priest not of the Zadokite family (probably in 152 B.C.), they had in large part withdrawn from Palestinian Judaism and formed their own community, known for the purity of its life, the sharing of goods, and its expectation of the coming of two Messiahs, one priestly and one of David's line.

A fourth group, certainly in existence by the time of the Jewish War against Rome in the late sixties, was the *Zealots.* Between the accession of Herod (37 B.C.) and the Jewish revolution there were incidents of resistance in the form of some uprisings around a leader, assassinations, and banditry by groups of robbers; but it is improbable that there was a continuing movement through this whole period that could be called the Zealot party. For these resistance groups holiness could be achieved only by driving Rome out of Palestine; similarly, taxes for Rome were anathema. These four movements cannot be called only "religious" movements; they were political as well as religious, for they were forms of organizing the Jewish community. And there was not the separation then of religion and politics that has wide currency today.

There were also the "people of the land," who were not identified with any of these groups. Palestine was 90 percent agricultural at that time. Society was divided between an elite with their retainers and the common people. There was no real middle class, but some of these common people were financially better off than others. There was a "rural proletariat," some of whom had previously owned property but because of a bad year had gone irreparably into debt and so lost their farms. The people of the land included most of the common people, many farmers, artisans, villagers, day laborers, and landless peasants. They were not able to observe all the laws the Pharisees identified.

The Pharisees called those "sinners" who did not observe the Torah as expanded by oral tradition (see John 7:34). The worst of the nonobservants were the "outcasts"; this included murderers, prostitutes and such, as well as tax collectors. The people were subject to a number of taxes, those that went to Rome and those that went to

Herod for his building projects and those that went to the Temple and the priests. Even without the one for Herod, this has been estimated at about 35 percent for farmers.[18] Pharisees insisted on the Temple tax as part of fidelity to the Law, but there were accusations at the time that much of this was being used by the high priests and aristocracy for themselves without being equitably distributed among the lower-order priests. Some scholars hold that many farmers were not able to pay this tax and so were subject to social ostracism as nonobservers of the Law. In fact, the extent of the overall taxation resulted in a number of farmers losing their farms and an increase in banditry and sedition.[19] Thus the exploitation of the poor by the aristocracy among the Jews added to the distress of the period. Marcus Borg concludes:

> The generation in which Jesus lived was heading toward war, not because it was a particularly warlike generation or because it was dominated by "men of violence." Rather, the most fundamental causes were twofold. There was the perception of real injustice—Roman rule was chronically oppressive and could be brutal. And there was loyalty to a deeply ingrained way of life, namely to the ethos of holiness understood as separation from all that was impure.[20]

II. Jesus' Proclamation of the Kingdom

What did Jesus proclaim was being offered people through his ministry? Mark, in a statement that is taken by most exegetes to re-

---

[18]See Borg, *Jesus,* 84–5.

[19]See Richard Horsley and John Hanson, *Bandits, Prophets, and Messiahs: Popular Movements at the Time of Jesus* (San Francisco: Harper & Row, 1985); Richard Horsley, *Sociology and the Jesus Movement;* Overman and Green, "Judaism in the Greco-Roman Period," 1044. There is a dispute about how serious poverty and banditry were in Galilee at this time. However, as noted by Sean Kealy in *CBQ* 52 (1990) 557, Gerd Theisen "concludes from Antipas' fear of a rebellion before his murder of the Baptist (Josephus, *Ant.* 18, 118), the desertion of Antipas' soldiers in the Nabatean War (*Ant.* 18, 114), and the decline in peasants' income leading to an increase of robberies in A.D. 39 (*Ant.* 18, 274) that a condition of instability had persisted [in Galilee] for many years." For evidence that the earlier Israelite call for periodically releasing debtors and restoring property in Jubilee years was strongly resisted in Jesus' time, see Sean Freyne, "The Geography, Politics, and Economics of Galilee and the Quest for the Historical Jesus," *Studying the Historical Jesus,* ed. Chilton and Evans, 75–122; see also Fraade, "Palestinian Judaism," 1060; Meyer, "Jesus Christ," 777.

[20]Borg, *Jesus,* 92–3.

flect substantially the ministry of Jesus and not merely Mark's own theology, gives a summary of Jesus' proclamation as follows: "After John had been arrested, Jesus came to Galilee proclaiming the gospel of God: 'This is the time of fulfillment. The kingdom of God is at hand. Repent, and believe in the gospel'" (Mark 1:14-15). Each part of this summary is important. In the ministry of Jesus the time of fulfillment has arrived. The kingdom of God is what is offered the people. This is God's definitive eschatological salvation, his exercise of sovereignty on behalf of his people and his judgment. It is future, but imminent. In fact, it seems to be more than imminent: "If the time before the kingdom is finished, the time of the kingdom has begun. . . . '[T]he new aeon has in its present-future identity of operation already broken in'" (73–4).[21] Jesus calls for people's acceptance of this gift through their repentance and belief in him and his message.

We are engaging in our introductory study here of this proclamation in the context of the dispute between those who claim that Jesus' proclamation of the kingdom was a function of his effort to renew Israel in the present and those who interpret this proclamation as apocalyptic. What we propose as our basic thesis is that initially in his proclamation Jesus did present himself primarily as anointed by the Spirit to renew the people by God's definitive intervention to save them; but when it was apparent to him that the leaders were not going to accept him he proclaimed the kingdom more in the apocalyptic mode, showing thereby that even if they reject and kill him God's kingdom will indeed come and come through him, now for the benefit of those who will be the community of believers in him. We will reflect on (1) how Jesus proclaimed the kingdom; (2) what this kingdom was, initially in its mode of renewal; and (3) what it was in its apocalyptic mode, though still with a present impact.

1. How Jesus Proclaimed the Kingdom

Jesus proclaimed the kingdom of God, or God's offer of salvation for which the Jews had been waiting, by his words and his deeds. He proclaimed it by macarisms, such as the Beatitudes; by parables; by

---

[21]The page references in the text in this section refer to Beasley-Murray, *Jesus and the Kingdom.* The enclosed quotation is from G. Gloege. I use Beasley-Murray's book in reference to the apocalyptic character of Jesus' proclamation of the kingdom but put this in the context of Jesus' understanding of his ministry as one of renewal or restoration of Israel.

sayings, for example, in controversies; by teaching his disciples how to pray, as in the Lord's Prayer; and by his moral teaching. But he also proclaimed it by his actions, such as by his healings, as he expresses to the disciples of John the Baptist when they ask him whether he is the one who is to come (Matt 11:5-6); by his exorcisms (Matt 12:28; Luke 11:20); by his table fellowship with sinners, as with Zacchaeus (Luke 19:1-10); and by his teaching the gospel to the poor.

These actions were symbols of a deeper healing and fellowship God was offering the people through Jesus. So he proclaimed it not primarily as a teacher in a classroom that students might have clear concepts but rather through symbols and metaphors in word and action that appealed to the heart as well as to the mind, that conveyed experientially what was being taught, that offered a kind of participative knowledge rather than simply intellectual knowledge, and that invited transformation of life. Jesus speaks of the kingdom of God as a "mystery" (Mark 4:11). As Beasley-Murray notes: "[T]he background for its [the word *mysterion*'s] appearance in Mark 4:11 is clearly the context of Jewish apocalyptic, in which it denotes the purpose of God in the history of the world, which will be realized in his universal rule revealed in the last times" (104). Jesus is proclaiming something that is coming somehow in the context of his own ministry. And he is proclaiming it so that the people will *believe* in it, not primarily that they will understand it. In the fourth chapter we shall reflect at greater length on how Jesus' proclamation of the kingdom is offered as a revelation.

2. The Kingdom, Primarily as Renewal in the Present

We shall first show evidence that Jesus mediated the presence of the kingdom by his ministry and then specifically relate this to the socioeconomic-political circumstances of his time and place. Hope for the kingdom of God was pronounced in the Judaism of Jesus' day, as seen, for example, in Jewish prayers, the *Kaddish* and *Tefillah,* or Eighteen Benedictions (147–8). We see in the prayer Jesus taught the disciples that concern for the kingdom was to take precedence over concerns for needs of this life: "Father, hallowed be your name, your kingdom come. Give us each day our daily bread" (Luke 11:2-3). Matthew adds in the first part of this prayer "your will be done on earth as it is in heaven" (Matt 6:10). Beasley-Murray writes in reference to the petition, "your kingdom come":

All the Old Testament prophetic pictures of deliverance through another Exodus and salvation in the kingdom of God come to expression in this brief petition. It entails the revelation of God's glory (Isa 40:1-11), the universal acknowledgment of his kingship (Isa 26:1-15), the universal sway of his righteousness (Isa 4, 11, 32, etc.), universal peace in his creation (Isa 2), and above all, in the latest reaches of Old Testament hope, the conquest of death and the wiping away of tears from all eyes (Isa 25:8). Brief as it is, no more comprehensive prayer than this can be prayed. . . . Needless to say, this prayer can be answered positively only by an act of God. Deliverance from all evil, including the ultimate enemy of man, and resurrection for life in God's kingdom can come about solely through God's intervention and recreative activity. In the final analysis, "Your kingdom come" is a prayer for God himself to come and achieve his end in creating a world (151).

This prayer presupposes that this condition does not exist now, and it prays for this as a future condition but as one that starts in the present. The kingdom of God and salvation are synonyms, as shown by the apostles' response to Jesus' statement, "How hard it is for those who have wealth to enter the kingdom of God." They asked, "Then who can be saved?" (Mark 10:23, 26). It is worth more than all else, and to give all one has for it is the only wise thing to do—as for a pearl of great price (Matt 13:44-46). It is social and universal, as the metaphor of the banquet to which people from east and west will come indicates (Matt 8:11). It is simply a gift from God, totally due to his initiative and his love; it is gained by those who receive it as a child receives a gift (Mark 10:15).

This saving event is present in the ministry of Jesus. The future saving event is already present in its beginnings during his ministry. At his baptism Jesus is anointed by the Spirit to bring salvation to his people, and Luke recounts the beginning of his ministry in Nazareth with Jesus' quotation from Isaiah 61:1-2: "The Spirit of the Lord is upon me, because he has anointed me to bring glad tidings to the poor. He has sent me to proclaim liberty to captives and recovery of sight to the blind, to let the oppressed go free, and to proclaim a year acceptable to the Lord." Jesus is the bearer of the Spirit in his ministry. As he says in reference to his exorcisms, "If it is by the Spirit of God that I drive out demons, then the kingdom of God has come upon you" (Matt 12:28; Luke 11:20 has "finger of God").

That overthrowing of powers opposed to God's rule expected in the eschatological future is already beginning to happen. Similarly, Jesus' answer to the disciples of John the Baptist who came to him that "the blind regain their sight, the lame walk, the deaf hear, the dead are raised, and the poor have the good news proclaimed to them" (Matt 11:5) shows that John's apocalyptic expectation of the kingdom was beginning to be realized in the present, apparently to the great surprise of John and his disciples. Jesus' remark on this occasion that "the least in the kingdom of heaven is greater than" John (Matt 11:11) supposes that some are already in the kingdom; thus Jesus "countenanced entrance into the kingdom prior to the judgment" (180). He said of Zacchaeus that "[t]oday salvation has come to this house" (Luke 19:9), and to those who asked when the kingdom would come that "the kingdom of God is among you" (Luke 17:21). The great feast that was a metaphor for the kingdom was already spread; it is already present (Matt 22:1-14; Luke 14:16-24).

This kingdom is mysteriously, humbly, and hiddenly present as a mustard seed, but powerfully so, like leaven in the dough (Mark 4:30-32; Matt 13:31-33). In fact, it seems that "the community of the Messiah can be equated with the community of the kingdom of God. . . . [T]hose who enter the community thereby enter into the kingdom of salvation" (185; see Matt 16:19). It is true that tares remain among the wheat, and the separation will come with the judgment at the end.

Jesus' proclamation was centered on the kingdom, but indirectly this tells us something about Jesus himself. The interpretation of his role in the kingdom of God is tied in largely with the interpretation of the Son of Man sayings, apparently Jesus' favorite form of self-reference, which we will reflect on below. But it would be to misinterpret Jesus if we were to look only at these passages. There are other Old Testament titles that Jesus seems to have reinterpreted directly or indirectly to refer to himself. Together with Marcus Borg and other exegetes, we can agree that it is important to recall other titles if we are to do justice to Jesus' aim to renew his own people in his own time.[22] With Beasley-Murray we can say: "In his own teaching, Jesus appears as the representative (Luke 17:20-21), the revealer (Mark 4:11-12; Matt 11:25-26), the initiator (Matt 11:12), the instru-

---

[22]See Borg, *Jesus,* passim. Also see Edward Schillebeeckx, *Jesus: An Experiment in Christology* (New York: Crossroad, 1979).

ment (Matt 12:28), the champion (Mark 3:27), the mediator (Mark 2:18-19), and the bearer (Matt 11:5) of the kingdom of God" (269).

Jesus was considered by others to be a prophet (Mark 8:28, para.), and he referred to himself at least indirectly as anointed by the Spirit and a prophet, with a prophetic ministry for this people (Luke 4:17-21, 24; 11:32; 13:33). The ministry of a prophet was to give the people a word from God in a time of crisis—a word that would help them receive salvation and avoid judgment in that historical crisis.

Jesus was also a sage, in continuity with the Wisdom figures of Israel's past; he taught in proverbs, parables, and lessons from nature to give the people a diagnosis of the human condition and teach them a way of transformation (Luke 11:31, para.). The Gospel of John, even more than the Synoptics, presents Jesus as a proclaimer of Wisdom which or who gives life to those who believe (e.g., John 6:44-47), but John's Gospel has a basis in the Synoptics' association of Jesus with Wisdom (e.g., Matt 11:28-30), who gives life (Matt 7:14). We will come back to this theme in the fourth chapter, when we reflect on revelation. As we shall see also in that chapter, Jesus accepted the designation "Messiah," even though he was much more than this and he did not use it directly of himself, in part because of some nationalistic misunderstandings attached to it in his time.

It may well be that Jesus also accepted the designation "Son of God" during his ministry, not explicitly in the sense of an ontological son of God but because this term was used of the Messiah (Luke 20:9-19, para.; Mark 14:61-62, para.).[23] Also, Jesus' normal term in prayer addressing God was "Abba," a familiar and tender word a child would use to address the father within the family (e.g., Mark 14:36; Matt 11:25, para.). This usage, not found in the Judaism of his time, shows his profound sense of intimacy with God as his Father in a way different from the way God was Father for the rest of humankind (Matt 6:9, para.). This relationship was the secret, source, and support of his life and his ministry, as is shown particularly in John's Gospel (though not exclusively, see Mark 1:11, para.; Luke 9:35, para.) with its deeper penetration into the person of Jesus.[24]

We have seen above that the future kingdom was having an impact in the ministry of Jesus. But an important question concerning this

[23]See Dunn, *Unity and Diversity,* 45; Beasley-Murray, *Jesus and the Kingdom,* 295. See also Marinus de Jonge, *Jesus, the Servant-Messiah* (New Haven, Conn.: Yale University Press, 1991).

[24]See Schillebeeckx, *Jesus,* 246–70.

present impact remains. Was this impact simply in the arena of a person's relation to God and with those immediately around him or her? Or was it a saving impact that was to change people's relations with one another in the sociopolitical-economic orders and thus to change systemic structures in these areas? Some who have stressed the apocalyptic nature of the kingdom that Jesus proclaimed and some who have interpreted Jesus' proclamation from a modern perspective of individualism and separation of religion and politics have not seen Jesus' offer of salvation as touching these spheres of societal life. And some who have stressed Jesus as concerned for a restoration of his people within the social oppression and conflicts of his day have tended to deny the apocalyptic character of the kingdom he proclaimed.

In the context of the tension between these views we will later suggest that his concern for the social renewal of his people was fully consistent with his apocalyptic interpretation of the messianic mission; here we indicate some aspects of this social renewal present in his proclamation, particularly as it affected the economic order.

I have written elsewhere, relying largely on a book by Lloyd Gaston,[25] that we must acknowledge that Jesus' ministry had relevance to the oppression his people were suffering during his lifetime. He could scarcely have been exercising a messianic ministry, even within the context of an apocalyptic understanding, without addressing this issue. The notion of peace that he proclaimed in continuity with previous prophets was not simply one that was interior to the individual or limited to the interrelation among neighbors but one that meant wholeness and harmony within the social order in the political, social, and economic interrelations among people and among peoples. In fact, the messianic promise of peace also projected a harmony between humanity and the physical world itself. It was opposed to injustice, whether individual or institutionalized.

The apocalyptic kingdom that was promised, for example, in Daniel, was not irrelevant to the oppression the people experienced at the time, as though it would be simply a peace in the realm of the resurrection in another world. It was a promise that God's saving action would give the kingdom to God's people, taking it away from those who unjustly oppressed them, and that it would be a kingdom

---

[25]See Lloyd Gaston, *No Stone on Another: Studies in the Significance of the Fall of Jerusalem in the Synoptic Gospels* (Leiden: Brill, 1970) 244, 425–6, passim. Also see Farrelly, "Peace of Christ," cited in note 10.

of justice and peace here in this world. Gaston points out that central to the Jews' self-understanding from 168 B.C. to A.D. 35 was a theology of martyrdom. In their situation as a small community amid the powers of their time, their alternatives were armed resistance to the Hellenistic world or accommodation with it.

In the book of Daniel they were directed to a path that lay between these two extremes. Daniel called the people to a confidence that God would save them and that they would be vindicated. On the basis of this hope they were called to remain faithful to their covenantal relation to God and by this fidelity witness their faith to the world—even at the cost of death. In his proclamation of the kingdom Jesus called not primarily for a strict observance of the Jewish purity code as it had developed but for a code of justice and compassion among the people. As he himself shared with others, particularly with the poor (Luke 7:22), meaning not only those who had nothing but also those held in contempt by the opponents of Jesus, he called others to share with the needy on every level, and he indicated that they would be judged on this basis when the Son of Man came (Matt 25:31-46). The righteous then will be those who fed the hungry, welcomed the stranger, clothed the naked, and visited the sick or those who were in prison. If the kingdom to come is to be one of wholeness, then it is imperative for those who put the kingdom first in their lives (Luke 12:31) to instantiate those qualities of the kingdom in the present.

Jesus' teaching, if accepted, would change the relations the rich had to the poor, the religious authorities had to the ordinary people of the land, and those richly endowed with God's gifts had to the needy on every level. His teaching called his followers to respect and love each other as brothers and sisters and so to overcome the divisions among individuals and groups. This message and the impact of Jesus' life did, we know, through his Spirit create a human community among his followers. If accepted on a larger scale among the Jews at that time, it would have had a much wider effect upon them and their social structures and so also on their relation to Rome. At the least it would have placed the political domination they experienced from Rome in a different perspective. Though painful to the Jews, it would not have been so to the extent that it would provoke them to a suicidal military uprising against Rome.

To speak more specifically about Jesus' attempt to change economic relations in Palestine at his time, we can follow Richard Horsley in much that he writes in *Jesus and the Spiral of Violence:*

Popular Jewish Resistance in Roman Palestine.[26] We have recalled above something of the circumstances of the Jews in Palestine during the ministry of Jesus. One significant factor that caused a great deal of distress was the economic burden carried by the farmers. Many of them had been reduced to tenant farmers or day laborers by their indebtedness due to the large taxes put on them as well as by other factors such as "foreclosings" by larger landholders.

Jesus shows in his parables and sayings a full consciousness of these economic conditions. He speaks of the rich man who is not aware of the impoverished at his very gate, of the man who has a great harvest and uses it simply to store up more for himself, of tenant farmers who kill the absentee landlord's son to take possession of the vineyard for themselves, of how hard it is for the rich to enter the kingdom of God because of their attachment to their wealth. He proclaimed his message largely to the villages of Galilee. Much of his message can be seen, if we are aware of the conditions of the time, to be addressed to a renewal of their local communities in the direction of more egalitarian communities of mutual help, with warnings to them not to go to court with others over problems but to settle them locally and generously. He encouraged them to overcome the mutual antagonisms that easily develop among people scraping out a marginal existence, to forgive each other's debts—and this did mean financial debts and not simply sins—and to be compassionate as their Father in heaven is compassionate.

In Jerusalem he attacked those who supported a system that impoverished many—those who sought to grow rich through the offerings made in the Temple. He overturned their tables in a symbolic prophetic action and predicted judgment upon them (Mark 11:15-17, para.).[27] This was to attack an unjust economic system at the source, because high priestly families at the time were forcing tithes even on the poor and keeping more than their rightful share, thus impoverishing both farmers and the lower priesthood.

---

[26]Richard Horsley, *Jesus and the Spiral of Violence: Popular Jewish Resistance in Roman Palestine* (San Francisco: Harper & Row, 1987).

[27]See Craig Evans, "Jesus' Action in the Temple: Cleansing or Portent of Destruction?" *CBQ* 51 (1989) 237–70. This article is opposed to E. P. Sanders' view that Jesus' action was a symbol of the coming destruction of the Temple.

3. The Kingdom Proclaimed in the Apocalyptic Tradition

If Jesus spoke of mediating the kingdom by his own ministry and was concerned with the renewal of his people, does this mean that the apocalyptic cast of many of his sayings comes from the early Church? First we note that we cannot identify eschatological and apocalyptic. Both refer to God's definitive and not-to-be-transcended inbreaking to save his people, but the apocalyptic does this in a way more marked by a dichotomy between the present age dominated by evil and the age to come in which God's universal and eternal kingdom will be brought about. A period of eschatological distress separates these ages. Daniel presents the installation of the Son of Man as preceded by a period of eschatological distress. We do not have reason to think that for Jesus to mediate God's definitive kingdom it had been necessary that the Jews reject him. What was necessary for the eschatological salvation to be brought about was their acceptance of him by faith in response to his ministry and gift of the Spirit.

We are suggesting that the apocalyptic cast of Jesus' sayings was more marked as he became more aware of the probability that the leaders of the Jews were unalterably opposed to him and were seeking his death. By proclaiming the kingdom in the apocalyptic mode, he was showing he shared the experience of those faithful Jews who, for example at the time of Antiochus IV, persevered in fidelity to the point of death and did so with the conviction that God would still bring about his kingdom and would raise them up even from the dead to share in that kingdom. If the present age is dominated by powers of evil opposed to God, this will not deflect God from his purpose; the age to come will subvert the present age and reveal clearly God's gift of the kingdom to his faithful people. Jesus was proclaiming that whether his people accepted him or not, God would bring his kingdom into being through him.

It is true that the predictions by Jesus of his *suffering and death* and specifically his expression of this in terms of the Son of Man (e.g., Mark 8:31) are ascribed by some exegetes to the early Church. But there is much that could lead Jesus to expect rejection of his ministry from the growing opposition of Pharisees and Sadducees to his teaching and his conduct, from the fate of John the Baptist, from his own popularity with the crowds, and so on. And there is much in the Old Testament that could help him to interpret this. There is the theme of the righteous man who suffers (Wis 2:5), which may be a homily based on the fourth Servant Song of Deutero-Isaiah (Isa 52:13–53:12); the theme of the rejected prophet; that of the Servant of the Lord; and the atoning power of the martyrs (e.g., 2 Macc 7:37-38). Each of the three predictions of his passion is followed by a prediction of his resurrection; and this corresponds to Israel's expectation of vindication that would come for the righteous sufferer, the Servant of the Lord, the rejected prophet, and the martyrs. We saw earlier, for example, in Daniel 7, that the reign that is to be given to one like a Son of Man is an event of the age to come as distinct from an event of this age dominated by evil powers.

There is much in the Synoptics that supports the view that Jesus' understanding of salvation and the kingdom was in the line of apocalyptic. It is widely acknowledged that John the Baptist's understanding of the kingdom was apocalyptic—with a greater stress on judgment than on salvation—and that the early Church's understanding was apocalyptic,[28] as we shall show in chapter 5. If this is the case, it is a strong argument that Jesus' own understanding of the kingdom was apocalyptic. The Q document and, some add, the Q community, apparently saw Jesus as a representative of Wisdom but also that "God's kingdom is imminent; the Son of Man will come soon and carry out the final judgment. Those who belong to Jesus on earth will be confirmed for salvation by the Son of Man at his coming."[29] This would support the Synoptics' portrayal of Jesus as having a ministry of renewal and then, as he becomes more aware of the threat to his ministry, a proclamation more in the apocalyptic vein.

We shall reflect further on this when we speak of Jesus and the Son of Man. Here we note the parables of the kingdom that presuppose some absence and then a coming of the Master, who will reward or accept those who are prepared for him. For example, the kingdom of God is likened to ten virgins who took their lamps and went out to meet the bridegroom (Matt 25:1-12). Kümmel comments on this: "[I]t follows also from all these exhortations to be on the alert and to be prepared that Jesus describes the coming of the Son of Man, and therewith the entry of the kingdom of God, as possibly very imminent, and in any case pressingly near, although its actual date was completely unknown" (quoted by Beasley-Murray, 213).

[28]See Dunn, "Apocalyptic Christianity" (see n. 6 above).

[29]Arland Hultgren, *The Rise of Normative Christianity* (Minneapolis: Fortress Press, 1994) 33; on the Q community, see 31–41.

This comparison of the Day of the Son of Man and the ensuing salvation or judgment to an event that will come at an unexpected time is also found in the parables of servants awaiting the return of their master or of masters who should be prepared for a thief who breaks into a house (Luke 12:35-40). And the parable of the talents and the pounds has the same implication (Matt 25:14-30; Luke 19:11-27): "Without doubt the evangelists understood the parable to signify the departure of Christ from this world and his return at the parousia" (217). We can say that this proclamation of the kingdom of God or of that salvation and judgment to which it referred designated primarily what would happen at the end of history, at the parousia of the Son of Man (Matt 15:31-46; 19:28).

This is not opposed to Jesus' continuing sense that God was operating through him for salvation in the present but puts this in a more apocalyptic context, now that it seems evident that the Jews will reject him and his ministry. The promise of the kingdom will be fulfilled, nevertheless, in the lives of those who come to believe in him. Even if he is rejected, he will be vindicated and exercise his saving and judging role from beyond this death. This means that his present ministry is a participation in that which is to come. Thus Beasley-Murray can appropriately write:

> The kingdom that comes in Jesus is *the kingdom of God promised for the end of the times*. . . . That which is at work in the present of Jesus is the future kingdom of God. It is the saving sovereignty of which the *revelation* is coming in the not-distant future (227).

> The glory and the grace set beyond the horizon of history is also operative in all its transforming powers now—*God's* glory, *God's* grace, *God's* transforming power (113).

> The emancipating power of God at work in Christ shows that the divine sovereignty that is destined to bring deliverance in the future is operative for that purpose in the present (80).

It is thought at times that the decisive shift of eschatology from the future alone to the present was the achievement of Paul and John, but it was rather the work of Jesus (see 338). We can look at the relation of the present and the future in two ways. It is the future saving action of God that is operating in the present. And this beginning of his saving action will inevitably lead to its triumph in the future (see

195). The parable of the dragnet that catches good and bad fish, which the fisherman will separate (Matt 13:47-50), supports this. It "is likening the kingdom of heaven to the *whole* process of catching fish, not merely the separation. The casting of the net, the gathering of fish of every kind . . . all this represents the sovereignty of God in action" (200).

To gain this kingdom one needs *faith* (e.g., Mark 2:5; Matt 13:58; 9:22). It is a matter of accepting it as a child receives a gift, and one needs to be willing to bear the cost of opposition and the cross, as Jesus himself bore these in his ministry (Matt 10:16-39). We will see more of the conditions for reception of the kingdom below, and particularly in the fourth chapter when we discuss revelation and faith.

As we mentioned above and will explore below, the Synoptics present Jesus' favorite self-designation as "Son of Man." There is a great deal of controversy about whether this designation came from the early Church or from Jesus, and if the latter how many of the Synoptics' uses of this came from Jesus and referred to himself and how many of these were influenced by the seventh chapter of Daniel. One can look elsewhere for this controversy.[30] It is a fact that the early Church did not use it as a title for Jesus, and while the Aramaic expression behind the expression could be used to designate a man, as in Psalm 8, there is a good deal of agreement (e.g., Dunn, Beasley-Murray, Meyer, Brown) that Jesus used it of himself in relation to Daniel's apocalyptic message to refer to his coming glory and parousiac judgment.

This is particularly the case in Jesus' answer to the high priest during his trial before the Sanhedrin. The high priest asked him, "Are you the Messiah, the Son of the Blessed One?" and Jesus answered: "I am; and you will see the Son of Man seated at the right hand of the Power and coming with the clouds of heaven" (Mark 14:62; see para.). Setting aside issues such as whether there was a trial of Jesus before the Sanhedrin (see Beasley-Murray 296–7), we can see this response as Jesus' stripping away his messianic reserve "in a context of total rejection and doom. From a position of utter humiliation before his foes he claims God's vindication for himself in a coming revelation of his right to rule" (287). He interrelates Psalm 110:1 and Daniel 7:13 in a reference to his exaltation and his coming to rule

---

[30]See, for example, Dunn, *Unity and Diversity,* 35–40; Meyer, "Jesus Christ," 788–90; Raymond Brown, *An Introduction to New Testament Christology* (New York: Paulist Press, 1994) 89–100.

and judge the world. This is a reference to the parousia, where those who accepted him and those who rejected him will *see* him as Son of Man. He is interpreting the Messiah as the Son of Man. Beasley-Murray sees this usage as in accord with his own interpretation of Luke 12:8-9 as forming "the bridge between sayings relating to the ministry and sufferings of the Son of Man and sayings that speak of his role in the coming of the kingdom at the end" (304).

There are also self-designations by Jesus as Son of Man in the Synoptics that present his sufferings as those of the Son of Man (e.g., the triple predictions of his coming passion, death, and resurrection after Peter's confession of him as Messiah). Can these come from Jesus with an indirect reference to Daniel 7? There is multiple attestation to this usage by Jesus, and we saw that he could have foreseen his coming suffering. Could "the Son of Man" have been viewed at that time "as a humble and humiliated man, the subject of prophecies of rejection, suffering and death" (247)? Perhaps it could have been by Jesus in light of the service to the kingdom of God given by such figures as the Suffering Servant, the persecuted wise man, and martyrs.

The Last Supper offers "the most important evidence in the New Testament as to how Jesus interpreted his death" (258), though passages concerning it are much disputed. Without going into all these disputes here (see Beasley-Murray 258-73), we can say that they show once more that Jesus considered his ministry as one of service and viewed his death similarly. He saw his life as redemptive (Luke 4:17-19); he knew that the fourth Servant Song recognized the death of the Servant as an efficacious vicarious death on behalf of humankind; he could then view his own death as a means by which the eschatological gift is made possible. In fact, this and the fact that the passages concerning the Last Supper place this meal in the context of the Passover, which recalled to Israel God's redemption of them from slavery in Egypt, argue that Jesus was engaging in prophetic action (see e.g., Mark 10:45):

> In the teaching of Jesus the Son of Man represents the kingdom of God among men precisely in terms of his coming to serve, and in Mark 8:31 that service consists in suffering death and then being vindicated by God in eschatological power. . . . [T]he Son of Man who suffers binds together the features of the Righteous Sufferer, the Servant of the Lord, the rejected Prophet, and the Martyr. It is likely that the same is true of the Son of Man in Mark

10:45, who gives up his life as a *lutron anti pollōn,* a freely offered
sacrifice, in order that the kingdom of God might be opened for
mankind in its totality (283).[31]

There is some reason to believe that this interconnection between
the Son of Man and suffering was used by Jesus, particularly after
Peter's confession of him as Messiah, when he began to prophesy his
suffering, death, and resurrection.

There are uses also of the Son of Man as a self-designation by
Jesus in reference to his present ministry, for example, in reference
to his healing of the paralytic (Mark 2:10) and to his power over the
Sabbath (Mark 2:28). Similarly, Jesus' statements about the Son of
Man as one who feasts (Matt 11:19), as one who is homeless (Matt
8:20), and as one who seeks and saves (Luke 19:10) are all in their
contexts reflections on his own ministry. It may be that these were
originally self-designations in the more general sense of "man" (see
Ps 8:4b; Heb 2:6) but later understood by the Church in the Danielic
sense.[32] Or Jesus could have used the phrase in a purposely ambiguous meaning. It is true that in Daniel 7 the Son of Man and the kingdom of God come simultaneously, but to whom should we ascribe
the greater creativity, Jesus or the early Church? And what would the
corollary be "for one who believed that the kingdom of God was
coming in his God-appointed and God-inspired ministry" (221)?

Perhaps we can relate this question to the interpretation of the Son
of Man saying in Luke 12:8-9: "I tell you, everyone who acknowledges me before others the Son of Man will acknowledge before the
angels of God. But whoever denies me before others will be denied
before the angels of God." Some deny this is a Son of Man saying
because Matthew's parallel (10:32-33) has "I" for "Son of Man." But
if Jesus believed that God's definitive and never to be surpassed—or
eschatological—salvation was being mediated through him, as we
are arguing he did, could he not with studied ambiguity have used
such an expression? In this, did Jesus point away from himself or toward himself?

John the Baptist did look toward a figure who would come after
him and who would be greater, but Jesus did not. Jesus affirms that

---

[31]Beasley-Murray, *Jesus and the Kingdom,* 299–300, notes a Midrash on Psalm 2:7 that relates
to one another Old Testament passages on Israel, the servant of the Lord, the king who is Son of
God, and the Son of Man, showing by this that Jesus too could have done this in his own way.

[32]See Dunn, *Unity and Diversity,* 38.

the future kingdom of God is present in his work and word, and he calls for people's "allegiance to himself only by virtue of his authority as the representative and mediator of the kingdom of God among men" (227). There is a parallelism between these verses. Jesus is saying that the one who confesses him as representative and mediator of the kingdom will be acknowledged by the Son of Man; this surely suggests that Jesus and the Son of Man are the same. The failure to see this could come from the failure to see how the words and deeds of Jesus mediate the kingdom. The enigmatic character of Jesus' use of the designation "Son of Man" had its advantages. There are different degrees of probability that Jesus used the Son of Man designation of himself; more exegetes would hold that he did use this to refer to his parousia, fewer that he used it of his suffering, and still fewer that he used it of his ministry.

Did Jesus expect the parousia to occur during the lifetime of his accusers? Many have interpreted Matthew 10:23 in this fashion: "When they persecute you in one town, flee to another. Amen, I say to you, you will not finish the towns of Israel before the Son of Man comes." But to interpret this passage in this sense does not do justice to the universalism of Matthew (see Matt 28:16-20). Also, it is to forget that the kingdom and judgment the Son of Man will exercise when he comes is already being exercised in part even now in history—in the very ministry of Jesus. It will be seen too in such events as the destruction of Jerusalem, prophesied as a judgment on Israel but one within history (see, e.g., Luke 19:41-44).

God's saving acts in history and his judgments in history are seen in this perspective, as we shall see more clearly in the fifth chapter, on the early Church's proclamation, as anticipatory of and partial expressions of *that* salvation and judgment that the Son of Man will bring when he comes again. In fact, these judgments in history and saving acts are themselves "comings" of the Son of Man, because they are shares in that judgment and salvation he will bring at the parousia. In this sense, the urgency to respond to his saving coming has its origin not simply in that final salvation and judgment he will bring to the world but in those anticipations of the final event that he visits upon his people within the course of history. Therefore to speak within the symbolic character of apocalyptic language of the *imminence* of the coming of the Son of Man is appropriate and does not imply that Jesus expected his final coming to be within the generation of his listeners.

In conclusion, we have argued in this chapter that Jesus proclaimed that the definitive kingdom of God, or salvation, was being offered to his people through him on the condition of their belief in him, that he understood this to be effective for renewal of his people in the circumstances of his time and place, and that as he came to anticipate his rejection by his people he proclaimed this in a more apocalyptic form, in the sense that even if he were to be killed he would be vindicated and mediate the kingdom for those who would come to be his believers and disciples. Vatican II's and the World Council of Churches' teaching to this effect, as well as that of many exegetes, is supported by the Gospels.

4

The Revelation Jesus Offered, and the Faith He Called For

In this chapter we ask what Scripture shows Christian revelation and faith to be, and we do so within the context of the second volume of *Foundational Theology*. That is, we take the perspective of Christians of the late twentieth century, and more specifically Catholics in the era of Vatican II, and we ask whether Scripture, the primary norm of Christian faith, supports what Vatican II taught concerning Christian revelation and faith. We do this in view of difficulties posed against such teaching in our time and in dialogue with our theological colleagues, who themselves are seeking to mediate Christian revelation and faith to our world, particularly that of the Atlantic countries and, more specifically, North America. In our first chapter, as well as in our earlier volume, we did analyze briefly what Vatican II—and the World Council of Churches—taught on this issue, major contemporary problems against this, and some major ways Christian theologians try to mediate belief in Christian revelation in our time and place. We will introduce this chapter by briefly recalling this.

Vatican II gave as reasons for belief in Jesus Christ the fact that it is through him that we gain salvation, the fact that God has revealed through him, and the fact that we have access to what Jesus said and did through the Gospels. Revelation through Jesus Christ is the basis for our belief in God through him, and the meaning of our faith depends upon the meaning of this revelation. In the present chapter we are primarily concerned with the *meaning* of Christian revelation and faith, though in a way restricted to the limits of foundational theology. In this matter we are supposing a view of the norm of Christian faith that will be critically defended only in a later part of *Foundational Theology*, namely, that one cannot propose a meaning of revelation and faith as Christian in a way divorced from what Jesus actually said and did in his ministry but rather only in dependence on this. So we ask: did he proclaim the kingdom of God, or salvation, as a divine revelation? In what sense did he do this, and what is the meaning of revelation implicit and explicit in his words and actions?

We are thus not answering all the difficulties against the Church's view of revelation and faith in this chapter. We shall have a later chapter in which we seek to relate revelation to an understanding of God and the human that we developed in the first volume, and so answer objections that come from views that the Church's interpretation of Christian revelation and faith is impossible, is counter to our realization that world religions mediate a revelation of God, and is opposed to the nature of the human person and human autonomy. The present chapter will, we trust, begin to answer these difficulties, but more through recalling the concrete story of the Christian beginnings than a theoretical analysis of revelation and faith.

What Vatican II taught about Christian revelation and faith is contained particularly in the prologue and chapter 1 of the Dogmatic Constitution on Divine Revelation *(DV).*[1] The council explicates revelation so that all may come to believe, have hope and love, in short that they may be saved. It asserts that "[i]t pleased God, in his goodness and wisdom, to reveal himself and to make known the mystery of his will (cf. Eph 1:9)" (2), namely, "that men should have access to the Father, through Christ, the Word made flesh, in the Holy Spirit, and thus become sharers in the divine nature" (2). Moreover, it teaches something on the motivation, the purpose, and the character of this process of revelation:

---

[1]See Austin Flannery, ed., *Vatican Council II: The Conciliar and Post Conciliar Documents* (Collegeville: The Liturgical Press, 1987) 750–3. The numbers in the text at this point are to the paragraphs of this constitution. See also Joseph Ratzinger, "Dogmatic Constitution on Divine Revelation: Origin and Background," and commentaries on the preface and chapter 1, *Commentary on the Documents of Vatican II,* ed. Herbert Vorgrimler (New York: Herder & Herder, 1969) 3:155–80; René Latourelle, "Revelation and Its Transmission According to the Constitution *Dei Verbum,*" *Theology of Revelation* (New York: Alba House, 1966) 453–88; Giles Lafont, "La Constitution 'Dei Verbum' et ses précédents conciliaires," *La nouvelle revue théologique* 110 (1988) 58–73 (hereafter cited as *NRT*).

> By this revelation, then, the invisible God . . . , from the fullness
> of his love, addresses men as his friends . . . , and moves among
> them . . . , in order to invite and receive them into his own com-
> pany. This economy of Revelation is realized by deeds and words,
> which are intrinsically bound up with each other (2).

There are stages to this divine revelation in history. This revelation
of who God is and the salvation he offers us finds its completion "in
Christ, who is himself both the mediator and the sum total of revelation" (2). For, after God had spoken many times and in varied ways
through the prophets, "in these last days he has spoken to us by a
Son" (Heb 1:1-2), "the eternal Word who enlightens all men" (4).
Jesus Christ

> completed and perfected revelation and confirmed it with divine
> guarantees. He did this by the total fact of his presence and his
> self-manifestation—by words and works, signs and miracles, but
> above all by his death and glorious resurrection from the dead, and
> finally sending the Spirit of truth. He revealed that God was with
> us, to deliver us from the darkness of sin and death, and to raise us
> up to eternal life (4).

Thus "no new public revelation is to be expected before the glorious
manifestation of our Lord, Jesus Christ (cf. 1 Tim 6:14 and Titus
2:13)" (4).

"To God as he reveals himself" (5) we must give the obedience of
faith. The council explains the nature of this faith: "By faith man
freely commits his entire self to God, making 'the full submission of
his intellect and will to God who reveals' (Vatican Council 1,
Dogmatic Constitution on the Catholic Faith *[Dei Filius]*), and willingly assenting to the revelation given by him" (5). To respond by
this faith to God, the human person needs grace and interior helps of
the Holy Spirit, who moves the heart, converts it, enlightens the
mind, and "makes it easy for all to accept and believe the truth" (5;
a quotation from Second Council of Orange). What the council
teaches here on revelation and faith depends on advances since
Vatican I in exegesis and theology, in the study of the liturgy and the
Fathers of the Church, and on writings of Catholics and Protestants.
Many Protestants have found this articulation of revelation and faith
in a personal, historical, scriptural, and concrete vein acceptable.

But this teaching is opposed by people who accept the Enlightenment position that the only knowledge accessible to human beings is that within the scope of our native human abilities, by those who go further and hold that pragmatism and/or praxis is the basic guide for human practical knowledge and who dismiss the Church's teaching by an ideology critique, and by those who say all knowledge is relative to the historical conditions of its origin. These viewpoints are particularly opposed to the Church's teaching that God's free and personal revelation is perfected and completed by Jesus Christ's life, words, deeds, death, and resurrection and his gift of the Spirit; that this revelation given through this mediator is definitive, though we can grow in the understanding of it and we do not expect another public revelation until Jesus comes again; and that while modern knowledge can contribute to our understanding of this revelation, for God reveals himself by the world also and the signs of the times, such knowledge cannot detract from the primacy of God's revelation through Jesus Christ or contradict it.

Many cannot conceive that something taught by a man two thousand years ago has a greater value than what is learned by the advances of our time. Similarly, the council's teaching on faith is rejected by many for similar reasons from the Enlightenment, pragmatism and ideology critique, and relativism. Many deny that Christian faith has any adequate confirmation and assert that such faith constrains us rather than gives us the freedom we most need, that it diminishes persons' concern for this world and its economic, political, cultural, and social needs. People with these views jettison their ancestors' view that God has definitively revealed himself to us through Jesus Christ and that this relationship of faith has primacy in our lives.

On the other hand, many who keep to the views of their ancestors in this matter identify "revelation" with some earlier articulation of it and so would not accept the nuanced view proposed by the council. Such are some fundamentalist Christians who do not accept what modern knowledge (e.g., scientific, or scriptural, or of world religions) can contribute to our understanding of Christian revelation, and some who have an individualistic view of salvation or who do not relate Christian salvation to the rampant injustices suffered by oppressed and marginalized groups in our time.

In addition, some theologians who seek to mediate the Christian faith to men and women of our century have difficulty with elements of the council's teaching in this matter. For example, we spoke earlier of differences among theologians before Vatican II on the question of how God reveals. Some stressed revelation as a communication of doctrine verbally from the divine to the human mind, even considering the resurrection as an apologetic proof rather than primarily as a medium of God's revelation. They assimilated God's revelation too much to an intellectualist form of communication, losing its mystery character and the symbolic character of its mediation. This difficulty has diminished greatly within the Church, but it persists in some evangelical groups.

Some stressed revelation as dialectical (Barth), and while this preserved the transcendence and mystery of God's revelation, it did not integrate, as the council does, its dialogical character or the way that words and deeds that are historical mediate this. Certainly Bultmann's view of revelation as mediated by the kerygma of the Church but not by Jesus in his public ministry, his view that this kerygma is the objectification of an inner religious experience but not of an experience mediated by historical words and deeds of Jesus and his resurrection appearances, his making modern science normative for what is possible in history, his view that for faith to be genuine it must be based simply on God's revelation but not on external signs that make this revelation credible—all of this is opposed to essential elements of Vatican II's interpretation of Christian revelation and faith.

Some post–Vatican II views of Christian theologians concerning revelation and faith similarly seem to reflect great difficulties with one or another element of the council's teaching. There are some who have subsumed Christian revelation under their preferred philosophy, and there are those who, reacting against the seeming arbitrariness or authoritarianism of Barth's and Bultmann's views of bases for Christian faith, have interpreted revelation as occurring through historical actions open to historical reason even, seemingly, without the inner aid of the Holy Spirit (Pannenberg), thus unwittingly assimilating revelation once more too much to an intellectualist communication. And there are those who base the faith on revelation's promise to answer the problem of evil in our lives (Moltmann, and, in some ways, some liberation theologians) while excessively separating the order of praxis from that of *theoria* and neglecting to face objections to Christian faith based on theory.

There are those too who view Christian statements about God as metaphors but interpret these as not normative for Christians but rather as susceptible to change as this is called for by pragmatic tests of today, such as what liberates those who are oppressed. Some of these theologians view Scripture as so sociologically conditioned and biased (e.g., against women) that it has lost its primacy as mediating God's revelation; its statements are wholly human efforts to express the mystery of God's loving and saving attitude toward us, and so they are dispensable and replaceable, if this basic truth is retained.[2] Also, some hold that one can have a genuine Christian identity without accepting a definite content of the message of salvation that Vatican II—and the Christian tradition more generally—considers essential, because Christian doctrines do not normatively articulate the reality of the Christian mystery but rather define rules for how we as Christians are to speak of God (Lindbeck).[3] Finally, there are those who, aware as never before of world religions, cannot agree with Vatican II that God's definitive revelation has occurred through Jesus Christ; they consider this claim triumphalism and an obstacle to interreligious dialogue.[4]

How can we evaluate whether Vatican II's interpretation of revelation and faith is genuinely the Christian view, given these serious objections to it? The present chapter is not the complete answer to this question, for it centers simply on the scriptural meaning of Christian faith and revelation. But within the limits of this chapter, I propose we must ask *how* Jesus reveals the kingdom of God, or salvation, and implicitly in this, God. Is it revealed symbolically by his words and deeds, his presence, his crucifixion and resurrection, and his gift of the Spirit? Is it revealed both through dialogue with those formed by God's earlier revelations and through dialectic? Is it revealed by a person to persons in community in a specific historical context? Does it demand from these people a breaking open of their perspec-

---

[2]See, for example, Edward Farley and Peter Hodgson, "Scripture and Tradition," *Christian Theology: An Introduction to Its Traditions and Tasks,* 2nd. ed., ed. Peter Hodgson and Robert King (Philadelphia: Fortress Press, 1985) 61–87. On diverse twentieth-century theological interpretations of revelation see Avery Dulles, *Revelation Theology* (New York: Herder & Herder, 1969), idem, *Models of Revelation* (New York: Doubleday, 1983).

[3]See George Lindbeck, *The Nature of Doctrine* (Philadelphia: Westminster Press, 1984). As a critique of this view, see Alister McGrath, *The Genesis of Doctrine: A Study in the Foundations of Doctrinal Criticism* (Oxford: Blackwell, 1990).

[4]See, for example, John Hick and Paul Knitter, eds., *The Myth of Christian Uniqueness: Toward a Pluralistic Theology of Religions* (Maryknoll, N.Y.: Orbis Books, 1987). For more mainline Christian responses to this challenge, see, for example, Les Newbigin, "The Christian Faith and the World Religions," *Keeping the Faith: Essays to Mark the Centenary of Lux Mundi,* ed. Geoffrey Wainwright (Philadelphia: Fortress Press, 1988) 310–40; Gavin D'Costa, "Revelation and Revelations: Discerning God in Other Religions, Beyond a Static Valuation," *Modern Theology* 10 (1994) 165–83.

tives and a reenvisioning of who God is, who they are, and what their call is for them to be able to respond to God by faith? This focus supposes that resistance to accepting God's revelation through Jesus Christ is primarily that we are locked into a view of human fulfillment that blocks out a good deal of God's vision and who we are and thus cannot incorporate the limits of the immediate, the flesh, and the individual. Secondarily, some of the Church's traditional forms of articulating the vision contribute to this resistance through the fact that they do not meet people where they are today—with what is wholly legitimate in their modern historical consciousness.

The main reason, I suppose, is not "reason" but "addiction"[5] to partial visions of human fulfillment. The need, then, is to allow our presuppositions to be challenged, to admit *levels* of the self, to acknowledge a vision beyond *our* power to accept. This is to accept experiences of weakness, vulnerability, and insecurity and to believe in the reality of God's love, call, and promise. We suggest that if we show that Scripture strongly affirms this then we are integrating what many theologians have taught about revelation, validating Vatican II's view as scriptural and Christian and showing that those theological views that contradict the council in this matter are not adequately Christian.

How can one show that this is what Scripture affirms? For this we depend on what we have studied in chapter 2, namely, on the literary character of the Gospels and their relation to history as justifying a view that we can, through them, have a valid historical witness to what Jesus substantially did and said in his ministry. We similarly depend on what we have studied in chapter 3, namely, what Jesus proclaimed when he proclaimed God's offer of the kingdom to the people through him and thus, both indirectly and directly, who God was and who he himself was as mediator of God's kingdom. We will seek to show what Christian revelation and faith are by a kind of phenomenology of faith that uses Peter's growth in faith as central and paradigmatic for Christians. Through studying Peter's faith we study the revelation that is its source. But we shall first reflect briefly on revelation and faith in the Old Testament and later on some major reasons for disbelief in Jesus during his ministry. Our next chapter, on the resurrection, is essential for an adequate sketch of the position we develop here, and there we shall look at some other New Testament

---

[5]See Gerald May, *Addiction and Grace* (San Francisco: Harper & Row, 1988).

perspectives on faith and lack of faith. All this we do within the limits of an introduction to our study of foundational theology.

I. Revelation and Faith in the Old Testament

We are asking for the meaning of revelation and faith in the Old Testament. It is only through those who believe that we are offered the meaning of revelation. Scripture itself is not revelation; revelation and faith occur before Scripture is written. If we simply look back to Scripture as though it were itself revelation, we might miss the "feel" of revelation and faith on the part of those whose experience is witnessed to in Scripture. The books of Scripture are generally written after the events to which they witness and after those who claimed revelation and acted on it had been vindicated. In our treatment here of the Old Testament we are not trying to prove that events happened as they were claimed to have happened but rather that this is the tradition from which Jesus came and so is essential for understanding his own claim to *reveal* God and the kingdom.

We shall recall briefly characteristics of revelation in the founding events of Israel as a people, in the prophets during the monarchy, the Exile and early postexilic period, in Israel's view of creation and some implications of this in Wisdom literature, and in apocalyptic literature. Our question here is, what does the Old Testament mean by revelation and the response due to it?

Before we treat these characteristics, we should recall that Israel had traditions of God revealing to the patriarchs before the Exodus. Abraham was the model of faith for Israel and for Christians. By God's revelation of his call and his promises, Abraham left Haran and in faith was on pilgrimage for many years before he received progeny through whom the promises were to be fulfilled (Genesis 12–23). Abraham's response to revelation was the experience and response of one facing the future, the unknown or largely unknown, and doing so in ways that frequently went beyond the bounds of the known and accepted.

Abraham and Sarah, like Moses and many prophets, were more like pioneers and explorers than like settlers in an established land, more like those venturing into an unknown new world that would transcend their expectations and stretch them to the limit than like those settled peacefully in a discovered land. They were like those venturing into an untamed and largely unexplored area that had already swallowed up some who ventured foolishly into it and that was taboo and totally off-limits to most. They had intimations that were the bases for their venturing beyond the known limits of the time and the accepted, but these did not give them a sense of security because there were so many questions within them and outside of them that tended to undercut the validity of these intimations and because they had to risk everything to respond to them. What was intimated to them by a revelation, whether it came through a dream, a vision, or some other mediation, was wholly beyond their control and it made them feel small and insufficient rather than triumphant. Acceptance was unsettling and filled with risks.

Because of this they have become paradigms of faith for us who follow, part of a cloud of witnesses who were to follow them (Hebrews 11). Revelation for many of these was not a vindication of what was already accepted by the people with whom they identified but something that set the recipients in tension with their surroundings. They were, by this, probers of the future, an advance guard who were to report on what they found to a skeptical and, indeed, frequently hostile world—hostile, because what these seers had to report threatened them and their accepted way of life.

1. Israel's Founding Revelation

Scripture's account of Moses, the Exodus, the covenant, and entrance into the Promised Land offers an important phenomenology of what revelation and faith are for the Old Testament.[6] To pick out a few elements of this formative experience for Israel, we can note that "an angel of the Lord appeared to him [Moses] in fire flaming out of a bush" (Exod 3:2). Actually, Moses is not said to have seen the Lord but to have heard the Lord speaking to him: "God called out to him from the bush, 'Moses! Moses!'" (Exod 3:4). Yahweh gave Moses the mission of liberating his people from Egypt and leading them into the land of milk and honey, and he revealed his name to him: "I am who am . . . the LORD, the God of your fathers, the God of Abraham, the God of Isaac, the God of Jacob" (Exod 3:14-15). The

---

[6]See H. Haag, "Révélation.- l'Ancien Testament," *Supplément au Dictionnaire de la Bible* (Paris: Letouzey & Ané, 1985) 10:586–600; M. John Farrelly, *Belief in God in Our Time* (Collegeville: The Liturgical Press, 1992) 73–99.

people themselves receive God's revelation through the mediation of Moses. In Moses' proclamation to them, in the rite of the sacrifice of the lamb on the night of the Passover of the Lord (Exod 12:11), and in the gradual fulfilling of the Lord's promises, they too have a revelation from the Lord through the events by which they were liberated and the words of Moses by which they were interpreted—thus by the mediation of what we can call *actual or real symbols* of Yahweh's dispositions toward them, promises to them, and of who Yahweh was.

The theophany surrounding the entrance into the covenant was also such a revelation to the people. When Moses laid before the people "all that the Lord had ordered him to tell them, the people all answered together, 'Everything the Lord has said, we will do'"(Exod 19:7-8). After the people had prepared themselves, "[o]n the morning of the third day there were peals of thunder and lightning, and a heavy cloud over the mountain, and a very loud trumpet blast, so that all the people in the camp trembled" (Exod 19:16). Mount Sinai was covered with smoke and the whole mountain trembled, filling the people with fear. They received through Moses the Law of the covenant and entered into a covenant, ratified by the sprinkling of blood, whereby God chose them to be his people and they chose him to be their God (Exodus 24). We see in this whole foundational act a central meaning of both revelation and faith for Israel. And we see in the subsequent events what was understood to be an adequate response to him and what was an inadequate response to his election, revelation, and covenant.

Thus the actions that constituted Israel as a people were understood to be the result of a revelation. And this revelation was an irruption into the lives of Moses and this people. It was a free act of God, of the God of their Fathers, of Yahweh, the one who is, a sovereignly free gift that came from his election of them as his people. It was an act in history at a particular time and place—God's entrance into the history of this people. It was an act that was a promise of a future for the people, a future that was this-worldly but one in which they would be his people, a holy and priestly people (Exod 19:6). It was an act that demanded a great deal of Moses and this people—an act that transformed their lives, distinguished them from the world about them, and called them to be God's faithful people in a unique way. It was a personal act on the part of God and called for a personal response of Moses and the people, a surrender to Yahweh, whom they accepted as their God. They were to accept the moral order that he prescribed and were to be faithful in the hope that God's promise to them would be fulfilled. Faith here is primarily having confidence in God, but this presupposes accepting the basis for such confidence, namely, that he had chosen them and made promises to them—that God is loving and faithful.

One dimension of this revelation important to underline is the following. The surrounding peoples of that age lived in symbolic universes articulated by their myths. These were imaginative constructions of dimensions of reality most important for them, of how the sacred impinged on their lives, how the power of the sacred was present and available to them, and how they should act toward the sacred to integrate their lives into the ultimate.[7] These myths were related to the origin of the gods and the universe and to the fertility of the fields. In Israel it was their history and interpretation of this history of their deliverance from Egypt, their wandering in the desert, their covenant and entrance into the Promised Land, that had the primary defining importance that myths had for other peoples of their time. Their interpretation was that God was the source of their deliverance, their call to be his people (election and the covenant), their guidance and support, and the gift of the Promised Land. This founding event was proclaimed and recalled frequently, and it constituted God's revelation as an act and as what God made known—namely, his way of salvation and dispositions to them and God's own elusive mystery as they knew him. It offered them the symbolically expressed world in which they were to live faithfully.

This history was constructed by the creative imaginations of those who passed on their traditions, the editors of the documents that came to enshrine these traditions, and the editors who came to unite these documents into the Pentateuch as we now have it. The epic form of these stories was the result of such creative imaginations, but it was the belief of these editors that they were faithfully organizing the traditional materials based on the founding events of Israel and were doing so to make known to the people the true meaning and implications of these founding events. They understood that the primary creative imagination to which they were faithful in this process

---

[7]See John McKenzie, "Aspects of Old Testament Thought," *NJBC* 1288–1315, especially 1288–90; Aylward Shorter, "God's Word, Our Guide," *Revelation and Its Interpretation* (London: Geoffrey Chapman, 1983) 34–67; Haag, "Révélation," 594–5.

was that of Yahweh, who was the agent and source of these saving and revealing events. There were such depths of meaning in these foundational acts that they needed deeper and deeper penetration, and their implications needed to be spelled out in ever new ways for succeeding generations. God had unveiled something hidden through them; he had confronted Moses and this people with what he unveiled. And he did so by both the events and the words by which Moses interpreted these events; both together were revelatory. God revealed through such mighty saving actions "so that you may know that I am the LORD" (Exod 10:2). The "knowledge" here is not simply an intellectual knowledge; the word used is the word used for sexual intercourse (Gen 4:1, 17, 25; Gen 19:8); it is to know Yahweh through experience, to live intimately with Yahweh, to recognize him, to be faithful to him.

While the primary mediation of God's revelation to his people was this founding historical event with the word that interpreted it, Israel had traditions of God revealing himself also to the judges after the entrance into the Promised Land, and finally to Samuel, even as a young boy (1 Sam 3:4f.). At times God was understood to reveal himself through dreams (as in the case of Joseph, Genesis 40; 41), the Urim and Thummin through which priests consulted God (Num 27:21; Deut 33:8; 1 Sam 14:41), and divination (Gen 44:2, 5). Israel did not use other means that people of the time used to divine their gods' directions such as reading animals' livers. And Saul was condemned for calling up Samuel's ghost through a medium (1 Samuel 28).

2. The Prophets and Revelation

Prophecy was a primary though not the sole medium of God's revelation during the monarchy, Exile, and early postexilic period. Even before the monarchy there were bands of prophets (1 Sam 10:10-13). And there were the prophets before and other than the literary prophets, some of whom were women, for example, Miriam (Exod 15:20), Deborah (Judg 4:4), and Huldah (2 Kgs 22:16). Nathan was a prophet in David's court who received a message from the Lord promising to build a house for David that would last forever (2 Sam 7:4-16), and later a message convicting David of sin (2 Sam 12:1-12). Gad, too, was a prophet with messages for David (2 Sam 24:11f.). In the divided kingdom, Elijah prophesied in the middle of the ninth century during the reigns of Ahab and Ahaziah. He sought particularly to rid the northern kingdom of the worship of Baal (1 Kgs 17–19:21); Elijah also had a revelation of God in a theophany of nature—not in the fierce wind, nor in the earthquake, nor in the fire, but in "a tiny whispering sound. . . . A voice said to him, 'Elijah, why are you here?'" (1 Kgs 19:12-13). Elisha succeeded him as prophet in Israel (2 Kings 2–9), but there were also groups of prophets at the time (2 Kgs 9:1-3).

Prophecy existed in the world around Israel, but the classical prophecy in Israel is set apart—both from its surroundings and from false prophets in Israel itself—by "the fearless revelation of the moral will of Yahweh, the God of Israel's covenant."[8] Latourelle writes:

> What really constitutes the authority and originality of the prophet is the fact that he has been the object of a privileged experience: he knows Yahweh, for Yahweh has spoken to him and entrusted his word to him. He has been admitted to a particular intimacy with God: he has been called to share his knowledge, his plans, his will, to be his interpreter among men. . . . [T]he prophet "has stood in the counsel of Yahweh" (Jer 23:18, 22; 1 Kgs 22:19-23) and Yahweh has revealed his plans (Amos 3:7). He knows the secrets of the Most High (Num 24:16-17), for he has understood the words of Yahweh (1 Sam 15:16). Yahweh has spoken to him and he possesses Yahweh's word.[9]

The prophets were called by Yahweh, and a number of them recount their inaugural vision (e.g., Isaiah 6; Jer 1:4-19). God addresses them, and they receive the *word* of Yahweh, at times expressed graphically, as in the experience of eating a scroll (Ezek 2:9-3:4). The prophet becomes the "mouth" of Yahweh (Jer 15:19). And it is this word that they proclaim—frequently to kings and people who do not wish to hear the message. In the preexilic period it is in large part a message of judgment against God's own people for sins against the poor and sins of idolatry: "Are you to steal and murder, commit adultery and perjury, burn incense to Baal, go after strange gods that you know not, and yet come to stand before me in this house which bears my name, and say: 'We are safe: we can commit all these abominations again'? Has this house which bears my name become in your eyes a den of thieves?" (Jer 7:8-11; also see Amos 2:4f.).

---

[8] Bruce Vawter, "Introduction to Prophetic Literature," *NJBC*, 190.

[9] Latourelle, *Theology of Revelation*, 32.

The prophet is a man who feels fiercely. God has thrust a burden upon his soul, and he is bowed and stunned at man's fierce greed. . . . Prophecy is the voice that God has lent to the silent agony, a voice to the plundered poor, to the profaned riches of the world. . . . God is raging in the prophet's words. . . .

As a witness, the prophet is more than a messenger. As a messenger, his task is to deliver the word; as a witness, he must bear testimony that the word is divine. . . . The prophet not only conveys; he reveals. He almost does unto others what God does unto him. In speaking, the prophet reveals God. This is the marvel of a prophet's work: in his words, the *invisible God becomes audible.* He does not prove or argue. The thought he has to convey is more than language can contain. Divine power bursts in the words. The authority of the prophet is in the Presence his words reveal.[10]

Because his message was frequently unpopular and forceful in the hope of overcoming people's callousness, the prophet was often a lonely man, burdened with a mission distasteful to himself and repugnant to others. Nothing, however, will stand in the way of God's word, whether people accept it or not. The prophet does not primarily tell the future but speaks for God *(nabi),* and he does so in immediate relation to the events of the time and place where he speaks. He interprets these events in relation to God. He conveys this message by a proclamation in words and, at times, in symbolic actions. For example, Jeremiah broke a flask to symbolize what God would do to Jerusalem (Jer 19:10-11), and Ezekiel symbolically journeyed into exile to show what God would do to the people of Jerusalem (Ezekiel 12). Particularly before the Exile the prophet's message was more dialectic than dialogue, more confronting than comforting for Israel.

The message the prophet has comes from God's love for Israel, even though she is unfaithful to his covenant (Hosea), and is more a message of hope for Israel's conversion than a threat of judgment. There are also promises of God's mercy and salvation; this is found, for example, in the messianic prophecies of Isaiah (e.g., Isa 7:14; 9:1-6; 11:1-9). But Israel rejected the prophets' warnings, and both the northern and the southern kingdoms fell. The Exile was the great rift in Old Testament history. The main tenor of the prophetic message after the Exile was one of comfort and hope for a depressed and even

---

[10]A. J. Heschel, *The Prophets* (New York: Harper Colophon ed., 1975) 2:3–4.

despairing people. Through the new depth of reflection on God and his relation to Israel that it occasioned, the experience of the Exile brought Israel (e.g., through Deutero-Isaiah and, later, Third Isaiah) to know that Yahweh was the only God, the one whose power extended through the whole world, that he was still faithful to his promises and indeed made greater promises to them than in the past. This led them to be faithful to God in a more stable way than in the past.

We should not conclude that it was only through the prophets that God's revelation was thought to reach his people. The priests proclaimed the Law and celebrated the cult, and both of these mediated God's revelation and became central to the postexilic Jewish community's identity. In the seventh century the book of Deuteronomy represents an important effort to organize Israel's life on the basis of the covenant Law. The Law was a revelation of God's moral will, and it was the priests' function to teach it. Cult, too, as with other peoples in the Middle East at the time but in a distinctive way for Israel, mediated revelation:

> The basic elements of cult are myth and ritual. By myth is meant the recital of the saving event, and by ritual, its symbolic reenactment. Through these two elements of cult the society establishes and maintains communion with the deity. Such recital and the reenactment appear in Israelite cult with one essential difference: the saving event that is recited is not the mythological event in nature but the saving deeds of Yahweh in history, viz., the actions by which he delivered Israel from Egypt and established Israel as the people of his covenant in the promised land. In the recital Yahweh reveals himself anew as the God of Israel. Apparently the narratives of the Pentateuch had much of their origin in such ritual recitals.[11]

3. Wisdom Literature and Revelation

The Pentateuch was assembled and edited in the early postexilic period, and the written word tends more and more to replace the spoken word as the spiritual center of Israel. It was thought that the people should rule their lives by revelation, as it had been written in the Torah.[12] But also, the writing of Genesis shows how Israel

---

[11]McKenzie, "Aspects of Old Testament Thought," 1300.

[12]See Haag, "Révélation," 594.

thought God was revealed not simply to Israel but to other peoples, and not simply by the Law and prophets but by creation and particularly by human beings whom God created by his word and his spirit in his own image (Gen 1:27; Psalm 104). The created world is the source of Wisdom's insights, and thus the experiences of the created world are divine experiences for Israel; creation has a language that is revelatory. The psalmist sings, "The heavens declare the glory of God, and the firmament proclaims his handiwork" (Ps 19:1).

There is a problem of how to integrate revelation through history and revelation through creation for Israel. Some exegetes identify revelation with salvation history and so do not consider creation to be a medium of God's revelation for Israel. But the Wisdom literature of the Old Testament, and specifically the personification of wisdom in Lady Wisdom, does not seem to support this. It does not seem sufficient to identify Lady Wisdom with the self-revelation of creation as the mysterious order of creation addressing humanity:

> One may question whether the lyrical description of Lady Wisdom is adequately captured by the concept of order. She certainly cannot be viewed apart from the Lord from whom she originates. Her authority also suggests that she is the voice of the Lord, the revelation of God, not merely the self-revelation of creation. She is the divine summons issued in and through creation, who finds her delight among the humans God has created (8:31). Lady Wisdom, then, is a communication of God, through creation, to human beings.[13]

This revelation cannot be made totally secondary to that which comes through Israel's historical revelation, since the Wisdom literature of Israel in Job and Wisdom (1:15) was able to go beyond Deuteronomy's understanding of the mystery of evil.[14] There is not an opposition between Wisdom and Torah; in fact, in some texts Wisdom is identified with Torah (Sir 24:8-10, 22; Psalm 19). This view is counter to some exegetes, particularly Protestant, who identify Judeo-Christian revelation as coming through salvation history alone, and to some theologians, particularly Catholic, who reduce

---

[13]Roland Murphy, "Introduction to Wisdom Literature," *NJBC* 450. Also see his "Wisdom and Creation", *JBL* 104 (1985) 3–11; and his book, *The Tree of Life* (New York: Doubleday, 1990) 121–6.

[14]See Murphy, "Introduction to Wisdom Literature," 449.

what can be known of God through nature to natural theology. It would be wrong, then, to identify Judeo-Christian revelation with what characterizes the prophets—knowledge mediated by one person that is frequently and necessarily adversarial. Revelation also comes to those who are open to the way God speaks through human experience. And the teaching of Lady Wisdom, who is closely associated with "spirit" (e.g., Wis 7:7; 7:22-23; 9:17), through these means is frequently pictured as winning, persuasive, and inviting; there is an immanence to this form of revelation that differentiates it from much of prophetic revelation (Proverbs 8). In Wisdom literature Wisdom is as much God's gift as salvation and, indeed, is identified with salvation.

4. Apocalyptic and Revelation

Finally, we should note a form of revelation found in Old Testament apocalyptic. There is some disagreement concerning how many of these writings should be considered apocalyptic, but there is agreement that the book of Daniel has substantial apocalyptic passages, and it is on this that we concentrate here.[15] We treated some content of Daniel's teaching in the preceding chapter. Here we ask how revelation is present in Daniel. Daniel is written to encourage Jews subject to persecution for loyalty to their Jewish traditions to persevere in fidelity even at the cost of death, and the author makes use of enigmatic visions and symbols for this purpose. In his time God did not seem to be revealed by what was happening in Jewish history. History seemed rather to be under the control of demonic forces opposed to God and so obscured God's fidelity and tended to undercut faith. Daniel taught that history was a sphere of conflict between divine and demonic wills. By his visions and their interpretation he proclaimed that in the age to come, which was imminent, God would overturn the forces controlling the present age and give the kingdom to one like a Son of Man and the holy ones of God—a kingdom that would be universal and everlasting (Daniel 7) and would mean resurrection from the dead for those who have been faithful (Dan 12:1-3). Daniel had comparatively a lack of interest in the saving deeds of God in Israel's history. For him and apocalypticism

---

[15]On the growth of apocalyptic, see John J. Collins, "Old Testament Apocalypticism and Eschatology," *NJBC,* 298–304.

more generally, "the whole salvation-happening *(Heilsgeschehen)* is eschatological-futuristic."[16]

Did this revelation come to Daniel by the visions and the interpretations of these visions by angels? It seems rather that this is a literary form because of the pseudonymous authorship of the book, which is a report of visions given to one who lived centuries earlier than its author. As Murdock writes of Jewish apocalypses:

> The *Gattung* apocalypse may be defined as a reading revelation, a book of divine wisdom in which the mysteries and secrets of God were unfolded before the reader's eyes as he experienced the visions, dreams, and celestial journeys described by the apocalypticist. . . . [T]he revelation with which the apocalypticists were concerned was the disclosure of the divine mysteries—ostensibly to some ancient seer directly by God himself or indirectly through visions and angels, but, in fact, to the reader of the apocalypse.[17]

Daniel promised through this that there would be that future revelation of God's salvation and judgment in the age to come: "[T]he eschatological revelation was understood, not as the sum of all historical revelations, but as the *doxa* of God bursting in upon this aeon of darkness from the aeon of light."[18] The first Christians would interpret the resurrection of Jesus through this apocalyptic tradition as the beginning of that age to come bursting in upon the present.

We have seen the Old Testament's claim that God's founding revelation for Israel came through the Exodus, covenant, and entrance into the Promised Land. This came through God's symbols—his acts and the words mediated through Moses and others who interpreted these acts. And it established a symbolic world, a world of meaning basic for Israel's life. Through the prophets as God's spokespersons God made known to Israel the implications of his relation to them and their relation to him as it was appropriate for their circumstances, at times through correcting their way of acting and at times through giving them comfort in affliction and hope in despair. This message called for a faith and fidelity frequently at odds with their surround-

---

[16]William Murdock, "History and Revelation in Jewish Apocalypticism," *Interpretation* 21 (1967) 180, quoting from G. von Rad.

[17]Murdock, "History and Revelation," 184.

[18]Ibid., 187.

ings. Israel's cult and the psalms so important in this cult and its Law were other mediators of God's revelation that fostered this relationship and Israel's identity as God's people. Through the message of creation as coming from God's word and spirit, the Wisdom tradition saw God's revelation as coming also through creation and human experience, a revelation that was expressed under its personification as Lady Wisdom as soliciting or persuasive, as immanent and leading men and women further in their relationship to God, even to being friends of God.

II. Revelation Through a Phenomenology of Peter's Growth in Faith

We now ask for the *meaning* of Christian revelation and faith as shown in the ministry of Jesus and beyond. We are examining the meaning of revelation and faith in view of Vatican II, difficulties raised against it, and some mutually opposed interpretations of it. We can only understand this meaning through the witness of those who believe, since it is these who are able to say what it is, and what is normative for Christians is Scripture. Scripture is written by believers for believers. The New Testament is a witness to their faith, how they came to faith, what they believed, and its implications for life. Revelation is available to us through those who believe, and Christian revelation through those who first believed in Jesus Christ. There is much reason to think that Peter is presented in the Synoptics as the first who began to believe in the distinctiveness of Jesus during his ministry (after, of course, Mary) and that he is offered to us as a paradigm and model of coming to believe in Jesus and the difficulties of such belief. He has been compared to the Abraham of the New Testament[19]— as blessed in the gift of his faith and further blessed because of his faith, as the one, with the other disciples, of course, through whom the new people of God would come to believe in Jesus, and thus as the foundation in a special way of the community of believers in Jesus.

A study of the stages of Peter's faith as presented to us in the Gospels gives us also a unique perspective on a number of issues that have divided theologians, such as the means by which Christian revelation

[19]See M. Chevallier, "A propos de 'Tu es Pierre, tu es le nouvel Abraham (Mt 16/18)," *Etudes théologique et religieuse* 57 (1982) 376–87; and 58 (1983) 354; J. Massingbird Ford, "Thou art 'Abraham' and upon this Rock . . . ," *Heythrop Journal* 6 (1965) 289–301.

is mediated, dialogue and dialectic, experience and authority, the objective and the subjective, *theoria* and praxis. So we shall approach the question of the meaning of Christian revelation and faith particularly through an analysis of the stages of Peter's faith: (1) Peter's confession of Jesus as Messiah, (2) his resistance to Jesus' teaching on the suffering Son of Man, and (3) his belief after Jesus' resurrection and the coming of the Spirit. The last of these depends on what we more fully develop in the next chapter.

1. Revelation and Peter's Confession That Jesus Is the Messiah

Can we take the Synoptic Gospels' account of Peter's confession of Jesus as Messiah as historically occurring in the ministry of Jesus and as a genuine response of Peter to a divine revelation? For us to use the passages recounting this event for our purposes here, we must answer these questions. So we shall first show what a currently widely received interpretation of this story is, then give reasons why the passages can legitimately be used for our purposes, and then analyze their implications for the nature of Christian revelation and faith.

a. A current interpretation of Peter's confession. Mark writes that Peter confessed Jesus by saying, "You are the Messiah" (Mark 8:29). Matthew, however, has a fuller confession, and adds that Jesus blessed Peter, chose him, and made him a promise. To Jesus' question "Who do you say that I am?" Peter replied:

> "You are the Messiah, the Son of the living God." Jesus said to him in reply, "Blessed are you, Simon son of Jonah. For flesh and blood has not revealed this to you, but my beloved Father. And so I say to you, you are Peter, and upon this rock I will build my church, and the gates of the netherworld shall not prevail against it" (Matt 16:16-18).

A full account of the modern history of the exegesis of this passage can be found elsewhere.[20] The main elements of this as relevant to our concerns are the following. In the early part of this century there was skepticism that Jesus could have founded his Church on Peter because it was thought that Jesus expected the kingdom in a

---

[20]See Gérard Claudel, "Première Partie: État de la Question," *La Confession de Pierre: Trajectoire d'une péricope évangelique* (Paris: J. Gabalda, 1988) 7–45.

sense that included the end of history to occur very soon. After the first quarter of the century, there was an increasing consensus among Protestants on the authenticity of Matthew's passage, in part because of the Semitisms it contained, including verse 19; but Bultmann rejected the authenticity as did Kümmel. In mid-century its authenticity had increasing favor. Oscar Cullmann wrote extensively on this passage.[21] He thought that Matthew 16:17-19 was a redactional insertion by Matthew into the Marcan account. There was nothing against the authenticity of this passage for Jesus, but Cullmann thought that what Jesus says of Peter as rock was meant for him alone; and he came to place this macarism and promise (Matt 16:17-18) at the Last Supper. Now exegetes more generally place it in an appearance of Jesus to Peter after the resurrection.[22]

Among the reasons for denying that it could be a tradition due initially to Peter's original confession are the following: It is thought that if Mark knew that Peter confessed Jesus to be "Son of the Living God," he would have added it. This designation of Jesus seems to many exegetes to be a postresurrection Christian title for Jesus. And many continue to think that Jesus expected the end to come soon and so would not have envisaged a structured community such as a "church" (*ecclesia* is an early Christian word) during his ministry. Moreover, many think that Jesus rejected Peter's confession of him as Messiah and that the source of Mark's account joined Peter's confession (Mark 8:29) and Jesus' rebuke (Mark 8:33). According to this view it was Mark rather than the tradition on which he depended that separated these two parts of this passage and made Jesus' rebuke seem more directed to Peter's resistance to Jesus' announcement of his coming suffering and death than to Peter's confession itself. The above interpretation, including variations within it, is a widely accepted one today but not the sole interpretation.

b. Can we use Peter's confession of Jesus as Messiah as historical and commended by Jesus? There are two steps in which we will answer this question. First, we note that there is a growing agreement among many exegetes that an essential critical method in approaching

---

[21]See Oscar Cullmann, *Peter: Disciple, Apostle, Martyr: A Historical and Theological Essay,* 2nd ed. (Philadelphia: Westminster Press, 1962).

[22]This is the opinion adopted in Raymond Brown, Karl Donfried, and John Reumann, eds., *Peter in the New Testament* (New York: Paulist Press, 1973) 85ff.

the Gospels is, as we saw in chapter 2, that of literary criticism.[23] It is not sufficient, for example, to search Mark's Gospel to find the sources behind it and view it as a window through which we can see the history of the first century, or even to investigate it by redaction criticism to see how Mark redacted the traditions he received. Both of these miss seeing his Gospel as a unitary and literary work, the work of an author who composed a narrative to convey a message. It is the literary-critical study that enables New Testament scholars to view Mark's Gospel "as a unified story, a literary work rather than a collection of disparate traditions . . . [and] literary criticism has made NT students more aware of the rhetorical devices present in Mark's narrative."[24]

There is not full agreement among those who approach Mark's Gospel by way of literary criticism; but while differing in their interpretations of Mark's rhetorical devices, many agree largely on the overall thrust and theme of his Gospel in view of which he organizes his narrative. And many agree that Peter's confession of Jesus as Messiah constitutes a point to which the preceding narrative leads and at which Jesus begins a new teaching about his own destiny and discipleship.

Recognizing Mark's Gospel as a literary work and similarly the other Gospels as such, we can see more clearly that some of their differences are due to their varied perspectives on the inexhaustible mystery of Jesus, his ministry and his person, and its meaning for the Church. Each evangelist by his creative imagination and the way he structures his narrative seeks to bring out certain central dimensions of this mystery. But, as we indicated in chapter 2, what they organize and explicate is what the tradition recounted in substantial fidelity to what Jesus said and did in his ministry. Thus the overriding "creative imagination" at work was that of Jesus Christ himself rather than those of the evangelists. Also, what is normative for Christians is not simply the bare facts of what Jesus said and did but the interpretation of these that the apostolic age reached and mediated to us in the New Testament. These had bases in the ministry of Jesus and not only in the experiences of the early Church. Thus the message each of the

---

[23]See, for example, Frank Matera, *What Are They Saying About Mark?* (New York: Paulist Press, 1987), especially chapter 5, "The Narrative of Mark's Gospel," where he discusses two approaches to Mark's narrative. Also see Augustine Stock, *Call to Discipleship: A Literary Study of Mark's Gospel* (Wilmington, Del.: Michael Glazier, 1982); idem, *The Method and Message of Mark* (Wilmington, Del.: Michael Glazier, 1989).

[24]Matera, *What Are They Saying About Mark?* 91.

evangelists gives us, by the way he structures his narrative of Jesus' ministry, is a legitimate interpretation of Jesus and normative for Christians. This holds, too, in their interpretation of what Christian revelation and faith are, the issues we are concerned with here.

The approach to the Gospels by way of literary criticism does not constrict us to the narrative world of the author and block us from questions of what actually happened in the ministry of Jesus. Rather, it seems to help us approach these questions. Specifically, as pertinent to our questions as to whether Peter actually confessed Jesus as Messiah and whether his confession was commended by Jesus, we do have multiple attestation from different traditions. If we accept the two-source hypothesis, we have Mark's witness to this. Matthew and Luke (9:18-21) also attest it, perhaps relying in part on traditions other than Mark. And John shows us Peter as spokesman for the faith of the Twelve in another critical context (John 6:67-69).

Also, by literary criticism we recognize that Mark's narrative understood the title "Son of God" as a more adequate title for Jesus than "Messiah." It is one he made known to the reader from the beginning of his Gospel (1:1); it is the title God used of Jesus at the baptism (1:11) and the transfiguration (9:7); it is used of Jesus by demons (5:7); the first human to ascribe this title to Jesus was the centurion at the foot of the cross when Jesus died (15:39). Since Mark wishes, as we will show, to indicate that Peter did come to the first stage of faith when he confessed Jesus to be the Messiah but that his faith was insufficient, even if the evangelist had in his sources a fuller expression of Peter's confession such as that which Matthew gives, he would not have used it. His not using it is not evidence of itself that it was not original. As we saw in the last chapter, the title "Son of God" was most probably used in a messianic sense in Judaism at the time of Jesus' ministry,[25] so it could have been part of the historical confession of Peter.

---

[25]See G. R. Beasley-Murray, *Jesus and the Kingdom of God* (Grand Rapids: Eerdmans, 1986) 299–300. Claudel argues that this title was one of royal messianism, was in Matthew's source, was the original, and was shortened by Mark (240–4). Also see James Dunn, *Unity and Diversity in the New Testament* (Philadelphia: Westminster Press, 1977) 45 and notes; Ben Meyer, "Jesus' Ministry and Self-Understanding," *Studying the Historical Jesus,* ed. Bruce Chilton and Craig Evans (Leiden: Brill, 1994) 350: "The object of Jesus' esoteric teaching was, generically, 'the secret of the reign of God,' . . . Penetration of Jesus' messianic identity (presented by John as among the first moments in the story, but retained by the Synoptic tradition as its dramatic turning point) was the crucial condition of receptivity on the part of the disciples. *The key to Jesus' view of 'new covenant,' 'new temple,' and 'new cult' was precisely his identity as 'new king.'*"

Finally, the use of literary criticism supports the view that Peter's confession of Jesus as Messiah was indeed accepted by Jesus, even though it was inadequate. Mark places immediately before Peter's confession Jesus' two-stage cure of the blind man of Bethsaida (8:22-26). After the first stage of his cure, this man saw but did not see clearly. This seems to presage both the truth of Peter's confession and its inadequacy.[26] The inadequacy of Peter's faith at this point is not reason to interpret Jesus' rebuke to Peter as motivated historically by his confession rather than by Peter's resistance to Jesus' prediction of his coming suffering.

c. Implications of Peter's confession for the meaning of Christian revelation and faith. First, we must ask whether Peter's confession is considered by the evangelists to be an instance of a response of faith to a revelation mediated by Jesus. Matthew, of course, interprets it as such in verse 17, but many exegetes hold that this verse is redactional and should be placed rather in a postresurrection appearance of Jesus to Peter. A full discussion of this issue can be found elsewhere,[27] but here we limit ourselves to evidence that Peter's confession is accepted by the evangelists as a faith response to a revelation. Matthew's passage asserting this (v. 17) may be original, but what was prominent in Matthew's organization of the tradition here was more its relevance to the founding of the Church than Peter's confession itself. Jesus' promise to Peter (v. 18) was more significant for this than even Peter's confession in terms of Matthew's message.[28]

This was not the significance of the passage for Mark. He was writing for a Church suffering persecution and seeking to encourage the people to fidelity in the midst of it, showing for this purpose the insufficiency of belief in Jesus as a wonder-worker and the necessity of seeing him as a suffering Messiah and of accepting discipleship as involving suffering. Thus it could well be that Matthew's account that Jesus explicitly stated that Peter's confession was due to a revelation and his addition of a change of Peter's name and promise to him (vv. 18, 19) came from a biographical apothegm of Jesus at this

---

[26]See Stock, *Method and Message of Mark,* 227–35; idem, *Call to Discipleship,* 130–4.

[27]See Claudel, *La Confession de Pierre,* 311, 387–8. Claudel opposes the view that verse 18 is redactional. He holds that it is the original ending of the biographical story of Peter's confession and that verses 17–19 are a redactional enlargement of the original ending with a strong paschal coloration.

[28]See ibid., 179.

point in his ministry. If the confession and its commendation occurred in the ministry of Jesus, it would seem that that is the most appropriate point at which Jesus would change his name. Abram's name was changed to Abraham after he believed, the latter form traditionally implying that he would be the father of many nations (Gen 17:5). It is at least Matthew's message that Peter's confession was indeed due to a revelation, so even if it is redactional it is normative for Christians to understand it as due to a revelation.

Also for Mark, Peter's shorter confession of Jesus as the Christ is understood to be a positive affirmation about Jesus, an ascription to Jesus of something more than "the people" did. Mark understood this title in a positive manner (Mark 1:1; 14:61-62), and the early Church did the same. Moreover, by the way that Mark situates this passage, he shows that he considers Peter's confession to be the result of a revelation, though he does not use the word. In the passage just preceding Peter's confession, Jesus cures the blind man of Bethsaida in two stages (8:22-26). Each of these stages was the result of Jesus' initiative; each was a curing that gave sight, though the first one gave only imperfect sight.

Mark had shown a number of instances in which the disciples of Jesus were blind to the significance of his actions and words. He now shows that Jesus cures this blind man in two stages, and he then recounts Peter's confession of Jesus as Messiah, which he takes as a positive affirmation about Jesus beyond that of the people, but Peter quickly shows how limited and confused his vision is. When Peter resists Jesus' teaching that he must suffer and die, Jesus tells him, according to Mark: "You are thinking not as God does, but as human beings do" (8:33). This is similar to what Matthew states at the same point of the narration (16:23) and is just the opposite of what Jesus says, according to Matthew, immediately after Peter's confession: "Flesh and blood has not revealed this to you, but my heavenly Father" (16:17). Though this verse of Matthew is not in Mark's account, it is implied by the context and by what Mark quotes Jesus as saying when Peter resists Jesus' proclamation of his suffering. In his confession Peter was thinking as God thought; his confession was due to God's opening his eyes, though partially—his revelation.

Luke's account, we may add, puts Peter's confession in the context of Jesus' prayer (Luke 9:18-21), which shows the importance of what follows. According to Luke, Peter responds to Jesus' question with "The Messiah of God" (9:20) and thus without even a whole sentence. Though for Luke this has significance and marks a turning point in Jesus' teaching, it seems to be less central than it was for Mark and even Matthew.[29] Luke omits Peter's rejection of Jesus' prediction of his suffering. We conclude, particularly from Mark and Matthew but also from Luke, that the evangelists present Peter as being spokesman for the faith of the apostles at this point and thus as responding to a revelation in a way beyond what the people's response to Jesus showed. It is as though Jesus finally found the beginnings of that faith that he came to stir up and that was the condition for his people's reception of the kingdom he was mediating.

Granted that the evangelists teach us that Peter's confession is an instance of faith in response to revelation mediated by Jesus and that this most probably reflects, both in fact and in valid interpretation, an important event in the ministry of Jesus, what are some things that a phenomenology of this event makes known to us about the nature of Christian revelation and faith? Peter's faith is a *response* on Peter's part to an act of God through Jesus that is called revelation. Peter's coming to believe in Jesus is in the context of and made possible by his earlier acceptance of the revelation God had given to Israel, the expectation of the Jews that God would send them one who would liberate them as he had promised, the severe sense of being oppressed that was experienced by the Jews in Palestine at the time of Jesus, their eager hope for liberation from this oppression, and Peter's sense of his own sinfulness and need (Luke 5:8). As we shall show below, the context is also Jesus' ministry.

First we should note that Peter's confession of faith, "You are the Messiah," expressed a judgment on Peter's part—a proposition about Jesus and who he was. These words express a knowledge of Jesus. The judgment is an intellectual act. It is belief *that* Jesus is the Messiah. This is an acceptance of what God had revealed. The Messiah has preeminence over the other mediators from God such as John the Baptist, Elijah, or one of the prophets that some of the people thought Jesus to be (Mark 8:28). It is an act on Peter's part that is an interpretation of Jesus in ambiguous historical circumstances, and it was other than the interpretation given by the people generally. It was a breakthrough on the part of this individual to a deeper knowledge of Jesus. But this act on Peter's part is in no way an isolated intellectual act. It is a commitment of Peter to Jesus, an

---

[29]See ibid., 239–40.

expression of discipleship, a belief *in* or *on* Jesus. By this act Peter becomes a disciple in a new way. So Peter's response is a whole human response; he expects God's kingdom to come through the Messiah; he confesses Jesus to be the Messiah; and he commits himself to be his disciple in hope. This is not simply an intellectual knowledge of Jesus or simply a commitment. It is *personal knowledge* in that he knows something of Jesus' person, and his knowledge is one that is not simply objective but subjective in the sense that he is involved. This knowledge comes from his involvement, and it promises an involvement as a disciple. It is the result of a discernment, and it expresses, establishes, and solidifies a personal relationship to Jesus.

It is a discernment and confession that is the result of a *dialogue*. Jesus did manifest himself as Messiah to those who had eyes to see, but he did not choose the word that Peter would use to identify Jesus—and in the process would identify himself in his relation to Jesus. Rather, Jesus asked his disciples, "But who do you say that I am?" He allowed and indeed invited his disciples to choose the specific expression they at this stage thought fitted Jesus among the varied ways in which the tradition had expressed the mediator of God's promises. This is genuine inculturation. Further, Peter's belief is both a *gift* to Peter ("Blessed are you"—a macarism), and it is a *free act* on Peter's part, because Jesus rewards him for this act of faith.

This act of Peter was a response to an act of God through Jesus Christ that is called "revelation": "Flesh and blood has not revealed *[apekalupsen]* this to you, but my heavenly Father" (Matt 16:17). This word means "to unveil," "uncover," "reveal." Elsewhere Matthew cites Jesus' words: "I give praise to you, Father, Lord of heaven and earth, for although you have hidden these things from the wise and the learned you have revealed them to the childlike. Yes, Father, such has been your gracious will. All things have been handed over to me by my Father. No one knows the Son except the Father, and no one knows the Father except the Son and anyone to whom the Son wishes to reveal him" (Matt 11:25-27).[30] It is the Father, who out of his gracious will has acted to make this known to Peter. The agency that made it known is contrasted to "flesh and blood" (see Gal 1:12, 16).

---

[30]See S. Légasse, "Le logion sur le Fils révélateur (Mt., XI, 27 par. Lc., X, 22). Essai d'analyse prérédactionelle," *La notion biblique de Dieu,* ed. J. Coppens (Gembloux: J. Duculot, 1976) 245–74.

The agent who revealed this to Peter is not human, he is divine; he is the Father. As we noted earlier, Mark is not so explicit in ascribing Peter's faith to God, but he does so implicitly by the context and by the way he later designates Peter's resistance to Jesus' predictions of his suffering: "You are thinking not as God does, but as human beings do" (8:33).

The agent who gave this revelation is the Father not in a way that excludes Jesus, but rather through Jesus. In the Old Testament we saw that God's revelation came through prophets, wise men, and teachers of the tradition. Jesus was acknowledged by many people to be a prophet (Mark 8:28; Luke 7:16; Matt 21:11), perhaps even the prophet like Moses promised in Deuteronomy 18:15. But he was more than a prophet (Matt 12:41), greater than Moses and Elijah (Mark 9:2-10; Matt 17:1-3; Luke 13:33). He does not speak like the prophets, who preface their messages with "Thus says the Lord," but speaks on his own authority, even in correcting the Law: "You have heard that it was said. . . . But I say to you" (Matt 5:27-28). And Jesus was not simply in the tradition of teachers and wise men; he was greater than Solomon, the paradigm of Israel's wise men (Matt 12:42); in fact, what is ascribed to the Old Testament figure of Wisdom is ascribed by Jesus to himself (Matt 11:28-30).

This message of part of the identity of Jesus was revealed in the *context* of God's *purpose* or design to save people through Jesus Christ. This was a new stage in God's design—in continuity with his earlier relationship with the people of Israel but also in fulfillment of it and of the promises of salvation God had earlier given. It was a new and definitive initiative on God's part. In the preceding chapter we saw that Jesus' mission was to mediate God's kingdom or his salvation, how he went about offering this, and how the response of faith was essential for people's participation in this great gift. Thus this revelation came from God's love and desire to save his people and indeed all peoples (John 3:16-17).

What was the content of this revelation? It was, as we said above, the identity, or part of the identity, of Jesus—a *mystery* that only the Father knows and those to whom he reveals it (Matt 11:27). Through this there is revealed much of the Father's design and its implications for Peter, the Jews, and implicitly, other human beings. It is revealed that God would establish his kingdom, would fulfill his great promises through this man, and that people would share the great hope of Israel through becoming disciples of this man. This man has more authority than any in the past. It was given to him to be the pre-eminent agent through whom God's loving purposes for his people would be fulfilled. Through him God's people would indeed be liberated. Peter's hope to this effect was not misplaced. In fact, through his belief he and those for whom he was spokesman would be the foundations of the community of those who were to inherit the kingdom.

How did the Father reveal this through Jesus? Jesus certainly made known who he was through his powerful deeds of mercy. When the disciples of John the Baptist came to him and asked, "Are you the one who is to come, or should we look for another?" (Matt 11:3), Jesus answered, "Go and tell John what you hear and see: the blind regain their sight, the lame walk, lepers are cleansed, the deaf hear, the dead are raised, and the poor have the good news proclaimed to them" (Matt 11:4-5; see Isa 26:19; 29:18-19; 35:5-6; 61:l). Jesus refers to Old Testament passages that describe the time of salvation in terms of saving acts that Jesus is engaged in. Similarly, when Jesus exorcised devils and his enemies ascribed this to Beelzebul, Jesus ascribed it to the Spirit of God or the finger of God (Luke 11:20) and stated, "If it is by the Spirit of God that I drive out demons, then the kingdom of God has come upon you" (Matt 12:28).

Thus Jesus' deeds of saving people were the way in which God revealed who he was. But we see from the above, these were *deeds* as interpreted by *words.* It is by both together that the presence of the kingdom and the identity of Jesus was unveiled. It was not simply by words, as by a teacher, or simply by deeds that gave encounter, but by deeds and words that spoke to mind and heart, that addressed the whole person. The message was revealed therefore by a *symbolic mediation,* by actions and words that pointed to a greater mystery, that contained this mystery, that showed and contained God's dispositions of love toward his people, that appealed to a full human response, and that transformed those to whom this appeal and manifestation was addressed. Indeed, it was not simply in his words and deeds that this symbolic mediation occurred but in the very *person* of Jesus, expressed in his whole ministry. The depths of the mystery of Jesus' person as revealing is more central to John's Gospel of the Word made flesh than to the Synoptics, though it is present in the Synoptics as well, as shown above.

These were substantively Jesus' *historical* words and deeds, his testimony, *external* and at a particular point in time and space. But revelation did not occur exclusively through them. There was an *interior* dimension to this revelation, as noted at times in the Gospels. For example, John's Gospel intimates this when he quotes Jesus as saying, "No one can come to me unless the Father who sent me *draw* him" (John 6:44). And Matthew implies as much when Jesus erupts into a praise of the Father: "I give praise to you, Father, Lord of heaven and earth, for although you have hidden these things from the wise and the learned you have revealed them to the childlike" (Matt 11:25). Mark shows Peter's faith is due to God's act, as the recovery of sight by the blind man of Bethsaida was due to Jesus' cure (Mark 8:22-26). The contrast between flesh and blood on the one hand and the Father's revelation on the other shows that it was not simply by the external works and words of Jesus that the mystery was revealed but by an interior teaching and gift (ascribed by the early Church to the Spirit; see 1 Cor 2:10-12) that illumined Peter's mind to the implications of Jesus's deeds and words and drew him to discipleship.

We can see through all of this that the revelation was made not by sheer authority but rather by the mediation of a genuine *religious experience* given to Peter through the symbolic mediation and interior illumination and drawing we have described. It is not religious experience as this has frequently been understood by modern writers, that is, an individual experience that is simply from some interior source or from natural phenomena. It came to Peter and others through historical actions of Jesus and interior illumination in virtue of which believers were able to understand and accept the reality and significance of the gift they received.

In a real sense, by believing in Jesus as Messiah Peter and the Twelve *entered into a new world symbolically mediated* to them by Jesus. This new world was opened to them by God's revelation and their acceptance of it. It was a new relationship to God, his kingdom, and the mediator of this kingdom, Jesus the Messiah. But it was in continuity with their past, and their acceptance of it depended on their acceptance of God's earlier revelations. Thus it was a paradigm shift in their own identities, for they accepted Jesus as the focus of their discipleship. To be a believer in God now meant to be a believer in Jesus Christ. We can see by this also that the Jesus of history was already the Christ of faith, though not to the extent that he would later be. Peter's faith was not the distinctively Christian faith. But it was a first step toward such a faith, an intermediate step between Peter's earlier Jewish faith and his later fully Christian faith.

2. Peter's Resistance to Jesus' Predictions of His Coming Suffering

According to Mark and the other Synoptics, immediately after Peter's confession of Jesus as Messiah, Jesus began to predict his own suffering and to prepare his disciples for suffering, and Peter resisted his teaching:

> He began to teach them that the Son of Man must suffer greatly and be rejected by the elders, the chief priests, and the scribes, and be killed, and rise after three days. He spoke this openly. Then Peter took him aside and began to rebuke him, "God forbid, Lord! No such thing shall ever happen to you." At this he turned around and, looking at his disciples, rebuked Peter and said, "Get behind me, Satan! You are thinking not as God does, but as human beings do" (Mark 8:31-33; see Matt 16:21-23; Luke 9:22).

In the preceding chapter we gave reasons to hold that this passage represents a prediction made by Jesus in his ministry of his approaching death.[31] It is most likely that Peter resisted such predictions. Such resistance would scarcely have been ascribed to Peter in the Gospels if it did not occur.

Here, then, we see Peter's lack of faith, a refusal of the response of belief to Jesus' words. Such an outcome of Jesus' ministry was radically opposed to Peter's understanding of who the Messiah was and how he would establish God's kingdom, just as it was opposed to the common understanding at that time of the Messiah. And it was opposed to the kind of discipleship that Peter envisioned for himself and to which he committed himself by his confession of Jesus as Messiah. While Jesus had commended Peter's confession of him as Messiah, here he rebukes him publicly and strongly, even calling him "Satan" and saying that he is thinking not as God does, but as human beings do. The later gospel story shows us the consequences of Peter's resistance here and his persistence in this resistance, namely, his and the other apostles' abandonment of Jesus when he was apprehended and his denial in the high priest's courtyard that he even knew Jesus (Mark 14:66-72; Matt 26:69-75; Luke 22:54-62).

Was there a revelation in Jesus' prediction of his suffering? The evangelists present this prediction as such; and there is not sufficient

---

[31] See chapter 3 above, pages 113–4.

reason to think that historically this did not happen. Jesus did make known a dimension of the mystery of his identity and the manner in which God would establish his kingdom. He is saying in effect that in the circumstances of the Jewish leaders' rejection of him, he will allow this to run its course. As those Jews for whom the book of Daniel was written suffered death because of their fidelity to God, so too would he. But this would not frustrate God's designs; it would rather be used by God to gain his designs, though in a way other than Jesus sought.

Jesus would be vindicated in the age to come and would from there establish God's kingdom. Thus he unveiled for the Twelve something further about his identity and that of the kingdom. It is as though he had brought them to the first stage of belief and was now seeking to lead them further to a belief more adequate to who he was and what his mission was. He made it known by words here what would later be confirmed by actions—by his actually being delivered into the hands of his enemies and undergoing death at their hands. But before this fulfillment of his prediction occurred, there was already a revelation offered. It was a clear statement, not cloaked as some parables were. And according to the evangelists he repeated this prediction two more times (Mark 9:31-32; 10:32-34; Matt 17:22-23; 20:17-19; Luke 9:43-45; 18:31-34). Revelation can happen in such a way and by such means. He made it known to prepare his apostles for what would happen and to bring them to a deeper discipleship and commitment.

We see by this several elements of Christian revelation and faith. Christian revelation is a *process;* it involves stages. In the initial stage it was dialogical; Jesus asked Peter and the Twelve, "Who do you say that I am?" But this second stage is dialectical. Jesus *tells* his apostles in no uncertain words what kind of Messiah he is, and his message shocks, disillusions, confronts, and corrects them. He denies, in effect, that he is the kind of Messiah they envisage, or at least that he is *only* that kind of Savior or that he will establish God's kingdom in the way they expect. He shows them how inadequate the category was that they had taken from their past to designate Jesus. And he shows them how inadequate their view of what discipleship was (see also Matt 20:20-27; Mark 10:35-45).

Peter and the others failed here in faith; otherwise, Jesus would not have rebuked them. Their failure was not through lack of a revelation but because this was so contrary to their expectations and their desires. Their experience of revulsion was not a religious experience, if by this one means a confirmation of what is revealed by interior experience. Rather, it was of emptiness and denial. But their experience could not be taken as an overriding criterion of whether what Jesus predicted was part of his identity and true discipleship. The significance of this experience was different; it showed how much in them resisted acknowledgment of the full dimensions of Jesus' identity and the acceptance of the discipleship to which they were called. It showed how profound the *mystery* was of Jesus himself, the kingdom, and their discipleship. It was not something they could accept by their human resources. It shows too that subjectivity is involved in both the acceptance of Jesus' message and its rejection; the question is whether this subjectivity will be open to God's revelation or resist it.

3. The Resurrection Appearances, the Coming of the Spirit, and the Distinctive Christian Faith

What we present here depends in part on what we will examine in the following chapter. We are once more offered an account of Peter as spokesman for the faith of the apostles, now the distinctively Christian faith though in a primitive form. In Luke's account of Pentecost Peter proclaims to the people: "Let the whole house of Israel know for certain that God has made him both Lord and Messiah, this Jesus whom you crucified" (Acts 2:36). James Dunn writes of the early Christian belief: "The distinctive feature which comes to expression in all the confessions we have examined, the bedrock of the Christian faith confessed in the NT writings, is *the unity between the earthly Jesus and the exalted one who is somehow involved in or part of our encounter with God in the here and now.*"[32]

Peter's faith was both faith *that* Jesus was Messiah and Lord and faith *in,* or discipleship of, Jesus as Messiah and Lord. It was a much deeper *personal knowledge* of Jesus than he had arrived at at the time of his first confession. He had by now integrated the acceptance of his suffering and death. As Luke recounts it, the risen Jesus explained to the disciples on the way to Emmaus why it was "necessary that the Messiah should suffer these things and enter into his glory" (Luke 24:26). Peter now acknowledged Jesus not only as Messiah but as Lord. Moreover, the discipleship that he offered to Jesus was similarly

[32]Dunn, *Unity and Diversity,* 57.

much deeper; it had integrated the dimension of his own insecurity insofar as hopes for the present life were concerned. His center was now on a larger understanding of God's salvation and rule than he had earlier had as his horizon when he first acknowledged Jesus as Messiah. There is not reason to think that his earlier hopes had been simply rejected, but he now saw them as part of a larger, more important, and inclusive whole. We have treated this in part in the preceding chapter and will return to it in the following chapter, and in a still later chapter on the meaning of salvation for our own time. Peter's faith in Jesus restructured his personality and made him an instrument for restructuring the faith and community of his own people and, eventually, of other peoples.

This stage of Peter's faith was a response to God's revelation, one conveyed through the death of Jesus, his resurrection appearances, and the coming of the Holy Spirit. As James Dunn writes:

> After Jesus' death the earliest Christian community sprang directly from a sequence of epochal experiences of two distinct sorts—experiences in which Jesus appeared to individuals and groups to be recognized as one who had already experienced the eschatological resurrection from the dead, and experiences of religious ecstasy and enthusiasm recognized as the manifestation of the eschatological Spirit. . . .
>
> Above all, the distinctive essence of Christian experience lies in the relation between Jesus and the Spirit.[33]

This revelation, according to Luke, occurred through the appearances of the risen Jesus and his interpretation of his suffering, death, and resurrection *and* through the experience of the gift of the Holy Spirit. Before this gift but after the appearances of the risen Jesus, the apostles were still able to ask him, "Lord, are you at this time going to restore the kingdom to Israel?" (Acts 1:6). Thus they still showed a lack of understanding of what the kingdom was, the salvation that God had in store for them. This distinctively Christian revelation was mediated to them both by the appearances of the risen Jesus and by the gift of the Spirit; without the Spirit's drawing and illumining they could not have the full Christian faith—that personal knowledge of Jesus, faith *that* and faith *in,* that we see characterized the disciples after

---

[33]James Dunn, *Jesus and the Spirit* (Philadelphia: Westminster Press, 1975) 357, 358.

the coming of the Spirit. It is John's teaching also that the Spirit is necessary (John 14:26; 15:26). Once more, Christian revelation is mediated by external, historical events and words and internal influence, and these as organically united. The inner illumination was of a message conveyed to them externally and objectively. But this message could not be received without the gift and acceptance of the Holy Spirit.

III. Disbelief During Jesus' Ministry

It may well seem astounding to us that people actually disbelieved Jesus during his ministry; or, in light of the disbelief from every section of society that greeted him, it may seem implausible to us that Jesus acted substantively as the evangelists said he did. It is important to reflect briefly on this disbelief; for disbelief, too, shows us something of the nature of Christian revelation and faith. In fact, each of the evangelists reflected on this. They accounted for this disbelief not by the lack of genuine authentications of Jesus but by how far he transcended the limited expectations and desires of different factions among the Jews. He could easily be interpreted as other than the one expected to liberate Israel. As Schillebeeckx writes: "The veiled, ambiguous character of Jesus' historical manifestation—sharing the ambiguity of everything one could call historical—is amplified by Mark . . . a historical opaqueness is cast over Jesus' life."[34]

In seeking to understand a bit why people disbelieved in Jesus during his ministry, we must bear in mind that the evangelists composed their narrative accounts of Jesus' public life for communities of Christians who were themselves facing threats to their perseverance in belief, and this concern of the authors affected the way they highlighted elements of Jesus' ministry and the response to him. For example, Mark probably wrote for a community that admired Jesus the wonder-worker but was facing persecution and was shaken by this.[35] Thus he showed the imperfect faith of the disciples of Jesus and how they failed the test posed by Jesus' suffering.

Matthew was probably written for a group of predominantly Jewish Christians in the decade of the eighties in lower Syria who had continued to feel a part of the larger Jewish community but who

---

[34]Edward Schillebeeckx, *Jesus: An Experiment in Christology* (New York: Seabury, 1979) 295.

[35]See Stock, *Call to Discipleship,* 45.

now were met by exclusion of the followers of Jesus from the synagogue and by the renewed rabbinic or Pharisaic emphasis, after the
destruction of Jerusalem, on all elements of the Law as essential for
fidelity to God and Jewish identity.[36] Thus Jesus' polemic against the
Pharisees is perhaps given greater prominence in Matthew than it actually had in the ministry of Jesus, though other traditions show that
it had a basis in history. In this controverted question we shall first
reflect on some sources offered by the evangelists for the apparent
failure of Jesus' Galilean ministry and then on sources indicated for
his rejection in Jerusalem.

The first part of Jesus' public ministry was, according to the Synoptics, in Galilee. Toward its conclusion Jesus reproaches the towns
"where most of his mighty deeds had been done, since they had not
repented" (Matt 11:20; see Matt 11:20-24; Luke 10:12-15 [from Q]).
At the same time, Jesus rejoices in the Father, "for although you have
hidden these things from the wise and the learned you have revealed
them to the childlike" (Matt 11:25; see Luke 10:21 [from Q]). What
led up to this disbelief that Jesus met? E. P. Sanders discounts conflicts
over the Law as the root of Jesus' difficulties with his contemporaries:
"[T]here is no substantial conflict over the law."[37] Though Sanders
contributes to redressing an imbalance in Christian interpretations in
this matter, his view is tied in with his claim that Jesus threatened to
destroy the Temple, which, as we shall see below, is not in accord with
all the relevant data. The Pharisees' part in opposing Jesus is given
more emphasis in this part of his ministry than in Jerusalem; and from
multiple attestation and extrabiblical accounts of excesses of some of
the Pharisees in the first century, it seems to have a basis in fact.

Mark puts together a series of controversies with scribes and
Pharisees that led to their active opposition to Jesus (Mark 2:1–3:6).
The first of these results from Jesus' declaration to the paralytic that
his sins are forgiven; the second is occasioned by Jesus eating with
tax collectors and sinners; the third from the fact that Jesus' disciples
do not fast; the fourth and fifth from the disciples of Jesus and Jesus
himself "working" on the Sabbath (see also Luke 14:1-3). This result
was that "[t]he Pharisees went out and immediately took counsel
with the Herodians against him to put him to death" (Mark 3:6). Such
actions on Jesus' part and his words about the Law relativized it and

---

[36]See, for example, Benedict Viviano, "The Gospel According to Matthew," *NJBC,* 631.

[37]E. P. Sanders, *Jesus and Judaism* (Philadelphia: Fortress Press, 1985) 275.

in part reformed it, for example, in the Sermon on the Mount (Matthew 5–7). Even though he stated: "Do not think that I have come to abolish the law or the prophets. I have come not to abolish but to fulfill" (Matt 5:17), his actions and words were bound to appear to contest the authority of the Pharisees and to be a claim to an authority greater than that of the Law.

We do not have to condemn the Pharisees as a whole to recognize that, in reaction against past Jewish infidelities that brought tragic sufferings upon the Jews, their efforts at fidelity and at putting a "hedge about the law" led to a kind of fixation on the material law that at times blocked out its deeper meaning and the priority that love (Matt 22:34-40) and compassion for those in need should have. "The sabbath was made for man, not man for the sabbath" (Mark 2:27). "Those who are well do not need a physician, but the sick do" (Mark 2:17).[38] It is historically plausible and most probable that many Pharisees thought that Jesus' attitude to the Law disqualified him as one sent by God. This would not be only an individual belief. They were, after all, a part of a close-knit group, and we know from much experience of our own time how people of such a group feel the pressure of their peers to stick with the group's evaluation of "outsiders," and how an outsider's questioning can make them close ranks and exaggerate their own positions to find further reasons to oppose the one who questions them. They were part of a system, and a system has its own defense dynamisms (see John 12:42-43); insofar as there was evil in their interpretation of the Law, this evil was systemic as well as personal.

It was not only the Pharisees who opposed Jesus in this early part of his ministry. Jesus' own townsfolk found him too much for them (Luke 4:16-30; Matt 13:54-58; Mark 6:1-6). The common people followed him to hear his words and reap the benefits of his healings, but there is some evidence that what they wanted was a national leader rather than the kind of Savior or Messiah that Jesus was (see

[38]Sanders himself indicates some exegetes who differ from his view in this matter: Aulén, Käsemann, Bornkamm, Jeremias, and Barrett (271–5). Also see Ben Witherington, *The Christology of Jesus* (Minneapolis: Fortress Press, 1990) 56–9, on different degrees of rigidity among the Pharisees of Jesus' day; and Ben Meyer, *The Aims of Jesus* (London: SCM Press, 1979) 22: "In the view of the Pharisees . . . the mass of the people were non-observant. . . . The Pharisees laid a claim on all Israel and the response fell short; the result was tension on the Pharisaic side between condemnation and the sustaining of the appeal." Also see Eduard Schweizer, *The Good News According to Mark* (Atlanta: John Knox, 1970) 75–7.

John 6:14-15, 27; Mark 6:34ff. may refer to the same event). Later, the common people were easily subject to manipulation by the Jewish leaders (Mark 15:11-14). The response of many of them to Jesus was superficial and fickle, like seed that fell on rocky ground (Mark 4:16-17). Without seeking to identify all the opponents of Jesus in his early ministry, let us proceed to reflect briefly on his later ministry as he approached and entered Jerusalem. The opposition there was surely present in part in his earlier ministry.

After Peter's confession that Jesus was the Messiah, Jesus made the first of three predictions of his suffering and death. In this he ascribed leadership in opposing him to the "elders, the chief priests, and the scribes" (Mark 8:31; see para.; also see Mark 9:30-32 and 10:33-34, where his opponents are said to be the "chief priests and the scribes"). We have given reason in the preceding chapter to think that these predictions had a basis in history. When Jesus entered Jerusalem shortly before his death, he is said to have done so seated on a donkey (Mark 11:1f.; see para.), in all probability a prophetic gesture that recalled Zechariah: "See, your king shall come to you, a just savior is he, meek, and riding on an ass, on a colt, the foal of an ass" (9:9). This reflected the character of his Messianic self-understanding. The people acclaim him (Mark 11:8-10; see para.) as "he who comes in the name of the Lord" (Mark 11:9) or as "Son of David" (Matt 21:9). The chief priests and scribes were indignant (Matt 21:15).

Either that day or the next Jesus entered the Temple and "began to drive out those selling and buying there. He overturned the tables of the money changers and the seats of those who were selling doves" (Mark 11:15; see para.). The "chief priests and the scribes came to hear of it and were seeking a way to put him to death" (Mark 11:18; see para.). As we mentioned above, Sanders considers Jesus' action here a prophetic sign of threatening to destroy the Temple, a threat that inevitably would be taken very seriously by the chief priests and the Sanhedrin.

Others do not agree with Sanders in his interpretation. Craig Evans presents a convincing account showing that Jesus' action was, as the evangelists all note it to be, a cleansing of the Temple.[39] It may seem that the trafficking in the Temple area was simply what was needed to

---

[39]See Craig Evans, "Jesus' Action in the Temple: Cleansing or Portent of Destruction?" *CBQ* 51 (1989) 237–70.

facilitate people making their sacrifices. But there are Jewish sources complaining about the greed of the priests and their extortion of funds from the lower priesthood; the Jews of Jesus' time could easily have expected it to be part of the Messiah's mission to purify the Temple. As Evans writes of some Jewish texts contemporaneous with Jesus:

> These texts would surely suggest to a Palestinian Jew of Jesus' day the possibility that the Messiah might purge the city of Jerusalem of corrupt officials, which would likely include priests, as part of an act of "cleansing" Israel for the messianic kingdom. Note also [Psalms of Solomon] 8:11-13, a passage that likely describes the priestly activity at the time of Pompey's capture of Jerusalem and the temple: "They stole from the sanctuary of God. . . . They walked on the place of sacrifice of the Lord. . . . [T]hey defiled the sacrifices as if they were common meat. There was no sin they left undone in which they did not surpass the Gentiles."
>
> *Testament of Moses.* The *T. Mos.* (early first century) contains scathing criticism of the Jerusalem priesthood.[40]

The chief priests, scribes, and elders (Mark 11:27-28) contested Jesus' authority to act as he did in the Temple, showing by this that they resented his undercutting of their authority. Also, they had reason to see Jesus' action as one aimed against their economic exploitation of the Palestinian peasantry. We treated this question briefly in the preceding chapter. Here we can simply quote from Richard Horsley:

> The principal conflict in Palestinian Jewish society was thus clearly between the rulers, domestic and foreign, on the one hand, and the ruled on the other. . . . The Romans, the Herodian rulers, and the priestly aristocracy all extracted produce from the peasantry through mechanisms of tribute, taxes or rents, and tithes and offerings. They were able to do this because they had political power and/or religious-cultural legitimation. . . . Jerusalem in particular enjoyed explicit religious legitimation, with the religious-economic-political domination of the priestly aristocracy based in the Temple as the form through which the theocracy was mediated.[41]

---

[40]Ibid., 255. See the other evidence Evans brings forward.

[41]Richard Horsley, *Sociology and the Jesus Movement* (New York: Crossroad, 1989) 88.

Jesus was a threat both to the authority of the chief priests and to their system of economic exploitation in Palestine. Jesus must have known the opposition he would provoke by this demonstration.

This action of Jesus and the controversies he engaged in with the Jewish leaders at that time (see Mark 12; para.) led the chief priests and scribes to plot to put him to death (Mark 14:1) and, with the aid of Judas, to arrest him and bring him before the Sanhedrin (see Mark 14:43, 53ff.).[42] Before this body, the final question addressed to Jesus by the high priest was, "Are you the Messiah, the son of the Blessed One?" (Mark 14:61). Jesus' reply, "I am, and 'you will see the Son of Man seated at the right hand of the Power and coming with the clouds of heaven'" (Mark 14:62; see para.), led the high priest to declare him guilty of blasphemy and thus deserving of death (Mark 14:63-64; see para.). Pilate sought to release him, "for he knew that it was out of envy that the chief priests had handed him over" (Mark 15:10), but the chief priests put pressure on him, and Pilate, probably in fear for his own position (see John 19:12-16), handed him over to death, inscribing the charge against him as being "The King of the Jews" (Mark 15:26; see para.).

To accept Jesus as Messiah demanded a relativizing of the criteria and interests the Sanhedrin brought to bear in the question of the identity of Jesus. Jesus certainly was a threat to the special interests of a number of groups. And though these groups were opposed to one another, they came to agree that Jesus was their enemy. Apparently some secretly believed in Jesus but were not willing to be public about this because of the opposition it would bring upon them (see John 3:1-2; 13:42; 19:38).

Conclusion

This scriptural study of revelation and faith, which will be supplemented in the following chapter, shows that Vatican II's interpretation is fully in accord with Scripture. For example, it shows that the Christian understanding is that God has revealed in a personal manner through words and deeds in a dialogue of love that began at the

---

[42]See Ben Meyer's identification of the Sanhedrin: "The chief priests (the current high priest, the retired high priests, the captain, overseers, and treasurers of the temple), the elders (the family heads of Jerusalem's lay aristocracy) and the scribes (Sadducees and Pharisees). In the time of Jesus the balance of power in the Sanhedrin was held by the Sadducees." *The Aims of Jesus,* p. 237.

beginning of human history and through stages prepared for his definitive revelation, which occurs through Jesus Christ. It shows that this revelation is both dialogical and dialectical, that it is mediated by symbolic actions—real symbols that are the effect of God's creative imagination such as the Exodus and the life, death, and resurrection of Jesus Christ—and that a faith response is the condition for the reception of God's salvific gift. It shows too the character of the faith response it calls for as personal knowledge and commitment, and it shows some of the factors that can prevent this faith from being forthcoming.

5

The Resurrection of Jesus, and Early Christian Understanding of Salvation and Revelation

In this chapter we will reflect on (I) the resurrection of Jesus as related to our theme of the meaning and foundations of faith in God through Jesus Christ and on central aspects of the early Church's interpretation of (II) salvation and (III) revelation and faith. The resurrection of Jesus is central for Christian faith and current evaluations of it. And the early Church's understandings of salvation and faith are important for us to recall, since they are corrective of some later interpretations. These themes are not separate from those treated in the preceding chapters, since the evangelists wrote the Gospels from that fuller understanding they had of Jesus after their experience of the appearances of the resurrected Jesus and the coming of the Holy Spirit. But there is a distinction, since the experience of the early Church did lead to deepening understanding and new articulations of these realities. We treat these issues here only in an introductory fashion, and we suggest further studies where they are treated in greater depth.

I. The Resurrection of Jesus

In the second chapter of volume one and more briefly in the first chapter of this volume we saw diverse interpretations and uses of the resurrection of Jesus by theologians of the twentieth century as they mediated faith in God through Jesus Christ. The variety of such interpretations and uses shows how critical this question is. This has been studied in a multitude of books and articles in recent decades.[1] As context for our own study we shall recall some major interpretations of the resurrection in our century, following here primarily the schema of Peter Carnley.

A first interpretation of the resurrection is as *a historical event,* for example, that of Scholastic theologians, Westcott and Pannenberg.[2] These hold that objectivity is essential for the dogmatic significance of the resurrection of Jesus, that the tomb was empty, and that the visions of Jesus were objective rather than subjective. Pannenberg holds that the resurrection must be considered in the context of the Jewish eschatological expectation and of Paul's ascribing the emergence of Christianity to the appearances of the resurrected Jesus, and that in the case of Jesus "an event that is expressible only in the language of the eschatological expectation is to be asserted as a historical occurrence."[3]

Second, the resurrection is understood as an *eschatological event* by Barth and Bultmann.[4] They agree that faith must be independent of critical historical enquiry. For Barth the resurrection is a fact of the objective order and clearly revelatory, while for Bultmann Jesus has risen in the kerygma, and the stories of the resurrection are a mythical way of expressing the meaning of the crucifixion. For both, faith is a commitment of obedience and trust in response to what is understood

---

[1]See E. Dhanis, ed., *Resurrexit: Actes du symposium international sur la résurrection du Jésus. Rome 1970* (Vatican: Libreria Editrice Vaticana, 1974); J. Schmitt, "Résurrection du Jésus dans le kérygma, la tradition, la catéchèse," *Supplément au Dictionnaire de la Bible* (Paris: Letouzey & Ané, 1985) 10:487–582; Raymond Brown, "The Resurrection of Jesus," *NJBC,* 1373–7; Francis Schüssler Fiorenza, "The Resurrection of Jesus," *Foundational Theology: Jesus and the Church* (New York: Crossroad, 1984) 1–55; Reginald Fuller, *The Formation of the Resurrection Narratives,* 2nd ed. (Philadelphia: Fortress Press, 1980); John Galvin, "The Origins of Faith in the Resurrection of Jesus: Two Recent Perspectives," *TS* 49 (1988) 25–44; Donald Goergen, *The Death and Resurrection of Jesus* (Wilmington, Del.: Michael Glazier, 1988); Gerald O'Collins, *Jesus Risen: An Historical, Fundamental, and Systematic Examination of Christ's Resurrection* (New York: Paulist Press, 1987); idem, *Interpreting the Resurrection: Examining the Major Problems in the Stories of Jesus' Resurrection* (New York: Paulist Press, 1988); Pheme Perkins, *Resurrection: New Testament Witness and Contemporary Reflection* (New York: Doubleday, 1984).

[2]See Peter Carnley, "The Resurrection as an Historical Event," *The Structure of Resurrection Belief* (Oxford: Clarendon Press, 1987) 29–95.

[3]Wolfhart Pannenberg, *Jesus—God and Man* (Philadelphia: Westminster Press, 1968) 98.

[4]See Carnley, "The Resurrection as Eschatological Event," *Structure of Resurrection Belief,* 96–147.

to be a call or word of God. Barth discounts Paul's apologetic intent in 1 Corinthians 15:3-8, and Bultmann dismisses Paul's efforts as inappropriate because faith is based only on God's word. Both react against the nineteenth-century historical quest for Jesus, but the end result of the way they do this is to make faith quite voluntaristic. Pannenberg's initial theological thrust was largely in opposition to this.

A third approach is to understand the resurrection as *a non-event:* "The primitive Easter faith is not to be understood as a response to a post-mortem event in any sense at all. . . . [F]aith is based upon the completed life of Jesus."[5] This view was advanced in varied forms from the time of the eighteenth-century rationalist Reimarus and is based largely on the fact that historians operate on the principle of the uniformity and rational intelligibility of history, which a physical resurrection seems to contradict. It is more recently present in Willi Marxsen, among others. Marxsen asserts that historically we can get as far back as the claims of Jesus' disciples to appearances of Jesus after his death, interpreted by stories of an empty tomb and by Jewish apocalyptic beliefs. There are various interpretations possible. The stories of the appearances are externalizations of the disciples' having found faith after Good Friday, and what they mean is that Jesus' cause still lives. Faith is itself a miracle and is caused by God; it does not depend on reason; Peter's coming to faith must be explained by analogy with our own.

Rudolf Pesch has a view similar to this.[6] He argues that at the time of Jesus there was a widespread Jewish belief that the messianic prophet would come, would be martyred, and would be raised from the dead and exalted to heaven. This belief is witnessed in Mark 6:14: "Some said, John the baptizer has been raised from the dead." Jesus understood himself as such a prophet, and his disciples shared his belief. They did not lose this faith through the death of Jesus but expressed it through the formula "he appeared," which in reality means that the identity of Jesus had been revealed to them by his prophetic lifestyle and martyrdom. So the basis for the resurrection stories is what happened during the lifetime of Jesus; they are to be taken as expressions of Christian belief, not its source.

---

[5]Carnley, "The Resurrection as Non-Event," *Structure of Resurrection Belief,* 168–82; quotation is from page 148. See W. Marxsen, *The Resurrection of Jesus of Nazareth* (Philadelphia: Fortress Press, 1970).

[6]On Pesch, see Galvin, "Origins of Faith," and Fiorenza, *Foundational Theology,* 18–21.

Still another interpretation of the resurrection is as *a postmortem revelation of Jesus as living, but not necessarily through objective visions.*[7] We can include both Edward Schillebeeckx and Peter Carnley under this heading, though differently. Schillebeeckx does agree with Pesch that there were bases in the life of Jesus, the precedents of the Old Testament, and expectations of Jews at the time of Jesus for the disciples of Jesus to expect his being raised from the dead as the eschatological prophet. But they did fail in their belief at the time of Jesus' death, and they did have an experience of conversion after his death, which they appropriately ascribed to God's eschatological grace through Jesus still living. Thus they did have an experience of Jesus after his death but not, or not necessarily, objective visions of him. The appearance stories are secondary.

Carnley holds that we cannot decide whether the appearances of the raised Jesus were based on objective or subjective visions but that this is not crucial. "What was actually perceived or seen was the activity of the Spirit which they traced to Jesus as the heavenly source and origin of it." Paul identified the Spirit and the activity of the glorified Jesus. "On the basis of this experience they inferred not only that Jesus was himself alive and exalted in heaven but that this was where he would come from at the time of his eschatological return."[8] The ground for belief in Jesus' resurrection "is not found only in appearances but in the presence of Jesus as well."[9] When attempts were made to express these christophanies, a variety of images were formed.

As final examples of interpretations of the resurrection of Jesus we can cite both Karl Rahner and Jon Sobrino, who are alike in not denying the appearances of Jesus to his disciples but who consider these as *grounds for faith secondary to our search for fulfillment and liberation in life in the midst of the evil that threatens our hope* and our finding in the message of the resurrection of Jesus an answer to this hope. In accord with his anthropological starting point in theology and his transcendental method, Rahner envisions the human

[7]See Carnley, "The Raised Christ: Glorified but Disappearing," *Structure of Resurrection Belief,* 183–222, where he discusses, among others, E. Schillebeeckx; Carnley, "The Raised Christ: Appearance and Presence," *Structure of Resurrection Belief,* 223–65, where he shows his own view, somewhat similar to that of Schillebeeckx; Edward Schillebeeckx, *Jesus: An Experiment in Christology* (New York: Crossroad, 1979) 379–97; idem, *Interim Report on the Books Jesus and Christ* (New York: Crossroad, 1981) 74–93.

[8]Carnley, "The Raised Christ: Appearance and Presence," 260.

[9]Ibid., 264.

being as oriented to the Absolute and receiving a transcendental revelation from God, which is quite generally accepted. Specifically, this human thrust and revelation is challenged by the prospect of death that faces us all. But men and women find in the resurrection of Jesus a historical or categorical symbolic expression of the transcendental revelation already received. Thus the resurrection in its meaning as an object of faith is also a ground of faith. This is all the more important because the complexity of the historical question of the appearances of the risen Jesus makes that approach inaccessible to all but the expert.[10]

Similarly, Sobrino finds the hermeneutic context for understanding the resurrection of Jesus to be the adversity that suffering poses to our deepest human orientation toward fulfillment and liberation. But he includes the experience of social injustice and not only the experience of death in this suffering: "Basic discussion of Jesus' resurrection . . . has to do with the triumph of justice. Who will be victorious, the oppressor or the oppressed?"[11] Sobrino does not attempt to answer the difficulty with the resurrection of Jesus based on the historian's principle of analogy, except to claim that "[t]he analogical supposition that the new is to be known on the basis of the old . . . at the very least . . . is inadequate."[12] The disciples' faith in Jesus was shattered by their experience of God leaving him on the cross to die, but their experience of his appearances showed them "that God had not abandoned Jesus on the cross after all."[13] The resurrection of Jesus gave rise to mission for the transformation of the world and is a hope not yet fulfilled: "It is possible to verify the truth of what happened in the resurrection only through a transforming praxis based on the ideals of the resurrection. . . . The resurrection can be understood only through a praxis that seeks to transform the world."[14]

The above examples show us major ways in which theologians of the twentieth century use the resurrection of Jesus to mediate Christian belief to our age. These are quite disparate ways, but perhaps we can say that each has something to offer in this matter, though some

[10]See Fiorenza, *Foundational Theology,* 13–18; O'Collins, *Jesus Risen,* 77–86.

[11]John Sobrino, *Christology at the Crossroads* (Maryknoll, N.Y.: Orbis Books, 1978) 244, cited in O'Collins, *Jesus Risen,* 94.

[12]Sobrino, *Christology at the Crossroads,* 249.

[13]Ibid., 169.

[14]Ibid., 255.

are far from accepting the wholeness of the Christian message or in relating that to our world.

This very disparateness leads us to ask how the kerygma of the resurrection was presented in the primitive Church and how such kerygma interrelated the resurrection as object of faith and as grounds for faith, the life of Jesus before and after death, a spiritual and a physical experience of the risen Jesus, and *theoria* and praxis. Can we know how they did this, and can we critically accept the way they mediated the resurrection of Jesus? Too often theologians or exegetes search the New Testament message about the resurrection of Jesus from excessively restricted presuppositions or questions. Their contexts lead to excessively restricted approaches to the evidence. What we need is an *integrative* interpretation of the New Testament on this question. In search for this we will look briefly at (1) the Old Testament foundations for resurrection belief, (2) the earliest Christian kerygma of the resurrection, and (3) other early testimonies and the Gospels' narratives of the resurrection appearances and empty tomb. Once more this will be only an introductory account, and I will indicate where these issues are more adequately treated.

1. Resurrection in the Old Testament and Intertestamental Period

The earliest clear affirmation of the resurrection of the just is found in Daniel 12:2-3.[15] In the early Old Testament period death did not seem a problem for those who died full of years and with progeny, because the future of the people was their own future. A notion of resurrection is perhaps found in the eighth-century B.C. prophet Hosea (6:2) and certainly in Ezekiel (37:14), but it seems to be a symbol of the restoration of Israel rather than a prophecy of the resurrection of the individual just person. There is a question of whether the fourth Suffering Servant Song of Deutero-Isaiah includes resurrection as part of the vindication and reward for the prophet (Isa 53:10-12). Certainly the postexilic small apocalypse of Isaiah speaks of a resurrection: "Your dead shall live, their corpses shall rise; awake and sing, you who lie in the dust. For your dew is a dew of light, and the land of shades gives birth" (Isa 26:19). This seems to

---

[15]On the Old Testament and intertestamental period, see R. Martin-Achard, "Résurrection dans l'Ancien Testament et le Judaïsme," *Supplément au Dictionnaire de la Bible,* 10:437–87; and Perkins, *Resurrection,* 37–70.

be an antecedent of Daniel, but whether resurrection is being used here as an image of hope or a reality affirmed is still in question. Some see in the passage a nature milieu that represents a tradition of Canaanite origin, though put into the service of the God of Israel.

In an apocalyptic genre and message Daniel writes of the resurrection: "Many of those who sleep in the dust of the earth shall awake; some shall live forever, others shall be an everlasting disgrace. But the wise shall shine brightly like the splendor of the firmament, and those who lead many to justice shall be like the stars forever" (Dan 12:2-3). Most exegetes find this to be a clear affirmation of the resurrection of the individual to new life after death. This belief arose in the midst of Antiochus Epiphanes' persecution of the Jews in the mid-160s B.C. Many Jews at that time accepted death rather than renounce their fidelity to God. And the author of Daniel, most probably from the Hasidim, or pious ones among the Jews, knew that God would not be unfaithful to those who were faithful to him. As this crisis led him to affirm that God would give the kingdom to one like a Son of Man, as we showed in chapter 3, so here it leads him to affirm that God would raise the just of Israel to new life after death.

The future of Israel was no longer a sufficient future for the people who have been faithful to God; this future happiness and vindication must include the faithful who have died. This prediction is made not for all but for the faithful among the people of Israel. This life of the future is not simply a return to the dimensions of this life but has a dimension of transcendence and finality about it; it is not simply a renewed life but a life shared with the angels and a communion with God. This teaching of the resurrection of the faithful Jew is found also in 2 Maccabees' account of the martyrdom of seven sons and their mother; the author bases himself (7:6) on Deuteronomy 32:36, where it is said that the Lord "will have pity on his servants"; thus God will vindicate those faithful to him and recompense them.

Toward the end of the Old Testament period the Hellenistic teaching on immortality and incorruptibility was adapted to express Jewish hope in God's vindication of the just (Wis 2:22-23; 3:1-9; 5:15-16). Because of the influence of Hellenism on the Jews, the traditional Jewish anthropology that made the possibility of future life depend totally on a resurrection no longer imposes itself as the only way to express hope for future life with God after death. External influences continue to be present in the Jews' expression of this great hope: "however, the determining element came from Israel itself, in its faith in the living God, as he had revealed himself little by little to his own."[16] The God who created human beings could re-create them, and in his justice and fidelity he would do so for those who had been faithful to him.

The main point to make concerning Jewish belief in life after death during the intertestamental period is that, contrary to those who would place a contradiction between resurrection and immortality, "one finds oneself in the presence of a great variety of witnesses on the destiny of the deceased that is impossible to reduce to one or two common denominators, even in the midst of the Jews of Palestine."[17] Writers use a terminology and imagery that the surrounding world affords them, and they do not attach a decisive importance to a single expression. What is primary is that the just will share the triumph of their God and will live in his presence. We pass over many elements of this teaching to note that the Pharisees of Jesus' time and later accepted the doctrine of the resurrection and dealt with questions it raised, some emphasizing more the earthly and some the transcendent dimensions of this life to come.

In his own public ministry Jesus shares this Pharisaic belief. His story of Lazarus and the rich man (Luke 16:19-31) presupposes a post-mortem judgment and describes the diverse fortunes of the rich man and the poor man in terms familiar to his audience.[18] The prediction of the sign of Jonah, at least in Matthew's version (12:39-42), which may have been modified from Q (Luke 11:29-32), presents the resurrection as a sign of judgment for a disbelieving generation. The only direct discussion of the resurrection by Jesus is found in Mark 12:18-27 and parallels; here Jesus sides substantially with the Pharisees against the Sadducees in expressing belief in the resurrection. His miracles of raising the son of widow of Nain (Luke 7:11-17), Jairus' daughter (Mark 5:21-24), and Lazarus (John 11:1-46) show God's power over death itself and Jesus' compassion. We have reflected on the Son of Man passages in chapter 3 of this volume and on Jesus' predictions of his resurrection in chapter 4. Suffice it to say that Jesus is reported to have expressed confidence that he would be vindicated after having been delivered into the hands of his enemies and put to death.

---

[16]Martin-Achard, "Résurrection dans l'Ancien Testament," 468.

[17]Ibid., 473. He is here referring to the work of H. Cavallin, with which he agrees.

[18]See Perkins, *Resurrection,* 71ff.

2. The Earliest Christian Kerygma of the Resurrection

For an example of the early Christian kerygma of the resurrection we propose that we look briefly at the sermon that Luke ascribes to Peter in Acts 2:14-41. Some preliminary questions we can ask are the following: Why do we turn first to this text rather than to a text on the resurrection of Jesus that is chronologically earlier and a first-hand account such as 1 Corinthians 15:1-11? The reason is that the speech in Acts 2 is probably more representative of the primitive Christian kerygma than Paul's account in 1 Corinthians 15 because the latter was composed to answer a specific problem, namely that of Greek disbelief in the possibility of a resurrection. We use Paul's text later, however, to corroborate Luke's statement that proclamation of the resurrection of Jesus was indeed central to its first message.

Also, our primary interest here is to investigate how early proclaimers of the word used their witness to the resurrection of Jesus to invite others to share their belief in Jesus as Messiah and Lord. In this volume we are critically evaluating the meaning and grounds for our faith in Jesus. An answer to this calls for an integral approach to the earliest Christian missionary proclamation rather than an analytical approach to elements of this such as the list of witnesses given by Paul.

We may also ask whether the speech Luke ascribes to Peter really represents a historical speech. A number of recent exegetes compare Luke's Acts to the work of contemporary Hellenistic historians, who did compose speeches in their works but in a way that was true to the historical situation.[19] Many earlier exegetes had thought that Luke

---

[19] See Richard Dillon, "Acts of the Apostles," *NJBC* 722ff.; R. Dillon and J. Fitzmyer, "Acts of Apostles," *Jerome Biblical Commentary* (Englewood Cliffs, N.J.: Prentice Hall, 1968) 2:165ff. (hereafter cited as *JBC*). Dillon, in *NJBC* (724), agrees with many exegetes who hold there is an analogy between Luke's work in Acts and Hellenistic historians of the time. Specifically, "the mission sermons . . . illustrate, together with their scenic frameworks, how the apostolic preaching and its reception carried earliest Christian history toward the outcome intended by God. . . . Closer determination of the sermons' traditional background remains an open question." As affirming a substantial historical reliability in this matter, see W. Ward Gasque, "Luke the Historian and Theologian in Recent Research," *A History of the Criticism of the Acts of the Apostles* (Grand Rapids: Eerdmans, 1975) 251–305; I. Howard Marshall, *The Acts of the Apostles: The Tyndale New Testament Commentaries* (Grand Rapids: Eerdmans, 1980) 34–44; L. R. Donelson, "Cult Histories and the Sources of Acts," *Biblica* 68 (1987) 1–21; Robert Tannehill, *The Narrative Unity of Luke-Acts: A Literary Interpretation,* vol. 2, *The Acts of the Apostles* (Minneapolis: Fortress Press, 1990) 33–4: "The speeches in Acts 2–5 . . . are intended to be appropriate to the audience addressed and to focus on the primary issue emerging at this stage in the story. I mean, of course, appropriate in the eyes of the narrator, which does not guarantee historical accuracy in the pre-

was working with written sources in Acts as he had in his Gospel, but form critics (e.g., Dibelius) contested this view. One factor specifically relevant to Peter's speech at Pentecost is that the text of the Old Testament used here is the Septuagint translation. Thus the text as it stands seems to reflect a stage later than the first days of the Church when it was confined to Jerusalem. Some exegetes consequently think that Peter's speech is completely Luke's literary composition.

Perhaps there is sufficient reason to say that it is basically Luke's composition. But many aspects of the speech can be shown to manifest traditions that preexisted the time (perhaps A.D. 80–85, or earlier, around 70) of Luke's composition, for they are found in early epistles of Paul and reflect the primitive Church's expectation of an imminent parousia. In fact, some passages are incorporated though they are, in the views of some exegetes, in tension with Luke's own theology. We shall see some of this data below, but it can be found more fully in the interpretations of the passage that I cite. An examination of this data supports Fitzmyer's view that although this discourse and some others in Acts "are best regarded as Lucan compositions, intended for his readers and designed to further his own story," they "reflect the missionary preaching of the first apostolic generation [and] . . . echo the primitive apostolic kerygma, [while] they do not necessarily reflect it in detail."[20]

Finally, we can ask what reason Luke had to write Acts, or what the point of his account of the early Church was. He selected and organized material from a particular perspective. One central interest Luke had was to tell how the "word of the Lord" spread till his own time in continuity with and as a fulfillment of Jesus' prophetic promise to the apostles: "[Y]ou will receive power when the Holy Spirit comes upon you, and you will be my witnesses in Jerusalem, throughout Judea and Samaria, and to the ends of the earth" (Acts 1:8).

We saw in chapter 2 that in the preface to his Gospel Luke showed concern that his own contemporary second-generation Christians might have "certainty" or assurance about the message they received.

---

sentation of the early Jerusalem church. Although the speeches doubtless have some relevance for later times, it is dangerous to assume that Peter, for all practical purposes, steps outside his narrative context and preaches the gospel directly to the author's situation." And, "Educated authors would want to compose speeches for their narratives that, in their opinion, were appropriate to the speaker and audience, for appropriateness was an important criterion of a good speech in Greco-Roman rhetoric" (42).

[20]Dillon and Fitzmyer, "Acts of Apostles," 2:166.

This seems also to be a central purpose of his account of the early Church. There, too, we find emphasis on this "assurance" (e.g., Acts 2:36). Luke shows that the word of the Lord spread in accord with God's designs and through his chosen instruments to reach even Gentile believers of his own time. This had a particular significance when second-generation Christians were questioning whether, due to the widespread rejection of Jesus by the Jews, the Christian message might seem to be in discontinuity with Old Testament promises that the Messiah would save his own people. Thus Luke is concerned to show that there is continuity between the disciples of Jesus of his own time and Judaism (e.g., his insistence that the message started being proclaimed in Jerusalem and was first proclaimed to the Jews) and also that it could be expected to meet rejection in part, as Jesus' own ministry had. It does not seem that dealing with a loss of Christian faith due to the delay of the parousia was a major concern for Luke.

In Peter's missionary discourse at Pentecost (Acts 2:14-41) we have the elements of the basic missionary kerygma: the name, the works, the death, and the resurrection of Jesus proclaimed. The core of the climactic verse of the discourse is pre-Lucan kerygma, shown in Pauline passages (e.g., Rom 1:4; 10:9-13): "Therefore let the whole house of Israel know for certain that God has made him both Lord and Messiah, this Jesus whom you crucified" (Acts 2:36). This kerygma is not simply or primarily narrative. Nor is it myth divorced from history. It is not a symbolic expression of a restrictedly internal religious experience. It is a proclamation with a kind of sacramental value insofar as it makes available to the people the saving presence of Jesus. And it can be called symbolic because it proclaims this through the mediation of interpreted events—the death, resurrection, and exaltation of Jesus—as manifesting what God has proclaimed Jesus to be: Lord and Christ. Thus it is in the context of a narrative with a split reference, namely reference to acts in space and time by Jesus and concerning Jesus, but these *as* manifesting God's action, which thereby declares him to be Lord and Christ with the implication this has for Israel and for others.

These actions are shown, as we shall see below, to be such a revelation through their interpretation by prophetic statements of the Old Testament. This mystery is presented symbolically in the sense that the reality proclaimed is both logos and life and thus speaks to human mind and desire, for it is presented by those who have not only encountered the risen Christ but have been animated by the Holy Spirit.

The early witnesses proclaim this message with conviction and at the cost of opposition from the Jewish leaders; they do so with evident concern for the people, and thus their very lives as individuals and as a community are symbols of the reality of God's loving presence to them and, through them, to the Jewish people. Their own transformation by their belief is understood to be God's testimony to the truth and value of their message. It is symbolic in the sense that this reality is to be participated in by those to whom it is proclaimed; it is participated in not simply by objective knowledge but by participative knowledge, by knowledge that comes from desire as well as intellect. It is symbolic, too, in the sense that it is transformative, for it immediately leads to a call for conversion so that the people may be saved (Acts 2:38, 40). We shall reflect more fully in the next section on what this salvation is according to the early Church.

How does the missionary preacher mediate this message? We shall examine this speech in three sections. The *first* (Acts 2:14-21) anchors the discourse in the narrative context of the Pentecost event, showing that this event is the fulfillment of God's eschatological promise of an outpouring of the Spirit. It is not only the appearance of the resurrected Jesus to the apostles but their being animated by the Spirit that is intrinsic to the mediation of revelation that their proclamation offered. The experience of the violent wind that drew the people to where the apostles were and their speaking in tongues were ambiguous signs and needed interpretation for them to be symbols of the presence of God's salvation.

Peter offers this through Joel's prophecy of the coming of the Spirit (Joel 3:1-5), cited according to the Septuagint version with some adaptations to make it more pertinent to the present experience. This too argues for this speech being basically Luke's composition, but his interpretation of the Pentecost event in a context of an expectation of an imminent parousia shows him to be faithful to a pre-Lucan tradition. This event that the people were witnessing was a fulfillment of God's promise that "in the last days" he would pour out a portion of his Spirit on all humankind, their young men and women would prophesy, there would be signs and wonders in the heavens and on earth before the "coming of the great and splendid day of the Lord," and "everyone shall be saved who calls on the name of the Lord."

This event is a symbol of God's saving presence only if its meaning is unveiled by the prophetic word of the Old Testament. Through the application to this event of such a prophecy the Jewish symbolic world is changed; they live now within a new universe. It is the event of the appearances of the resurrected Christ *and* the coming of the Spirit that generates this application and this new symbolic universe. We may recall here a statement from James Dunn concerning the origins of Christianity:

> After Jesus' death the earliest Christian community sprang directly from a sequence of epochal experiences of two distinct sorts—experiences in which Jesus appeared to individuals and groups to be recognized as one who had already experienced the eschatological resurrection from the dead, and experiences of religious ecstacy and enthusiasm recognized as the manifestation of the eschatological Spirit. . . .
>
> *Above all, the distinctive essence of Christian experience lies in the relation between Jesus and the Spirit.*[21]

As we showed earlier, Luke wished to present in his Gospel an "orderly" sequence (Luke 1:3) that would bring out the *meaning* of the acts and words of Jesus. Similarly, in Acts it is this kind of order that he presents. We do not know whether the outpouring of the Spirit occurred fifty days after the resurrection. From John's tradition, we hear that there is a distinction between Jesus' resurrection and ascension and that it is in virtue of the latter that he sends his Holy Spirit on his disciples (John 20:17, 21-22), though John places all these events on Easter itself. Indeed, in his gospel, Luke, too, places the resurrection and the ascension on Easter itself. Like Luke's chronology, John's may have been theologically motivated, for he presents later accounts of Jesus' resurrection appearance (John 20:24-29; 21). We know that Paul also lists a number of appearances of Jesus (1 Cor 15:1-8) that would not fit into a single day.

There may be a historical basis for Luke in Acts placing the event of the outpouring of the Spirit and beginning of the Church's ministry fifty days after Easter, or he may have chosen that day because the Spirit is the law of the new covenant and Pentecost may have been celebrated by the Jews at that time, as it was later, as remem-

---

[21] James Dunn, *Jesus and the Spirit* (Philadelphia: Westminster Press, 1975) 357, 358. On the relation between the ascension and resurrection in Acts, see Joseph Fitzmyer, "The Ascension of Christ and Pentecost," *TS* 45 (1984) 409–40.

brance of Moses coming down the mountain to give the people the Law of the old covenant.

The *second* and central section of the speech is Acts 2:22-32. This reflects the kerygma of the missionary discourses: name, works, death, resurrection, and exaltation of Jesus. Jesus the Nazorean was a man *attested* by God with "mighty deeds, wonders, and signs, which God worked through him in your midst, as you yourselves know" (22). These actions are noted *as* God's commendation of him or attestation concerning him; thus God was acting through Jesus. This is presented as something those in Jerusalem knew—and, indeed, later Jewish tradition did not deny the great deeds of Jesus, though it ascribed them to sorcery or magic.[22] "This man, delivered up by the set plan and foreknowledge of God, you killed, using lawless men to crucify him" (23). Peter does not point out how Jesus' death was itself salvific but does indicate it was a part of God's providential plan. And this sentence gives a basis for the call to repentance with which the discourse ends.

Then Peter discourses on the fact and meaning of the resurrection (vv. 24-32). "God raised him up": once more it is God's action that is involved here, and this too had been foretold. Psalm 16:8-11 is interpreted as David's foretelling that God would not allow his holy one to see corruption; that this was not fulfilled in David himself, whose tomb was in the Jews' midst; that as a prophet David knew "that God had sworn an oath to him that he would set one of his descendents upon his throne" (30), and thus in this passage he "foresaw and spoke of the resurrection of the Messiah; that neither was he abandoned to the netherworld nor did his flesh see corruption" (31). And Peter attests: "God raised this Jesus; of this we are all *witnesses*" (32), using "witnesses" as Paul does in his list of witnesses (1 Cor 15:3-8, 15). The apostles bore official testimony to this event that the risen Jesus had appeared to them.

"Witness" is important for Jewish legal tradition; to be a "false witness to God" (1 Cor 15:15) is a great sin. The testimony of Peter and the apostles occurred not only through their words but by their lives and ministries under the Spirit. And their words of proclamation encompassed both the event of the resurrection and its meaning. The event and the prophetic word of Scripture are together God's

---

[22]See Howard C. Kee, *Jesus in History: An Approach to the Study of the Gospels,* 2nd ed. (New York: Harcourt, Brace, Jovanovich, 1977) 48–54.

declaration that Jesus is the Messiah; by his testimony under the Spirit that embraced both, Peter was a witness for God.[23] We do not find this psalm used elsewhere in the New Testament to this effect, but the "peculiarly rabbinic brand of exegesis that Peter employs in verses 29-31" makes it quite improbable that Luke was the first to find a resurrection argument in it.[24]

In a *final* section, verses 33-36, Peter distinguishes Jesus' exaltation from the resurrection itself: "Exalted at the right hand of God, he received the promise of the Holy Spirit from the Father and poured it forth, as you [both] see and hear" (33). This understanding that Jesus was "exalted at the right hand of God" was pre-Lucan, though perhaps in the earliest period its significance was not distinguished from that of Jesus' resurrection (see Rom 8:34; Eph 1:20; 1 Pet 1:21). Luke, like John, temporally distinguished the ascension from the resurrection itself. The ascension is an externalization of Jesus' exaltation, that is, his being placed at "God's right hand," or receiving power to rule from him. Also, the view that the risen Christ becomes powerful in the Spirit is a pre-Lucan teaching (see Rom 1:4; 1 Tim 3:16). The view that Jesus received the "promise of the Holy Spirit" from the Father and poured her out is a Lucan expression of this earlier teaching.[25] This exaltation and exercising of saving power—shown in the very proclamation by the apostles—too is in accord with Scripture, for David, who did not go up to heaven, said: "The Lord said to my Lord, 'Sit at my right hand until I make your enemies your footstool'"(34-35). The use of this psalm verse is also found in the controversy over the Messiah's Davidic sonship (Mark 12:35-37a, para.).

---

[23]See Enrico Castelli, ed., *Le Témoignage* (Paris: Aubier-Montaigne, 1972); see also Xavier Tilliette's comment on this colloquium in "Le Témoignage," *Gregorianum* 54 (1973) 179–88; Allison Trites, *The New Testament Concept of Witness* (New York: Cambridge University Press, 1977); René Latourelle, "Testimony," *DFT* 1044–60. Latourelle writes (1048): "'Testify' and 'witness' are found chiefly in the vocabulary of Acts and in the theology of Luke. 'Testifying' is a characteristic activity of the apostles in the period after the resurrection. There are four traits that cause them to be so described. First, like the prophets they have been chosen by God. . . . Second, they have seen and heard Christ. . . . Third, Christ has given them the mission of testifying to him . . . , and in order that they may carry out their commission, they have been invested with the power of the Spirit. . . . A final trait of the apostles as witnesses is commitment, an attitude that finds expression in an absolute fidelity to Christ and to his teaching, which is seen as the truth and as the salvation of humanity."

[24]Dillon and Fitzmeyer, "Acts of Apostles," 2:174.

[25]I ask the reader's permission to refer to the Holy Spirit in this work by the feminine personal pronoun. I defend this in "Feminine Symbols and the Holy Spirit," *God's Work in a Changing World* (Washington, D.C.: The Council for Research in Values and Philosophy, 1994) 49–76.

The distinction between the titles of lordship *(kyrios)* and messiahship is part of the most primitive Christian kerygma (see Rom 1:3); this refers back to the earlier quotation from Joel (3:5) that whoever calls upon the name of the Lord will be saved. Peter concludes with a proclamation: "Therefore let the whole house of Israel know for certain that God has made him both Lord and Messiah, this Jesus whom you crucified" (36). The substance of this verse, too, is part of the traditional kerygma (see Rom 10:19; Phil 2:9-11). It is through his resurrection and exaltation that God has declared Jesus to be both Messiah and Lord. This is what the people are called to believe; this is what Peter and the Twelve and the whole early Church proclaim.

In the conclusion of the account of Peter's missionary discourse (37-41), Luke presents the question of Peter's hearers, who were "cut to the heart": "What are we to do, my brothers?" and Peter's response: "Repent and be baptized, every one of you, in the name of Jesus Christ for the forgiveness of your sins; and you will receive the gift of the Holy Spirit. . . . Save yourselves from this corrupt generation." Thus Peter calls for (1) repentance, or turning away from sin—here repentance for the death of Jesus; (2) baptism—here in the name of Jesus Christ; (3) the forgiveness of sins; and (4) the reception of the Holy Spirit. So the whole discourse is oriented to this praxis and through this to salvation and is acceptable only to people open to conversion.

We see that through the kerygma the early Church offered a new paradigm for Jewish experience that integrated their past but transcended it. It reconfigured the world for Jews through finding in the Christ-event, when interpreted by the Old Testament prophecies, a real symbolic manifestation of God's definitive saving action. The Church presented a symbolic universe that had continuity with Judaism but discontinuity also, though this discontinuity became explicit only later. In the first years of its existence those who accepted Jesus as the Messiah were simply another Jewish faction in the pluralistic Judaism of the time. We stress this because the *meaning* of the Christian faith for the first Christians is manifested through this.

3. Other Early Testimonies and the Gospel Narratives of the Resurrection Appearances and Empty Tomb

The apostles' witness dependent upon the appearances of the risen Jesus to them and the gift of the Spirit is essential to the most primitive Christian kerygma, as we see in all the early Christian traditions.

James Dunn concludes that amid the diversities of early Christian kerygmata there is what can be called "a common kerygma," which includes three elements: "the proclamation of the risen, exalted Jesus . . . the call for faith, for acceptance of the proclamation and commitment to the Jesus proclaimed . . . [and] the promise held out to faith—whether it be put in terms of Spirit, or of its various aspects (forgiveness, salvation, life) or of a continuing relation thus established between the exalted Christ and the believer."[26] To interpret the Christian kerygma as though it is not essentially dependent on this witness to an encounter with the resurrected Jesus is to depart from what has been from the beginning the basis for Christian belief and its meaning. The fact that it is proclaimed in diverse ways shows that there were different appearances and that accounts about them are literary compositions.

The different forms, or literary genres, are related to different contexts or purposes. We can distinguish as literary genres the short formulas in the Pauline writings from the appearance traditions in the Gospels.[27] The earliest texts we have are the short formulas, either one-clause, which are theocentric, such as "God has raised Jesus from the dead" (e.g., Rom 4:24b; 8:11a and 11b; 2 Cor 4:14; Gal 1:1; Eph 1:20; Col 2:12; 1 Pet 1:21), or two-clause, which add a christological emphasis, such as 1 Thessalonians 1:10, which refers to the Thessalonians' conversion to God and awaiting "his Son from heaven, whom he raised from [the] dead, Jesus, who delivers us from the coming wrath" (see also Rom 1:3 and 10:9). Perhaps one use of the one-verse form was as a eulogy within a liturgical service; the two-phrase form may have been used as a belief formula, a part of missionary preaching, and in a baptismal liturgy. We shall reflect briefly

---

[26]James Dunn, *Unity and Diversity in the New Testament: An Inquiry into the Character of Earliest Christianity* (Philadelphia: Westminster Press, 1977) 30. Also see idem, *The Parting of the Ways Between Judaism and Christianity and Their Significance for the Character of Christianity* (London: SCM Press, 1991) 184: "Of course, it is technically possible to see Easter faith as a projection or expression of some other more basic conviction about Jesus. But the fact remains that its irreducible formal expression is of something having happened to Jesus, not just to the disciples. God raised *Jesus;* he did not simply bring comfort to the disciples. If 'the resurrection of Jesus' does not mean that something happened to Jesus himself, then the character of Christian faith becomes so radically different from what it has been understood to be from the beginning that it has actually become something else—not simply a difference in degree, but a difference in kind." Interestingly, Pinchas Lapide, a Jew, accepts a resurrection of Jesus as the vindication of a just man, though not the implications that Acts 2:36 sees in this; see P. Lapide and J. Moltmann, *Jewish Monotheism and Christian Trinitarian Doctrine* (Philadelphia: Fortress Press, 1981) 60, 68.

[27]See Fiorenza, *Foundational Theology,* 33–42; Schmitt, "Résurrection du Jésus," 493ff.

on Paul's list of witnesses to the appearances of the risen Jesus and the gospel narratives of the appearances and the empty tomb.

a. Paul's list of witnesses. In writing to the Corinthians in the year 54 or 55, Paul reminds them of what he had handed on to them when he evangelized them, probably in the year 50:

> I handed on to you as of first importance what I also received: that Christ died for our sins in accordance with the scriptures; that he was buried; that he was raised on the third day in accordance with the scriptures; that he appeared to Kephas, then to the Twelve. After that, he appeared to more than five hundred brothers at once, most of whom are still living, though some have fallen asleep. After that he appeared to James, then to all the apostles. Last of all, as to one born abnormally, he appeared to me (1 Cor 15:3-8).

We will make several comments on this critically important testimony, dependent largely on an article by Jerome Murphy-O'Connor, who refers to many other exegetes in his analysis of this passage.[28]

The occasion for Paul's writing this passage was a denial of the resurrection by some Christians of Corinth, probably from their attaching little importance to the body and their view that they already had eternal life. Paul answers with the Church's kerygma that Jesus had risen from the dead. Paul's reference to "what I also received" probably points to the time of his first visit to Jerusalem after his conversion (ca. 35 or 36). In articulating this, Paul repeats an early creed (3b-5). The "third day in accordance with the scriptures" is usually interpreted as a reference to Hosea 6:2, though J. Christensen finds in it a reference to the third day of creation as the creation of Eden (Gen 1:11-13; Isa 11:6-9).[29] The word *ōphthē* is the middle voice form of a word *(horaō)* meaning "I see"; thus it means "he appeared" visually; it emphasizes the initiative of Jesus more than the experience of those who saw him.[30] Paul adds verse 6 to this traditional

[28]See Jerome Murphy-O'Connor, "Tradition and Redaction in 1 Cor 15:3-7," *CBQ* 43 (1981) 582–9; also see Schmitt, "Résurrection du Jésus," 498.

[29]See J. Christensen, "And That He Rose on the Third Day According to the Scriptures," *Scandinavian Journal of the OT* 4 (1990) 101–13.

[30]For a discussion of *ōphthē* see John Galvin, "Jesus Christ," *Systematic Theology: Roman Catholic Perspectives,* ed. Francis Schüssler Fiorenza and John Galvin (Minneapolis: Fortress Press, 1991) 1:301f.

creed "to underline the objectivity of the experience. . . . Paul's purpose was apologetic . . . those who enjoyed this privilege are still accessible."[31] Verse 7 is a traditional fragment. In verse 8 he identifies the type of appearance of the risen Christ to him with the appearances to the others mentioned. When he later refers to visions he had (2 Cor 12:1), he uses not *ōphthē* but *optasia;* thus the appearance of the risen Jesus was a unique event in his life. Similarly, the appearances of the risen Jesus to others that he recounts are not to be identified with experiences of the early Christians generally.[32] After thus recounting appearances of the risen Jesus, he asserted that such proclamation was common to all the proclaimers of the gospel: "Whether it be I or they, so we preach and so you believed" (1 Cor 15:11). He added:

> If Christ has not been raised, then empty [too] is our preaching; empty, too, your faith. Then we are also false witnesses to God, because we testified against God that he raised Christ, whom he did not raise if in fact the dead are not raised. . . . If for this life only we have hoped in Christ, we are the most pitiable people of all (1 Cor 15:14-15, 19).

Christian belief in Jesus as Christ and Lord is essentially dependent upon the appearances of the risen Jesus to select followers, above all the apostles, among whom Paul counts himself. It was through his resurrection and ascension that God declared him Christ and Lord (Acts 2:36).

b. The gospel narrative accounts of the resurrection appearances and the empty tomb. The gospel narratives (Mark 16; Matthew 28; Luke 24; John 20 and 21) are a different genre from the pre-Pauline list of witnesses. We shall mention some elements these narratives have in common and then some elements in which they differ. They are narrative in form, anthropomorphic, dependent in form on Old Testament anthropomorphic theophanies rather than on Greco-Roman appearances of divine men, and permeated with motifs of apologetics, identity, and commissioning. There is discontinuity and continuity between the Jesus who appeared after his death and resurrection and Jesus in his ministry.

---

[31]Murphy-O'Connor, "Tradition and Redaction," 586.

[32]See Daniel Kendall and Gerald O'Collins, "The Uniqueness of the Easter Appearances," *CBQ* 54 (1992) 287–307.

Discontinuity is shown by the initial lack of recognition on the part of his disciples, or the doubts they showed, or Jesus appearing through locked doors and disappearing or ascending from their midst. There was transcendence and mystery about the resurrected Jesus; his resurrection was not a resuscitation like that of Lazarus, who returned to the same form of life that he had departed through death. Jesus' new life was the life of the age to come as distinct from the present age; Paul would say that Christ's resurrection was "the first fruits of those who have fallen asleep" (1 Cor 15:20).

Continuity is indicated by his inviting Thomas to put his finger into his wound in John 20, or by eating in Luke 24,[33] thus showing that he is flesh and bones; he is recognized by them as Jesus of Nazareth. And he commissions them for the ministry he has given them. In reference to the question of identity of the risen one with Jesus of Nazareth, we may again call upon James Dunn, who after examining early Christian confessional formulas of Jesus as Son of Man, Christ, Son of God, and Lord notes that "the distinctive feature which comes to expression in all the confessions we have examined, the bedrock of the Christian faith confessed in the NT writings, is *the unity between the earthly Jesus and the exalted one who is somehow involved in or part of our encounter with God in the here and now.*"[34] The evangelists are basically much more concerned with this identity and the commission that establishes continuity between Jesus and the early Church than with the apologetic motif.

Some major differences among the narratives are the placing of Jesus' appearances in Galilee (Mark 16:7), which points to such an appearance though he does not recount it (see, too, Mark 14:28; Matt 28:16-20; Matt 26:32; John 21), or in Jerusalem (Luke 24; Matt 28:9-10 [Jesus' appearance to the women]; Mark's longer ending [16:9-20]; John 20). As far as appearances to the Twelve go, R. Brown suggests along with A. Dechamps that "in a certain way, *as far as substance is concerned,* all the Gospels are narrating the same appearance to the Twelve."[35] Perhaps there was a theological reason for each to present the appearance to the Twelve in the locale he did. Their unity and differences show their sense of responsibility to what happened and their freedom to organize it to bring out some deeper

---

[33]On this see O'Collins, "Did Jesus Eat the Fish?" *Interpreting the Resurrection,* 39–52.

[34]Dunn, *Unity and Diversity,* 57. His italics.

[35]Brown, "Resurrection of Jesus," 1375.

meaning of God's saving action manifested through these events. Or, more probably, there were different appearances. There is multiple attestation to this, so there seems less reason to say that there was only one appearance of the resurrected Jesus, even to the apostles.

The Gospels also have narratives of women discovering the tomb of Jesus empty on the morning of the third day (Mark 16:1-8; Matt 28:1-8; Luke 24:1-12; John 20:1-10). Paul does not mention this in 1 Corinthians 15. But, as R. Brown comments, "[T]he disciples' preaching of the resurrection (and therefore their understanding of the resurrection) supposes that the tomb was empty. . . . This preaching would have been quickly refuted if there were any tradition of a tomb where Jesus' corpse still lay. Even the Jews who sought to refute the followers of Jesus never suggested that the tomb was not empty."[36] There are differences among these accounts concerning the number of angels the women found at the tomb, the number of women who went there, what the angels said, and so on. But their unity is complete on the emptiness of the tomb. Historical veracity is supported by the fact that women were the witnesses; if the stories were constructed simply for apologetic reasons, men would have been the witnesses. This tradition was secondary to that of the appearances of the resurrected Jesus, and it was the latter that was the basis for the early Christian kerygma.

In conclusion, we will address an objection to the credibility of the appearances of the risen Jesus as we have presented it—an objection that comes from a naturalistic tincture to the historical-critical method as practiced by many historians and exegetes. In reliance on a treatment of this issue by Francis Schüssler Fiorenza,[37] we note the following. Our general experience does not give us access either to the meaning or the truth-claim of the resurrection of Jesus. Assertions that Jesus had risen differ from our ascription to someone of an event or attribute of which we do have general experience (e.g., Jack has pneumonia). We cannot explicate the resurrection as an example because we do not have experience of it elsewhere, nor as a symbol—in the sense of an objectification of a restrictedly *interior* religious experience—because this loses the uniqueness and event character of it. It is only testimony that can give us access to it. And

[36]Ibid., 1374. Also see O'Collins, *Jesus Risen,* 123–7.

[37]See Fiorenza, "A Reconstructive Hermeneutic of Jesus' Resurrection," *Foundational Theology,* 29–55.

this testimony is not simply witness to an event but interpretation of the meaning of the event, for the meaning and the event do not exist separately.

Modern historians who accept a critical-historical approach frequently think that there cannot be historical testimony to the resurrection of Jesus because historical testimony must show analogy with our other human experience and be in a chain of cause and effect with that experience. But historians should be open to the unique event in history, and historical accounts do call upon interpretation—even when some event is not publicly accessible—if this is necessary to make the sequence of events intelligible. For example, if a battle plan is manifest, historians suppose decisions behind them even if these are not publicly accessible. So too, the apostles' testimony to the appearances of Jesus to them does not give us access to publicly verifiable events, but they do give us an intelligible account of how the early Church emerged from a group of men cast into depression and profound disappointment by the death of Jesus. "The historical issue would then become not whether the documents have a demonstrative force and apologetic function independently of [openness to] faith, but whether they give the most appropriate narrative accounts of extant publicly accessible materials and whether these accounts disclose the meaning of events in relation to reality and human existence."[38]

James Dunn and many others support such an approach. Dunn points out that the historian seeks to give a narrative account explaining the origin and development of significant movements in the past, one of which is the emergence of Christianity. How can the historian explain the emergence of this movement from within Judaism and its endurance, propagation through the Mediterranean world, and even development to the point of being the major religion within three hundred years? The first Christians explained the origin of Christianity by the resurrection of Jesus from the dead. Can historians dispense with this explanation in their reconstructions of the beginnings of Christianity? Dunn makes a helpful distinction in this matter between event, data, and reconstruction. The event of the past is not repeated, and so historians cannot directly perceive it. They have data, however, from which they can reconstruct the beginnings of a movement such as Christianity by a narrative account that never exactly imitates the events themselves:

[38]Ibid., 32–3.

> The historian must *interpret* his data in order to achieve the most satisfactory reconstruction. He must allow for distortion in the data and bias in himself. And there will always be something tentative or provisional about his reconstruction, since there is always the possibility that new data will emerge which will require a realignment of other data and a reassessment of the reconstructed event.[39]

The event of Jesus' resurrection is irretrievable. Actually, no Christian even in the beginning claimed to have experienced Jesus' rising from the dead. The data the historian has to go on are the witnesses to the appearances of the resurrected Jesus, the transformation of apostles, and the origin and development of the early Church.

Historians may dismiss this explanation of the origin of Christianity, but what they put in its place seems totally inadequate to account for it, counter to the evidence we have, and due to the presuppositions they bring from philosophy or fear of the implications that the resurrection of Jesus can have for human life even today. We can agree that critical history as such cannot acknowledge the resurrection, since it methodically limits its criteria and methods. But this is a philosophical question. Neither can physics acknowledge the existence of God, since it methodically limits itself to the specifically physical antecedent cause or condition of an event. Also, we are not claiming that acknowledging the resurrection of Jesus is simply an intellectual act. In fact, we think that it is not possible, at least in the way that accepts its implications, without God's gift of the Spirit that enables us to be believers. But we do claim that the call to conversion is not without God's testimony through the resurrection of Jesus to the truth of what we are called to believe.

From what we have written here it is clear how our interpretation of the resurrection compares with those we presented at the beginning of this section. What stands out in the early Christian kerygma and missionary discourses as genuinely reflected in Luke's account of the first missionary discourse in the Church, Paul's list of witnesses, and the gospel narratives is that the proclamation comes from a religious experience the apostles had through the appearances of the risen Christ and the gift of the Holy Spirit. It is made in a way that conveys this experience through their quasi-sacramental witnessing for the purpose of inviting people to faith in Jesus as Messiah

---

[39]James Dunn, *The Evidence for Jesus* (Philadelphia: Westminster Press, 1985) 55.

and Lord and fellowship with him as such through the gift of the Spirit.[40] The point of the discourse is not so much apologetic as to proclaim what God has *declared* through raising Jesus from the dead and through the sending of the Spirit, as this is illuminated by the words of Jesus and the Old Testament. Thus it is through God's actions and words that he declares this saving message, and it is through mediating these in the power of the Spirit that the apostles fulfill their mission of proclaiming the message.

This message began to be preached in Jerusalem, and its context is Jewish apocalyptic expectations (see Dan 12:1-3 on the expectation of a resurrection in the last times) rather than Greek myths. One cannot say, however, that the apostles had some experience after Jesus' death that they proceeded to interpret in apocalyptic categories, as though this is simply *one* possible interpretation, but not demanded by the experience. There is no experience without interpretation, and what they give us indicates that this interpretation was evoked by the experience they tell us evoked it, namely the physical yet transformed Jesus encountering them after his death.[41]

Certain modern interpretations of religious experience, as though it was something individual and interior that was expressed externally by symbols, have supported the contrary position of Bultmann and others. But to impose this as a grid to interpret the early Church's witnessing to Jesus' resurrection is now widely recognized as distorting. The apostles did have a religious experience that led them to belief in Jesus as Christ and Lord, but one mediated by the appearances of Jesus and the gift of the Spirit. Similarly, others came through their preaching to a religious experience and thus to belief, but one mediated by the apostles' and others' witnessing to the resurrection of Jesus and the gift of the Spirit.

The early proclamation of the resurrection is not presented simply as a fact that forces belief. It is mediated only by *witnessing,* or testimony, and is available by no other path; it is witnessed only within the larger context of a call to faith. It was the mystery of a person that was being revealed by this witness, namely who Jesus was and what the way was that God offered us for salvation. As Jesus had made this

---

[40]For an analysis of the early Christian proclamation in this way see Luke Johnson, "The Resurrection Faith," *The Writings of the New Testament: An Interpretation* (Philadelphia: Fortress Press, 1986) 98–113.

[41]See Fiorenza's critique of Schillebeeckx's attempt to get behind the New Testament interpretation to a different and more primitive experience, Fiorenza, *Foundational Theology,* 20–8.

known through a personal witness during his ministry, his apostles did so after his resurrection and the coming of the Spirit. In a later chapter we shall see how appropriate such mediation is for such a revelation. And it could only be evaluated positively by those who were open to faith. This is counter to the way the resurrection was used by many Catholic manualists through the first half of this century, who presented it as an apologetic miracle rather than as God's symbolic act declaring who Jesus was and accompanied by the gift of the Spirit.

We should note that there is a distinction between the early Christians' belief in the resurrection and their belief that Jesus was Lord and Messiah. It is the latter they were called to believe at the climax of the missionary discourse. This could not be seen. The apostles presented their witnessing to the resurrection of Jesus to the people together with Old Testament texts as a share in their own religious experience to mediate what they were called to believe. Others had to accept this human witness if they were to accept the Christian faith that Jesus of Nazareth was Messiah and Lord. The encounter with Jesus that the apostles witnessed to was historical in the sense that it was an event within a specific time and space. To believe that Jesus is Messiah and Lord is to believe something that is transhistorical. The witness to the appearances of Jesus could be considered "evidence" justifying faith in him, but it could also be considered God's sign or testimony or declaration concerning Jesus, which people were called to discern.[42] Discernment of God's testimony led many Jews and, later, Gentiles to restructure their lives.

II. The Meaning of Salvation in the Early Church

We now ask what meaning salvation had for the early Church. Peter and the apostles had a new or deeper understanding of Jesus through the resurrection and the coming of the Holy Spirit upon them. How did this affect their understanding of the meaning of the salvation God offered through Jesus? Several contexts for this question are the following, all expressed earlier. We ask this in the context of contemporary Christian divisions in the interpretation of

---

[42]See M. John Farrelly, *Belief in God in Our Time* (Collegeville: The Liturgical Press, 1992) 216–20, 230–4, where the question of God's manifestations and discernment, or "evidence," are discussed in reference to belief in the existence of God.

salvation. Many Christians keep to an earlier cultural interpretation of this that was centered on the individual, otherworldly, and interior; this is associated in many cases with a traditional *exitus-reditus* theology, which we will treat in the next chapter. Some do accept modern historical consciousness, and among these, some see Christian salvation as irrelevant to our historical concerns. There are also some who almost reduce this salvation to human fulfillment within history or give this dimension priority.

Parallel to these widespread divisions among Christians, there are theologians who, while differing among themselves, interpret the early Church's view of salvation in a way disengaged from modern historical consciousness—abstracting from concerns to transform history rather than simply the individual. This includes Neoscholasticism, the early Rahner, and Bultmann. There are others who so interpret Scripture's view of salvation as answering the need for human fulfillment that they may seem to continue, in a form of neoliberalism, the Protestant liberalism of the last century (e.g., much process theology, some American theology marked by pragmatism, and statements of some liberation theologians). We have sought to get beyond these divisions in our interpretation of Jesus' ministry, and we now seek to do so in reference to early Christianity, though our study is only introductory.

We begin by noting that among exegetes "there is a widespread consensus that the earliest Christian community was an apocalyptic community."[43] Käsemann, who called apocalyptic the mother of Christian theologies, writes: "The heart of primitive Christian apocalyptic . . . is the accession to the throne of heaven by God and by his Christ as the eschatological Son of Man—an event which can also be characterized as proof of the righteousness of God."[44] The interpretation of salvation in this perspective is quite different in part from theologies prominent in our century such as existentialist eschatology, realized eschatology, and forms of salvation history.[45] And there

---

[43] Adela Yarboro Collins, "Apocalypses and Apocalypticism. Early Christian," *ABD* 1:289.

[44] Ernst Käsemann, "The Beginnings of Christian Theology," *Apocalypticism,* ed. Robert Funk (New York: Herder & Herder, 1969) 43–4, also page 40, where Käsemann writes, "Apocalyptic . . . was the mother of all Christian theology." See also Klaus Koch, *The Rediscovery of Apocalyptic* (Naperville, Ill.: Alec R. Allenson, 1970) 73ff.

[45] On different meanings of "salvation history" see Thomas McCreesh, "Salvation History," *The New Dictionary of Theology,* (Wilmington, Del.: Michael Glazier, 1987) 929–31 (hereafter cited as *NDT*).

is still lacking an answer to the question of whether there is organic unity among diverse early Christian interpretations of salvation, and if so what that organic relationship is.

In our brief study of this question, our thesis will be that the prime meaning of salvation in the early Church was what Jesus would do when he comes again; that gradually they realized that what he would do then he is, from his exaltation in that future kingdom, doing in part even now; and that a major aspect of this is the inner transformation by the Spirit, whom he has sent into this present age as the "power of the future age" for those who believe. We shall first look to Paul and then to some differing contexts of early Christian interpretations of salvation. We start with Paul because his writings are the earliest literary witnesses to the primitive Christian Church's belief. We see by his emphasis on the tradition that he accepts together with the other apostles (e.g., 1 Cor 15:1-3) that his writings reflect the pre-Pauline primitive Church's belief.

1. Salvation in Paul

What did salvation mean for Paul? While this is our central question here, the answer to it is contained in a larger theocentric basic belief of Paul, described by J. Christiaan Beker:

> Paul is an apocalyptic theologian with a theocentric outlook. The Christ-event is the turning point in time that announces the end of time. Indeed, Christ has become "Lord" since his exaltation and is now God's appointed world ruler who bears the divine name (Phil 2:10), but—as Paul adds—"to the *glory* of God the Father." . . .
>
> The climax of the history of salvation is not the resurrection of Christ and his present glory (cf. John) but the impending glory of God. . . . Both the Spirit (Rom 8:26) and Christ (8:34) are the executors of God's purpose and "intercede" for us to hasten the final state of glory. Paul's apocalyptic theocentrism, then, is not to be contrasted with his Christocentric thinking, for the final hour of the glory of Christ and his Parousia will coincide with the glory of God, that is, with the actualization of the redemption of God's created order in his kingdom.[46]

---

[46]J. Christiaan Beker, *Paul the Apostle: The Triumph of God in Life and Thought* (Philadelphia: Fortress Press, 1980) 362–3. See also Joseph Plevnik, who criticizes Beker in part in "The Center of Pauline Theology," *CBQ* 51 (1989) 461–87. Our position does not fully agree with Beker.

We propose that an analysis of Paul's view of the meaning of salvation substantially supports this interpretation and that the later interpretations of the apostolic age are organically related to it.

In 1 Thessalonians, the first of Paul's letters, the theme of justification is not present. Paul draws the Thessalonians' attention again and again to "the coming of our Lord Jesus Christ" (4:23; 1:10; 2:16; 3:13), namely the parousia and the Day of the Lord (5:2). It is *then* that the followers of Jesus will receive salvation and be delivered from God's wrath: "[T]he dead in Christ will rise first. Then we who are alive, who are left, will be caught up together with them in the clouds to meet the Lord in the air. Thus we shall always be with the Lord" (4:16-17). "Salvation," then, is a *future* word that signifies primarily what Jesus will give when he comes again; it has an apocalyptic meaning in continuity with Daniel 7. The primary analogue for salvation is what will happen then. This seems to be correlated with what may be the earliest meaning of the ascription of lordship to Jesus in the primitive Church. As Raymond Brown writes:

> The prayer *maranatha,* "Our Lord, come!" (1 Cor 16:22; cf. Rev 22:20 . . .), *may* be early and may have arisen among the first Aramaic-speaking Christians. It may have implied that when Jesus came then he would be Lord ruling the earth. Some scholars maintain that future sayings with Jesus returning from heaven as the Son of Man in order to judge the world were the earliest Son-of-Man usage. . . . [F]uture christology may have enjoyed relatively short preeminence.[47]

It may well be that in the primitive Church Jesus was initially called Lord in virtue of the exercise of divine power that will be given him when he comes again, namely the power to save and to judge. As the primary meaning of salvation was what Jesus will do when he comes again, the primary meaning of Jesus' lordship or rule or coming into his kingdom was his exercise of saving and judging power when he comes again. The earliest Christians did not think that this event was far off because the resurrection of Jesus was an event of the age to come, the fulfillment and liberation of history, and what it signified would quickly follow, as the harvest follows the first fruits.

---

[47]Raymond Brown, "Aspects of New Testament Thought. Christology," *NJBC,* 1357.

In 1 Corinthians, Paul is addressing Christians who seem to feel that they have already been saved and received their inheritance and are filled with God's gifts of wisdom (1:5-7). In answer to this mis-understanding, Paul continues to use the word "save" in reference to what Jesus *will* do for them and his other disciples *when* he comes again (3:15; 5:5; 15:22f.; 15:51f.). They are already justified, washed clean, and are temples of the Holy Spirit (e.g., 6:1; 12:13), but victory is in the future. And the divisions and immorality among them show too clearly that the victory is not yet assured. Through his obedience and the cross, Jesus, the new Adam, did gain what they will receive and have al-ready received (1:21-23; 15:22). But the life that Jesus gained for them, he offers to them only as risen and exalted, as having entered that fu-ture age, for it is from there that he acts as "a life-giving spirit" (15:45).

It is as though Paul continues to use "save" and "lordship" in ref-erence primarily to what occurs at the parousia but recognizes that Jesus is exercising that lordship even now through the gifts he gives now to his followers, especially the gift of the Spirit. He exercises that saving power even now and will exercise it till he comes again and completes his work: "[T]hen comes the end, when he hands over the kingdom to his God and Father, when he has destroyed every sov-ereignty and every authority and power. For he must reign until he has put all his enemies under his feet" (15:24-25). Paul seems to say that the sovereignty most primitive Christians thought Jesus would exercise when he comes again he is now exercising through begin-ning to save and to judge (11:31-32). He is already exalted and given the name "Lord" (Phil 2:9-11) and has begun that salvation and judg-ment that will happen at the end of history when he comes again— present participations in what he will do then. His present exercise of lordship is a partial exercise of that future reign.[48]

The presence of the kingdom exercised by the exalted Christ is shown in part by the power used by the apostles (1 Cor 4:20), who are ambassadors for Christ (2 Cor 5:23) calling people to repentance and to be reconciled with God, for "now is the day of salvation" (2 Cor 6:2). Future salvation depends on and is initiated in the present for those who believe; the not yet is in part, but only in part, already.[49]

---

[48]See É. Cathenet, "Règne de Dieu: Épîtres pauliniennes," *Supplément au Dictionnaire de la Bible* (1985) 10:165–87, 171–80.

[49]See Beker, *Paul the Apostle,* 162–3, 172. The apocalyptic future is also present in part in Paul's expectation that after his death he will be with Christ before the end comes. See Phil 1:23; 2 Cor 5:1-5.

We shall see further reason for interpreting the relationship between future and present in this fashion. The primacy of the future lordship of Jesus and of salvation is not lost as its presence is stressed more and more; it is precisely this future that is in part present now, and it comes from that future age.

Paul uses the terms "salvation" and "kingdom of God" somewhat interchangeably, more the former than the latter. Thus the kingdom of God for him, too, is primarily future—what Christ will do when he comes again, though God is exercising that reign even now through the exalted Christ and the Spirit. The kingdom of God will be inherited in the future or, in the case of the unjust, will not be inherited (1 Cor 15:50; 6:9-10; Gal 5:21). But the kingdom, too, is already in part present. The exalted Christ is reigning in part: "For he must reign until he has put all his enemies under his feet" (1 Cor 15:25). There are other agencies contesting his reign at present, but at the end all such agencies will be converted or destroyed. We can say here what Karl Donfried writes in another context: "Already now, partially and proleptically, through Christ and his gospel, God's rule and glory have broken into this transient world and are at work in them."[50] Or as J. Beker writes of the Church: "Because the church has an eschatological horizon and is the proleptic manifestation of the kingdom of God in history, it is the beachhead of the new creation and the sign of the new age in the old world that is 'passing away' (1 Cor 7:29)."[51]

In Romans Paul writes to Christians who have been justified and, he hopes, will be saved. It is Jesus who by his death and resurrection has gained this for us (3:24-25; 5:10); it is by our belief and being baptized into Christ that we share his life (6:3-4). The kingdom is present in part (14:17). It is particularly through the Spirit that this is transformative of us (Romans 8). As James Dunn writes, "The Spirit is the future good which has become present for the man of faith—the power of the not yet which has already begun to be realized in his present experience."[52] Paul even uses an aorist here: "In hope we were

[50]Karl Donfried, "The Kingdom of God in Paul," *The Kingdom of God in 20th Century Interpretation,* ed. Wendell Willis (Peabody, Mass.: Hendrickson, 1987) 182. I differ in part from Donfried in the interpretation of Paul.

[51]Beker, *Paul the Apostle,* 313. We need not agree with his following sentence, where he states that the Church will not "enter into the kingdom as a supratemporal reality." This does not follow from the fact that the Church is not to be identified with the kingdom of God.

[52]Dunn, *Jesus and the Spirit,* 310. Also see M. John Farrelly, "Holy Spirit," *The New Dictionary of Catholic Spirituality,* ed. Michael Downey (Collegeville: The Liturgical Press, 1993) 492–503;

saved" (Rom 8:24), but in a way that orients us to the future salvation. It is all too obvious that this salvation is something we still strive for: "[W]e ourselves, who have the first fruits of the Spirit, we also groan within ourselves as we wait for adoption, the redemption of our bodies" (Rom 8:23).

We add here that at times salvation is ascribed by theologians in a one-sided manner to Jesus Christ, whereas Paul ascribes it to both Jesus Christ and the Spirit, but in different ways. For example, Jesus Christ won salvation for us and commissions his apostles to proclaim the message as his ambassadors so that through faith we may be sons and daughters in the Son. But the Spirit—the gift of the exalted Christ—mediates salvation by beginning from the interiority of the Church and the individual person, enabling them to appreciate what the Father and Christ have done for us and to respond by love, a love that expresses itself externally in many ways.

Salvation is, indeed, something still to come (10:9, 10, 13; 5:9, 10), though "our salvation is nearer now than when we first believed; the night is advanced, the day is at hand" (13:11-12). God's designs in history are oriented toward the salvation of all, and he even uses Israel's lapse to forward his design (Romans 9–11), a design that includes God's fidelity to his promises to Israel and its eschatological salvation.[53] Like salvation, judgment primarily signifies what will occur on the Day of the Lord (2:5-9). The present age is the age of God's patience with us (9:22), but in part God's eschatological judgment is already being exercised in the present age (1:18f.; 11:22).

We conclude this brief account of Paul's view of the eschatological nature of salvation by noting that this is a social more than an individual reality for him; he emphasizes its transformative impact in the present age primarily within the Church itself. Paul states one aspect of this impact when he notes that those reputed to be pillars in the Church accepted the validity of his message but told him, "[W]e were to be mindful of the poor, which is the very thing I was eager to do" (Gal 2:10). He states that the Christian mystery makes an end to divisions between Jew and Greek, male and female, free and slave (Gal 3:28); and he expresses an ethic of how this should change re-

---

Farrelly, "Feminine Symbols," 66–8, where I compare and contrast how Jesus Christ and the Spirit mediate salvation in Paul's teaching.

[53]See E. Elizabeth Johnson, *The Function of Apocalyptic and Wisdom Traditions in Romans 9–11* (Atlanta: Scholars Press, 1989) for Paul's use of the Wisdom tradition as well as apocalyptic.

lations within the worshiping community and between Christian master and slave (Philemon). This is revolutionary in the Greco-Roman society of Paul's time (e.g., in marriage; see 1 Cor 7:3-5). Though Paul did not seek to overthrow externally or directly social structures of his time and place, "the revolution within the church carried within itself important seeds of revolution for the structures of society . . . 'pockets' of a life-style that—as in the case of marriage—could and did penetrate the mores of the larger society."[54] Evangelization and the upbuilding of the Church were the central means for him to bring about God's designs for the larger world.

2. Later New Testament Interpretations of Salvation

Though it is widely agreed that Paul's primary interpretation of salvation and the kingdom was apocalyptic, it is also agreed that later New Testament writings seem to move from this perspective, putting the main emphasis not on the parousia but rather on the present or the preexistent Son of God coming into the world. James Dunn notes

> what is probably *the chief contrast within NT christology*—namely, that between the christology of the very first Christians and the christology that began to develop as Christianity began to adopt (and adapt to) more of the conceptualizations of the wider religious philosophy of the time. . . . *The christology of earliest Christianity* seems to have been *essentially forward looking.* . . . *The developments in christology* after this earliest period can be characterized as *the beginning of a shift of the decisive "christological moment" backwards in time from the eschatological double event of resurrection-exaltation-parousia.* . . . Much the most important shift in the christological moment is heralded by the introduction of *the language of pre-existence* into the talk about Christ. . . . [W]ith the use of the language of pre-existence the concept of *incarnation* becomes part of christology. And the door is thereby opened to that christology which sees Jesus not only as the incarnation of divine Wisdom or divine Logos, but which also reckons the incarnation as the decisive moment in salvation—the taking of humanity into the godhead and thereby sanctifying it."[55]

[54]Beker, *Paul the Apostle,* 326.

[55]Dunn, *Unity and Diversity,* 216–7, 219, 220, 221–2. His italics.

The later loss of the apocalyptic understanding of salvation, which we will document in Christian history, begins, Dunn says, in the New Testament itself. Beker expresses this summarily:

> In the New Testament we notice this movement away from the temporal tension inherent in Paul's apocalyptic theology. Two solutions seem to present themselves: (1) a diffusion of the tension between the foci, or (2) a conflation of the foci. The first solution postpones the apocalyptic hour (cf. esp. 2 Peter, 2 Thessalonians, Luke-Acts); the second solution spiritualizes it (cf. esp. Colossians, Ephesians, John).
>
> Second Peter alters the conception of time from historical chronology into a divine conception of time, in order to come to terms with the delay of the Parousia. . . . At the other end of the spectrum, the apocalyptic future is not postponed but conflated with the Christ-event. Here the "not yet" focus disappears in favor of the "already." Present and future are not stretched apart but collapse into each other.[56]

We will illustrate the thesis, a thesis held by a number of exegetes, that this shift, as real as it is, does not deny what we have shown in Paul's apocalyptic theology, namely that the prime moment in which Jesus Christ exercises his reign to save us is the parousia. Our salvation comes from the age to come. We will reflect briefly on this theme in Colossians and Ephesians, in the theologies of the evangelists, and in the Apocalypse.

In Colossians and Ephesians, which many exegetes today see as representing a Pauline school but not written by Paul himself, there is a definite shift from Paul's view. There is a preexistence Christology in Colossians (1:15-20), and what Paul expected to happen in the future is expressed in these epistles as having already occurred. God has already "transferred us to the kingdom of his beloved Son" (Col 1:13); we "were also raised with him [Christ] through faith in the power of God" (Col 2:12); God "raised us up with him, and seated us with him in the heavens in Christ Jesus. . . . For by grace you have been saved through faith" (Eph 2:6, 8). Consequently, "[i]f then you were raised with Christ, seek what is above, where Christ is seated at the right hand of God" (Col 3:1). This is called a realized eschatology.

---

[56]Beker, *Paul the Apostle,* 160–1, 162.

We will see in the next section that there is reason to think that these epistles are addressed to Christians who are influenced by Jewish apocalypticism and who thus look to sources other than Jesus Christ for wisdom. The author emphasizes, then, that preexistent wisdom is fully in Jesus, and this emphasis tends to inculturate the Christian message of salvation for a culture where the dichotomy was more that of the material and the spiritual order, the earthly and the heavenly, than that of the present age and the age to come. This leads to an emphasis that in a sense we are already saved and raised to new life in Christ.

Counter to some exegetes this message does not deny what was central to Paul's soteriology. There is still the acceptance of the distinction between the present age and the age to come (Eph 1:22).[57] Our salvation and sharing in Christ's resurrection even now comes to us from Jesus, who has gained this for us through his own death (Eph 1:7) and who gives it to us only from having gone into his reign of the age to come by being exalted to the right hand of the Father (Eph 4:8-10), not in his condition as preexistent. The Spirit who is sent to us from Christ in the age to come remains "the first installment of our inheritance" (Eph 1:14).

Even Paul recognized that the saving and judging power Jesus would exercise when he came again he was already exercising in part through having been exalted at God's right hand and given the name "Lord." He came to realize that even if he died before Jesus came again he would share the presence of Jesus (2 Cor 5:8; Phil 1:23) without waiting for the parousia. The power of the resurrection is operating even now, and there are passages in Paul that represent a pre-existent Christology (e.g., Phil 2:6). The emphasis has changed in Colossians and Ephesians, but the new life or new creation continues

---

[57]Adela Collins points to "the vacillation in Jewish and Christian eschatology between temporal and spatial imagery. The Hebr. word *'ôlam* and the Gk. word *aion* could both be translated either 'age' or 'world' . . . 'the age to come' or 'the world to come'" ("Eschatology and Apocalypticism," in "Aspects of New Testament Thought," *NJBC,* 1363.) Collins would not contest the primacy for early Christian apocalypticism of the temporal imagery. What she does not perhaps sufficiently develop is that the present exercise of God's saving power in this context is an anticipation and participation in that final saving act of Christ's parousia. In the next section we will refer to Thomas Sappington, *Revelation and Redemption at Colossae* (Sheffield, England: Sheffield Academic Press, 1991), who argues that the error against which the author of Colossians writes is more Jewish apocalypticism than Hellenistic syncretism. He notes (21, 56ff.) with Collins the use of spatial imagery of heaven and earth in Jewish apocalypticism, and he holds (225f.) that the contrast between the eschatology of Colossians and the undisputed letters of Paul is exaggerated.

to come to us from the agent Christ in his position as having gone into the age to come. From the perspective of us who are still "in via," Paul also emphasizes the present by telling the Philippians to "work out your salvation with fear and trembling" (Phil 2:12). And he is convinced that in giving us the beginnings of salvation, God has given us through Christ its fulfillment, though we can still lose this great gift (cf. Rom 8:28-30).[58] It is possible to overemphasize the difference between Paul's genuine epistles and those of the later Pauline school.

In an earlier chapter we examined Jesus' own preaching on the kingdom. But here it is also worthwhile to indicate summarily the eschatologies of the evangelists as relevant to our theme. The dividing line is particularly between the Synoptics and John. In what is probably its original form, Mark's Gospel does not even end with a resurrection appearance. The reason for this is that "[t]he eschatological hope of Mark centers on the coming Son of Man. . . . [T]he resurrection of Jesus is not significantly the fulfillment of eschatological hope. It is a preparation for the second coming, an event for which Mark expresses imminent expectation (9:1; 13:24-37)."[59] Matthew puts more emphasis on the resurrection of Jesus. And for him the risen Christ is present to the Christian community (18:20; 28:20). Collins writes: "In the postresurrection period the world is the kingdom of the Son of Man (cf. 13:38 with v. 41). But that kingship will not be exercised until 'the close of the ages,' when the general judgment will occur (cf. 13:30 with vv. 40-43)."[60]

The primary analogue for the kingdom of God is that which Christ will exercise when he comes again. But it seems we must also say, as the parable of fishermen (Matt 13:47-50) does in marking all the stages of their task as illustrative of the kingdom of God, that the Son of Man is already exercising *in part* that kingship he will exercise then (also see Matt 28:18-20). Luke–Acts rejects the kind of apocalypticism that seeks to identify exact times of the coming of the Lord, but this is "by no means a rejection of apocalypticism as such. . . . The kingdom of God will be manifest in the revelation of the Son of Man (cf. 17:20 with vv. 24 and 30). Like Matt, Luke places more em-

---

[58]For a development of this theme see M. John Farrelly, *Predestination, Grace, and Free Will* (1964; available through Washington D.C.: The Council for Research in Values and Philosophy, 1994) 54–60.

[59]Collins, "Eschatology and Apocalypticism," 1363.

[60]Ibid.

phasis on the presence of the risen Lord with the Christian communities than does Mark,"[61] particularly in the Eucharist (24:30-31) and the sending of the Spirit (Acts 1:4-8; 2:32-33). These effects in the present are not a substitute for the parousia but a partial exercise of the saving presence and power that Jesus will manifest then, for he has already been exalted to the right hand of the Father (Acts 2:33).

John has been understood as interpreting eschatology as wholly realized in the present. There is some basis for such an interpretation. Francis Maloney writes:

> This [Jewish] dualism of the present evil age resolved by the rule of God in the age to come is replaced in John with another form of dualism. A traditional temporal dualism has been (partly) replaced by a cosmic dualism. Underlying the Gospel story are a series of contrasts: e.g., light and darkness (1:5), above and below (8:23), spirit and flesh (3:6), life and death (3:36), truth and falsehood (8:44-45), heaven and earth (3:31), God and Satan (13:27). These opposing forces do not simply coexist but are locked in conflict. . . .
>
> There are indications that this form of dualism was not foreign to 1st-cent. Jewish thinking. . . . John built bridges out of the Judaism of its birth into the new world of Hellenistic syncretism.[62]

The weight of God's saving action seems to shift to the past and present. Out of love God sent his Son into the world to save us (3:16-18). And the one who believes in him already has eternal life (6:47); the one who does not believe is already condemned (3:18). John spoke much more in terms of life than of the kingdom of God. This Gospel comes from the Johannine community toward the end of the first century, and its purpose was to lead people to believe in Jesus, the Messiah and Son of God (20:31). Hence it underlines the importance of the present time of decision for or against faith.

Still, there is throughout the Gospel an expectation of a future judgment by the Son of Man that will lead to a resurrection to life or to condemnation (5:28-29). As in Paul and Luke, the coming of the Spirit is mediated only by the death, resurrection, and exaltation of

[61]Ibid., 1363–4. Hans Conzelmann had proposed that the central problem for Luke was the delay of the parousia and that Luke, in answer to this, developed a theology in which the end was not so important. What took its place was a salvation history in three stages, the period of Israel, the period of Jesus, and the period of the Church. Many exegetes have now withdrawn from this view.

[62]Francis Maloney, "Johannine Theology," *NJBC*, 1421–2.

Jesus (7:39; 20:17, 22). In that sense the Spirit continues to come from and to be the power and presence of the age to come. John accentuates the abiding of the Spirit with the disciples of Jesus, the abiding of the Father and Jesus through the Spirit (14:16-17, 23), and the effects of the Spirit in guiding his disciples, witnessing to Jesus, and judging the world (14:26; 15:26; 16:8). Rather than thinking of Christ's present impact on us by the image of a ruler, John emphasizes the influence through interior life, as the branch lives from the vine and as the Spirit, or Paraclete, gives us communion with the Father and the Son. This is a necessary balance for some of the images of the kingdom given by the Synoptics, and it once more calls us to see the Father's present saving influence on us as coming both through the Son as exalted Christ and from the Spirit.

We can say that in John, as distinct from many later Christian writers, the age to come has not been made simply an appendix to Christian life by over-assimilation to a Greek cyclic view of reality. While John bridges these two cultures, he still affirms the primitive Christian apocalypticism. To evangelize, it was necessary to relate the Christian message to the Hellenistic culture, and it was necessary to preserve the initial Christian message that was apocalyptic in character. John did both.

The book of Revelation, written for Christians under persecution toward the end of the first century, "is evidence that intense and imminent eschatological expectation was still a major factor in the 90s."[63] There is both spatial and temporal dualism. There will be a vindication of those who are faithful to Christ because his reign will appear on the earth (19:11-21). This coming reign of Christ "also includes a new cosmic creation and an eternal, intimate relationship between God, Christ and the faithful (21:1–22:5)."[64] There is in Revelation, as in many New Testament books, an effort to relate that ultimate exercise of saving and judging power by Christ to a more immediate and temporal phase of his exercise of messianic kingship in a passage that has been frequently interpreted in a millenarian sense (20:1-10). But if we take apocalyptic language as largely symbolic, we cannot interpret it in the concrete forms and in correlation with current events that fundamentalists have often used.

---

[63]Collins, "Eschatology and Apocalypticism," 1364.

[64]Ibid.

III. Revelation and Faith in the Apostolic Age

We will now give very briefly some representative views on revelation and faith in the early Church. We will find that they are in accord with what we saw in chapter 4 on revelation and faith as reflected in Peter's stages of faith, particularly the third stage, which was mediated by the appearance of the resurrected Jesus and the gift of the Holy Spirit. That is, Christian revelation is mediated by God's symbolic deeds and words through Jesus Christ and by the Spirit, particularly by the appearance of the resurrected Jesus and the gift of the Spirit, and the words, both of the Hebrew Scripture and of Jesus, that interpreted these events. It was mediated, then, by exterior historical deeds and words and by interior movement by the Spirit. What was revealed was the mystery that God's salvation comes through Jesus Christ and the Spirit, that Jesus was Lord and Christ, and thus the mystery of God's love and saving design and through this who God is. This revelation called for a faith that was both a faith in Jesus Christ and faith that he was indeed Lord and Christ; it called for acceptance of a content revealed and for discipleship; salvation was gained through such a transformative faith, and it was a personal knowledge of Jesus and God.

In the West we have all too frequently lost this integral view of revelation and faith through our analytical approach and our emphasis on conceptual knowledge. There was reason given to believe, primarily the appearance of the resurrected Jesus and the internal witness of the Holy Spirit, but also signs in Jesus' public life by which the Father testified for him. The response of faith was not possible save through the Holy Spirit. This revelation was the fulfillment of God's earlier revelations to his people. We find that this understanding of revelation and faith accords with that of Vatican II, is more integral than some major interpretations offered in twentieth-century Christian theologies, and helps to overcome their oppositions to one another. The development in the articulation of revelation and faith that occurred in early Christian writings was in part stimulated by the problems posed to the proclaimers of the faith in different contexts and the gradual movement of this proclamation into Hellenistic culture. We will briefly recall aspects of Paul and the Pauline school, the Letter to the Hebrews and the Gospel of John.

1. Paul and the Pauline School

Paul began where the other apostles began, that is, with receiving a revelation from God through the appearance of the risen Jesus and the gift of the Holy Spirit (Gal 1:11-17; 1 Cor 15:8; Acts 9:3-6, 17).[65] Through this he received the revelation that Jesus was Christ and Lord and that God was saving people through Jesus Christ and his Spirit, a message interpreted initially by the apocalyptic tradition, as we explained briefly in earlier sections of this chapter. Paul responded to this revelation with faith, and his whole later life shows how transforming this faith was for him and the world about him.

Second, he *proclaimed* this revelation to others, first to the Jews and later to the Gentiles (Acts 9:20; passim). He did so, like the other apostles, as a *witness* to God in testifying that God raised Jesus from the dead (1 Cor 15:15) and from Christ's commission given him (1 Thess 2:4; Gal 1:16) as an ambassador for Christ (2 Cor 5:20). He proclaimed the gospel or good news or the word of God (1 Thess 1:5; 2:13) as a *mystery*. The gospel is not "a wisdom of this age" but rather "God's wisdom, mysterious, hidden, which God predetermined before the ages for our glory . . . this God revealed to us through the Spirit" (1 Cor 2:6-7, 10).[66] In fact, it is a scandal to the wisdom of this age, because God has chosen to save us through "Christ crucified, a stumbling block to Jews and foolishness to Gentiles" (1 Cor 1:23). We note once more that though Paul emphasized the cross of Christ as the preeminent sign of God's love for us (Rom 8:32) and because it was such a stumbling block, the center of his proclamation was that the ultimate, and so apocalyptic, expectation of the Jews was being offered by God through the exalted Jesus Christ and the Spirit to those who believe.

Third, he proclaimed it so that others might hear and believe and be saved (Romans 10), because it is through believing in the authentic message that they are saved (1 Cor 15:1-2). This faith is possible to all only through the Holy Spirit (Romans 8; 1 Cor 2:11-16). Paul's

---

[65]Paul uses the words *apocalypsis* and *apocalypto* in Galatians 1:12, 16. See Colin Brown, "Revelation," *The New International Dictionary of the New Testament*, ed. Colin Brown (Grand Rapids: Zondervan, 1978) 3:306–40; J. Guillet, "Révélation. - II. Nouveau Testament," *Supplément au Dictionnaire de la Bible* 10:600–18; and R. Latourelle, *Theology of Revelation* (New York: Alba House, 1966) 59–86, on revelation in Paul, Hebrews, and John; see also Latourelle, "Revelation," *DFT,* especially pages 912–7.

[66]On this notion of "mystery" and its roots in the Old Testament and Jewish apocalyptic writings, see J. Fitzmyer, "Pauline Theology," *NJBC,* 1389.

emphasis on faith is frequently within the context of the problem posed by the Judaizers, namely their view that Gentiles could not be saved unless they accepted the Jewish Law. Against this Paul taught again and again that it is through faith that one is saved (e.g., Rom 1:16-17). But he also proclaimed this message in other contexts. For example, he proclaimed it to Jews as the fulfillment of God's promises to their ancestors (Acts 13:16-43) and to Gentiles in dialogue with them as those who had previously received God's care and his self-manifestation through nature and conscience (Acts 17:22-31; Rom 1:19-20; 2:14-15).[67] Revelation through Jesus Christ is not God's first revelation, and it does not contradict his earlier revelations but fulfills them. Paul appeals to people to believe on the basis of his witness to Jesus' resurrection and on the basis of his hearers' acceptance of the earlier revelations God has given them.

We note that Paul asserts that he received revelations in the course of his ministry through visions (2 Cor 12:1-4) and for the purpose of guidance (Gal 2:2), and that the gifts of the Spirit given to Christians are "manifestations" (*phanerōsis;* 1 Cor 12:7) of the Spirit. Reception of revelations through the Spirit was not unusual in the early Church (see, e.g., Acts 21:10-11; 1 Cor 14:26, 30), though these were not at all confused with the foundational revelation that came through Christ's public life, death, and resurrection. They were to be discerned by the Christian community and accepted only if they were in accord with the Christian belief (1 Cor 12:1-3; 14:29). Paul called Christians to grow in faith as in love. There were profound depths to the Christian mystery into which they were to grow (1 Cor 2:6–3:3; 2 Cor 3:18; see also Eph 1:17-23). Paul himself burst into praise at the depth of the wisdom of God shown in his designs through Christ: "Oh, the depth of the riches and wisdom and knowledge of God! How inscrutable are his judgments and how unsearchable his ways!" (Rom 11:33). The full revelation to which we look forward with great longing is that which is to come when Christ comes again and when faith gives way to vision (1 Thess 4:16-17; Rom 8:23-24; 1 Cor 13:8-12).

If we look to Colossians and Ephesians, we find a somewhat different emphasis from the generally accepted Pauline epistles, though some have overstressed this difference. There is reason to think that the error Paul (or the author) was addressing in Colossians was a form of Jewish apocalypticism, as Thomas Sappington argues. For

[67]See Farrelly, *Belief in God,* 101–12.

example, Sappington points out the similarity in vocabulary between this epistle and some Jewish apocalyptic writings. The author of the epistle stresses his concern that his addressees "have all the richness of fully assured understanding, for the knowledge of the mystery of God, Jesus, in whom are hidden all the treasures of wisdom and knowledge" (Col 2:2-3). Sappington points out that 2 Baruch writes of "the treasures of wisdom" and that "such a phrase is rare in Greek, hellenistic-Jewish and early Christian sources. Yet concepts which would give rise to such a phrase pervade the thought-world of Jewish apocalypticism."[68] Sappington emphasizes the Semitic background of the author's use of the word "mystery," for example, in Colossians 1:26-27, "the mystery hidden from ages and from generations past. But now it has been manifested to his holy ones . . . Christ in you [Gentiles], the hope for glory."[69] "Mystery" is a word used extensively in Jewish apocalyptic literature.

The author sought to correct the Christians at Colossae who, misled by Jewish apocalypticism, sought wisdom from media and asceticism to which such apocalypticism ascribed it. He emphasized that in Jesus all the treasures of God's wisdom are found; this wisdom does not need the supplement that the purveyors of error at Colossae propagated. To bring his message home to these Christians, the author used and adapted a hymn to Christ as the preexistent wisdom of God: "He is the image of the invisible God, the firstborn of all creation. For in him were created all things in heaven and on earth, the visible and the invisible, . . . in him all the fullness was pleased to dwell" (Col 1:15-16, 19).

This concentration on the preexistence of Christ as the wisdom of God descending to earth has led a number of exegetes to ascribe to Colossians and Ephesians a "realized eschatology." But it is one thing to say that a *revelation* that is superior to all others and is sufficient has already been fulfilled in Jesus; it is another to say that *salvation* is located in the Jesus of the public ministry or the resurrection as a past event. Salvation is still future for these epistles (see, e.g., Col 3:4, 24; Eph 1:13-14, 21; 2:7; 3:6), even though its blessings have already been given in part: "Christians at Colossae have been qualified to receive their inheritance through faith in Christ, and this blessed state exists even now in the heavenly realms. Yet they must wait to

---

[68]Sappington, *Revelation and Redemption,* 178.

[69]Ibid., 184.

receive their inheritance at the revelation of their glory, when their participation in Christ's victory over the powers will be realized."[70] There is nothing in Colossians or Ephesians counter to what we have seen, namely that the Father offers salvation now to Christians through Jesus, who has gone before us into the kingdom through his death, resurrection, and glorification and through the Spirit. Also, insofar as revelation occurs now when Christians come to faith and more deeply understand the mystery, it is this glorified Christ and his Spirit who is communicating with them. And it is to the future communion with Jesus that they are oriented, because only there is their communion with him and knowledge of him complete.

2. Epistle to the Hebrews

The author of the Epistle to the Hebrews may have been a Hellenistic Jewish Christian influenced by middle Platonism, as is shown by his emphasis on the earthly as an image of the heavenly. And he may have been encouraging a community of Jewish Christians tempted to return to Judaism because of the grandeur of Jewish institutions. He seeks to prevent such a failure by showing how superior the Christian dispensation is when compared to the Jewish. Among the elements he compares is that of revelation: "In times past, God spoke in partial and various ways to our ancestors through the prophets; in these last days, he spoke to us through a son, whom he made heir of all things and through whom he created the universe" (Heb 1:1-2).

There is continuity and contrast between these dispensations, continuity because *God spoke* in both, contrast because in the past his revelation was partial and fragmentary and through prophets and angels (2:2), while in these last days he has spoken to us through his Son, a name "'inherited' by Jesus at his exaltation"[71] though he was preexistent as Son. Jesus is made the leader for our salvation through his suffering, death, resurrection, and exaltation (2:9-10; 8:4). As glorified, he had entered the holy of holies and intercedes for us (8:1-2). If we have a revelation superior to that of the past, there is a greater exigency that we listen to it, believe it, and obey it, lest we fall under the judgment of God (2:1-3).

---

[70]Ibid., 227–8.

[71]Myles Bourke, "The Epistle to the Hebrews," *NJBC*, 923.

What is this faith? "Faith is the realization of what is hoped for and evidence of things not seen" (11:1). It allows us to realize what is not seen; it is the realization of what constitutes true reality and is proof of such reality.[72] The author's examples of the many witnesses to faith in the Jewish past (11:4-38) show that the heroes of faith lived by what God had promised but they did not see, and so they were pleasing to God and gained his promises. Similarly, he exhorts his addressees to accept the suffering that is their lot: "For here we have no lasting city, but we seek the one that is to come" (13:13).

3. Johannine Writings

First, it is important to realize that historically the message of the Gospel of John was generated by the appearances of the risen Christ and the coming of the Spirit, as was the existence and message of the primitive Church. The very marked development of this initial faith of the Church found in John's Gospel is examined by recent exegetes within the context of the Johannine community.[73] The Gospel comes from this community in its stage of development toward the end of the first century. Christology was a central issue for its identity. This community found that certain titles ascribed to Jesus such as that of Messiah were not adequate, and it was opposed to those Christians who concealed their belief in Jesus for fear of expulsion from the synagogue; it affirmed the preexistence and divinity of the Word (John 1:1) who became flesh in Jesus (1:14); thus it distinguished its belief also from gnosticizing elements and affirmed its unity with the community shepherded by Peter (John 21:15-19).

Though exegetes have speculated on different possible backgrounds for John's Gospel (e.g., the philosophy of the period, pagan religious cults, hermetic writings, early Gnosticism), the Jewish Wisdom tradition and the Dead Sea scrolls show parallels to some characteristic Johannine themes such as the preexistence of Wisdom, who comes to human beings, and a kind of moral dualism between light and darkness, the heavenly and the earthly, which help to explain the Gospel's scheme without accounting for its identification of God's revelation with Jesus.

---

[72]Ibid., 940.

[73]See Pheme Perkins, "The Gospel According to John," *NJBC,* 945–6; Francis Maloney, "Johannine Theology," *NJBC,* 1418–9.

Second, so much of the thrust of the Gospel seems to differ from the belief of the primitive Church. This difference is characterized by some exegetes as the difference between a consistent eschatology and a realized eschatology. While the Christian community initially looked for the salvific moment to come with the return of Jesus at the parousia, John's Gospel seems to push this back to the incarnation by its emphasis on the preexistent Word who "became flesh and made his dwelling among us, and we saw his glory, the glory as of the Father's only Son, full of grace and truth" (1:14). For the Beloved Disciple, the "Word" designates not only what Jesus says and does but Jesus himself. Whatever revelation there was in the past—and there was such because the true light enlightens everyone and God gave the Law through Moses (1:9, 17)—finds its completion in Jesus, through whom we receive grace and truth and the power to become children of God (1:12, 17): "No one has ever seen God. The only Son, God, who is at the Father's side, has revealed him" (1:18).

Jesus' life is the revelation of God and particularly of God's love for the world: "God so loved the world that he gave his only Son, so that everyone who believes in him might not perish but might have eternal life" (John 3:16; see 1 John 4:9). "God is love" (1 John 4:16). Jesus reveals this through signs *(semeia),* such as the miracle of Cana and the raising of Lazarus, that have sacramental value—showing symbolically how God gives life and salvation through Jesus—and that are the Father's testimony to Jesus (5:36-37; 8:18; 9:30-33; 11:25). Above all, Jesus reveals the Father's love through his own suffering and death, where he brings to perfection what his Father had sent him to do (John 17:4; 19:30). As Paul stressed the scandal of the cross, so John stresses that it is on the cross that Jesus is glorified (12:32); what initially was a scandal to the apostles themselves is now proclaimed as the ultimate sign of God's love for us and of Jesus' love for the Father. God's revelation, then, has occurred through Jesus. Those who accept Jesus already have eternal life (John 6:47), and the one who does not accept Jesus has already been judged (John 3:18; 12:31).

It would be improper to characterize John's Gospel as fully realized eschatology. We must distinguish between salvation and revelation. Revelation in John's Gospel is ascribed to the eternal Word of God become flesh in Jesus. As Francis Maloney expresses it:

> John built bridges out of the Judaism of its birth into the new world of Hellenistic syncretism. . . .

> Given . . . the dualistic presentation of God and "the world," of
> "above" and "below," such a mission involves the descent of the
> revealer from above (3:13) and his subsequent ascent to where he
> was before (6:62; 17:5; 20:17). The Johannine Jesus comes from
> the Father, reveals him in a unique way as his Son, and returns to
> the Father, to have again the glory that was his before the world
> was made.[74]

However, the moment of salvation continues in John's Gospel to reflect the early Christian apocalypticism. Jesus will raise those who
believe in him on the last day (6:39), and those who reject him will
be condemned on the last day (12:48). Moreover, salvation is
through the gift of the Spirit, and that gift comes only through the
death, resurrection, and exaltation of Jesus from the age to come (see
John 7:39; 20:22). Salvation and judgment as occurring in the present are not unrelated to this future apocalyptic event but are rather
anticipations and participations in it, as we found in Paul. John's
stress on the importance of the present time of decision is not for the
purpose of diminishing the reality or centrality of the future Day of
the Lord, but to show that that day already is in part present.
Moreover, the community to which John's Gospel was addressed
lived toward the end of the first century:

> The Johannine community, at the end of the 1st century, could not
> "look upon" and "hear" the historical Jesus. They were living in an-
> other stage—the stage of the Holy Spirit, an outflow of living water
> that would be received by those who believed in Jesus, but only
> after he had been glorified (7:39). . . . The Johannine community
> experienced the revelation of the Father through the action of the
> Spirit, not through direct contact with Jesus himself. However, it
> is still the story of Jesus telling the story of God that they are to
> hear, since the Paraclete does not bring a new revelation.[75]

The glorified Jesus is present to the addressees and speaks to them
through the Spirit, who recalls to them everything that Jesus did and
said (14:18, 26; 16:13-15).

---

[74]Maloney, "Johannine Theology," 1422.

[75]Ibid., 1424–5.

Third, it is through faith in Jesus and in his words that we have eternal life and are children of God (1:12; 6:24) and are released from blindness so that we might see (9:39-41). The lives of followers of Jesus are a paradox, like that of their Master; but we look forward to the fulfillment of his promises: "We are God's children now; what we shall be has not yet been revealed. We do know that when it is revealed we shall be like him, for we shall see him as he is" (1 John 3:2).

We conclude by reaffirming that there is every reason to continue faithful to that long line of Christians that goes back to the year 30, when Jesus in all probability died, in the faith and life of faith they lived on the basis of the appearances of the risen Jesus to chosen witnesses, the coming of the Holy Spirit upon the whole body of Jesus' first disciples, and their testimony to his appearances in the power of the Spirit. And there is reason to interpret the salvation and revelation mediated by these central events in history in their relation to the expected parousia of Jesus Christ shown in the early Christian canonical writings.

6

Soundings in Christian History
on the Understanding of Revelation,
Faith, and Salvation

We now turn to examine some representative interpretations of revelation, faith, and salvation, or the kingdom of God, through the ages of Christian history. This study presents rich resources for our understanding of these themes today, for there has been here as in other areas of Christian belief a development of doctrine, though at times a loss as well. Also, this helps us to understand better the emergence of the contemporary state of the question in this area of Christian belief and theology. For example, it helps us account for the fact that many Christian theologians have developed mutually opposed interpretations of revelation, faith, and the kingdom of God. And it shows us some of the reasons for the erosion in our age of Christian belief in God's revelation and salvation as this is presented in Scripture. What follows is no more than an introductory analysis, but we will indicate where the themes we treat may be studied at greater length and depth. We shall ask (I) how the patristic age interpreted these themes in the Greco-Roman culture, (II) how these themes were viewed in the High Middle Ages and the Reformation period, and (III) how the turbulent reflection on these themes developed from the Enlightenment to the early twentieth century. We presuppose here what we treated in volume one on the development of Christian reflection on belief in God during these periods, though what we say here can be understood independently of our treatment in the earlier volume.

I. The Patristic Period

In our earlier volume we showed how the early Fathers were in dialogue with Roman and Hellenistic polytheism and official cult, with Jews, with Gnostics, and with middle Platonism; how they used middle Platonism as an ally in defending belief in God; and yet how they transcended it. They believed that God had revealed himself in part through the logos to all humanity but that he had fulfilled this revelation through the Logos incarnate. Here we shall primarily dwell on their teaching on this latter revelation but also recall their teaching on salvation. We shall say something of these themes first in selected authors and liturgical documents through the third century, and then, after an aside on Eusebius of Caesarea's understanding of the kingdom, in Augustine.

1. Some Selected Witnesses Through the Third Century

We are not here discussing adequately the reasons for which the great majority of people became Christian but rather the way certain representative writers reflected on this belief and articulated it. Perhaps many people, particularly women and slaves, became Christian in large part because their human dignity was acknowledged in Christianity more than in their own culture.[1] We will treat consecutively Ignatius of Antioch as a representative of the Apostolic Fathers, Justin and Irenaeus as representatives of Apologists, Origen as representative of the Alexandrian school, and some fragments from the early liturgy pointing to the apocalyptic meaning of the kingdom that the liturgy preserved.[2]

---

[1]For a larger, social study of the encounter of Christianity with Greco-Roman culture, see, for example, Wayne Meeks, *The First Urban Christians: The Social World of the Apostle Paul* (New Haven, Conn.: Yale University Press, 1983); John Gager, *Kingdom and Community: The Social World of Early Christianity* (Englewood Cliffs, N.J.: Prentice Hall, 1975); Karl Baus, *From the Apostolic Community to Constantine,* vol. 1, *History of the Church,* ed. Hubert Jedin (New York: Crossroad, 1980); Robin Lane Fox, *Pagans and Christians* (New York: Alfred Knopf, 1987).

[2]For treatment of the theme of revelation among the Fathers, see particularly René Latourelle, *Theology of Revelation* (New York: Alba House, 1966), which I have used extensively; idem, "The Theme of Revelation in the Fathers of the Church," *DFT* 917–23; Jaroslav Pelikan, *The Christian Tradition: A History of the Development of Doctrine,* vol. 1, *The Emergence of the Catholic Tradition (100–600)* (Chicago: University of Chicago Press, 1971); M. John Farrelly, *Belief in God in Our Time* (Collegeville: The Liturgical Press, 1992) 114–27. On the theme of the kingdom or salvation, see Everett Ferguson, "The Kingdom of God in Early Patristic Literature," *The Kingdom of God in 20th Century Interpretation,* ed. Wendell Willis (Peabody, Mass.: Hendrickson, 1987)

Ignatius of Antioch (d. 107) understood that God did manifest himself by the creation of the world and through the prophets of the Old Testament who announced the gospel to come. But the full revelation of God comes through Christ: "There is only one God who manifests himself through Jesus Christ his Son, who is his Word come out of silence" (Ign. *Magn.* 8:2). Christ is the "undying mouth through which the Father has spoken in truth" (Ign. *Rom.* 8:2) and the "gate to the Father" (Ign. *Phld.* 9:1). Jesus offers us the whole of revelation and salvation. This salvation, in continuity with Paul, has a future character: Ignatius speaks of the kingdom of God as something one will inherit or not inherit (see Ign. *Eph.* 16:1). But with John, he speaks too of the kingdom as eternal life already given in part: "The old kingdom was destroyed, for God was manifest as man for the newness of eternal life" (Ign. *Eph.* 9:3). When he was facing his own martyrdom, Ignatius welcomed it as leading to union with Jesus. Ignatius' expression of these themes is close to the ways that Paul and John expressed them.

The Apologists presented Christian revelation as the fulfillment not only of the Old Testament but of Greek philosophy. The key here is that Jesus Christ is the Logos; Platonic and Stoic philosophies had explained the order existing in the world by logos, whether this is immanent in the world or is the reasoning of God, who shapes the world. Justin Martyr (d. ca. 165), for example, related the Logos in John's prologue to the theme of logos as the reason behind order in the world. God had his Logos before creation but conceived his Logos as Son to be his agent in the creation and organization of the cosmos (2 *Apol.* 8:1; 12:51). Through him God continues to speak. In all human beings there is "a seed of the Logos" (2 *Apol.* 13:5), which permits them to come to a partial knowledge of the truth and expression of it. Thus the pagan philosophers were able to conceive some rays of truth (1 *Apol.* 46:2-3). The Logos' revelation is seen better in Moses and the prophets: "Jesus is the one who appeared and spoke to Moses, Abraham, and, in a word, to all the patriarchs" (*Dial.* 113:4). But it is only Christians who live "according to the entire knowledge and contemplation of the Logos who is Christ" (2 *Apol.*

191–208; Brian Daley, *The Hope of the Early Church: A Handbook of Patristic Eschatology* (New York: Cambridge University Press, 1991); Benedict Viviano, "The Kingdom of God in the Church Fathers," *The Kingdom of God in History* (Wilmington, Del.: Michael Glazier, 1988) 30–56; Geoffrey Wainwright, *Eucharist and Eschatology* (New York: Oxford University Press, 1981). I refer in the text to writings of the Fathers by the usual abbreviations.

8:3). "We have the whole Logos in Christ who has appeared to us, body, Logos, soul" (*Apol.* 10:1-3).

Irenaeus (d. ca. 202) defended Christianity against the Gnostics, who claimed a special esoteric knowledge and opposed the New Testament to the Old. Against them, Irenaeus taught that "[n]o one can know the Father except the Word of God, that is, unless the Son reveals him" (*Adv. Haer.* 4:6, 3). Revelation is an epiphany of the Father through the Word made visible in Jesus Christ: "Through the Word, become visible and palpable, the Father also appears" (*Adv. Haer.* 4:6, 6). The Son had revealed the Father from the beginning, but this revelation has taken place progressively, as the Father in his goodness educates human beings through stages. Creation is the first stage: "Through creation itself, the Word reveals God the Creator; through the world, it reveals the Creator as builder of the world; through its work, it reveals the workman; through the Son, it reveals the Father" (*Adv. Haer.* 4:6, 6). Then, "Through the Law and prophets as well, the Word proclaimed himself and proclaimed his Father" (loc. cit.). The Old and New Testaments are part of one economy of salvation. But the Old is preparatory for the New, as "servants who are sent before the king announce his coming, so that his subjects will be prepared" (*Adv. Haer.* 4:34, 1). Revelation finds a new stage and its completion in Jesus Christ, who recapitulates all things in himself. This revelation is a work of God's love and grace; it is a work of salvation for sinful humanity. For those who do not believe, it is judgment; for those who do believe, it brings salvation and life: "It is impossible to live, if we do not have life; we possess life only by sharing in God; now sharing in God means seeing God and enjoying his goodness. Men will see God in order to live, becoming immortal through this vision and arriving at the very presence of God. . . . For the glory of God is man alive, and the life of man is the vision of God" (*Adv. Haer.* 4:20, 5–6, 7). Of this message, which both unveils God and leaves God veiled until we see him face to face, Irenaeus states that "the prophets announced it, Christ established it, the apostles handed it down, the Church offers it to her children" (*Dem.* 98). We see that it is the incarnation of the Word, or Son of God, by which the invisible descends to us and leads to our ascent to God through being educated by the Word. Though he primarily emphasized the role of the Son of God, Irenaeus shows different ways in which the Spirit acts in the economy of salvation and writes of God acting through the Son and the Spirit as his two hands, or ministers (see *Adv. Haer.,* pref. 4; 4:7, 4).

What is the understanding of salvation, or the kingdom of God, in the second century? Everett Ferguson notes a number of the earliest noncanonical Christian documents (*Epistle of Barnabas, Pastor of Hermes*, the *Didache*, Papias) that preserve a duality between present and future and interpret the kingdom futuristically:[3]

> Apart from the Gnostics . . . , the interpretation of the kingdom as an interior, present possession hardly occurs before Origen. . . . [T]he overwhelming usage of "kingdom" in second-century Christian literature is eschatological. . . . The kingdom for second-century authors is almost uniformly future . . . , heavenly . . . , and eternal. . . . For several writers in the second century the future kingdom will be earthly and millennial: Cerinthus . . . , Papias . . . , Justin . . . , Irenaeus . . . , and others.[4]

Apologists were sensitive to possible misunderstandings in their talk of "kingdom," and they contrasted earthly kingdoms and the kingdom of God. But we see from their futuristic interpretations of the kingdom a continuing influence of early apocalyptic. An example of such an interpretation is found in Justin's *Dialogue with Trypho, a Jew*: "I, and all other entirely orthodox Christians, know that there will be a resurrection of the flesh for a period of a thousand years in a rebuilt Jerusalem, adorned and enlarged, as the prophets Ezekiel and Isaiah, and others affirm" (*Dial.* 80:4).

If we look briefly to Alexandria in the third century, we see the interpretation of revelation through the descent of the Logos and that of salvation as the transforming knowledge that faith and later vision give us. Clement of Alexandria (d. 215) understood the Logos as designed by nature to reveal the Father; this Logos reveals for the purpose of saving humanity, and he does so in stages that progress from the Mosaic Law to Jesus but also uses the philosophy of the Greeks that was given to them "to tune their ears for the kerygma" (*Str.* 4:44, 1). Christianity is superior to what has preceded it, either in the Law or in the Greeks, as the sun is superior in light to the stars of the night: "Let us receive the light and let us become disciples of the Lord"

---

[3]Also, see Viviano, *Kingdom of God in History,* 34–5, and Robert Grant's list of Christian believers in the millennium in the second and third centuries in his comments on Daley's book, cited above, in *Journal of Religion* 73 (1993) 86.

[4]Ferguson, "Kingdom of God in Early Patristic Literature," 199–200.

(*Prot.* 113:4). If we receive this revelation in faith and grow in this faith, we have the true gnosis. "Clement conceives of the order of salvation as a passing from darkness to faith, and from faith to gnosis."[5]

Origen (d. ca. 251) also interpreted revelation as coming through the Logos. God is unknowable to us, but he comes close to us only through Jesus Christ and his Spirit: "The Word was made flesh in order to dwell among us, and we can begin to understand him only in this way" (*Com. Jo.* 1:18). Jesus is sign and image of the invisible and spiritual Father. He teaches us "through his example and teachings" (*De Princ.* 4:4, 5). He comes to us for our salvation, and those who believe that he is "Truth itself, do not look for the knowledge of virtue and happiness anywhere but in the words and doctrine of Christ" (*De Princ.,* pref., 1).

Against Marcion, Origen taught the unity of the Old and New Testaments. Christ spoke to Moses and the prophets, though partially, and there was progression from the one Testament to the other. After his ascension Christ continues to speak through the apostles; he is present only through the Church. The gospel itself must be understood in the Spirit; only grace allows us to understand and grasp the meaning of the mysteries (*Com. Jo.* 20:18). Belief depends on our docility: "Christ sends his light into our minds, but the illumination will not take place if our blindness presents an obstacle" (*Hom. Gen.* 1:7). The gospel is an image of the eternal gospel; it will lead those who believe and are purified to vision. "What we now have only a foretaste of, in faith and hope, we shall then [at the parousia] grasp effectively in its substance" (*Hom. Jos.* 8:4). The theme we find in Clement and Origen of revelation for the salvation of sinful humanity through the Logos, the light of the world, brought to its culmination in the incarnation and looking forward to vision, is found also and developed further in Athanasius and the Cappadocians.[6]

The implications Origen and others drew from this for the meaning of salvation are significant. Pelikan notes that "by far the most widespread understanding of salvation in the church Catholic of the second and third centuries [was] salvation from death and the attainment of everlasting life," and he notes that "the definition of salvation as revelation and the definition of it as forgiveness were repeatedly

---

[5]Latourelle, *Theology of Revelation,* 112.

[6]See ibid., 121–32; Jaroslav Pelikan, *The Light of the World: A Basic Image in Early Christian Thought* (New York: Harper & Brothers, 1962).

linked."[7] We have shown that the main Christian writers of the second century preserved a sense of the future meaning of the kingdom. But Origen spiritualized the kingdom of God, and many later theologians who rejected some of his views largely followed his view of the kingdom. Origen writes:

> It is evident that he who prays that the kingdom should come prays with good reason that the kingdom of God should spring up and bear fruit and be perfected in him. For every saint who takes God as his king and obeys the spiritual laws of God dwells in himself as in a well-ordered city, so to speak. Present with him are the Father and Christ who reigns with the Father in the soul that has been perfected (*On Prayer,* 25).

Origen largely lost the apocalyptic understanding of the kingdom, even though he did accept the second coming of Jesus and a significance of this for our fulfillment. More influenced by Platonism than he was aware, Origen attempted "to demythologize the accepted apocalyptic tradition of the Scriptures and popular Christian belief." He was opposed to the millenarian interpretation of the Apocalypse, and he found that the most important part of the "future" was what it could tell us "in a symbolic way, about the individual Christian's growth toward salvation."[8]

We cannot but agree that Christ comes to us now and not simply at his second coming, but the question is whether Origen sees Christ's present coming as simply the relation of transcendence to immanence or mainly, as Paul did, of his future advent, in part anticipated in the present. Everett Ferguson writes:

> Origen marks the change in Christian usage of "kingdom" to the interior meaning of the rule of God in the heart. . . . In the deepest sense what Origen meant by the kingdom of God was the rule of the divine Spirit in the world of spirits. . . . Accompanying the interiorization of the kingdom was a change in emphasis from a general eschatology to an individual eschatology, also evident in Gnosticism. Origen achieved a synthesis of the present and the future, the dynamic and static features of the kingdom, but he did so

[7]Pelikan, *Emergence of the Catholic Tradition,* 153.

[8]Daley, *Hope of the Early Church,* 48–9.

in the framework of a philosophy and world view quite different from the thought world of Jesus and the early Church.[9]

Origen interpreted the kingdom within a Platonic and nascent Neoplatonic philosophy. Joseph Trigg notes that Origen recognized that "simple acceptance of this [Christian] rule of faith did not go very far toward meeting the intellectual and spiritual needs of his time. That rule of faith, in order to meet those needs, would have to be explained in terms of a larger world view; otherwise it would remain for the learned an irrelevant formula."[10] In his culture the basic dichotomy for the religious searcher was between the sphere of divinity or incorruptibility and that of matter and the corruptible. A large problem was both how the former could communicate with the latter and how the latter could be liberated from matter and corruptibility. The doctrine of Christ as Logos incarnate and of that salvation as deification, making us children of God by adoption, which comes through illumination, faith, and purification, was an answer to this cultural problem that could be understood and found very inviting.

We should note that a sense of the kingdom more in continuity with the early Church's apocalyptic interpretation seems to have been preserved in elements of the Liturgy of the Eucharist. Evidence for this is brought out well by Geoffrey Wainwright's *Eucharist and Eschatology,* in which he examines the eschatological significance of the Eucharist in both Scripture and the patristic Church. Through the symbols and words of the Eucharist, the liturgy expresses that what Christ will give us when he returns he is already giving us in part now. For example, in discussing the fourth petition of the Our Father, Wainwright writes: "Where . . . the Fathers reckon with 'bread of the coming day' as a possible meaning of *epiousios,* they usually see it as giving the fourth petition an eschatological significance: 'Give us already now the bread of the future age.' What is more, the same Fathers usually, though not always, make a eucharistic application of the petition of these lines of 'bread of the future age.'"[11] Similarly, "Sometimes the eucharist is pictured as Christ's banquet, at which

---

[9]Ferguson, "Kingdom of God in Early Patristic Literature," 198–9.

[10]Joseph Trigg, *Origen: The Bible and Philosophy in the Third-Century Church* (Atlanta: John Knox, 1983) 131–2.

[11]Wainwright, *Eucharist and Eschatology,* 32. See the texts he gathers concerning the bread and the cup.

He is present not only as food and drink . . . but also as host or participant in the meal."[12]

If we ask what the relation is between Christ's coming at the Eucharist and his final coming, Wainwright concludes from the examination of three liturgies (*Testimonium Domini, Apostolic Constitutions* 7, and the Byzantine liturgy of St. John Chrysostom) that "the *Benedictus qui venit* found its place in the eucharistic liturgies for the good reason that it can suggest, in a usefully ambiguous way, the present coming of the one who has come and is to come. To this extent it may be considered the legitimate replacement of *Maranatha*."[13] Wainwright therefore expresses the relation between the final advent of Christ and his coming in the Eucharist as a "projection" in two senses: "Christ's coming at the eucharist is a projection in the temporal sense that it is a 'throwing forward' of Christ's final advent into the present. . . . [Also] Christ's coming at the eucharist is a projection of his final advent. . . . [I]t is a presentation of a large reality by means of a set of comprehensible symbols."[14] The liturgy then preserved central elements of the early apocalyptic understanding of salvation and its impact on the present that much of patristic theology, in its necessary effort to relate the Christian message to Greco-Roman culture, seems to have lost.

Before turning to Augustine, we should note another interpretation of the kingdom of God. There was in the fourth century one who, perhaps out of amazement that the emperor who had persecuted the Church now embraced it, gave a certain primacy to the state by describing the emperor in a way that almost confused him with the Son of Man in Daniel, suggesting that he was the image of God and that he exercised the sovereignty of God on earth, thus unconsciously supporting the later Caesaro-papism of the Eastern Church. This was Eusebius of Caesarea.[15] Later conflicts between Church and state in the West also harked back to the contrasting models of Augustine and Eusebius.

---

[12]Ibid., 51.

[13]Ibid., 71–2.

[14]Ibid., 92.

[15]See Viviano, *Kingdom of God in History*, 45–51.

2. Augustine's Understanding of Revelation and the Kingdom

We treat Augustine's understanding of these themes because he was as important for the Western tradition as Origen was for the Eastern tradition. His own conversion experience, the aid he found in Neoplatonism for this radical change in his life, and the break his conversion enabled him to make from his earlier self-indulgent life influenced his understanding of these realities. For his interpretation of revelation Augustine draws particularly from John's Gospel. While he recognizes that God manifests himself in the created world (*De Util. Cred.* 10:24) and that God spoke through Moses and the prophets, it is the Son, the "Wisdom begotten from the Father," who reveals to us the "secrets of the Father" (*De Fide et Symb.* 3:3). What is revealed is primarily "the history and prophecy of the way in which Divine Providence will realize in time the salvation of the human race, restoring and renewing it for everlasting life" (*De Vera Rel.* 7:13).

In the economy of the incarnation Jesus teaches us by action as well as by word, and he reveals not only himself but the Father. Christ "came above all to teach men how much God loves them and to make them realize that their heart should burn with love for God who has loved them first" (*De Cat. Rud.* 4:8). There is a double dimension to this revelation, both external and internal. Jesus had said: "No one can come to me, unless my Father draw him" (John 6:44); and "Whoever has heard the Father and learned from him, comes to me" (John 6:45). Augustine understands this coming to Jesus as our experiencing an attraction from the Father and believing; this is a gift of grace. The Father's teaching is an interior teaching or illumination, and the hearing is an interior response or belief (see *Tract. in Jo.* 26:5; 26:8; 106:6). As Avery Dulles comments, "Augustine's theology of revelation is closely bound up with his doctrine of illumination, which centers about God as the light of truth. . . . [H]e uses the term 'revelation' not so much for the external communication of the gospel as for the inner light by which men are enabled to believe it. In a famous text, Augustine says [as a] . . . preacher . . . 'Unless he who dwells within reveals, to what purpose do I speak?'"[16]

---

[16] Avery Dulles, *Revelation Theology* (New York: Herder & Herder, 1969) 37. The included quotation from Augustine is from his *Tract. in John* 26:7. Latourelle notes, "The council of Orange, expressing itself according to the views of Augustine, will say that no one can cling to the teaching of the Gospel and posit a salutary act, without 'an illumination and inspiration of the Holy Spirit, which gives to all men the sweetness of belonging and believing in the truth'" (Latourelle, *Theology of Revelation,* 140).

The apostles were witnesses of Christ and received from him the mission to preach to the whole human race; thus their words are the word of God and we must believe them (see *Tract. in Jo.* 109:5). If we wish the truth, Augustine advises us to follow "the Catholic rule which, from Christ in person, through the apostles, has come down even to us and from us will pass on to our posterity" (*De Util. Cred.* 8:20). Our response of faith, if allied with charity, will lead to vision.

If we ask what Augustine's understanding of the kingdom or salvation is, we can find central elements of an answer by looking first at his *Confessions* and then at *The City of God.* In the first, Augustine offers praise to God for his own conversion. He presents his life in the first nine books as having a circular pattern. Emmet Flood summarizes these books:

> He was born, ignorant of his Origin and Creator. He falls, then wanders like the Jews through a spiritual desert of snares and diversions; he is exiled in a Babylon of verbal unlikeness. Despite all this, God is mercifully at work and through his divine care and the prophetic activity of his mother and friends Augustine returns to Christ, the Word who was in the Beginning, in the act of conversion. . . . In Book IX he is actually baptized. [He recounts the mystical experience he had with his mother.] . . . The rapture of this vision was a fleeting participation in the life of Eternal wisdom itself, a momentary elevation to a plane beyond time and language."[17]

Augustine sees his life as distended in time:

> [C]onstantly beset by temptations, and insofar as he succumbs to the objects of his perverse desire, he tends to dissolve himself into randomness and chaos. He is, as he says, "distracted amid times whose order I do not know" (*Conf.* XI, 29). This inclination to fragment himself is latent in his very temporality and exploited by the desires that infect that distended condition. At the same time, however, Augustine, though temporal, is a man made in the image and likeness of God. . . . [T]here is always within him that divine spark goading, or trying to goad him toward ever greater unity with God. This charitable spark cannot abolish temporality *per se*

---

[17]Emmet Flood, "The Narrative Structure of Augustine's *Confessions:* Time's Quest for Eternity," *International Philosophical Quarterly* 28 (1988) 151–2.

but can redeem it from its centrifugal direction. As it does so, Augustine's temporal life more closely approximates the perfection of eternity, the mode of duration proper to God.[18]

Augustine sees time not primarily as linear but as a distended image of eternity; he interprets salvation as God's freeing him from the distention that comes from sin and even temporality and giving him a share in God's own being and eternity through the incarnate Word. His own literary activity by which he constructed the *Confessions* he sees as an act of imagination giving unity to distended events by language that is distended, somewhat on the model of how God in creation creates the world in time by the Word as an image of his own eternal being.

The relation between time and eternity, between text and author, that we see in the *Confessions* is also present in *The City of God*. In this book, written in response to those who held Christianity to blame for the fall of Rome in 410, Augustine disputes those who see Rome's greatness as due to Rome's honoring of the gods. And he rejects the cyclic view of history—the view that the world "over and over again . . . periodically disintegrates and begins again" (Book XII, 12). "Christ died once for our sins" (Book XII, 14) and dies no more. Moreover, a cyclic view would mean that there was never true beatitude because human beings would always revert to misery.

In this work, in which Augustine tells us of the origin, history, and destiny of the earthly and the heavenly cities, he deals with two societies. The *civitas terrena* designates both the community of earthly minded human beings and the world community in which the city of God exists on earth (Book XV, 2). "The two cities then were created by two kinds of love: the earthly city by a love of self carried even to the point of contempt for God, the heavenly city by a love of God carried even to the point of contempt for self" (Book XIV, 28). The earthly city does seek a good, even peace, but seeks one that does not remain and does so in a way that generally causes division within itself. "But that it should possess this peace meanwhile in this life is important for us, too, since so long as the two cities are intermingled we also profit from the peace of Babylon; and the people of God is by faith so freed from it as meanwhile to be but strangers passing through" (Book XIX, 26).

[18]Ibid., 143–4.

As in his account of his own life, so here Augustine also recognizes stages in the growth of the cities. For the city of God he sees six ages before the seventh age, which will not have an evening, namely eternity. He maps five ages in the Old Testament and sees the sixth age as lasting from the first coming of Christ to his second coming. He identifies the millennium of Revelation 20:1-6 with the age of the Church, this sixth age. And so he identifies the kingdom of God in this world with the Church, though he knows that there are weeds among the wheat and some outside the Church who are saved. Anthony Kemp comments: "These [stages] do not denote development in the modern sense, but abrupt changes in God's dealings with mankind. . . . [A]lthough there is progression of revelation that marks the boundaries between the millennia, within each millennium is essential uniformity, and this present age is the last before the end. There will be nothing new in time, and by this stasis all—divine events and historical events—is made simultaneously far and near."[19]

Augustine's sense of time in *The City of God* is similar to that in the *Confessions* as we briefly described that above. Thus though he speaks of the second coming of Christ, the parousia does not at all fulfill in his scheme what it did in the primitive Church's understanding of salvation. Also, although in the circumstances in which Augustine wrote his book it was appropriate for him to underline the fact that the destruction of Rome is not the ultimate evil, the way he did this seemed to undercut some intrinsic meaning of the earthly city in God's salvific designs. While Augustine put great emphasis on charity for one another as central to Christian life, he did not articulate salvation as implying the Christian's responsibility to humanize the earthly city in accord with its own intrinsic God-given task.

Augustine interpreted salvation much more through the incarnation than through the impact on the present of the age to come already initiated in the resurrection and glorification of Christ. God's saving activity is pictured as coming from transcendence and the past, but not from the future. Much the same is true of his view of revelation. Even though he emphasizes that God in the present illumines and draws people to belief, this activity is modeled on that of creation rather than on the redemptive activity that the glorified Lord and the Spirit whom he sends exercise on the present from the age to come. Augus-

---

[19] Anthony Kemp, *The Estrangement of the Past: A Study in the Origins of Modern Historical Consciousness* (New York: Oxford University Press, 1991) 20, 26.

tine's interpretation of salvation and revelation was marked by the Greco-Roman culture he contested. Anton-Hermann Chroust describes this culture: "The predominant and traditional Greco-Hellenistic ideal of man and his temporal existence within what was considered a closed universe of causal nexi could only maintain itself with reference to an essentially timeless and static present which fully absorbs human existence."[20] Although Augustine rejected the Greek cyclic view of reality and the fatalism that so frequently accompanied it, the primary Hellenistic dichotomy between the transcendent, immutable divinity and the sublunary order of time and mutability presented the context in which he interpreted salvation and revelation.

II. The High Middle Ages and the Reformation

It is important for us to take soundings in these later periods of theology on dominant understandings of revelation, faith, and the kingdom of God, or salvation, because the theologies of these periods affect the state of the question as it exists in our time more immediately than those of the patristic period. Thomas Aquinas' views on these subjects became almost paradigmatic for Catholics for centuries. And Luther's views have been similarly influential for many Protestants. The growth of disbelief in specifically Christian revelation and salvation in the eighteenth and nineteenth centuries developed in part as reactions to these earlier interpretations. What then were some dominant interpretations of these Christian mysteries during these periods? We presuppose here what we have written in our first volume on the interpretations of God and the knowledge of God during these centuries. We will recall some views on these issues first in the High Middle Ages, then in the Reformation period.

1. The Thirteenth Century

This period in the West, and it is only theologies in the West that we are now following, is in part in continuity with the patristic age,

---

[20]Anton-Hermann Chroust, "The Metaphysics of Time and History in Early Christian Thought," *The New Scholasticism* 19 (1945) 329. For a comparison of some aspects of Augustine's view of salvation with the apostolic Church's, see M. John Farrelly, "Trinity as Salvific Mystery," *Monastic Studies* 17 (1986) 81–100.

particularly with Augustine. This is especially the case with the Franciscan school of theology. Bonaventure uses the term "revelation" largely as Augustine did. Latourelle describes Bonaventure's view:

> Revelation is light to the mind. . . . "Reveal" means . . . to *illuminate the mind* on a subject which was darkness, secret, mystery. A second element, essential to the idea of revelation, is the certitude it engenders. . . . What makes the true prophet is the enlightenment he has to understand what is represented. . . . Faith is born of the combined activity of the external word and the internal word, the teaching and preaching which strikes the ear of the body and the teaching of the Holy Spirit who speaks to the heart in secret. . . . This inner illumination which does not show a new object, but enables the mind to grasp this object as it should be, Saint Bonaventure calls, in the words of Scripture, "revelation," "testimony," "inner inspiration."[21]

Bonaventure interpreted revelation and faith, as did Thomas, within the context of Augustine's *exitus-reditus* scheme, starting from the Word who becomes incarnate and enables us by revelation and salvation to share his sonship.

Thomas' theology of revelation, faith, and salvation became the dominant Catholic view in later centuries, and so we shall examine his interpretations in a little more detail, though still summarily. The context in which he presented the Christian message was primarily the university during an age when the Christian West was first aware of all the works of Aristotle. A primary problem for Thomas was how to relate the Christian mystery to the world of "reason" as understood and taught by Aristotle. This affects not only the order of reality known but the ways available to human beings to know, and particularly to know what is central to their own fulfillment, which is found ultimately in communion with God. Thomas writes:

> There is . . . a threefold human knowledge of things pertaining to God. The first is according to man's rising to a knowledge of God through creatures by the natural light of reason. The second occurs as the divine truth, transcending the human mind, descends to us

---

[21]Latourelle, *Theology of Revelation,* 155–8. On this period, see Farrelly, *Belief in God,* 127–34.

through revelation, not as demonstrated to be seen, but offered by word to be believed. The third occurs as the human mind is elevated to the vision of what is perfectly revealed" (*Contra Gentiles,* IV, 1).

Thomas is moving away from identifying revelation with inner illumination to identifying it with knowledge that is beyond human ability to know by the light of natural reason. As Dulles comments, in Thomas there is "an increasing tendency to restrict *revelation* to knowledge of a supernatural character and to employ the term in a more objective sense, corresponding to the content of official Church teaching."[22] Revelation of the supernatural mysteries is necessary because human beings are ordained to a communion with God that is supernatural, and they must know their goal to orient their actions toward it. It is necessary too that religious truths that do not in principle exceed the capacities of the human mind be revealed, because otherwise "the truth about God investigated by reason would come only to a few, through long effort, and admixed with many errors" (*ST* I, 1).

Thomas frequently speaks of the relation between God the revealer and human beings as that between teacher and students; revelation is passively received. Also, God reveals through both the external word and the internal word: "It is not only the exterior revelation or the object [of belief] that has the power of attracting, but also the interior instinct impelling and moving one to believe; therefore the Father draws many to the Son by the instinct of the divine activity moving the heart of man interiorly to believe" (*In Jo.* c. 6, lect. 5). Exterior revelation comes through words but also to the prophets through such things as dreams, symbolic actions, visions, and ecstatic experiences, and to us through Christ's visible presence, example, actions, passion, and resurrection (see *ST* II–II, 171–8). What is offered us by God through revelation is offered for our acceptance not on the basis of the natural light of our reason, though it is not opposed to reason, but on the authority of God who reveals. To testify to the fact that he is revealing, God gives us external signs such as miracles and prophecies: "He who believes has sufficient motives for belief; for he is moved by the authority of the divine teaching confirmed by miracles, and, what is more, by the interior instinct of God inviting him" (*ST* II–II, 2, 9, ad 3; see *CG,* III, 155; *ST* II–II, 2, 1, ad 1).

---

[22]Dulles, *Revelation Theology,* 38.

Thomas calls this interior invitation a "witness" to God, an illumination and a teaching (see *In Jo.* c. 5, lect. 6; *Quodl.* 2, 4, 6, ad 3) but, in this differing from Augustine, not normally "revelation." Faith is the human person's response to God revealing (the formal object) and what he reveals (the material object). This response is possible only through grace, or the interior attraction, which is called at times "the light of faith." For example, Thomas says that "the light of faith makes us see those things which are believed. As by other virtues man sees that which is appropriate to him according to that virtue, so also by the virtue of faith the human mind is inclined to assent to those things which are appropriate to right faith, and not to other things" (*ST* II–II, 1, 3, ad 3). This interior attraction, or virtue of faith, sets up a connaturality between the believer and God who calls and what God proposes for our belief. One does not appropriately believe unless one sees both that there is reason to believe and that it is good to believe. In consequence of the context of Thomas' reflection on revelation and faith, he emphasizes its character as an intellectual act, though moved by the will, rather than dealing with it primarily as the path to conversion or as a basis for justification distinct from works.

In comparing Thomas' interpretation of revelation with what we saw in Scripture, we can say that he preserved better than some later theologians that God reveals by deeds as well as words, that he contributed much by relating the theme of revelation to other forms of knowledge, and that he brought out well that we believe because it is good to believe and we have reason to think that God has revealed. While he was wholly in accord with Scripture to see revelation as mediated by the Word of God incarnate, it seems that he did not give sufficient place to the early Church's view that God continues to reveal in the sense of communicating with us through the mediation of Christ gone into the fullness of the future by his resurrection and exaltation and through the Spirit whom he sent, that revelation is a fully personal communication and essentially involves God's interior movement of the heart and illumination, and that it was mediated by religious experience as well as God's authority.

If we turn now to the question of what the meaning of the kingdom or salvation was in the High Middle Ages, perhaps the best way to articulate this briefly is to indicate first the interpretation of Joachim of Fiore and then the reaction to him by Thomas and Bonaventure, showing bases for their positions and concluding by

evaluating this basic difference of viewpoint through what we have
seen earlier in Scripture and the Fathers.

Joachim of Fiore (ca. 1135–1202) developed a theology of history
based on his spiritual interpretation of Scripture concerning the
Trinity's relation to successive stages of history. He found concordances between the Old Testament and the New. For example, he saw
seven persecutions that the Jews in the Old Testament were subject
to as types of seven major persecutions that the people of the New
Testament would be subject to through their history. And he saw the
entire book of Revelation "as presenting a historical message, and
not one that is generic and vague, but rather a revelation that can be
tied down to specific persons, events, and dates. In this Joachim
stands in resolute, if silent, opposition to Augustine."[23] He identified
the existence of three overlapping stages of history, each associated
by way of appropriation with one person of the Trinity, and he discovered in each of these stages an equal number of generations in
human history, though not all defined in the same number of years.

He also identified characteristics of each stage. The first stage is
that of the Father, and it began with Adam, bore fruit from Abraham,
and was consummated in Christ; it thus included the dispensation before the Law and under the Law and was the state of married people.
The second stage is that of Christ, and it began with Ozias, bore fruit
from Zachary, the father of John the Baptist, and was having its consummation in Joachim's time; this is characterized by the clerical
order and preachers. The third stage is that of the Spirit, and it had
its beginnings in St. Benedict, began to bear fruit in the twenty-sec-
ond generation after him, and will be consummated at the end of the
world. This stage is characterized by contemplatives, primarily monks,
and a spiritual understanding of Scripture. McGinn comments:

> The implications of this ascription of the individual orders to the
> Persons of the Trinity *(proprietate similitudinis)* is that although
> there is a progressive spiritualization of humanity represented in the
> three orders, each of the orders has its own unique and equal role
> in history. The monastic order will, of course, enjoy preeminence

---

[23]Bernard McGinn, *The Calabrian Abbot: Joachim of Fiore in the History of Western Thought*
(New York: Macmillan, 1985) 150–1. I depend primarily on McGinn for what follows. See also
Karl Löwith, "Joachim," 145–59, and "Modern Transfigurations of Joachism," 208–13, *Meaning
in History* (Chicago: University of Chicago Press, 1949).

in the dawning third *status,* which shows that the Holy Spirit is a divine Person fully equal to the Father and the Son; but the pre-eminence of the monks does not mean the end of the married or clerical orders, any more than the procession of the Holy Spirit cancels out the divinity of the other two Persons. In important passages in the *Psalterium,* Joachim stresses how individual members of both the married and the clerical orders can belong to the true monastic order, that is, "the real contemplatives."[24]

Joachim shifts the Christian focus from the period of Jesus Christ to the future age of the Spirit, but he does not state that this coming stage replaces that of Christ: "In speaking of the spiritual men of the third *status* whose Old Testament type is Solomon, Joachim says: 'all those wonderful things written about Solomon and Christ will be completed in them [the spiritual men] in the Spirit *because in this people Christ will reign more powerfully.'"*[25] Thus Joachim

was forward-looking, with an innerworldly hope for the future more profound than almost any other classical Christian theologian. By locating the magnet of reform in the future rather than the past, that is, in the coming *status* of the Holy Spirit rather than in any return to an apostolic ideal or some glorification of the present, he broke with previous theologies of history in a manner that has continued to be a source of inspiration for many and a bone of contention for others.[26]

In the middle of the thirteenth century Gerardo di Borgo San Donnino and several others interpreted Joachim's predictions in ways that "were overlaid with explanations and specifications which significantly altered and frequently gravely perverted the thought of the abbot of Fiore."[27] Seven statements from Gerardo's book were condemned by Alexander IV in 1255,[28] but this did not keep Joachim's views from spreading, particularly though not exclusively among the "spiritual" Franciscans.

---

[24]McGinn, *Calabrian Abbot,* 186.

[25]Ibid., 173; see also 137.

[26]Ibid., 236.

[27]Ibid., 208.

[28]See Viviano, *Kingdom of God in History,* 58–9.

Bonaventure did accept in part Joachim's method of interpreting Scripture by the use of concordances between the Old Testament and the New, and he used the traditional seven ages Augustine identified within this search for historical correlations. On the basis of the understanding of the past that this method allowed, he thought that we can know the future to some degree. He considered his own age to be approaching the seventh age of peace but thought that it would be preceded by an intensified conflict between good and evil that he saw in the crises of his own age: the efforts of emperors to dominate the Church and the misuse of unredeemed philosophy in Catholic theology. He considered St. Francis of Assisi to be foreshadowed in the angel mentioned in Revelation 7:2. Francis "appears as the initiator of a coming order of contemplatives that will flourish in the final age of the Church, but this coming order is to be distinguished from the actual historical Franciscan order of which Bonaventure was Minister General."[29] Thus Bonaventure developed a theology of history that has notes of an apocalyptic expectation of the coming of the end, and of a better age before that, though he rejected Joachim's expectation of the coming third stage of the Holy Spirit.

Thomas Aquinas was more curtly dismissive of Joachim than Bonaventure. He rejected the detailed concordances between the Old and New Testaments (see *In IV Sent.* d. 43, q. 1, a. 3, *quaestiuncula* 4, sol. I, ad 3) and so also predictions of the future based on these as found in Joachim. In *ST* I–II, 106, 4, he rejected the view that there will be a stage in history that succeeds the state of new law: "No state of the present life can be more perfect than the state of the new law; nothing can be closer to the final end." Though there can be changes of state in accord with persons, times, and places, and "insofar as the grace of the Holy Spirit is possessed more or less perfectly by certain people," "[i]t should not be expected that there will be a future state in which the grace of the Holy Spirit will be more perfectly possessed than it has been to this point, and above all by the Apostles, who received the firstfruits of the Spirit, that is prior in time and more abundantly than others."

This view of Thomas is to be understood within his whole theology, which has been organized on the *exitus-reditus* model he inherited from Augustine and which does not seem to integrate history in God's saving dispensation as the early Church's understanding of the

---

[29]McGinn, *Calabrian Abbot,* 219.

parousia and its present impact did.[30] He relates the Christian mystery more to a philosophy of being than a philosophy of history. He understands that human beings have a natural desire for the beatific vision and that God through Christ's redemption and the Church enables them to attain this goal by the infusion of grace with the theological virtues. By justification through faith and the virtuous life human beings move toward this goal.

The notion of the kingdom of God is not central for Thomas. In his commentary on Matthew 3:2 he finds four meanings of the kingdom: Scripture itself, the Church militant, the heavenly court, and immanent within us "because by means of the indwelling grace the way of the heavenly kingdom is begun in us" (*Super Evan. S. Matthaei,* lect.). The first meaning is rather arbitrary; the second and third meanings come from Augustine; and the fourth "is the familiar false start based on Luke 17:21 which becomes the basis for an individualist, private interior definition."[31]

What reflection does our earlier study of Scripture enable us to make on this dispute? In the first place, Joachim does catch something of Scripture's understanding of salvation, for he sees us as oriented to salvation through the future of history rather than through a kind of transcendence that makes the historical future unrelated to the ultimate. However, the foundation on which Joachim bases his theology of history seems to differ in part from that of the primitive Church. What we found in the earliest Church was an expectation of the return of Christ, and a view that Jesus as the exalted Lord and

---

[30]See M.-D. Chenu, "La Somme Théologique," *Introduction à l'étude de Saint Thomas d'Aquin,* 2e ed. (Paris: Vrin, 1954) 255–76. Max Seckler wrote on Thomas' view of salvation in history in *Das Heil in der Geschichte: Geschichts-Theologisches Denken bei Thomas von Aquin* (Munich: Kösel, 1964). Thomas was concerned for exact historical knowledge and did see historical events as having more than historical significance, especially the incarnation of the Word, and he saw the Church as a continuation of the incarnation of Christ. But this remains quite different from either Scripture or a modern philosophy of history. See also Jürgen Moltmann, "Christian Hope: Messianic or Transcendent? A Theological Discussion with Joachim of Fiore and Thomas Aquinas," *Horizons* 12 (1985) 328–48. For my own agreements with and differences from Thomas and Moltmann see Farrelly, "Trinity as Salvific Mystery." Moltmann's article was inspired in part by the attack by Hans Urs von Balthasar on his book *The Theology of Hope.* I expressed my reservations on von Balthasar's too-full acceptance of Augustine's *exitus-reditus* scheme in a review of his *A Theological Anthropology* in *Salesian Studies* 5 (1968) 98–100.

[31]Viviano, *Kingdom of God in History,* 62–3. On page 65 he writes, "Thomas' critique of Joachim's method of finding harmonies between the Testaments is trenchant and reasonable, but there is an alternative danger of spiritualizing, ahistorical exegesis of a kind dependent on the Pseudo-Denis. Thomas himself is not always immune from this danger."

Christ is exercising even now his saving activity upon us from our future in the kingdom into which he has entered. He is acting on the people of God through sending the Holy Spirit; through the proclamation of his apostles, which allows people the opportunity for faith; and through the sacraments. This saving activity is to have a transforming influence not simply in the individual or in the community of the Church but in society itself, and it gives his disciples the impulse to instantiate in the historical present such aspects of the kingdom as are possible.

There is not a promise of an age within history of full peace and justice, but there is an *adventus* of Jesus as Lord within history to impel his disciples to contribute to such an age in history, as there is also an *adventus* that is even now a share in the judgment he will exercise when he comes again. Thomas articulated God's causal influence on human beings from a model of God as creator and totally transcending the order of time as eternity. He seems to assimilate to this model the causal influence upon our justification and sanctification that he ascribes to Jesus' resurrection and ascension (*ST* III, 56, 2; 57, 6). But he does not seem to give place to an exercise of causal influence from the future of history, as the New Testament does. It is this that is necessary if we are to do justice to the apocalyptic character of the kingdom as the New Testament presents it to us. This is also essential if we are to integrate modern culture's appropriate concern for the intermediate historical future into the understanding and search for salvation that the Church proclaims. This may raise for some people philosophical problems of how the future can have an impact on the present, but we will address these in the next chapter.

2. The Reformation Period

To leap from the thirteenth to the sixteenth century is to skip what makes the Reformation understandable. We will make a brief statement about this intermediate period, but for the most part we direct the reader to other resources for a study of this period.[32] Certainly the syntheses in life, thought, and institutions of the thirteenth century did

---

[32]See Pelikan, *The Christian Tradition,* vol. 4, *Reformation of Church and Dogma (1300–1700)* 10–126. Also see Karl Fink, Erwin Iserloh, and Josef Glazik, "The Late Middle Ages," vol. 4, *From the High Middle Ages to the Eve of the Reformation: History of the Church,* ed. H. Jedin (New York: Crossroad, 1980) 291–624; Myron Gilmore, *The World of Humanism* (New York: Harper, 1952); Farrelly, *Belief in God,* 134–40.

not hold. Part of the reason for this was that there were urgent movements in particular areas of human life for more autonomy, as in the
states' new consciousness and search for an identity that the leaders
themselves controlled, and there were provocations by excessive
claims on the part of Church leaders that increased the resulting split.

Theology did not grow sufficiently to work toward new syntheses.
Rather, because of nominalism and the tendency of many to treat
possibilities of God's power more than the actual order of salvation
through Christ, it became more removed from Christian experience.
The popes' stay at Avignon and the Great Western Schism further undercut the capacity of the Church to provide leadership for an emerging new age. In the renewed interest of the early Renaissance in the
human achievements of ancient Greece and Rome, the popes tended
to be supporters, even to the extent that some acted more as Renaissance princes than as popes.

Much of the spirituality of the later Middle Ages also represented
a withdrawal from the larger world, and much religious practice was
marked by externalism and superstition. There were those, particularly in the fifteenth century, who sought reform in theology and life
(e.g., representatives of *devotio moderna,* Nicholas of Cusa, and a beginning of renewal of Thomistic theology in Capreolus and Cajetan),
but by and large Church intellectual and institutional leaders de-
faulted in providing suitable leadership for the age. Thus the tension
between the human dimensions of culture, life, and thought on the
one hand and the fully Christian mystery and life on the other grew
to the breaking point.

Some commentators see similarities in origin and consequence between the Renaissance and Reformation. Anthony Kemp holds that
in both there is a critical methodology that finds "history is dynamic,
and . . . early or original documents have more value than later
ones." Thus the humanists distinguish ancient, medieval, and modern
culture and esteem the ancient more highly than the medieval, or
"dark ages." Similarly, Luther distinguishes the apostolic age from
later Church tradition and uses the former to critique the latter. Kemp
suggests that "[t]he two movements began independently with
Petrarch and Wyclif respectively, and both sprang from the rhetoric
of a single writer [Valla], yet became shadows of each other." And,
"The Renaissance and Reformation precipitated a historical revolution (and it is essentially a single revolution) so profound that it re-
versed the Western perception of the past within a single generation,

from a perception of unity to one of division and difference, from a stillness to a dynamic motion."[33]

The sixteenth century saw varied forms of resolution of this tension. Luther found peace in a form of biblical theology that was enormously suspicious of the human and of philosophical thought. Some Renaissance humanists glorified or exploited the human in a way that diminished the place of the fully Christian. What appears to many to be the most successful effort to give a new integration of the Christian and the human appropriate for that time was the Council of Trent. There were combinations of various orientations, such as in those leaders of state who allied themselves with the reformers largely for the purpose of enhancing their own freedom from religious authorities who had previously been independent of their control, and in the leaders of Catholic states who kept the reformed papacy's control of the Church in their domains as minimal as possible. We shall limit ourselves here to sixteenth-century reflections on revelation, faith and the kingdom in Luther (with a note on the Anabaptists), and the Council of Trent, and we treat even these very briefly. We find the implications of the more humanistic wing of the sixteenth-century solutions worked out more explicitly as it affects our themes in the following period, called the Enlightenment, or "Age of Reason."

There are disagreements about exactly when Luther came to his discovery of the central theme of his theology, which generated much of his program and the Reformation as a whole, but there is not this disagreement about what this theme was. It was justification by faith alone. At some point before 1518 Luther had a kind of conversion experience, which he called his "tower experience," that resolved his anxiety about whether he was accepted by God or not, an anxiety that he had not been able to resolve by his efforts in accord with the sacrament of penance (involving contrition, confession, and satisfaction) or the Scholastic theology he knew. He recounts his wrestling with God's righteousness *(justitia Dei)* in Romans 1:17:

> I hated that word "righteousness of God," which, according to the use and custom of all teachers, I had been taught to understand philosophically regarding the formal or active righteousness, as they called it, with which God is righteous and punishes the unrighteous sinner. . . . At last, by the mercy of God, meditating

[33]Kemp, *Estrangement of the Past,* 101, 103, 104.

day and night, I gave heed to the context of the words, namely, "in
it the righteousness of God is revealed, as it is written, 'He who
through faith is righteous shall live.'" There I began to understand
that the righteousness of God is that by which the righteous lives
by a gift of God, namely by faith. *And this is the meaning: the
righteousness of God is revealed by the gospel, namely, the passive
righteousness with which merciful God justifies us by faith. . . .
Here I felt that I was altogether born again and had entered par-
adise itself through open gates.*[34]

Luther had felt terror before the law that stated he must have certain dispositions and make satisfaction for the sacrament of penance
to be effective or for him to be justified, because no man knew his
own dispositions. He was looking for a gracious God who would
forgive him. And he found peace and release from terror in *trusting*
that because of Christ's sufferings God did accept him, totally independent of any works of the law, including those conditions on
which Scholastic theology said that God's forgiveness depended. In
this position he saw himself as opposed to the Pelagians of his time,
who made God's justification of the sinner depend on the works of
the law. And in this he saw himself giving all the glory to God and
none to human beings.

At times in the heat of controversy he spelled out the rather extreme Augustinian anthropology associated with this interpretation,
namely that "the human will was not 'evil by nature, that is, essentially evil' but . . . it was 'nevertheless innately and inevitably evil
and corrupt' and therefore 'not free to strive toward whatever is declared good.'"[35] The divine image in human beings was lost through
original sin, and original sin remained in them after baptism. Against
Erasmus, he "confined free will to 'natural matters, such as eating,
drinking, procreating, governing' and the like."[36] He felt that to ascribe justification to God's grace *and* human beings' free response
was against ascribing it fully to God's grace.

---

[34]Martin Luther, "Preface to the Complete Edition of Luther's Latin Writings," cited in Eric
Gritsch, "The Origins of the Lutheran Teaching on Justification," *Justification by Faith: Lutherans
and Catholics in Dialogue, 7,* ed. H. George Anderson, T. Austin Murphy, and Joseph Burgess
(Minneapolis: Augsburg Publishing House, 1985) 164. Gritsch's emphasis.

[35]Pelikan, *Reformation of Church and Dogma,* 141. The enclosed quotation is from Luther's
Disputation Against Scholastic Theology.

[36]Pelikan, *Reformation of Church and Dogma,* 143.

We could go further into this matter, but that can be found else-where.[37] What we want to point out is that virtually the sole target of Luther's attack is the Pelagians, and thus he seems to fall into the opposite error of overstressing human depravity, ignorance, and incapacity for freely responding to God even under God's grace. Luther's disciples and Luther himself at times softened what he had said to this effect, but the substance of his views continued in his disciples.

What does this say, first, about Luther's views on revelation and faith? Faith for him is basically fiducia, or trust:

> It meant, above all, "a firm trust [fiducia]," for which "Christ is the object of faith, or rather not the object, but so to speak, the one who is present in the faith itself." . . . It was, then, believing "in" Christ; that included, as Luther's exposition of the Apostles' Creed showed, believing "that" the life, death, and resurrection of Christ were historically true—but above all that they were true "for me," a phrase that one was to "accept with a sure faith and apply to himself" without doubting.[38]

The "Word" of God for Luther was more God's deed and the proclamation of the Word than Scripture itself. His view of God's divine revelation, as shown in his acceptance of his particular interpretation of Romans 1:17, involved the sense that it struck him personally and indeed gave him a sense of God's compassion and his own peace.[39] The law too, of course, was God's revelation. But its purpose was to sow terror in sinners and thus induce them to throw themselves totally upon Christ by trust. Thus subjectivity was profoundly involved in Luther's interpretation of God's revelation, and he at times judged

---

[37]See ibid., "The Gospel as the Treasure of the Church," 127–82; B. A. Gerrish, *Grace and Reason: A Study in the Theology of Luther* (Oxford: Clarendon Press, 1962); M. John Farrelly, *Predestination, Grace, and Free Will* (1964; reissued, Washington, D.C.: The Council for Research in Values and Philosophy). In this work I show how justification is ascribed wholly to God's grace *because* the human being's truly free response is itself due to God's grace. The only initiative human beings can make on their own is to refuse God's call.

[38]Pelikan, *Reformation of Church and Dogma,* 154. The enclosed quotation is from Luther's 1535 commentary on Galatians. Pelikan adds (165): "Taken to its most radical consequences, such an interpretation of revelation and knowledge led to the following definition of faith: 'It is the nature of faith that it presumes on the grace of God. . . . Faith does not require information, knowledge, or certainty, but a free surrender and a joyful bet on his unfelt, untried, and unknown goodness.'" This quotation is from Luther's *Sermons.*

[39]See Dulles, *Revelation Theology,* 47.

parts of Scripture to be insignificant (e.g., his judgment that the epistle of James was an "epistle of straw") if they were counter to his interpretation of justification by faith.

In an earlier book I sought to show that, though Luther's view on the relation of predestination and grace on the one hand and our response on the other had some bases in Augustine, in important elements they were counter to Paul's message.[40] For example, there is no absolute divine predestination of an individual Christian. Rather, God predestines all who are justified in Christ to heaven; he gives them the fulfillment of grace when he gives them justification, but this gift is "frustratable," or resistible, and can be lost if the person freely refuses perseverance in response to God's call. There is no reason to doubt God's dispositions toward us, but we do have reason at times to doubt our dispositions toward God. God calls us to accept the insecurity that may come from such self-doubts without projecting them upon God, rather than blocking them out of consciousness by a kind of fiducia that appears to be counterphobic, and to leap over intermediate factors, stages, and mediations in the genesis of faith to establish a dialectical relationship between the human condition before justification and after. Neither in Paul is there a contradiction between God's grace and our merit under grace. Subjectivity is truly involved in revelation and faith, but as we saw in Peter's growth in faith, our subjectivity must accept as criterion God's word more than the reassurance our interpretation of God's word may give us.

What understanding of the kingdom of God do we find in Luther? He has a famous interpretation of two kingdoms, difficult to understand. I follow Benedict Viviano in what follows. In Luther's work "On Secular Authority, and How Far One Owes Obedience to It," he writes:

> Here we must divide the children of Adam and all men into two parts, the first belonging to the kingdom of God, and the second to the kingdom of the world. Those who belong to the kingdom of God are all true believers in Christ, and are subject to Christ. . . . All who are not Christians belong to the kingdom of the world and are subject to the law."[41]

---

[40]See Farrelly, *Predestination,* especially on Paul (52–70), Augustine (79–96), and Luther (133–8).

[41]Cited in Viviano, *Kingdom of God in History,* 88–9; see also pages 85–92.

Melanchthon, following Luther, emphasizes the "distinction between Christ's kingdom and a political kingdom. Christ's kingdom is spiritual; it is the knowledge of God in the heart, the fear of God and faith, the beginning of eternal righteousness and eternal life. . . . The Gospel does not introduce any new laws about the civil estate."[42] This is similar to the spiritual Neoplatonic interpretation of the kingdom of God in Origen and much of the mystical tradition of Christianity. The Christian lives in two kingdoms, but it is difficult to see in Luther's interpretation—or in that of many Catholic interpretations of the time—the socially transformative impact of the kingdom of God as it was taught by Jesus. In accord with this, Luther came to the point of forcefully opposing the German Peasants' Revolt for some measure of social justice, which they had initiated under the banner of Luther's call for Christian freedom. And he gave leadership in the Reformation of the Church largely to German political leaders. Socially Luther was conservative, and he needed the German princes for the success of his religious cause.

This is not the case with the Anabaptists. This left wing of the Reformation generally was opposed to infant baptism because it held to the New Testament's practice of baptizing adult believers, but it was divided by much else, particularly on the issue of whether or not violence should be used to change society in accord with the gospel. They not only opposed medieval traditions in the Church as corruptions as Luther did but even those of antiquity after the apostolic age. Thus some of them repudiated even Nicaea's trinitarian doctrine. The Anabaptists generally gave more room to the Spirit than Luther did, but what this meant differed among them. Thomas Müntzer thought that there were new revelations given after the apostolic age.

But the initial sense of the Spirit in this movement was that the local Christian assembly had the authority given it by the presence of the Spirit to make binding decisions concerning doctrine and practice without deferring to ecclesiastical or civil authority or to the professional scriptural scholar. This attitude is found among the radical Zwinglians in Zurich in 1523 and in the agreement at Schlechtheim in 1527. Also, "[c]omplementary to the congregational concept . . . is the concept of the Spirit as the power of subjective appropriation of the truths of scripture, tradition or preaching, not the source of

---

[42]Ibid., 86–7.

truth . . . but of power, witness and reassurance."[43] In effect, their emphasis on the Spirit over tradition and even the literal word of Scripture led to a rejection of Church structure and doctrine of the patristic age.

In reference to their understanding of the kingdom of God, Müntzer acknowledged the great influence on him of Tauler's mysticism and the spiritualist and chiliastic doctrine of Joachim of Fiore:

> Müntzer was profoundly convinced that faith must prove itself in testimony before the world and that the Christian bears an active responsibility for the world and the fate of his neighbor. For him there was no division into two sides as there was for Luther. The will of God demanded an immediate and absolute realization in all spheres. . . . [In] His "Sermon to the Princes" [1524] . . . the Kingdom of God is no purely eschatological thing and the princes are not "heathen folk" with merely secular duties; rather, the Kingdom of God is to be realized in this world and time, if necessary by the sword of princes.[44]

In fact, Müntzer forcefully supported the Peasants' Revolution, was captured, and executed. It was within pacifist communities of believers that the enduring communities of the Anabaptists integrated their view of the present impact of the kingdom, as we see in the Mennonites, Amish, and Hutterites.

The primary official Catholic response to the Protestant Reformation was the Council of Trent (1545-63) in its decrees on the reform of the life of the Church and on doctrines brought into dispute by the Protestants. At particular sessions the council began its discussions of particular doctrines by considering lists of statements from Protestant leaders, particularly Luther, against traditional Christian beliefs. It sought to define the Church's position on these issues without deciding issues among the diverse Catholic schools of theology such as the Dominicans, Franciscans, and Scotists. Most of Trent's teaching deals with issues other than those we treat here. But we shall refer to

---

[43]John Yoder, "The Enthusiasts and the Reformation," *Conflicts About the Holy Spirit,* ed. Hans Küng and Jürgen Moltmann, Concilium 128 (New York: Seabury, 1979) 45. Also see Pelikan, "Challenges to Apostolic Continuity," *Reformation of Church and Dogma,* 304–31; Erwin Iserloh, "The Struggle over the Concept of Christian Freedom," *Reformation and Counter Reformation: History of the Church,* ed. H. Jedin (New York: Crossroad, 1980) 5:116–38, 177–91.

[44]Iserloh, "Struggle over the Concept of Christian Freedom," 131–2.

the central teaching of Trent on revelation, on faith and justification, and more implicit than explicit, on the kingdom of God.

Trent deals with the question of revelation, because Luther rejected tradition in favor of the Bible and took his own interpretation of Paul's teaching on justification even though he found it was opposed in part by the epistle of James. Rather than the word "revelation," the council used the word "gospel," meaning the message of salvation, and it accepted as normative for its meaning both the written word in canonical Scripture and unwritten apostolic tradition:

> The Holy Council . . . having ever before its eyes the removal of error and preservation of the Gospel in its purity in the Church— the Gospel which, promised beforehand by the prophets in holy Scripture, *our Lord Jesus Christ first promulgated by his own mouth and then ordered to be preached by his apostles "to every creature" as being the source of all salutary truth and moral life;* realizing, too, that this same truth and code of morals is contained in written books and in unwritten traditions which, received by the apostles from Christ's own mouth or at the dictation of the Holy Spirit, have come down to us . . . ; this same Council . . . reverently receives with like devotion and veneration [Scripture] . . . as well as traditions concerning both faith and morals.[45]

Thus it rejected what it understood Luther's *sola scriptura* to involve—a rejection of apostolic tradition preserved by the Church as normative in its interpretation, a disrespect for some parts of the Bible (such as the epistle of James), and a subjectivism.

What then, according to Trent, is the faith on which our salvation and justification depend? It opposed statements of Luther that ascribed our justification to "faith alone," which denied human freedom in cooperating with grace and which seemed to measure our justification by our degree of trust. While it teaches that all the descendants of Adam inherit original sin, it does not have as negative

---

[45]DS 1501, as translated in Yves Congar, "The Meaning of Tradition," *Twentieth Century Encyclopedia of Catholicism* (New York: Hawthorn, 1964) 3:42. My emphasis. Congar explains there how this text substituted a less restricting "and . . . and" for an earlier text that had read "partly in written books and partly in unwritten traditions" to avoid deciding against a Catholic theological school that held that the full content of Christian faith was somehow contained in Scripture. Citations in the text at this place are to paragraphs in Trent's decrees according to Denzinger-Schönmetzer's numeration.

238 Soundings in Christian History

an estimate of the present state of human nature as Luther does. We have lost in Adam the holiness and justice originally meant for us and have been weakened in soul and body, but we have not lost free will (DS 1555). It is only by the initiative and help of divine grace that comes to us through Jesus Christ that the beginnings and the completion of our justification can be effected (DS 1551); neither Gentile nor Jew can be justified by works or natural powers. But this justification in the adult takes place only if he or she freely assents to God's grace (DS 1525). The process of justification begins when "stirred up and helped by divine grace, conceiving faith 'by hearing' [Rom 10:17], adults are freely moved toward God, believing those things that have been divinely revealed and promised to be true, above all, that the unjust is justified by God through his grace 'by the redemption that is in Jesus Christ' [Rom 3:4]."

The council here insists on historical faith, that is, faith in what is objectively revealed through Christ, though it goes on to include in this process adults' acknowledgement of their sins, fear of God, consideration of God's mercy, hope, trust in God's mercy, the beginning of love of God, and the turning away from sin (DS 1526). Thus justification is a process that includes much more than trust. And it terminates in "not only remission of sins but also a sanctification and a renewal of the interior man through his voluntary reception of grace and the gifts, by which man becomes just rather than unjust and a friend [of God] rather than an enemy" (DS 1528).

There is more continuity here in the steps by which the adult turns from sin to God than some statements of Luther (and some of his twentieth-century disciples) acknowledge. The council proclaims that this interpretation of justification does not detract at all from the glory of God or the merits of Christ but rather "reflects the truth of our faith and the glory of God and Jesus Christ" (DS 1583). One may see that, counter to humanism, the council asserted that human beings cannot become just by their human powers or acts without God's grace and the merits of Christ (DS 1551); counter to Luther, it asserted that God's glory is not diminished by the acknowledgment of a freely received interior justice in human beings through God's gift.[46] What is best in the human is here made an ally of God.

---

[46]For the very important present-day convergence statement on justification between Lutherans and Catholics and background articles for this statement, see *Justification by Faith,* cited in note 34.

If we ask what Trent had to say concerning the meaning of the kingdom of God, we would have to say that this is more implicit than explicit. But we can make two points. *First,* the center of the Reformation's critique of the Church concerned the justification of the individual, and so too Trent's decree on justification centered on the individual. And thus the center of the post-Tridentine Catholic theology of grace also was on the individual; the social dimensions of God's gift through Christ, namely the kingdom of God, did not have the central importance it had for the New Testament writers. But, more positively, by its teaching on the intrinsic character of justification Trent acknowledged more forcefully than Luther the transformative impact of God's salvation through Christ as already occurring in part in history. *Second,* while Luther used the scandals and corruptions in the Church as partial justification for his sectarian revolt, Trent's too-late reforms promoted a more Christian life and belief in the whole body of the faithful. Pelikan recounts Catholic responses to Luther:

> In 1 Corinthians Paul had warned against schism, in Ephesians against "heretical deserters," and Augustine had warned against those who accepted the authority of Scripture but violated unity. Now, with the growing "internal disorders of Christendom," it was incumbent on all parties to recognize that, evil as the abuses in the church were, they were not nearly so dangerous as schism and heresy. . . . As Augustine had said and as Luther had once agreed, there was no graver sin than sectarianism, which could not be justified even by the supposed centrality of the gospel.[47]

An implicit understanding of the kingdom of God is shown by how one reacts against tares among the wheat in the Master's field.

III. The Enlightenment to the Early Twentieth Century

On the whole during this period the Church or Churches lost leadership in Western culture and society. Pelikan introduces his *Christian Doctrine and Modern Culture (Since 1700)* with a recall of Goethe's *Faust* and the doubts it expressed about the Christian tradition: "It

[47]Pelikan, *Reformation of Church and Dogma,* 273–4.

was within such a tension between tradition and doubt or between dogma and relativism that the history of Christian doctrine developed during the eighteenth, nineteenth, and twentieth centuries. . . . This is, then, preeminently the period in which tradition stood in tension not only with doubt but with reason, including 'historical reason.'"[48] Christian tradition lost its authority for many. We can say that this happened both because of the attacks on tradition and because of the inadequacy of the Churches' response to these attacks. We will examine this briefly under the headings of the Enlightenment and the nineteenth to the early twentieth century.

1. The Enlightenment

We have already recalled in our earlier volume some influential individual authors who elevated reason above Christian faith during this period in England and then on the Continent. We have also recalled the context of both praxis and *theoria* for this attack upon the primacy of Christian faith. Here we restrict ourselves to giving an overview and a few key examples of the Enlightenment attack on Christian revelation, faith and salvation, and the largely inadequate Christian response.

The Catholic Reformation had strengthened the Church's doctrinal, institutional, and moral life. There was a reinvigoration of the life of the Church in many spheres, for example, in new and renewed religious orders, in saints, in new missions, in the multiplication of schools. But there were also the wars of religion that tore Europe apart, and there were serious and enduring conflicts within each Church, shown, for example, in Catholicism in the conflicts surrounding Jansenism. Moreover, neither the Catholic Church nor Protestant theological leaders was sufficiently responsive to the early development of modern science; witness the Church's condemnation of Galileo. We recall also the discovery of non-Christian peoples in the Americas and the Far East and the continuing search for human autonomy that had in part motivated the sixteenth-century religious divisions.

As an overview of the Enlightenment, we cite Peter Gay's *The Enlightenment: An Interpretation,* volume 1, *The Rise of Modern Paganism.* Gay shows the appeal of antiquity (e.g., Stoics, Lucretius,

---

[48]Jaroslav Pelikan, *Christian Doctrine and Modern Culture (Since 1700)* (Chicago: University of Chicago Press, 1989) 5–6. See our treatment of tradition in chapter 2 above, pages 46–48.

Cicero) for the intellectual leaders of the eighteenth century, the pre-history to the Enlightenment in Renaissance interest in the classics and in seventeenth-century Newtonian science, and the tensions with Christianity that accompanied these movements. Through several generations of Enlightenment leaders there was a movement from a rationalist Christianity to deism to full religious skepticism and a program for a new world. Gay writes of the late eighteenth-century philosophes:

> While the variations among the philosophes are far from negligible, they only orchestrate a single passion that bound the little flock to-gether, the passion to cure the spiritual malady that is religion, the germ of ignorance, barbarity, hypocrisy, filth, and the basest self-hatred. It is true that just as they disagreed on their diagnoses, the philosophes disagreed on their prescriptions for health: the atheists reduced the simple doctrines of natural religion to a mere expres-sive metaphor for the majesty of nature, and the skeptics doubted that the truth of natural religion could be reliably established. . . . But both groups conceded to the deists that natural religion alone —a religion without miracles, priestly hierarchies, ritual, divine saviors, original sin, chosen people, and providential history—was tolerable and intellectually respectable. . . . All other religions deserved to be extirpated: this was the meaning of Voltaire's slo-gan—*Ecrasez l'infame.*[49]

The erosion of the Christian faith that occurred for many cultural leaders during the Enlightenment began to gain force in England and spread from there to the Continent. The tension between Christian revelation and reason, between Christian faith and knowledge, is ex-emplified in John Locke, who tried on the basis of reason to justify Christianity in *The Reasonableness of Christianity* (1695). He used his understanding of reason to defend Christianity. External miracles testified to Jesus as Messiah and to his message, and so we should believe in him as Messiah and accept his resurrection. Locke tended to reduce Christianity to these dimensions, which he found more ac-ceptable to reason than such doctrines as the Trinity and predestina-tion. He did at times add arguments from the beauty and power of

---

[49]Peter Gay, *The Enlightenment: An Interpretation,* vol. 1, *The Rise of Modern Paganism* (New York: Norton, 1977) 373.

Christianity, but he did not develop these arguments.[50] Reason, particularly as interpreted by Newtonian physics and Locke, eroded Christian revelation for many intellectual leaders in England. To exemplify this, we quote from the Deist Matthew Tindal's *Christianity as Old as Creation* (1730):

> When Men, in defending their own, or attacking other traditionary Religions, have recourse to the Nature or Reason of Things; does not That shew, they believe the Truth of all traditionary Religions is to be tried by it; . . . and if there are such evident Truths, must not all others be tried by their Agreement with them? And are not these the Tests, by which we are to distinguish the only true Religion from the many false ones? And do not all Parties alike own . . . that Reason enables them to tell what is worthy of having God for its Author. And if Reason tells them this, does it not tell them every thing that God can be suppos'd to require?[51]

The evaluation of Christian revelation by such a method reduces it to the level of reason and to what accords with a particular culture's or individual's interpretation of reason. This approach has continued till our own time in some approaches found in religious studies, though it has developed as the physical and human sciences have developed.[52]

On the Continent, we may take as our examples of the Enlightenment's attack upon Christian revelation and faith and its substitution of a new hope for Christian salvation Lessing and Reimarus from Germany, Voltaire from France, and Kant, as summing up and transcending the Enlightenment.

Gothold Lessing (1729–81) was not influenced so much by the empiricism of England as by the rationalism of Descartes, Leibniz, and Spinoza, which took its understanding of reason from mathematics and viewed knowledge as genuine if it had the notes of necessity and universality. Consequently, Lessing questioned how the contingent particular events of history, and particularly as these were

---

[50]See Ronald Thiemann, *Revelation and Theology: The Gospel as Narrated Promise* (Notre Dame: University Press, 1985) 17–24 on Locke's argument for the reasonableness of Christianity.

[51]Matthew Tindal, *Christianity as Old as Creation,* 2nd ed. (London, 1732), cited in William Placher, *Readings in the History of Christian Theology,* vol. 2, *From the Reformation to the Present* (Philadelphia: Westminster Press, 1988) 90.

[52]See Peter Byrne, *Natural Religion and the Nature of Religion: The Legacy of Deism* (New York: Routledge, 1989).

accessible to a later age through questionable witnesses and documents, could give us an adequate basis for certainty about dogmatic truths of Christianity:

> Who will deny (not I) that the reports of these miracles and prophecies [of Jesus] are as reliable as historical truths ever can be? But if they are only as reliable as this, why are they treated as if they were infinitely more reliable? . . . That is: accidental truths of history can never become the proof of necessary truths of reason. . . .
>
> That, then, is the ugly, broad ditch which I cannot get across, however often and however earnestly I have tried to make the leap.[53]

Lessing concludes that it does not matter to him whether the Christian legend is true or false; the fruits are excellent, and it is the practical moral results that are enduring and of value. He accepts from Christianity the practical results that commend themselves to him in accord with his gospel of reason.

Hermann Reimarus (1694–1768) was a professor of oriental languages in Hamburg. From the presuppositions of the Enlightenment he made a critical study of Scripture that he left unpublished at his death. Lessing published fragments of this critical study without naming its author in 1774. Reimarus noted the great difference between developed Christian doctrine and Jesus as he can be grasped from the Synoptics by a critical historian. Viewing Jesus in the context of Judaism of his time, Reimarus took as his starting point Jesus' proclamation of the kingdom of God. He interpreted Jesus as proclaiming this in accord with Jewish expectations of a Messiah who would liberate them from the Romans. But Jesus failed to get the following he hoped for, and he died in despair. After initial shock his disciples ascribed to him a proclamation of the kingdom of God in accord with Daniel's apocalyptic message, made up stories about the resurrection, and promised the people an imminent parousia.[54] Reimarus thus forcefully raised the question of the seeming disparity

---

[53]Gotthold Lessing, *Lessing's Theological Writings* (London: A. and C. Black, Ltd., 1956) cited in Placher, *Readings,* 102. Also see Alister McGrath, *Christian Theology: An Introduction* (Oxford: Blackwell, 1994) 313–6; Peter Gay, *Enlightenment,* 404–12, on Hume's attack on miracles.

[54]See Albert Schweitzer, *The Quest of the Historical Jesus* (New York: Macmillan, 1968 ed.) 13–26. Schweitzer paraphrases Reimarus (22): "Inasmuch as the non-fulfillment of its eschatology is not admitted, our Christianity rests upon a fraud. In view of this fact, what is the evidential value of a miracle, even if it could be held to be authentic?"

between the Jesus of history and the Christ of faith, which was to remain a central issue till our own time.

In France, we simply mention the enormous impact of the eighteenth-century salons where many intellectuals who interpreted reason as undermining Christian revelation gathered, the encyclopedists who publicized such opposition, and individuals such as Pierre Bayle (1647–1706), Voltaire (1694–1778), and Jean-Jacques Rousseau (1712–78), who together had great cultural influence in discrediting Christianity.

Voltaire in 1718 wrote a version of Sophocles' *Oedipus* that "pointedly depicts God as a metaphysical villain, a cruel, despotic, and implacable being."[55] During his stay in England (1726–8) he wrote letters that commended the Quakers, whom he presented as believing Jesus to be a teacher of a simple rational religion that was later corrupted. He wrote against Pascal's view of humanity as having fallen from grace, a view he rejected "vehemently . . . in the name of human autonomy."[56] He used humor, sarcasm, irony, and all the literary forms at which he was so skilled to crush the infamy, that is, Christianity. He wrote: "Every sensible man, every honorable man, must hold the Christian sect in horror."[57] In his late work *Dictionnaire philosophique* he defined "superstition" as follows: "Almost everything that goes beyond the worship of a supreme Being, and the submission of one's heart to his eternal commands, is superstition." And, Gay adds, "that 'almost' was a last concession to prudence. This, as everyone recognized, was critical deism, accompanied, as such doctrine usually was, by its corollary, a naturalistic religion."[58]

Immanuel Kant (1724–1804) is considered to have summed up and concluded the period of the Enlightenment. He accepted elements of both the rationalist and the empiricist interpretations of reason, and in his *Critique of Pure Reason* he argued that reason could not transcend experience and thus could not give valid intellectual bases for knowledge of the existence of God. However, in his *Critique of Practical Reason* he argued that there is sufficient basis in a *rational faith* in the existence of God and that this is found in what we must postulate on the basis of the categorical imperative.

---

[55]Gay, *Enlightenment*, 385.

[56]Ibid., 389.

[57]Ibid., 391.

[58]Ibid., 396.

That is, we experience a sense of absolute obligation, but this is meaningless unless we can postulate the existence of a divinity who can assure us a happiness proportioned to our moral behavior.

In his *Religion Within the Limits of Reason Alone* (1793) he argued for the superiority of such rational faith over a historical faith such as that of Christianity. Our moral life is autonomous, and the adult should dare to live on the basis of experience and reason; the authority of revelation is for children. Kant recognized the importance of a historical revelation for most of humankind, but Christian doctrines have only a symbolic value insofar as they support a moral life; religion is morality, not doctrine.

The Enlightenment was not only an attack upon the Christian past; it was the beginning of modern historical consciousness, and one central part of its program was to envisage the age of the future and try to bring it about. In a genuine sense this was a substitute for the Christian hope for the kingdom of God; or it was a kind of immanentizing of the Christian hope for the kingdom, because the Christian linear sense of history oriented these philosophers toward the future. The philosophes looked for freedom and religious tolerance, and they expected these to come about through enlightened but absolute monarchs. They did not have much confidence in the populace at large, because they thought they were captives of superstition.

Voltaire is an example of one who looked to history as a historian, not as a believer in Providence. And he wrote a philosophy of history, a phrase he coined. He viewed progress in history to lie in "the progressive development of sciences and skills, morals and laws, commerce and industry."[59] He compared China and the West, and he found much reason to think the Chinese more civilized than the Jews. The main obstacles to civilization are dogmatic religions and wars. Science of his time, he thought, showed that human beings have a more modest place in the scheme of things than Christians thought. He "provided the rising bourgeoisie with a historical justification of its own ideals by suggesting that all history was leading up to the eighteenth century. In Voltaire's essay God has retired from the rule of history; he may still reign, but he does not govern by intervention. The purpose and meaning of history are to improve by our own reason the condition of man, to make him less ignorant, 'better and happier.'"[60]

---

[59]Löwith, *Meaning in History,* 107.

[60]Ibid.

Voltaire was realist enough, however, not to be too confident in this progress. We may note that Immanuel Kant too had this forward looking hope: "To found a moral people of God is . . . a task whose consummation can be looked for not from men but only from God himself. . . . Man [must] proceed as though everything depended upon him; only on this condition dare he hope that higher wisdom will grant the completion of his well-intentioned endeavors. The wish of all well-disposed people is, therefore, 'the kingdom of God come, that His will be done on earth.'"[61]

We may well ask how the Churches responded to these attacks upon basic Christian revelation and faith. To restrict ourselves to just several elements of this, we should note that there were indeed Christian apologists in the major Christian denominations who responded to religious indifference, to deism, to the philosophes, and to rationalistic attacks on Scripture. For example, in the seventeenth century Pascal developed an apologetic against religious indifference, and Richard Simon inaugurated modern biblical criticism of the Old and New Testaments while preserving his Catholic faith; in the eighteenth century the Anglican bishop Butler wrote a powerful defense of Christianity against deism, and the abbé Nicholas Bergier and others wrote against the philosophes. But with few exceptions, we agree with Dulles:

> The initiative in this period no longer lies with the protagonists of the Christian cause but rather with the adversaries. The apologists, rushing to answer one objection after another, are vexed and harassed, anxious and defensive. They seem unable to turn the tables on the adversaries by mastering and correcting the new currents of thought—as Origen had done for middle Platonism, Augustine for Neo-platonism, and Aquinas for Averroistic Aristotelianism.[62]

Also, the higher clergy in England, Germany, and France were too much a part of the system of government and society in the era of absolute monarchy and offended many by their wealth and privilege.[63] Moreover, Christians fought one another while their main adversary

---

[61]Immanuel Kant, *Religion,* cited in Viviano, *Kingdom of God in History,* 101.

[62]Avery Dulles, *A History of Apologetics* (Philadelphia: Westminster Press, 1971) 156. See chapter 4, "From the Sixteenth through the Eighteenth Centuries," 112–57.

[63]See Gay, "The Treason of the Clerks," *Enlightenment,* 336–57.

went insufficiently challenged. The seventeenth century had still been a religious age, but there came about

> a subtle shift of attention: religious institutions and religious ex-
> planations of events were slowly being displaced from the center
> of life to its periphery. . . . Cardinal de Bernis noted in his
> *Memoirs* that by 1720 it "was no longer considered well-bred to
> believe in the gospels," and only a few years later, in 1736, Bishop
> Butler sardonically reported, "It is come, I know not how, to be
> taken for granted by many persons that Christianity is not so much
> as a subject of enquiry; but that it is now at length discovered to be
> fictitious. And accordingly they treat it as if in the present age this
> were an agreed point among all people of discernment; and noth-
> ing remained but to set it up as a principal subject of mirth and
> ridicule, as it were by way of reprisals for its having so long inter-
> rupted the pleasures of the world."[64]

Thus the leadership in the "pursuit of modernity" passed largely into the hands of those who espoused the principles of the Enlighten-ment. It was no accident that major revolutions—the American and French Revolutions—occurred toward the end of the eighteenth cen-tury. Historical consciousness made the intellectuals more aware of how human and subject to criticism political institutions were and how they could be changed by human initiative.

While the philosophes thought that the objectives of the Enlight-enment—religious toleration, freedom of press and speech, fair and equal treatment before the law—could be assured by enlightened ab-solutism, "[a] minority of eighteenth-century thinkers thought other-wise. It was these thinkers who were mainly responsible for wedding the liberal concept of self-government to the Enlightenment's concern with personal freedom and legal equality."[65] John Locke, with what is called at times his "economic individualism," was particularly im-portant for the American Revolution; similarly, Montesquieu was im-portant as an advocate for the limitation of absolute government in France, though he did not have much concern for the economic needs of the populace at large. Religious and nonreligious people could and did unite on many of these goals and the revolutions they sparked.

[64]Ibid., 338–9.

[65]John McKay, Bennett Hill, and John Buckler, *A History of Western Society,* vol. 2, *From Absolutism to the Present,* 2nd ed., (Boston: Houghton Mifflin, 1983) 725.

The French Revolution in particular was taken over by antireligious forces, and much of nineteenth-century European liberalism took both the destruction of the Church and the promotion of liberal political goals as essentially united.

2. The Nineteenth and Early Twentieth Centuries

What were some major issues the Churches faced concerning the meaning and foundations of belief in Christ in this period, and what were some major responses the theologians gave? There has been an enormous amount of writing on these themes,[66] but our purpose here is no more than to take some representative soundings on these issues. Even with this, we are recalling rather than giving an adequate analysis of the views we mention. This recall shows us something of the background necessary to account for the problems the Churches face in our time and for the differences among current theological responses to these problems. We shall note some major alternatives both to the Christian goal of the kingdom of God and to Christian revelation and faith as these were proposed for Western culture in the nineteenth century. We shall then note responses to these from Protestant liberalism and Catholics. There were other and more conservative Protestant responses that we are not mentioning here but that are analyzed in writings to which we refer.

In our first volume we recalled the attacks on Christian belief in God that came from Hegel and left-wing Hegelianism, or the "masters of suspicion."[67] These men and others (e.g., Auguste Comte) proposed alternatives to the Christian kingdom of God as the future of humankind. These alternatives are in continuity with the eighteenth century's rationalistic envisagement of the just society such as Immanual Kant's ethical commonwealth, or kingdom of virtue. Hegel understood his own project as contributing to the realization of the kingdom of God on earth. His work was to transpose "the Christian expectation of a final consummation into the historical process as

---

[66]See Claude Welch, *Protestant Thought in the Nineteenth Century,* 2 vols. (New Haven, Conn.: Yale University Press, 1972, 1985); Ninian Smart and others, eds., *Nineteenth Century Religious Thought in the West,* 3 vols. (Cambridge: Cambridge University Press, 1985); Gerald A. McCool, *Catholic Theology in the Nineteenth Century: The Quest for a Unitary Method* (New York: Seabury, 1977); Joseph Fitzer, ed., *Romance and the Rock: Nineteenth-Century Catholics on Faith and Reason* (Minneapolis: Augsburg Fortress, 1989).

[67]See Farrelly, *Belief in God,* 152–6.

such [and] . . . to translate theology into philosophy and to realize the Kingdom of God in terms of the world's real history. He felt no difficulty in identifying the 'idea of freedom,' the realization of which is the ultimate meaning of history, with the 'will of God.'"[68]

This immanentizing of Christian eschatology continued in Hegel's left-wing followers such as Feuerbach, Marx, and Dewey. Theirs were not simply intellectual theories. They were largely praxis-based or philosophical articulations of large cultural forces operative in Western culture at the time, such as the development of the modern liberal state and of industrialization and the problems of justice it posed. Many cultural leaders had the sense that the knowledge by which this process would be guided was that of autonomous, practical, and historical reason incompatible with Christian revelation. They found their viewpoint supported by scientific discoveries later in the nineteenth century, particularly that of evolution, that seemed to them to undercut the Christian view and to do so by scientific method.

Positivistic historical studies accepted a similarly rationalistic context for interpretation, even of Christian origins. David Strauss, for example, interpreted the gospel accounts of Jesus in *The Life of Jesus Critically Examined* (1835) within the rationalistic confines of Hegel's philosophy. The Gospels give us a mythical interpretation of Jesus, because they present historical facts embellished by the faith of the early Church. Through social and scientific advances in much of the nineteenth century there was fostered in many people an expectation of inevitable progress and a sense of the adequacy of scientific forms of knowledge.

Protestant liberalism's manner of understanding Christian revelation, faith, and the kingdom, and of leading others to accept these in the mid- and late nineteenth century, derived largely from Schleiermacher and biblical criticism. We recalled Schleiermacher's approach in our earlier volume,[69] and so here we confine ourselves to the following remarks. His apologetic, addressed to Christianity's "cultured despisers," showed the influence on him of Romanticism, his pietistic background, and his acceptance of Kant's strictures against intellectual arguments for the existence of God. Ronald Thiemann shows the place and importance of Schleiermacher:

[68]Löwith, *Meaning in History,* 58. Also see McKay, et al., *History of Western Society,* 795–834, 865–74.

[69]See Farrelly, *Belief in God,* 37–8, 151–2, 156–8.

The modern doctrine of revelation in its classic post-Kantian form attempts to provide a theoretical justification for revelation by formulating a universally valid argument for a unique mode of access to God's reality. Schleiermacher is clearly the father of the mature modern doctrine, and his account of revelation marks the pinnacle of achievement in this tradition. Schleiermacher's turn to human consciousness as the locus for God's revelation uncovers a rich terrain which theologians are still plowing in search of an argument demonstrating the possibility of that revelation.[70]

The word "revelation" here points to the source of a religion's beliefs, and this source is an inner experience by which God's communication is mediated. This inner experience is not to be identified with a knowing or a doing but rather with an experience of *absolute* dependence that implies as its source and goal—its whence and whither—the Infinite, which then we call God. To be fully human is to accept this part of oneself. And among religions, that of Jesus represents best what union with God means and how we can move from a sense of alienation from God to one of union with him. The Christian community fosters this union, and its doctrines express this inner experience symbolically and so support this union. We can see in this interpretation an effort to relate Christian belief to a cultural mode of human self-understanding current in Schleiermacher's time and thus an effort to avoid sheer positivism. And we can see how different it is from the approach of Locke and the Enlightenment. The difficulty is that he seems to reduce the criterion of Christian revelation and faith to a universal, interior human experience. It is all dialogue and no dialectic. This is not what we found in Scripture.

Much biblical criticism in the nineteenth century used the historical-critical method and approached the Bible as it would any historical book. This criticism rejected a fixed Christian theological view as placing an obstacle to objective analysis. Hegelian dialectic, as we recalled above, influenced Strauss' interpretation of the New Testament. In the second half of the century, evolutionary theory influenced such interpretations.[71] Ritschl and Harnack can exemplify Protestant liberalism.

---

[70]Thiemann, *Revelation and Theology*, 25; see 24–31.

[71]See Alexa Suelzer and John Kselman, "Modern Old Testament Criticism," and John Kselman and Ronald Witherup, "Modern New Testament Criticism," *NJBC*, esp. 1117–22, and 1132–5.

Albrecht Ritschl (1822–89) accepted Kant's dichotomy between speculative and value judgments. He identified religious judgments with the latter; they do not state what things are in themselves but how they are for us. Ritschl sought to get behind metaphysics and dogmas, which are the result of the Hellenization of early Christianity, to the simple message of Jesus, particularly as this is shown in the earliest strata of New Testament writings. Here he finds the "kingdom of God" of great importance: "The kingdom of God is the divinely ordained highest good of the community founded through God's revelation in Christ . . . only in the sense that it forms at the same time the ethical ideal for whose attainment the members of the community bind themselves to each other."[72] He and his disciples assimilated the kingdom to the nineteenth century's optimistic sense that they were evolving toward a more perfect society on the basis of their human enlightenment. Revelation was assimilated to their envisaging this human ideal. In one sense they did relate the Christian message to modern historical consciousness, but once more we find only dialogue and not dialectic. And this interpretation of Jesus' understanding of the kingdom would quickly be undermined by the scriptural studies of Weiss and Schweitzer.

Adolf von Harnack (1851–1930) was the most famous of Ritschl's followers. His book, *What Is Christianity?* (1900) presented a non-dogmatic Christianity with an exclusively "high-minded" religious interpretation of the kingdom. In Protestant liberalism and the lives of Jesus that it gave rise to, Scripture is less normative than a general human religious experience and social ideal.

It is important for us to examine briefly some representative Catholic efforts in the nineteenth century to offer meaning and grounds for belief in Jesus Christ because Vatican II's teaching in this regard builds on these earlier developments, though it goes beyond them. We have treated some Catholic efforts to give meaning and grounds for belief in God in this era in our earlier volume,[73] and we do not wish to repeat that here, though there will necessarily be some overlap. We will first give Gerald McCool's expression of the problem Catholic theology faced during this century and then recall some varied responses. McCool writes:

[72]A. Ritschl, *Three Essays,* trans. Philip Hefner (Philadelphia: Fortress Press, 1972) 222, as cited in Viviano, *Kingdom of God in History,* 114. On Protestant liberalism see idem, *Kingdom of God in History,* 113–6; McGrath, *Christian Theology,* 92–6; Dulles, *Revelation Theology,* 77–82.

[73]See Farrelly, *Belief in God,* 158–64.

The theologians of the Catholic renaissance addressed themselves to two major tasks. The first was the defense of the Catholic faith against the rationalism and the religious skepticism of the Enlightenment. The second was the presentation of positive Christian revelation in a coherent, unified system that could stand comparison with the systems of Fichte, Schelling, and Hegel without compromising the supernaturality and the unique, historical character of positive Christian revelation. . . . All through the nineteenth century Catholic theologians would be trying to show that Hegel was wrong and that a synthesis of positive revelation and speculative thought was possible. In the first half of the century Catholic theologians would attempt to effect the synthesis on the basis of post-Kantian scientific method. In the second half, under the influence of the neo-Thomists, they would revert to the Aristotelian scientific method of St. Thomas.[74]

We will recall something of these efforts in the first part of the century, in Vatican I, in Newman, and in Maurice Blondel's alternative to both Neoscholastics and the Modernists.

In the first part of the century Romanticism was an influence in Catholic as in Protestant theology. From the perspective of Vatican I it may seem that most Catholic theological efforts of this period were erroneous. But from our post-Vatican II perspective we see the need for integrating the intuitive with the rational, and tradition with the discursive reason of the individual, and so we can see some enduring value in these efforts. For example, Francois-René de Chateaubriand's *Genius of Christianity* found grounds for belief in Christianity in the beauty of the Christian message and its effects. And there were French apologists who, opposed to the Enlightenment's confidence in human reason and not able to contest Kant's critique of metaphysics on its own grounds, based belief in God on a religious tradition that goes back to the origins of humankind (Louis de Bonald and Felicité de Lamennais) or on faith (Louis Bautain). These views were rejected by Pope Gregory XVI.

Johann Sebastian von Drey (d. 1853), the founder of the Catholic Tübingen school of theology, had a more moderate traditionalism that was not condemned. Dependent in part on the idealist Schelling, Drey situated the individual within an organic whole that included

[74]McCool, *Catholic Theology,* 32–4.

God who expresses himself, the whole order of creation, and the stages of history through which God expresses himself up to and including Jesus. In turn, Jesus gave to his community the overriding and identifying idea of the kingdom of God that directs its growth and self-realization. This is the only adequate context for the response of faith to God. Knowledge of God must derive from God's speaking directly or indirectly; it cannot derive simply from discursive reason.[75]

Georg Hermes (d. 1831), on the other hand, while accepting the faith, thought that we could prove our need to accept it only by the agreement of the alleged revelation with moral reason, that is, by showing that this message is necessary if human beings are to fulfill the categorical imperative. Even though Christian revelation did occur through historical acts, we cannot know these with the requisite certitude or prove our need to believe save through practical reason. Because of this he is described as a semi-rationalist, and his view was condemned by Gregory XVI (1835).[76]

We have been recalling some early nineteenth-century Catholic reflections on revelation and faith. But since the grounds of belief in Jesus include the hope that through such belief we receive the kingdom of God, we should ask whether there was some presentation of the kingdom in relation to the modern historical consciousness of the age. While there were strong forces in the Church, for example, in France, holding that the monarchical political order was more consistent with the Christian life than a republican order, there were also those who supported liberalism even when it was still wedded to a strong anticlericalism (e.g., Felicité de Lammenais). Also, some Catholics began to develop a positive analysis of the changed social and economic orders and to defend the rights of workers (see, e.g., Archbishop Wilhelm von Ketteler, *The Worker Question and Christianity,* 1864). Pope Pius IX himself in his first years accommodated himself to liberalism as head of the Papal States, but after the revolutions of 1848 he became reactionary. This reactionary strain was expressed strongly in Pius IX's *Syllabus of Errors* (1864), where many errors of the time were condemned, among them the following: "The Roman Pontiff can and should reconcile himself with progress, liberalism and modern civilization" (80). Concerning such opposition to modern developments, Walter Kasper writes:

[75]See ibid., ch. 2, "French Traditionalism," 37–58; on Drey see 67–81.

[76]On Hermes see Fitzer, *Romance and the Rock,* 125–35; McCool, *Catholic Theology,* 59–67.

The papal commission *Justitia et pax* has issued a working paper on *The Church and Human Rights* (1974), which states self-criti- cally that the church's attitude toward human rights in the last two centuries "has all too often been characterized by hesitation, ob- jections and reservations." It even speaks about open hostility and condemnation by certain popes.

Much of this is understandable, historically speaking. Yet we have to say that Christianity has often failed miserably to put across its own deepest concern: the message of the God who in his divinity liberates us for a humane humanity. And the tragedy of the modern development is that essential humane Christian impulses have had to be asserted in the face of Christianity in its mainstream form.[77]

We looked at Vatican I and John Henry Newman on the issues of revelation and faith in our earlier volume,[78] and we will not repeat that here. We will just recall some of their central teachings on these matters, showing there is a certain complementarity and tension be- tween the council and Newman, a tension largely overcome by Vatican II. Vatican I's teaching on faith and revelation in its constitu- tion, *Dei Filius,* was specifically directed against Enlightenment views and certain Catholic reactions to it that it correctly deemed in- adequate (traditionalism, fideism, and semi-rationalism). It made use of and fostered a resurgent Thomism.

It taught that God can indeed be known by the natural light of human reason but that "it has pleased [God] in his wisdom and good- ness to reveal himself and the eternal decrees of his will in another and supernatural way" (DS 3004). Such a revelation is absolutely necessary, "because God has ordained man to a supernatural end, to participate in divine gifts which totally transcend the understanding of the human mind" (DS 3005). This revelation is contained in the books of Scripture and in apostolic tradition. As creatures we must in faith give the full obedience of mind and will to God revealing, a faith in which "by the help of God's grace, we believe to be true those things that are revealed by him, not because their intrinsic truth is perceived by the natural light of reason, but because of the author-

---

[77]Walter Kasper, *Theology and Church* (New York: Crossroad, 1989) 38.

[78]See Farrelly, *Belief in God,* 158–64. On Vatican I's *Dei Filius,* see McCool, *Catholic Theology,* 216–26. We cite Vatican I in our text by the Denzinger-Schönmetzer paragraph numbers.

ity of God revealing, who can neither deceive nor be deceived" (DS 3008). That the obedience of our faith may be in accord with reason, God has given not only the internal help of the Holy Spirit but "external arguments for his revelation, namely divine deeds, and particularly miracles and prophesies, . . . [as] certain signs of divine revelation accommodated to the intelligence of all" (DS 3009).

Indeed, the Church itself is a perpetual motive of credibility because of its "admirable expansion, its outstanding holiness and inexhaustible fruitfulness in all good, its Catholic unity and unconquered stability" (DS 3013). Thus there is a double order of knowledge, distinct in principle and object. But there is not contradiction between faith and reason; indeed, they offer help to one another, "since true reason demonstrates the foundations of faith and, illumined by its light, develops a knowledge of divine things, while faith frees and protects reason from errors and gives it new knowledge" (DS 3019).

Vatican I's analysis of revelation and reason was primarily an abstract and nonhistorical contrast, an analysis of the mutual relationship between two orders of knowledge and their objects, showing their objectivity and the objectivity of bases for belief in God's supernatural revelation, though it did insist as well on the interior help of the Holy Spirit and the sign that the Church itself is. In this latter addition, the council fathers were influenced by the apologetics of Victor Dechamps, the archbishop of Malines, of which McCool writes: "Its appeal to the correspondence between the concrete reality of the Church and the 'interior fact' of man's subjective needs was the distinctive trait."[79]

Cardinal Newman's apologetic seems closer to Dechamps than to the main thrust of Vatican I in its incorporation of the subjective, the phenomenological, and informal reasoning. In language somewhat idiosyncratic, Newman spoke of revelation as an "idea," or impression, in fact, as "the initial and essential idea of Christianity."[80] By "impression" he meant that "the perception that God gives of himself in revelation is original, divinely produced, and conformed to the object it represents" (253). As "idea," it is an invisible principle that takes hold of the mind and leads it to a deeper understanding of itself. Christian revelation is an idea that is comprehensive in the sense that

---

[79]McCool, *Catholic Theology,* 223.

[80]In this section on Newman, I am depending on Avery Dulles, "From Images to Truth: Newman on Revelation and Faith," *TS* 51 (1990) 252–67. References to Newman's works can be found there. Page references in the text are to pages of Dulles' article.

it is a master vision that "unconsciously supplies the mind with spiritual life and peace" (Newman, *Oxford University Sermons*), though it is necessarily expressed part by part through creeds and dogmas. It is living in that it interacts in the human mind with the whole order of the person's other knowledge. It is real in that it preexists the human mind, for, "[t]hrough the appearances of nature and the symbols of Scripture, liturgy and dogma, God communicates mysterious and heavenly truth to which the human mind is receptive but nevertheless unequal" (254). It is the idea of Christ that is central and essential to Christianity. This idea is expressed by different dogmas that are necessary to give "unity and direction to the community of faith" (255). Through dogmas we have "supernatural truths irrevocably committed to human language, imperfect because they are human, but definitive and necessary because given from above" *(Development of Christian Doctrine)*.

This view of Newman reflects not relativism but the mysterious character of revelation given through Christ and the inviolate though imperfect and developing character of the Church's expression of revelation in its dogmas. Thus for Newman Christian revelation is objective and complete in apostolic times, and "God continues to speak His word today and . . . the revealed idea in the mind of any believer is an 'inward manifestation,' an 'inward impression'" (260).

The response to revelation is faith, which Newman described as follows: "As sight contemplates form and colour, and reason the processes of argument, so faith rests on the divine word as the token and criterion of truth. . . . By faith then is meant the mind's perception or apprehension of heavenly things, arising from an instinctive trust in the divinity or truth of the external word, informing it concerning them" *(Lectures on the Doctrine of Justification)*. Thus faith depends on an external word that mediates the revealed idea; faith is the correlative of dogma. It is an internal assent, and specifically a real assent (as distinct from notional) that involves conviction and commitment. Its object is not simply an intellectual content but one that appeals to the imagination and affections, as the words of Scripture do.

Newman responded to the Enlightenment's demand for strict reasons for what one accepts through faith by emphasizing not the external evidences for Christian faith, as Vatican I generally did, but the need for certain moral predispositions. "Only those with the requisite preparation of heart are in a position to judge the claims of religion. We are responsible for our faith because we are responsible for our likes and dislikes, our inclinations and repugnances" (262). Antecedent to faith we must be responsive to conscience and in doing so are already accepting what is beyond the visible and demonstrable.

Conscience implies the existence of a Supreme Power, and acceptance of this Power in natural religion disposes us toward worship, prayer, and obedience to the divine and even an anticipation that a revelation will be given. With these dispositions faith "acts promptly and boldly on the occasion, on slender evidence, as if guessing or reaching forward to the truth, amid darkness or confusion" *(University Sermons)*. Grace is operative here, of course. Newman wrote that "[w]e believe because we love." "Love, not reason, is the eye of faith" *(University Sermons)*. This was a kind of phenomenology of faith. He knew that most people's Christian faith did not depend on examination of the apologetic proofs for Christian revelation, and he thought that a stringent demand for evidences betrayed a disposition resistant to faith, as though human beings are judges rather than suppliants. Moreover, people act on an informal logic, and they may not be able to spell this out explicitly. Newman's teaching on faith was later contested by many Neoscholastics and misused by some Catholic Modernists to support their own positions, but the personalist perspective of Vatican II on faith has led to more positive evaluation of his teaching.

Finally we should say a word about the reflection on faith and revelation in the Modernist period, though we recall only the problem posed at the end of the nineteenth century, the initial response of Maurice Blondel in his philosophy of action, and then his extension of this response to include the problem of history raised by Loisy.

Roger Haight expresses well the problem posed to the Church at the end of the nineteenth century:

> Modernism was born out of the confrontation between traditional Catholic doctrine and theology, and the history, science and culture of modernity. One sees in the Church at the end of the nineteenth century an authoritarian structure, a world apart, whose official scholastic theology, with its hardened and static formulas, was isolated from modern intellectual culture but shared in the Church's authority. For this Church, the world of modern philosophy, the advances of critical historical scholarship, and the world of science were a grave menace. Given this situation, once the principle of immanence and the presuppositions of man's autonomy began

to be taken seriously in the domain of philosophy, the idea of a supernatural truth imposed on man from the outside and solely through a church authority became ambiguous. On the level of historical science, when the method and findings of biblical criticism began to be recognized, certain historical data seemed to contradict this authority. When this modern world came crashing in on Catholic theology, crisis was born. This is the general problematic of Catholic Modernism.[81]

It is only Blondel's responses to this crisis that we are recalling here, and they can be seen in two stages. In the first stage he responds as a philosopher to the modern question of how a philosopher could "take seriously a doctrine that demands the submission of mind and will to an external supernatural order . . . [and] be obliged to take account of an event that occurred so long ago in an obscure corner of the Roman Empire" (636). His doctoral dissertation, *L'Action*, presented at the Sorbonne in 1893, was an attempt to deal with this problem. In this book he develops a phenomenology of human action showing that action reflects a human desire for much more than the immediate purposes of discrete actions, in fact, that it reflects a desire for an absolute and infinite. Action shows an exigency for the supernatural. He concludes with a discussion of the hypothetical possibility that Christianity offers the response to this demand. Thus he develops an apologetic based on the method of immanence. This proposal evoked a great deal of opposition both from the philosophers of the time and from Scholastic theologians, and it led Blondel to further clarifications.

A further complication of the problem and a further stage of Blondel's own response was provoked by Alfred Loisy's use of the critical-historical method in his study of the Gospels. Blondel immediately attacked a historical method that would lead to Loisy's assertion of a limited consciousness in Jesus, which Blondel took to be a denial of his divinity. Blondel held that a strictly historical method could not be used on religious data because it would reduce this data "to events explicable in the natural order" (644).

---

[81]Roger Haight, "The Unfolding of Modernism in France: Blondel, Laberthonniere, Le Roy," *TS* 35 (1974) 632–66, especially page 661. Page references in the text here are to Haight's article. Also see Gabriel Daly, *Transcendence and Immanence: A Study in Catholic Modernism and Integralism* (Oxford: Clarendon Press, 1980).

Blondel was partially satisfied with Loisy's response that he was, as a historian, operating with a methodological reserve. Thus Blondel wrote his book *Histoire et Dogme* (1904), addressing it "to two abstract and ideal systems of ideas which he himself constructed, i.e., extrinsicism and historicism" (645). Extrinsicism refers to a decadent Scholasticism that seeks to prove the credibility of Christian revelation only by the external arguments of miracles and then imposes this on a passive believer from the outside. Historicism refers to the historian's attempt to explain religious data as he "would ordinary positive and empirical events, . . . [thus distorting] the religious or transcendent character of these events" (646). The problem "concerned the possibility and the necessity of normative Christian events and revelation in a world of historicity and historical consciousness and the way to interpret the past" (664). The way Blondel mediated the extremes he posits rested on "an existential view of the 'real history' behind its [Scripture's] historical and written record . . . and 'tradition,' grounded in the actual lives of Christians, as the continuous link in the development of dogma" (646).

Perhaps we can say that Blondel's effort to interrelate the philosophical and historical dimensions of foundations for Christian faith is a central part of what we are attempting in this and the preceding volume. But our post–Vatican II perspective gives us certain advantages. In our previous volume we did use a phenomenology of human action with the help of developmental psychology and social experience to show that human persons are indeed oriented to an absolute dimension of the good in their individual and social lives. We suggested, as Vatican II did, that God gives testimonies to himself through exterior and interior human experiences and that in the present order these are ordained to a supernatural goal and thus mediate, though incompletely, supernatural revelation and faith. The philosophical arguments we used are reflective, systematic evaluations of such intimations, contained within the person's question of whether these intimations of the divine are genuine.

Similarly, the way we interpreted Scripture in the present volume as proclamation of the good news that makes use of historical words and deeds of Jesus both accepts and transcends the historical-critical method. In chapter 8, on revelation, we will show more implications of this approach, while in chapter 7 we will relate salvation to our personal search, but we will integrate with this the social and the future perhaps more than Blondel did.

7

Salvation and Its Meaning in Our Time

In this chapter we seek to articulate theologically the meaning of Christian salvation for our time and place. Foundational theology studies the meaning and foundations of our belief in God through Jesus Christ. The study of Scripture is primary for both of these purposes, but it is not sufficient. One can still ask whether it is possible for God to raise Jesus from the dead, and we will treat this question later in this chapter. One can also note that the Gospels and epistles express the meaning of salvation, revelation, and faith in reference to the concerns and categories of their addressees.

The theologian of our time must similarly articulate the meaning and significance or value of salvation, revelation, and faith in reference to the concerns and categories—or preunderstandings—of our time and place, while being wholly faithful to Scripture. This is theology's contribution to the *inculturation* of our Christian faith.[1] We cannot a priori accept the articulation of some past time and place as adequate for our own, no matter how true and of what continuing authority this past articulation was and is. For example, Thomas and Luther were addressing concerns and using the conceptual tools of their times and places. The problem of articulating the faith today is different from relating it to a world opened up to the West by Greek philosophy or showing the terrified sinner a compassionate God.

[1] See Vatican II, *Gaudium et Spes* nos. 53–62; Paul VI, *Evangelii nuntiandi (On the Evangelization of the Modern World)* 20; Aylward Shorter, *Toward a Theology of Inculturation* (Maryknoll, N.Y.: Orbis Books, 1988); Robert Schreiter, "Faith and Cultures: Challenges to a World Church," *TS* 50 (1989) 744–60; Carl Starkloff, "Inculturation and Cultural Systems," *TS* 55 (1994) 66–81, 274–94.

The problem of inculturation is not only appropriate for missionaries who are proclaiming the Christian message to a non-Western culture. It is a problem for us in the nations of the North Atlantic, because our culture is not that of the sixteenth or thirteenth century. We have experienced a cultural revolution, one consequence of which is that there is a split between the Gospel and culture. Pope Paul VI wrote, "The split between the Gospel and culture is without a doubt the drama of our time, just as it was of other times" (*On Evangelization in the Modern World, [EN]* 20). Thus if we simply repeat the theology of an earlier age we fail to communicate with our own; in fact, we create an obstacle to the understanding and appreciation of the Christian message.

We have spoken of this cultural revolution primarily in terms of modern historical consciousness, which is, in practice at least, largely naturalistic. We realize that historical epochs differ, that our lives are lived not so much in the circle of the seasons of the year as in our individual and communal histories. Who we are depends on decisions of the past, and what will become of us depends largely on what we and our communities will decide or have already done. Meaning is largely found in the intermediate future, not the ultimate and transhistorical. This view becomes naturalistic when people act as though the only agents, knowledge, and resources active in history are natural or human and the only goal is what is contained in history. Theology, then, must relate the Christian message of salvation, revelation, and faith to this preunderstanding. Since theology must be faithful to Scripture, it cannot reduce the meaning of these themes to what our world will accept; it must relate it to this preunderstanding of our age if theology is faith seeking understanding for ourselves and others.

Jesus proclaimed the kingdom of God by his words and deeds, and thus it was through *symbols* that he presented this gift offered to us by him. "The symbol gives rise to thought," as Paul Ricoeur reminds us. If we accept, as I think we must, a structuralist dimension to the development of Christian doctrine (a matter we hope to explain and defend in a third volume of *Foundational Theology*), we must say that the articulation of Christian doctrine does not depend exclusively on the intrinsic significance of the Christian mystery but also on the resources of a particular culture such as its concerns and understanding of humanity and the cosmos.

For example, Nicaea's statement that the Son was *homoousios* (the same substance) with the Father depended in part on the philosophical concerns and concepts of Hellenism. This is not relativism, because there is something valid transculturally concerning what it means to be human, what being is, and who God is; and each culture from its perspective has something to contribute to knowledge of humanity, of being, and of God. God is related to all cultures, and so are being and humanity. The riches of a particular culture come from God and can contribute to our understanding of the inexhaustible Christian mystery. We do not, of course, say that the perspective of a particular culture should be simply affirmed rather than critiqued. There is error as well as truth in a culture, evil as well as good.

Of course, much of postmodernism contests what we have written in the preceding paragraph. In attempting to give proper weight to the pluralism among cultures in a multicentered world—a weight that was not given in earlier philosophies that sought to subsume all pluralism under one unitary perspective—many of the proponents of postmodernism fall into epistemological and axiological relativisms.[2] In my previous volume I presented a critical evaluation of belief in God that took these concerns into account, since it started from an acceptance of modern historical consciousness. I sought to show that on the basis of contemporary experience (as previously on the basis of experiences in the premodern world) we can critically justify a genuine objectivity in moral values, metaphysical knowledge, the validity of intimations of God based on experience of an evolving cosmos and of conscience, and God's relationship to a world in change.

Similarly, earlier in this volume we showed that the Gospels did have reference to what Jesus said and did historically and through this to what God was revealing and doing. The perspectives we bring from our different locations can enable us to see more through these writings than was seen previously. We can, for example, acknowledge a validity to intimations of the divine found in world religions without that undercutting the validity of our Western belief in a personal tran-

---

[2]See, for example, William Dean, *History Making History: The New Historicism in American Thought* (Albany: State University of New York Press, 1988); Jean-Francois Lyotard, *The Post-Modern Condition: A Report on Knowledge* (Minneapolis: University of Minnesota Press, 1984). For theological treatments of the issues raised, see, for example, David Griffin, William Beardslee, and Joe Holland, *Varieties of Postmodern Theology* (Albany: State University of New York Press, 1989); Thomas Guarino, *Revelation and Truth: Unity and Plurality in Contemporary Theology* (Scranton: University of Scranton Press, 1993); Jack Bonsor, "History, Dogma, and Nature: Further Reflections on Postmodernism and Theology," *TS* 55 (1994) 295–313.

scendent God. In fact, the perspectives of other religions can recall to us riches of our own that have been obscured by our culture. Our present study is based on our previous study of these themes. One can see what we studied in our first volume as based on revelations God has graced us with through the reality of the cosmos, of conscience, of our own humanity. These can form a *praeparatio evangelica,* a kind of preparation for the gospel in our time and place. This relation between pre-Christian revelation and Christian revelation will be further clarified by our treatment in the next chapter of Christian revelation and faith.

The *primary context* in which we seek to articulate the meaning of Christian salvation is the challenge that modern historical consciousness, in part naturalistic, presents to the traditional Christian interpretation of salvation. We have seen that pre-Vatican II twentieth-century Catholic theologies and Barth did not speak sufficiently to this challenge; Bultmann seems to have succumbed to it. Post-Vatican II theologies deal with it much more centrally, whether they are primarily based on objective intellectual grounds or on praxis. We have seen in Scripture that apocalyptic was central to the meaning of Christian salvation. This is a perspective different from creation. Yet Thomas and classical theology generally seemed to read the order of redemption with a perspective dominated by creation in the *exitus-reditus* scheme. In contrast, some recent theologians seem to read creation from the perspective of Scripture's apocalyptic interpretation of salvation. Here we refer to Moltmann and Pannenberg, who conclude that God is the power of the future. Moltmann, in fact, denies that there is such a thing as human nature; there is only a human history.[3] In this conflict we see once more the conflict between dialogue and dialectic.

---

[3]See Douglas Schuurman, "Moltmann: Eschaton, Creation, and Social Ethics," *Creation, Eschaton, and Ethics* (New York: Peter Lang, 1991) 125, where he speaks of Moltmann's rejection of the Lutheran theology of "orders" and philosophy's assertion of a human nature: "The anthropological corollary to this idea of the orders likewise denies history by affirming that human beings have a 'nature' which perdures throughout the changes of time. According to Moltmann, human nature 'cannot be identified by abstracting permanent characteristic traits from [its] history' as though these traits were the foundation for historical appearances. . . . More than ever before in human history, experience is characterized by the absence of permanent, changeless reality and the dominance of change. . . . The theology of orders wrongly attempts to construct an eternal foundation to what is essentially and exclusively temporal. Both the eschatological horizon of Christian hope and modern experience of reality as changeable affirm the fundamental historicity of human experience. This historicity and related openness to new possibilities is precisely what is denied by the theology of orders. . . . '[M]an does not have a nature but a history.' Christian eschatology and

A *second context* for our study here is to redress the imbalance an earlier theology showed between Christ and the Spirit in its interpretation of salvation. A *third context* is to redress the imbalance between the interpretation of salvation as ultimate union with God and the interpretation of it as release from oppression and injustice in history. One might see this last issue as a continuation of the tension found in the New Testament between the apocalyptic and the messianic interpretations of salvation.

In all of these we see ourselves as walking in the path opened up for us at Vatican II and thus as critically and positively evaluating its interpretation of salvation while, in some elements, going beyond its explicit articulation. The Churches teach that we should believe in Jesus Christ because it is through him that God has given us salvation. We ask then (I) whether we need salvation, (II) what Christian salvation is, and (III) how this interpretation compares to some other theological views and to some views of other world religions. We do this in simply an introductory fashion.

I. Do We Need Salvation?

Scripture shows us how one community, that of the Jewish people, came through time to realize more and more deeply their need for salvation from God. They recognized their inability on their own to keep from self-destruction as individuals and as a people and their need to turn to God, who alone could assure them of deliverance from hostile forces within and around them and could assure them of an enduring life together, characterized by that peace that is a *wholeness* of human beings with God, with one another, and with the rest of creation. We saw too that Peter and the first followers of Jesus did begin to believe in him because they viewed him as the one through whom God was going to give them the salvation they needed. And in our account of conversions in our earlier volume, we saw that there still continues in our time on the part of many a sense of a need for a salvation that only God can give.

---

contemporary experience provisionally confirm this maxim of historicism." For enclosed quotes from Moltmann, see Jürgen Moltmann, *Hope and Planning* (London: SCM Press, 1971) 117–8. On 118, Moltmann writes: "The recognition that man does not have nature but history means an overcoming of all the naturalistic or quasi-naturalistic ways of thinking." Moltmann frequently stresses discontinuity between creation in the historical order and Christian eschatology, even contradiction.

There are, however, in our age of modern and largely naturalistic historical consciousness, many who, while they sense that the world is not as it should be, look to human efforts to change it so that it is just, humane, and whole. They look to changes in the economy, in the government, in technology and its availability to all, and in education, as well as to such sources as psychotherapy and the development of supportive communities. We can acclaim much that they hold as necessary for a humane life, while we still question their naturalism. We contested a naturalistic anthropology in our first volume, and we rely on that here. Thus the human person is oriented through stages—in accord with a maturing human potential and in differing and enlarging social environments—toward a fulfillment in accord with a constitutive human good, and indeed toward God, who alone can fulfill the human heart. To be a human person is to seek these human values as participations in God in a way that does not separate us from God, union with whom is more deeply necessary to our fulfillment and the meaning of our lives than any other good. We are oriented to God through our orientation to human goods, and this includes the good of community. Thus too we are oriented to God through freedom and time, or history. The only good that can fulfill us is, as the symbols of Scripture indicate, wholistic.

We have similarly shown in our earlier volume that God is acting within us as individuals and communities through the goods appropriate for us—and thus through "the signs of the times" and through conscience—to lead us or orient us to himself through these goods. Respecting our freedom as co-creators with him and under him in history, he gives us responsibility for ourselves and others. He leads us as individuals and as communities.

However, there is much that obstructs our living in this way. Of course, not a few in our time think that human values are what human beings choose and that they themselves are the autonomous deciders of what will fulfill them. In fact, this view, as Nietzsche saw, leads to nihilism;[4] it is contradictory to the limited beings we are. Those who view life this way need salvation to accept themselves as their humanity shows them to be and to do so in thanksgiving to God.

There is much that obstructs our putting God first in our lives, that gets in the way of living by what is deepest in us and from accepting

---

[4]See Friedrich Nietzsche, *The Will to Power* (London: Weidenfeld & Nicholson, 1968) 9, 318; Johann Goudsblom, *Nihilism and Culture* (Totowa, N.C.: Roman & Littlefield, 1980).

a *wholistic* goal that includes respect for the dignity of all other human beings, a preference to fulfill the needs of the poor over the cravings of the rich, and a living in harmony with natural creation that sustains us as our environment. There is much that obstructs *hope* for a better human future for ourselves and for others, because this future depends on many other human beings and we are aware of our own weaknesses. The evils of individual and communal existence can easily overwhelm us and make us think that efforts to change the world are futile. The experience of these evils in a world where many people trample the individual in search of their own perceived needs saps many children's and adult children's basic trust in their own worth and future, in other people, in institutions whose function it is to promote human welfare, and in God. And what is the answer to death itself that seems to threaten all our hopes?

The inclinations in ourselves and in others to put first not God but, in a way that is destructive of ourselves and others, some particular felt need can be called *addiction*. Initially this word was used for alcoholics and drug addicts, and later it was extended to a whole range of needs such as addiction to food, codependency, and so on. But, appropriately I think, Gerald May suggests that it is a good metaphor for sin or the inclination to sin.[5] These addictions, for example, to security, to freedom from commitment, to past structures that are now counterproductive, to our small group to the exclusion of others, bring us to actions or to inactions that are destructive.

These addictions in us derive not simply from our own limitations and past sins but from the societies of which we are a part. Societies are structured forms of response that have been defined and institutionalized by past human free decisions about what is beneficial for that society or that part of it that exercises power. Roger Haight writes:

> Social arrangements are meant to enhance human freedom. . . . But institutions also limit and determine behavior. Moreover they invariably involve oppressive elements. . . . The identity of every group is defined by its boundaries over against other groups. . . . One is inclined to be loyal to one's family, tribe, caste, corporation, professional guild, economic class, regional society, race, nation, sex—right or wrong. The objective structures that define social institutions are internalized by those born into them or

---

[5]See Gerald May, *Addiction and Grace* (San Francisco: Harper & Row, 1988).

joined to them. . . . This objective determination of human beings . . . enters into the personhood of each individual as a "second nature." Thus every individual *is* social or socially constituted
in being. This accounts for the infectious quality of the sin of the
world and its contagion.[6]

Even to escape from one's society does not really answer this problem because one may thereby become responsible for one's group re-
maining in its inclination to injustice.

It is through such experiences in Israel's history and their seeing
them as the universal condition of human beings that the scriptural
foundations for the doctrine of original sin were laid. St. Paul expressed a universal human experience when he wrote: "I take delight
in the law of God, in my inner self, but I see in my members another
principle at war with the law of my mind, taking me captive to the
law of sin that dwells in my members. Miserable one that I am! Who
will deliver me from this mortal body?" (Rom 7:23-24). People can,
of course, block recognition of this condition in them, and they frequently do. But the result is that they become to some degree alienated from themselves and cut themselves down to what they feel
comfortable with.[7]

We propose in accord with what religions worldwide affirm that if
we are honest to our experience, we will recognize that we are individually and socially to some degree alienated from what is deepest
in our selves and from God and that we cannot of ourselves liberate
ourselves or our societies from such alienation.[8] We and our societies
need to be saved by a power greater than we have at our command.
Who can forgive us for our individual or communal sins except God?
Who can deliver us from death? Who can deliver us and our communities from the destruction with which our tendencies to evil
threaten us? If people do not acknowledge their spiritual sickness,
they obviously will not recognize their need for Christ's salvation
(Matt 9:12-13).

---

[6]Roger Haight, "Sin and Grace," *Systematic Theology: Roman Catholic Perspectives,* ed.
Francis Schüssler Fiorenza and John Galvin (Minneapolis: Fortress Press, 1991) 103–4. On original sin see Haight's article and the references there; see also G. Vandervelde, *Original Sin: Two
Major Trends in Contemporary Roman Catholic Reinterpretation* (Amsterdam: Rodophi N.V.,
1975), on which I wrote a review article in *The Thomist* 43 (1979) 482–8.

[7]See Ernest Becker, *The Denial of Death* (Macmillan/ Free Press, 1975) 181.

[8]See John Henry Newman, *Grammar of Assent* (New York: Doubleday, 1955) 308–11.

II. The Meaning of Christian Salvation

In our effort here to give an introductory theological explanation of Christian salvation, we are seeking to interpret what is mediated symbolically by Scripture through relating it to an understanding of humanity that emerges from our modern historical consciousness and of the evils that afflict us. Vatican I encouraged the theologian to seek some limited though fruitful understanding of the divine mysteries "from analogy with those things which human reason naturally knows, and from the relation of the mysteries among themselves and with humankind's ultimate goal."[9] We will use these varied ways in our effort to explain briefly the meaning of salvation. Specifically in a period of historical consciousness, we understand that human beings move toward their ultimate end through stages and conditions of history.

Relying on what we earlier found in our study of the New Testament, we recognize that Jesus may well have proclaimed the kingdom of God initially in a predominantly messianic meaning. But when it was evident that he was to be rejected by the Jewish leaders, he proclaimed it in a predominantly apocalyptic meaning that subordinated without rejecting the messianic meaning. It was in this sense also that the early Church proclaimed salvation, or the kingdom of God, and it is in this apocalyptic sense that we interpret it here. Thus we will interpret it (1) in its future meaning or as the ultimate gift it is; (2) in its present meaning, for it is in part already operative here in history. Here we shall examine it *(a)* as present in the Church and *(b)* in the wider society. There is, of course, some overlap among these themes. Finally (3) we shall reflect briefly on whether such salvation is possible.

1. The Salvation in Its Fullness That Christ Offers Us

In treating this question, we note once again that we are treating not the soteriological question, that is, how it is that Jesus merited salvation for us, an issue examined in Christology, but what the salvation is that he won for us and how he makes that available to us.[10]

---

[9]Vatican I, "Dei Filius," DS 3016.

[10]For recent studies of salvation from a more soteriological perspective, see, for example, Brian McDermott, *Word Become Flesh: Dimensions of Christology* (Collegeville: The Liturgical Press, 1993) 211–48; Elizabeth Johnson, "Jesus and Salvation," *Proceedings of the Catholic Theological Society of America* 49 (1994) 1–18.

Though we do seek to say something about what salvation is, we are not here dwelling at length on what Scripture tells us of heaven or our promised beatitude; that is studied by eschatology. Christ expressed this salvation through symbols, and particularly through the resurrection that is a parousiac mystery—an anticipation, a proleptic event pointing to and promising the resurrection of those who believe in him. The salvation he offers us is primarily that which he will give us when he comes again. Though he expressed this primarily through symbols, there are some things we can say about it in a more conceptual manner.[11]

God will give us his definitive and never-to-be-surpassed salvific inbreaking into history when Jesus comes again. It is here that he will fully liberate humankind. Through Jesus constituted as Lord he will save all who believe in him from sin, Satan, and death and establish the definitive kingdom of God. That is, Jesus will unite us forever to himself and to his Father and to one another; he will liberate us from all that is evil, all that obstructs this unity with God, with ourselves, and with others. There will be no more sorrow and no more tears. This is a universal kingdom and an everlasting kingdom. It is to be the end and the raising up (*aufhebung,* overcoming and elevation) of history as we know it. This is both a personal and a communal fulfillment and liberation.

God will give himself wholly to those who were faithful or who were converted and faithful till the end. He makes us his sons and daughters, and we will inherit the kingdom along with the Son. Thus he will fulfill and more than fulfill our orientation to God as human beings and overcome all that obstructs our relationship to God, that alone can give meaning and fulfillment to our lives. We have shown earlier in this and the preceding volume that through the process of history we seek union with a personal God and with one another and that this search and longing is obstructed by much that is within us and outside of us. In our treatment of the stages of our individual lives we saw that the meaning of this process, or history, was our search for an ultimate or absolute, which is God as personal. This represents the depth of our own person, varied dimensions of which are shown in the process of these stages, and it represents what God himself is leading us to in this same process.

[11]See Karl Rahner, "The Hermeneutics of Eschatological Assertions," *Theological Investigations* (London: Darton, Longman & Todd, 1966) 4:323–46.

In the salvation the exalted Christ will give us, what has total priority is his gift of this union. When Christ comes again he will give this as sheer gift to those who have received him in faith. As believers in Christ we already have as promised inheritance this union with God, which is the meaning, sustenance, and goal of all our life's longing. We are not first given an incremental movement to a particular new stage in our lives and in our transformation of the world about us so that it is more humane and less oppressive. In our conversion through faith and baptism we are given first a liberation from the enslavement that would give such a focus primacy in our lives. That is, we are liberated from a naturalism in practice. We are liberated from being controlled by the naturalism around us and within us.

We are given not only the union with God but, through the Holy Spirit, the interior disposition of love that enables us to put this value, this relationship, first in our lives. We are given first God's love for us, and by this we are given this opening in our interior lives to love God above all and love our neighbor as ourselves. We are given the gift of surrender to God through God's self-gift. This is an opening to the fullness of the future—our individual and our communal future—so that we are actually assured of this and are given the dispositions whereby we can prefer it and foster it in ourselves and in others.

This is the deepest healing of the human person and community, for it is the liberation from what is most destructive of the person and community. We are given this through our acceptance of union with the death of Christ, that is, our acceptance of holding everything else in our lives as a secondary value and our willingness to sacrifice all of this if the primacy of love entails it. It is only that response to God's love and call that makes us inheritors of the promise, and it is only by persevering in that disposition that we continue to be heirs of the promise. This promise is of a union with God that death itself cannot obstruct but can only further. It is then transhistorical, as the goal and meaning of history itself is transhistorical.

We will be given, as we said above, not only our individual personal fulfillment but a share in that perfect community with Christ and one another in which there will be one mind and one heart. The saved will see themselves as united with the justified of all ages, not only with those living at a particular time but with those who precede and follow them in history, for these too will rise. This community will overcome all that brings disunity among people and among peoples, all that brings opposition, separation, and alienation. This reunion will never be threatened again, never be broken, never be subverted by evil. This salvation, then, is both human and divine. It is wholistic too, for it involves not only our union with God, our unity within ourselves, and our union with one another but even a "new heaven and a new earth" (Rev 21:1), and thus our union with a wholly renewed natural world, healed from what has been inflicted on it as a result of human sin (Isa 11:1-9; 66:17, 25).

This community will be seen as that toward which the whole of evolution and history is moving as their secret source and meaning and goal. We earlier sought to show that the individual person is by his or her very humanity oriented to the human community and not simply to an individual fulfillment. Thus this community will be seen as the meaning of the whole course of history. It will be seen also as the goal and fulfillment of God's providence and governance of the world, and as the result of the salvation and liberation effected by Jesus Christ and the Holy Spirit.[12] It too is transhistorical, not as disengaging us from history and its tasks but as the fulfillment of the tasks of history and the liberation from all that obstructs perfect community. All of this is given to us not simply as something that frees us from the area of change and mutability but rather as the completion of the movement that occurs through evolution and history. It is not a return to the primordial but the fulfillment of all the potentiality of the primordial. Creation and its extension in history is fulfilled and liberated only through the redemption or salvation of Jesus Christ, which is the kingdom of God.

All of this communal and individual fulfillment and liberation is given us by the exalted Christ and the Spirit. It is not only a teleological fulfillment of our movement and hopes and a liberation from our fears; rather, it comes to us through the *advent* of the exalted Christ, who has been made Lord of history. It is the gift he himself brings when he comes again at the parousia to those who are faithful servants or, rather, sons and daughters of God. God the Father approaches us through Christ and the Spirit from the future when he offers us this salvation, and so meets us as we face the future and long for its fulfillment and our liberation from all that obstructs this within ourselves and outside of ourselves.

---

[12]On God's providence and the Lordship of Jesus in relation to this, see M. John Farrelly, "Providence," *The Modern Catholic Encyclopedia,* ed. Michael Glazier and Monika Hellwig (Collegeville: The Liturgical Press, 1994) 699–701.

One thing to note about this salvation that is offered us by God through Jesus Christ is that it is at present *absent.* We possess this in hope, but hope that is seen is not hope (Rom 8:24). And so people are able to interpret the world and history naturalistically: "Where is the promise of his coming? From the time when our ancestors fell asleep, everything has remained as it was from the time of creation" (2 Pet 3:4). We live now by faith, but faith that has grounds in the resurrection of Jesus, the presence of the Holy Spirit within us, and that crowd of witnesses who have preceded us in the way of faith (Hebrews 11). Thus, too, our belief in the assurance of salvation is not overcome by the sufferings we as Christ's followers endure in this life. We are enabled by the Spirit to follow the path of Jesus, who went through death to life. Experiences such as the Holocaust and other forms of genocide are critical experiences for faith, as the persecution of the Jews under Antiochus Epiphanes was and as the death of Jesus was, but they can deepen rather than undercut faith in God's salvation; they do not contradict Scripture's teaching on how God saves humankind.

This interpretation differs in part from those of St. Thomas and of Moltmann and Pannenberg. It differs from Thomas because it makes the parousia of Jesus Christ the definitive point of salvation, as Scripture does, and so interprets salvation as coming to us from Jesus as he has gone into the fullness of our future, namely the kingdom of God. This is counter to Thomas' large use in his *exitus-reditus* schema of Neoplatonism and the incarnation as his model for interpreting God's salvific activity. He interprets God's salvific action largely through his model of God's causality in creation. Counter to this, we have seen that God's present salvific activity comes to us through the advent of Jesus Christ. Thus too, it sets up in us a movement toward the Father through Jesus and the Spirit that fully integrates history— in fact, more fully integrates it than any philosophy of history does or can. In reference to this I would like to quote from a review I wrote on Hans Urs von Balthasar's *Theological Anthropology* (New York: Sheed & Ward, 1967) some years ago. Balthasar holds that:

> History has a cyclic character; it is from God and to God. Religious time is primarily vertical; the horizontal aspect of revealed time as a time of promise and fulfillment in Christ is a function of the vertical dealings between man and God. . . . Balthasar recognizes that Augustine Christianized the view of time in antiquity such as

that held by Plotinus. Is the solution today to go back to Augustine's view of time, or can modern futurism be Christianized through opening up the horizons of modern man to their full human and Christian dimensions? A number of contemporary Christian theologians (particularly Jürgen Moltmann and Johannes Metz) opt rather for this second approach.[13]

Modern philosophies of history such as communism and forms of capitalism take the future of history as their goals but in a very constricted sense, since it is not transhistorical and is one that will be enjoyed by some future privileged generation when present sufferings and efforts gain their purpose. These are not philosophies that answer the question of death or the longings of the human person and community.

While the view we propose in dependence on Scripture differs from Thomas' and classical theology's study of salvation within an *exitus-reditus* framework, it also differs from Moltmann's and Pannenberg's stress on the future and the advent of the future. They are indeed correct to give primacy to the New Testament's use of apocalyptic to interpret salvation. But they do not have a basis either to deny the reality of human nature (as Moltmann seems to do) or to interpret God's causal influence in creation by his causal influence mediated by the kingdom of God (as Pannenberg seems to do).[14] God is the power of the future in the sense that it is through Jesus Christ as he has gone into the fullness of our future and through the Spirit as the power of the age to come that God now exercises his saving influence upon humanity. Creation continues to have its own internal

[13]*Salesian Studies* 5 (1968) 99–100.

[14]On Pannenberg's views on these issues, see, for example, Carl Braaten and Philip Clayton, eds., *The Theology of Wolfhart Pannenberg* (Minneapolis: Augsburg Publishing House, 1988), particularly the essays by Philip Clayton, "Anticipation as Theological Method"; David Polk, "The All-Determining God and the Peril of Determinism"; Ted Peters, "Pannenberg's Eschatological Ethics"; and Pannenberg's response. Pannenberg does distinguish his position from that of Moltmann. For example, he writes: "While the reality of God, in my argument, is indeed bound up with God's kingdom so that God's activity in creation is seen as the ultimate future impinging upon everything present, this does not entail 'a radical negation of the present order of the world'" (Wolfhart Pannenberg, "Providence, God, and Eschatology," *The Whirlwind in Culture: Frontiers in Theology. In Honor of Langdon Gilkey,* ed. Donald Musser and Joseph Price [Bloomington: Meyer-Stone Books, 1988] 172). On Moltmann, see Douglas Schuurman, *Creation, Eschaton, and Ethics,* cited in note 3 above; Jürgen Moltmann, "Christian Hope: Messianic or Transcendent? A Theological Discussion with Joachim of Fiore and Thomas Aquinas," *Horizon* 12 (1985) 328–48. This article was motivated in part by Hans Urs von Balthasar's critique of Moltmann's integration of salvation and time as Jewish.

consistency, though it is indeed under the influence of alien powers because of human sin. One cannot presume to interpret creation by the causal influence God exercises in his redemption of us through Christ. And counter to some statements of Moltmann, there is not a total dichotomy between creation and salvation. Rather, salvation heals, liberates, and fulfills creation.

2. Salvation as Offered to Us Already in Part

The salvation that God will give us when Jesus comes again, he is already in part giving to us here and now, as we found in the New Testament. It is the exalted Christ as he has gone before us into the fullness of our history, the kingdom of God, who is even now exercising that salvific activity he will fully exercise when he comes again. The present exercise of that salvation is his as having gone into this future to which he invites us, of which he makes us inheritors. It comes to us from this future and draws us through history to this future. We will examine this briefly as it is present *(a)* in the Church and *(b)* in the wider society, that is, in reference to the economic, social, and political order.

a. In the Church. Christ who has gone into the future is *already* exercising *in part* that salvific activity that he will exercise when he comes again. And he does this uniquely and particularly in and through the community of his disciples, the Church. This historical community that we find in the primitive Church is presented in the New Testament as continually affected by the exalted Christ and the Spirit whom he has sent. If what we wrote in previous chapters on Scripture is accepted as the Christian meaning of salvation, then we can use Vatican II's teaching on the kingdom, or salvation, as explanatory for our time of the meaning of Christ's salvation we now in part already share. However, we must keep in mind the apocalyptic understanding of the kingdom and the fact that the salvation that is being exercised now comes from Christ as he has gone ahead of us into the fullness of the kingdom, as a participation in that future.

This perspective, which we justified in Scripture, gives a special significance to the relevant statements of the council that do not always keep this perspective. For example, the council teaches that the Church is "the universal sacrament of salvation" (*LG* 48). But if we recall that this salvation is not only transcendent but future and comes to us from that future as a sacramental presence of that kingdom, this explanation is both more in accord with Scripture and more appropriate for our culture of modern historical consciousness. The Church is and should be progressively reformed to be a symbol of salvation that is believable.

As the council teaches, this future kingdom is a communion of people with God and among themselves. Thus God through Christ "willed to make men holy and save them, not as individuals without any bond or link between them, but rather make them into a people who might acknowledge him and serve him in holiness" (*LG* 9). Thus Christ, who now reigns gloriously in heaven, "called a race made up of Jews and Gentiles which would be one, not according to the flesh, but in the Spirit, and this race would be the new People of God. . . . That messianic people has as its head Christ" (*LG* 9). This Church is "the universal sacrament of salvation" (*LG* 48), at once manifesting and actualizing the mystery of God's love for humankind. Thus "the Church has but one sole purpose—that the kingdom of God may come and the salvation of the human race may be accomplished" (*GS* 45). The Church is "the kingdom of God—already present in mystery" (*LG* 3). "Already the final age of the world is with us (cf. 1 Cor 10:11) and the renewal of the world is irrevocably under way; it is even now anticipated in a certain real way, for the Church on earth is endowed already with a sanctity that is real though imperfect" (*LG* 48).

This is what that body of disciples of Jesus Christ who gathered at Pentecost and received the Holy Spirit were. And this is what the descendants of those disciples are, even today. It already shares in part and in a way characteristic of its pilgrim status what it will become when Jesus comes again. For example, it overcomes the differences among people: "There is neither Jew nor Greek, there is neither slave nor free person, there is not male and female; for you are all one in Christ Jesus" (Gal 3:28). However, we must add that "Christ summons the Church, as she goes her pilgrim way, to that continual reformation of which she always has need, insofar as she is an institution of men here on earth" (*UR* 6).

This is true of the disciples of Christ, whether within the bounds of the Catholic Church or in the varied Christian Churches, for the council writes: "[S]ome, even very many, of the most significant elements and endowments which together go to build up and give life to the Church itself, can exist outside the visible boundaries of the Catholic Church: the written Word of God; the life of grace; faith, hope and charity, with the other interior gifts of the Holy Spirit, as well as visible elements" (*UR* 3)[15] such as sacraments and mission. Through being the sacrament of the kingdom to come and the present instrument of Christ's salvific activity, "that messianic people, although it does not actually include all men, and at times may appear as a small flock, is, however, a most sure seed of unity, hope and salvation for the whole human race. Established by Christ as a communion of life, love and truth, it is taken up by him also as the instrument of salvation of all; as the light of the world and the salt of the earth (cf. Matt 5:13-16) it is sent forth into the whole world" (*LG* 9). The Church is essentially missionary (*LG* 17).

To articulate the meaning of salvation in the present even in this introductory treatment, we must express briefly how the exalted *Jesus Christ* and the Holy Spirit are present to God's new people. The salvific activity Jesus will exercise when he comes again he is already exercising in part, for he has already gone into the fullness of our future, the kingdom of God, and is seated at the right hand of the Father. All power in heaven and earth has been given him (Matt 28:18), but he is now exercising that most definitely within the Church, the future kingdom present in mystery. He is the head of the Church, and it is his body.

We can see his action from the future particularly in the sacraments, for it is the exalted Christ who is the main agent acting symbolically in the sacraments; "when anybody baptizes, it is really Christ himself who baptizes" (*SC* 7). As this refers to the Eucharist we have seen evidence for this in the Fathers.[16] The Eucharist is an

---

[15]It is not our purpose to explain or evaluate the Church's teaching at Vatican II that "[t]he Church . . . subsists in the Catholic Church. . . . Nevertheless, many elements of sanctification and of truth are found outside its visible confines" (*LG* 8). Here we seek only to defend and explain how those who are genuinely disciples of Christ are saved by God through him.

[16]See chapter 6 above, pages 215–6. This understanding has been preserved by the Orthodox Church better than by the Western Church. See, for example, John Zizioulas, "The Mystery of the Church in Orthodox Tradition," *One in Christ* 24 (1988) 294–303: "[T]he *eschata* is the beginning of the Church's life, the *arche*, that which brings forth the Church, gives her her identity"; the Church is "an eschatological community existing in history." The Church's encounter with the Word is "not as a message coming to her as passed through the channels of historical experience, but as an echo of the future state of things." "All this makes the Church an *eikon* of the kingdom to come"; see also "Roman Catholic–Orthodox Dialogue, Valamo, 1988: The Sacrament of Order in the Sacramental Structure of the Church," ibid., 367–77: "[T]he ecclesial ministry is by nature sacramental. The word sacramental is meant to emphasize here that every ministry is bound to the eschatological reality of the kingdom." For example, the ordination of the bishop is "accomplished by the glorified Lord in the power of the Spirit at the moment of the imposition of hands."

anticipation of the messianic banquet, at which the exalted Jesus Christ is the host, in the sense of the one who presides at this banquet from beyond the veil that separates the age to come from the present age. He gives us the food of the age to come. Thus he who will come is coming now to be with us and to give us a share in that union with him and one another that we will have when he comes again, and he recalls to us what he did for us and thus his love for us and his Father's love for us. He does this sacramentally, in a way mediated by symbols and not face to face.

Also, it is Christ in the age to come who sends his ministers as ambassadors for him to give his message, or word of salvation, so that we may believe and be saved. This Christ who will come again is coming now in his word, in his ministers, in his community, and in the least of his little ones; we meet the one we will meet when he comes again as we respond to him by living belief as he is present now and converses with us and with his Bride the Church. Through Christ and the Spirit, "[i]n the sacred books the Father who is in heaven comes lovingly to meet his children, and talks with them" (*DV* 21), a theme we shall develop in the next chapter on revelation. And, of course, it is only when he has gone into the age to come that Christ sends from there his Spirit to the Church.

To understand in even an introductory fashion what Christian salvation and its present impact is, we must turn to the *Holy Spirit*. The mystery of salvation and other Christian mysteries have been interpreted in a too christocentric framework in the West in recent centuries as we have been split off from Eastern Orthodoxy.[17] Happily, the strong Pentecostal resurgence in its many forms is helping us to regain consciousness of the centrality of the Holy Spirit in Christian life and belief. It is essential that we begin our remarks here by recalling that Christian experience precedes reflection, theological or popular, on the Holy Spirit. Talk about the Holy Spirit in the primitive Church and today is secondary to the experience of the dynamic effects and presence of the Spirit in our Christian lives and has in a special way a symbolic character. To ascribe these effects to the Holy

[17]On the question of the Holy Spirit as this is relevant here, see M. John Farrelly, "Holy Spirit," *The New Dictionary of Catholic Spirituality,* ed. Michael Downey (Collegeville: The Liturgical Press, 1993) 492–503; L. Bermejo, *The Spirit of Life: The Holy Spirit in the Life of the Christian* (Chicago: Loyola University Press, 1989); Yves Congar, *I Believe in the Holy Spirit,* 3 vols. (New York: Seabury, 1983); Jürgen Moltmann, *The Spirit of Life: A Universal Affirmation* (Minneapolis: Fortress Press, 1993); Michael Welker, *God the Spirit* (Minneapolis: Fortress Press, 1994).

Spirit is still a matter of belief, but not a belief wholly dissociated from experience in the present.

First, the Holy Spirit comes to us individually and communally from Christ *as* he has gone into the fullness of the future, into the kingdom where he is exalted at the right hand of the Father (Acts 2:33-34; John 20:17, 22; 1 Cor 15:45). Thus James Dunn can write: "[T]he Spirit is the future good which has become present for the man of faith—the power of the not yet which has already begun to be realized in his present experience."[18] Through the Holy Spirit, the power of the age to come, we are oriented to God the Father not only as the transcendent source but through Christ's anticipated coming; indeed, we "groan within ourselves as we wait for adoption, the redemption of our bodies" (Rom 8:23). We are oriented to God not simply as the absent one but through the power and presence of God the Holy Spirit within us, as we will recall below.

This Spirit is given to us through being given to the Church (Acts 2) and our being incorporated into it by belief and baptism. Thus the Spirit is the principle of our communion with God the Father, Jesus Christ, and one another. As Vatican II says: "It is the Holy Spirit dwelling in those who believe and pervading and ruling over the entire Church, who brings about that wonderful communion of the faithful and joins them so intimately in Christ that he is the principle of the Church's unity" (*UR* 2). We are saved not only as individuals but even more as joined together in the kingdom that is present in mystery in the Church.

This Spirit is both a dynamic influence in our lives and a personal presence. We can see its dynamic influence bringing God's salvation in part even now into our lives by appropriating what Paul says of the Spirit. The Spirit enables us to do what the Law did not: "For the law of the spirit of life in Christ Jesus has freed you from the law of sin and death. For what the law, weakened by the flesh was powerless to do, this God has done" (Rom 8:2-3). "The love of God has been poured out into our hearts through the holy Spirit that has been given to us" (Rom 5:5). So too, through the Spirit we have an inner testimony to God's dispositions toward us: "The Spirit itself bears witness with our spirit that we are children of God" (Rom 8:16); thus we are inclined to cry, "*Abba,* Father!" (Rom 8:15). The Spirit gives us the freedom of the children of God in the sense that out of belief in

[18]James Dunn, *Jesus and the Spirit* (Philadelphia: Westminster Press, 1975) 310.

God's antecedent love for us we are able to respond to him with love in obedience and humility.

By the Spirit also we are able to pray in a way beyond what words can express (Rom 8:26-27). And by the Spirit we are enabled to "live according to the spirit" (Rom 8:5) and not be dominated by the flesh, even though the believer must acknowledge "that he is a *divided man,* a man of split loyalties. He lives in the overlap of the ages and belongs to both of them *at the same time.*"[19] Thus Paul calls upon us: "I say, then: live by the Spirit and you will certainly not gratify the desire of the flesh. For the flesh has desires against the Spirit and the Spirit against the flesh; these are opposed to each other, so that you may not do what you want" (Gal 5:16-17). This is the way that the present impact of future salvation upon us manifests itself. This gift enables us to overcome addictions that alienate us from God, from our own deepest selves, and from one another.

Another way this dynamism expresses itself is through the *charisms* that the Spirit distributes so generously throughout the Church. Each of these "spiritual gifts" is a "manifestation of the Spirit" (1 Cor 12:4, 7). Each is a "brilliant epiphany [of the Spirit], like the sparkling reflection of a crystal ball as it rotates in the light."[20] These gifts—apostleship, prophecy, the ministry of teaching, gifts of healing, different forms of service, varieties of tongues—are meant for building up the Church in love; they are impulses of the Spirit beyond the simply rational. They can be abused, and they are worthless and empty if they are not used in love (1 Cor 13).

This dynamism of the Spirit in our Christian lives is not dissociated from but rather comes from a *personal indwelling* of the Spirit. It is not only by a created grace that God effects our justification and sanctification as present participations in the salvation to come but by the indwelling of the Holy Spirit, Jesus Christ the Son, and the Father. Thomas taught this in his study of the missions of the Persons of the Trinity. There is a visible mission of the Son through the Incarnation and a visible mission of the Holy Spirit in the sense that her presence is indicated by visible signs, such as the dove at Jesus' baptism and the fire at Pentecost. But there is also an invisible mission of the Son and the Spirit, for they begin to be in graced human

---

[19]Ibid., 312.

[20]George Montague, *The Holy Spirit: Growth of a Biblical Tradition* (New York: Paulist Press, 1975) 148.

beings in a mode different from their presence through God's creative and sustaining activity. Thomas writes:

> Through sanctifying grace the whole Trinity indwells the mind, according to John 14: "We will come to him and make our dwelling with him." To send a divine person to someone through invisible grace means a new manner of that person's indwelling and the origin of that person from another. Thus since both to indwell through grace and to be from another are proper to both the Son and the Holy Spirit, each is invisibly sent. It is proper to the Father to indwell through grace but not to be from another and therefore not to be sent. . . .
>
> . . . if we speak of the mission according to its origin, the mission of the Son is distinguished from the mission of the Holy Spirit as generation is from procession. If however according to the effect of grace, the two missions share in the root of grace, but they are distinguished in the effects of grace, which are the illumination of the intellect and the inflammation of the affections. Thus it is clear that one cannot be without the other.[21]

While in traditional Scholasticism the tract on grace dwelt primarily on created grace, in our time, partially under the influence of Karl Rahner, the gift of grace has come to mean primarily God's self-gift with which there is essentially connected a created grace. Also, this self-gift has come to mean a gift of a proper relation to each of the Persons of the Trinity.[22] Without going further into this theme here, we wish primarily to note that Rahner as well as Thomas interprets grace and indwelling on the model of the Incarnation rather than on Scripture's apocalyptic understanding of how God the Father now exercises his saving influence on us through Christ and the Spirit. In this theology, just as the Word became flesh, so too, through the gift of grace we are divinized. Eternity entered time through the Incarnation, and we are empowered to transcend time through grace. The invisible missions of the Son and the Spirit now come to us from Christ exalted at the right hand of the Father, but the image attached

---

[21]Thomas Aquinas, *ST* I, 43, 5 and ad 3. The kind of illumination of the mind Thomas means here is "one that effects the affection of love" (ad 2) and so one that involves a certain experiential knowledge.

[22]See, for example, Karl Rahner, "Grace," *Sacramentum Mundi* (New York: Herder & Herder, 1968) 2:412–27; Roger Haight, "Rahner: Grace and History," *The Experience of Grace*, 119–42.

to this is one of transcendence entering time and raising those who dwell there.

Counter to this, we have been arguing throughout this book that Christ's and the Holy Spirit's—and thus the Father's—present influence on us to save us should be seen as coming primarily from the future. That is, the mission of the Son now is from that kingdom, our ultimate future, which Jesus Christ entered through his death, resurrection, and ascension and from which he comes to us through the Spirit, in word and sacrament and by the invisible movements of grace and indwelling. Similarly, the Spirit, who is the power of the age to come, acts within the Church and us individually from that same future kingdom, which is the fulfillment and salvation of time and history. The effect of this transposition is to show more clearly that the advent of Christ and the Spirit here in time is an invitation to a transcendence that deepens our engagement with the intermediate historical future rather than one that makes us more detached from it. It deepens it because we are called to be engaged with it within the context of the kingdom of God rather than, as many people of our time are engaged with it, in a way cut off from its full and only lasting meaning.

The coming of Christ and the Spirit, if seen in this context, dissociates this saving mystery from elements of an anthropology too tied with a previous culture more static than our own, more hierarchical, more cosmocentric, and involved with the cycle of nature's seasons. It presents it in a way that meets men and women in a period of historical consciousness where their primary concerns and legitimate self-understandings are. The Spirit gives us a love that frees us from being dominated by fixations on what is immediate to us or on our immediate future, so that we can be centered on the whole of God's plan for history and the God of history. Christ and the Spirit lead us to build the Church and make the kingdom present to the larger secular society in which we live. This is possible only on the condition that under the Spirit we adopt the mind of Christ and seek first the kingdom of God, even if this means losses in history and without having our confidence totally shaken by such losses.[23]

b. In the larger community. We have shown that the salvation or kingdom God offers those who believe in Jesus is future but already present, particularly in the Church through the gift of Christ and the

[23]See M. John Farrelly, "Trinity as Salvific Mystery," *Monastic Studies* 17 (1986) 81–100.

Spirit. In what sense is it present in the larger human community? The future world will be a restoration of all creation; in fact, all who are saved will be Church. But is that future restoration meant to be partially transformative here in reference to goals of the state, outside the Church as well as within? If Jesus is exercising within the Church in part that saving and judging power he will exercise when he comes again, is he already in part exercising that to release people, those both within and outside the Church, from political, economic, and social oppression? Is this constitutive of Christ's present exercise of his saving action and so of the Church's and Christians' participation in Christ's saving ministry? This is important also because it has a bearing on what living faith, or genuine discipleship, of Jesus really is.

This theme has been written about at great length and from many perspectives, particularly since Vatican II. We will only make two points. (1) We recall that Jesus' exercise of his saving ministry included the political, economic, and social concerns of his people. (2) We indicate some implications this has for today, dependent on the social teaching of the Church and liberation theology.

(1) In our study of the kingdom in the ministry of Jesus (ch. 3) we agreed both with those who interpret Jesus' ministry as one of renewal of his people and with those who consider his message to be in the apocalyptic tradition. There is evidence that toward the beginning of his ministry Jesus did particularly focus on the renewal of the Jewish community; thus Peter proclaimed him to be Messiah, and Jesus accepted this designation. Such renewal involved addressing, for example, economic issues that deeply divided the community. To make a dichotomy between the religious relation to the Father Jesus came to offer and an economic, political, and social relation among his people that was just and compassionate represents more a modern sense of the division between the religious and political orders than the culture of the Jews at the time of Jesus. When it became obvious to Jesus that the Jewish leaders would reject him and the kind of salvation God was offering them through him, his proclamation of the kingdom became more apocalyptic. By this he meant to convey the assurance to his disciples that even if the Jews killed him, the kingdom he offered would still come about.

The kingdom in its fullest sense was always the center of Jesus' teaching, and this sense is transhistorical. Thus if the Jews were to kill Jesus, he would be vindicated; and as the Son of Man he would establish his kingdom. This meant the resurrected life—the new heavens and the new earth. But it also meant that he would establish his new people here on earth, in and through whom he would reign even now. Thus the apocalyptic and the messianic senses of salvation did not cease to be interrelated in the primitive Church, but it was for his disciples rather than for the Jewish people as a whole that Jesus would most immediately exercise this saving role. The future eschatological community was to be already in part anticipated and present in and through his community of disciples. And that judgment that he would exercise when he came again would also be in part exercised even now. One example of this is the destruction of Jerusalem that he sought to avoid but that, the Gospels tell us, followed from the Jewish leaders' rejection of Jesus. A renewal of Israel had been a real possibility, but with the rejection of Jesus this renewal happened in the community of the disciples of Jesus, and they were to mediate it to the rest of the world.

(2) What does the symbol of Jesus' mediation of the kingdom mean for our own age? In this study we speak primarily from the perspective of the First World, specifically that of the North Atlantic states and more specifically that of the United States. The symbol of Jesus' ministry confirms the interpretation of the kingdom or salvation reflected in the 1971 Synod of Bishops' statement: "Action on behalf of justice and participation in the transformation of the world fully appear to us as a constitutive dimension of the preaching of the Gospel, or, in other words, of the Church's mission for the redemption of the human race and its liberation from every oppressive situation."[24]

Tragically, in some earlier periods of the modern Church such as in the eighteenth and nineteenth centuries, many Christian leaders did not make this connection between their responsibility to proclaim redemption and their responsibility to challenge structures that oppressed people. There was a great deal of work by Church leaders to free individuals from hunger, sickness, and ignorance. But there was not much challenging of unjust social systems. This failure was due in part to the fact that the present effect of Christ's salvific activity was explained largely through the gift of grace, and grace was understood to be given to the individual within an *exitus-reditus* theology, without a sufficiently articulated relation to the eschatological kingdom of God.[25] This was understandable before the advent of modern

[24]Synod of Bishops, Second General Assembly (1971), *Justice in the World,* 6.

[25]See Haight, "Sin and Grace," particularly "The Social Dimension of Grace," 126–35; Jean-Marc Laporte, *Patience and Power: Grace for the First World* (New York: Paulist Press, 1988).

historical consciousness, but one result was that the Church tended
to identify itself with the structures of traditional society, even when
they were unjust. Thus others took the leadership for social renewal,
and they frequently sought a renewal that was directed against the
Church as an oppressive force in society.

As we approach the end of the second millennium of Christianity,
Pope John Paul II has called upon the Catholic Church to acknowledge the sins of its sons and daughters and ask God's forgiveness.[26]
Surely the Church's failures to inculcate social reform sufficiently in
its sons and daughters must be included here. Even in 1968 the Latin
American Catholic bishops at Medellín acknowledged "complaints
that the hierarchy, the clergy, the religious are rich and allied with the
rich," and while they contested some of these complaints, they also
acknowledged that "all of us need a profound conversion so that 'the
kingdom of justice, love and peace,' might come to us."[27] Since then
many bishops, theologians, religious, and laity in Latin America have
shown a preferential love for the poor, denouncing their countries' and
other countries' economic policies oriented to favor the wealthy while
sacrificing or neglecting for this purpose the basic needs of the impoverished masses in both the rural and urban areas.[28] One key element in the raising of consciousness about how wholly opposed such
a social order is to what is humane and Christian is the explosion of
base communities, where predominantly lay and poor Christians
come together to reflect on their situations in the light of the Gospels.

Whereas before Vatican II, the Church had presented its social
teaching primarily on the basis of the natural law, since Vatican II it
has given much more place to the socially transformative implications of salvation mediated by Jesus or the kingdom and what disci-

---

[26]See his apostolic letter "As the Third Millennium Draws Near," *Origins* 24 (November 24, 1994), especially nos. 33–6.

[27]See "Medellín Documents," *The Gospel of Justice and Peace: Catholic Social Teaching Since Pope John,* ed. Joseph Gremillion (Maryknoll, N.Y.: Orbis Books, 1976) 471, 446.

[28]See for example, Edward Cleary, ed., *Path from Puebla: Significant Documents of the Latin American Bishops Since 1979* (Washington, D.C.: United States Catholic Conference, 1989). One can see the "preferential option for the poor" evident in many of these documents. To restrict our-
selves here to episcopal statements in one country, Brazil, see "The Message of Puebla"; "Basic Christian Communities"; "The Church and the Problem of Land"; "The Use of Urban Land and Pastoral Action," 37–9, 43–7, 349–56. For liberation theology, see particularly Arthur McGovern, *Liberation Theology and Its Critics: Toward an Assessment* (Maryknoll, N.Y.: Orbis Books, 1989). More generally, see Edward Cleary, ed., *Born of the Poor: The Latin American Church Since Medellín* (Notre Dame: University of Notre Dame Press, 1990).

pleship of Jesus means. For example, the Vatican's "Instruction on Christian Freedom and Liberation" (1986) shows the influence upon it of liberation theology when it writes: "It is the truth of the mystery of salvation at work today in order to lead redeemed humanity toward the perfection of the kingdom which gives true meaning to the necessary efforts for liberation in the economic, social and political orders and which keeps them from falling into new forms of slavery."[29] In our view the kingdom, or mystery of salvation, mentioned here should be understood apocalyptically. That is, Jesus Christ who has gone into the fullness of the future is even now in part effecting from there that salvation he will give when he comes again, and is doing so through his disciples in their efforts to exorcise forces, individual and communal, that bring oppression upon people in the political, economic, and social orders.

The Church has not abandoned natural law, though it has recognized that natural rights and duties are historically conditioned; the whole emphasis in the Church's teaching on the signs of the times indicates this awareness in accord with modern historical consciousness. The Church does not make a dichotomy between redemption and creation as Moltmann at times does, and it does not simply call upon the values of the kingdom while neglecting bases for human rights grounded in the nature of the human person. Redemption or salvation includes the healing of nature and its restoration, its liberation from being controlled by powers antithetical to the purposes of the God of creation and history. In fact, the *dignity of the human person* is absolutely basic to the Church's claim for justice and solidarity with the poor.[30]

The issues that face us on these questions in the First World and as Christians of the First World seem monumental. Here we take note

[29]The Congregation for the Doctrine of the Faith, "Instruction on Christian Freedom and Liberation," *Origins* 15 (April 17, 1986) no. 99, 714–28.

[30]See the American bishops' use of both of these resources in their pastoral on peace, *The Challenge of Peace* (1983), and on economic justice, *Economic Justice for All: Catholic Social Teaching and the U.S. Economy* (1986). Also see the bishops' tenth-anniversary reflection on the first of these pastorals, *The Harvest of Justice Is Sown in Peace* (1993). In *Public Religions in the Modern World* (Chicago: University of Chicago Press, 1994), Jose Casanova argues that religion could help modernity save itself: "[N]ormative traditions constitute the very condition of possibility for ethical discourse. . . . [W]ithout normative traditions neither rational public debate nor discourse is likely to take place. It seems self-evident that religious normative traditions should have the same rights as any other normative traditions to enter the public sphere as long as they play by the rules of open public debate" (cited by John Coleman in *Commonweal* [September 23, 1994]).

only of the issues of economic justice, of political peace based on justice, and of ecology. Many of us are overprivileged citizens of the world in these matters, while much of the world lives in poverty, war or the threat of war, and ecological degradation. For example, a religious sister who is a missionary in northeast Brazil and with whom I have been in correspondence for many years told me after being there for some years that she did not know one family that had not lost a child to malnutrition. Many of us are aware of the severe and widespread poverty that exists in many countries, and we know that the differential between the poor and the rich in our own country has been growing; the rich have been becoming richer and the poor and those of moderate means have been becoming poorer.

There is something seriously and morally wrong in political and economic systems where this happens. In justice we must acknowledge the efforts made to address the poverty of so many people in our own country and in those of the Southern Hemisphere. But the unconscionably large and increasing differential between the living standards of people in countries of the North Atlantic and most people of the Southern Hemisphere is a major issue of justice and charity in constructing "the new world order" in the period of decreased tensions between the West and Russia after the collapse of the Soviet Union (1989). In an acclaimed book on the coming economic order (or disorder) Robert Reich suggests the serious problem that facing poverty even in our own country poses:

> The question is whether the habits of citizenship are sufficiently strong to withstand the centrifugal forces of the new global economy. Is there enough of simple loyalty to place—of civic obligation, even when unadorned by enlightened self-interest—to elicit sacrifice nonetheless? We are, after all, citizens as well as economic actors; we may work in markets but we live in societies. How tight is the social and political bond when the economic bond unravels?[31]

This shows us a theme of Catholic social teaching, for example, in Pope John Paul's *Centesimus annus* (1991), on the one hundredth anniversary of Leo XIII's *Rerum novarum*. But proposals for economic

---

[31]Robert Reich, *The Work of Nations: Preparing Ourselves for 21st Century Capitalism* (New York: Knopf, 1991), cited in Dennis McCann, "The Shape of Economic Justice in the 21st Century," *The Christian Century* (October 30, 1991). The following comment in the text from McCann is from the same article.

reform like that of Reich are, as Dennis McCann notes, "unsustainable unless they are rooted in our common search for the ultimate truth about human persons and societies. When our most promising paradigms of social analysis point to the need for sacrifices beyond the boundaries of enlightened self-interest, political economy itself becomes a religious enterprise." This certainly shows us that the Church's new emphases in interpretation of what Christian salvation and discipleship mean are, aside from being valid interpretations of the Gospels, necessary for our time.

The issue of war and peace has not disappeared; it has simply taken new guises, as wars based on ethnicity and religion as well as on economic issues in the former Yugoslavia, sections of the former Soviet Union, and Africa show us.[32] The conflict of identities among those who identify themselves by blood, flesh, and past memories and between these and those who seek a larger society based on principles of universal justice has not diminished.[33] It is very relevant that the peace Jesus came to give as a constitutive part of salvation was not simply a peace of mind but a social, political, and economic order among people who were called to accept themselves as brothers and sisters, even though they differed as much as Jew and Gentile, slave and free, and male and female in a patriarchal culture. It is also relevant that we see in Scripture that the future salvation to which the exalted Christ invites us calls for an instantiation of values of the kingdom here and now in our world. This vision can perhaps help to liberate people from addiction to a peace organized by a social order identified with some past condition or even a present state in our changing world.

One crisis of our age is ecological degradation brought on by industrial pollution of the atmosphere, waterways, and the earth itself, by deforestation and by putting a weight on the planet by economic expectations and population explosion that is not sustainable. There have been multiple studies of this crisis and of the technical, political, and economic means needed to address it effectively. But the use of these means depends upon motivation. Does the gift of salvation

[32]See, for example, Robert Kaplan, "The Coming Anarchy," *The Atlantic Monthly* (February 1994); Samuel Huntington, "The Clash of Civilizations?" and responses to this article in *Foreign Affairs* (summer 1993 and September/October 1993).

[33]See M. John Farrelly, *Belief in God in Our Time* (Collegeville: The Liturgical Press, 1992) 346–7, referring to Clifford Geertz's study of the new states after World War II and decolonization in his *Interpretation of Cultures: Selected Essays* (New York: Basic Books, 1973) chapters 9–12.

to those who believe in Jesus Christ have much to offer here? Some think it does not because they see Christianity as in large part the source of this crisis. Christianity teaches that God gives human beings dominion over the earth (Gen 1:28); it has supplanted earlier religions that did have a sense of the sacredness of the earth; and the Catholic Church's population policy is part of the problem.

There is much to say to counter such an estimate.[34] Here we simply make the following points. *First,* modern mechanistic science had a great deal to do with a loss of the human sense of kinship with nature because it denied finality or intentionality and purpose in creation lower than humans. Contemporary science is seeking somehow to redress this imbalance and to restore a sense of some unity between the physical world and human beings that premodern societies largely possessed, though now from the perspective of the achievements of present-day science. Much of the work of A. N. Whitehead, Teilhard de Chardin, and more recently, Thomas Berry and Brian Swimme has brought modern science to bear in helping this reintegration.[35] The theological recovery of the place of the Holy Spirit in the human process of conversion, sanctification, and salvation has enormous untapped potential to help us toward an ecological consciousness, because it helps us to see God's saving activity within us as happening through an inner and immanent empowerment, and to see ourselves as part of a community that even includes lower creation (Rom 8:9-23). All this can help us also to a more contemplative appreciation of nature that may temper our exploitative approach to it.

Second, the promise of a salvation that includes "new heavens and a new earth" and the assurance of this to his disciples by Christ who has gone before us into the kingdom has through the centuries helped vast numbers of Christians to relax a grasping attitude toward possessions (cf. the Beatitudes) and to accept a solidarity with those in need in imitation of Jesus—a spirituality of *care.* Creation will be integrated into the eschatological salvation; there is no need to revert

---

[34]See, for example, the May 23, 1992, issue of *America;* Al Gore, *Earth in the Balance: Ecology and the Human Spirit* (New York: Houghton Miffin, 1992); Bill McKibben, *The Age of Missing Information* (New York: Random House, 1992); James Nash, *Loving Nature: Ecological Integrity and Christian Responsibility* (Nashville: Abingdon Press, 1992).

[35]I have made use of the work of Adam Koestler in some brief reflections on this question in *God's Work,* 149–51, and *Belief in God,* 243–55. In the latter book I also note the religiously based sense of the sacredness of the earth in Native American peoples and Asian cultures (258–9, 290–9) and its contribution to an ecological consciousness.

to the primordial for this integration. In fact, as we shall point out later, to identify respect for nature with a primordial sense of the sacred rather than with religion that also accepts modern historical consciousness is counter to the kind of integration and use of the resources of the physical world needed in our time. Care of the human community demands that we use modern industrial and technological advances, though within the context of a sustainable economy and ecology.

Finally, in the view of many the Catholic Church has shown great courage and care for the human community in rejecting abortion as an instrument of population control, and indeed in rejecting any means that are counter to the dignity of the human person and what we can know of God's law. This is a very complicated issue which we cannot address here.[36]

3. Is Such Salvation Possible?

Is it really possible that God could act in the way we have represented him acting and, indeed, as Scripture represents him acting in offering us salvation? In the next chapter we will address this question as it relates to revelation, but here we ask it in reference to salvation. There has been a long history of rejection of essential aspects of Scripture's account of Jesus' ministry, death, and resurrection since the Enlightenment, which continues till today, not only on the part of non-Christians but even on the part of a number of Christian theologians and exegetes. In our earlier volume we recalled that Bultmann rejected the possibility of miracles. Here we can recall a statement of Langdon Gilkey:

> The canon of the autonomy of human understanding, and thus the integrity of the sciences, which we all accept in our daily life and therefore must accept in principle in theology as well, requires us to admit that a dogmatic statement, a doctrine, even a sacred "story of the incarnation," cannot assure us of any of the factual elements ingredient to the doctrine. To deny this is to deny our own integrity as assenting members of a modernity that trusts in science and autonomy,

---

[36]See, for example, a whole issue of *Theological Studies* 35 (1974) 3–163, devoted to this subject; and Farrelly, *God's Work,* chapters 4 and 5; and "An Impasse in the Church," *America* (May 24, 1986).

an assent in ourselves that is undeniably apparent every time we
go to a doctor or fly in an airplane.[37]

Gilkey's Christianity does not depend upon the "factual elements" of
the gospel accounts of any of the genuine miracles of Jesus Christ or
of the resurrected Jesus encountering his disciples. Like many of
those who reject Christianity on grounds of science and the philosophy of the Enlightenment, he considers the acceptance of miracles a
denial of our integrity as members of modernity and people who accept science. We respond briefly to this difficulty here by recalling
the "preunderstanding" of God that we presented in our first volume,
the context of the gospel accounts of miracles in the ministry of
Jesus, and our capacity in our time and place to accept the miraculous.

In our previous volume we critically developed an interpretation
of the human being and of God in relationship, beginning with modern historical consciousness. Accepting our experience of change—
individual, cultural, and historical—we showed that each of us
starting from a particular time and place, through the process of personal development and within different communities, both seek and
are challenged to seek a horizon of infinite being through time. We
also showed that God is both personal and really related to the changing world and to the history that he brings to be and to change—from
his own free and genuine love for each human to whom he gives existence. This, then, indicates the reality of God's providence with regard to human beings.

And as there is a hierarchy of physical beings in the universe, so
too there is a hierarchy of intentions that God has in his relation to
this world. While he establishes an order in the physical world, the
ultimate source and purpose of this is personal. God's purpose is
more the communion of human beings with him in love and knowledge than the order of the physical world. Thus it is in accord with
God's more profound purposes in relating to the physical and human
world for him at times to act freely in the physical world beyond its
natural capacities by a miracle, in order to communicate with human
beings, to stir them to belief in his presence and saving love, and to
attest one he has sent as a witness to this love. The physical sciences

---

[37]Langdon Gilkey, *Catholicism Confronts Modernity: A Protestant View* (New York: Seabury,
1975) 98. I evaluate Gilkey's view in "Christian Interpretation of History: A Dialogue," *God's
Work*, 34–48.

are not a metaphysics of what is possible in the world, nor do they express all the agency operative in the world. Scientists of our time are more willing to acknowledge this than in an earlier age, and the people of our time very commonly accept the possibility of the miraculous. A Gallup poll in 1989 showed that over 80 percent of Americans accepted the possibility of miracles.

Miracles are so central to the ministry of Jesus that his impact on the people and the opposition of the Jewish leaders to him make no sense without them. Even Jewish tradition acknowledges that Jesus performed wonders.[38] It is true that the history-of-religions school in the study of the Gospels relegated

> all the material treating of miracle in the Gospels to later tradition. According to this hypothesis, the real, historical Jesus was a teacher of pious wisdom, and it was the later converts to Christianity from Hellenistic culture who transformed the image of Jesus into that of a wonder-worker, thereby conforming him to the putatively universal image of a "divine man." . . . The argument is purely deductive, however. The initial assumption is that the real Jesus could not have done such an intellectually embarrassing thing as performing miracles.[39]

All the criteria accepted broadly as authenticating words and deeds of Jesus as historically true are found in reference to the miracles, such as multiple attestation, discontinuity (because Jesus performed miracles in his own name, while prophets did in the name of God), conformity with the basic teaching of Jesus on the kingdom of God, and divergent interpretations by different evangelists within substantial agreement among them. There are different types of miracles ascribed to Jesus, such as exorcisms, healings, miraculous rescues and gifts (e.g., multiplication of loaves), raising from the dead, and accreditation miracles (e.g., Matt 11:2-6). Jesus performed these miracles for the purpose of the salvation of the human person, in

---

[38]See René Latourelle, "Miracle," *Dictionary of Fundamental Theology,* ed. R. Latourelle and R. Fisichella (New York: Crossroad, 1994) 690–709. He cites the Babylonian Talmud (Sanhedrin 43a) on page 695. Idem, *The Miracles of Jesus and the Theology of Miracles* (New York: Paulist Press, 1988). My treatment here is particularly dependent on his article. Also see above, chapter 2, pages 84–7.

[39]Howard C. Kee, *Miracle in the Early Christian World: A Study in Sociohistorical Method* (New Haven, Conn.: Yale University Press, 1983) 291–2.

view of the call to the kingdom. The person so called has a part to play in this interaction with Jesus through his or her faith, through which a new and transforming relationship with Jesus is established. By his miracles, the power of the kingdom is present to cast back the powers of evil (e.g., in exorcisms), to show symbolically, through a physical healing, a deeper healing offered by the kingdom, and to reveal something of the person of Jesus as mediator of the kingdom. They are acts of compassion. Jesus refuses simply to give a sign when people, particularly those in bad faith, call for it (Matt 16:1-4).

We can accept Latourelle's definition of a miracle: "A religious wonder that expresses, in the cosmic order [human beings and the universe], a special and utterly free intervention of the God of power and love, who thereby gives human beings a sign of the presence of his message of salvation in the world."[40] A miracle is an act that appeals to the human person as evidence attesting the worthiness of one who brings a message of salvation from God. But more than this, it is itself revelatory of the presence of God's free, loving, saving presence; it is a *sign* that is "interpersonal and conveys a challenge; it is the vehicle of a divine intention and addresses human beings like a divine utterance, a concrete, urgent message in which God seeks to make them understand that salvation is at hand."[41]

Human beings are, as the history of Christianity shows, capable of discerning and responding to the fact and meaning of the miraculous. The story of the healing of the man born blind in John 9 shows the varied reactions that may be given to the miraculous. People can resist it and seek doggedly to find some other explanation of what is before their eyes, no matter how fragile such an explanation is. To be able to respond positively to the truly miraculous, one has to acknowledge one's own insufficiency and need of salvation and allow one's presuppositions to be overturned.

An encounter with the miraculous is an encounter with the *mysterium fascinans et tremendum,* the sacred; to accept it and its invitation is frightening because it opens one to what cannot be controlled and what may make demands upon one that are very costly. This conversion is not possible, Christians generally hold, without God's grace. This grace is not a substitute for the intrinsic reality and intelligibility of the miraculous but an aid to open the mind

---

[40]Latourelle, 701.

[41]Ibid., 703.

and heart so that one is enabled to accept God speaking and calling through such an event. An uneducated person can be so open, and an educated person can refuse such openness. The use of critical reason is completely appropriate, as the Church's investigation of cures claimed at Lourdes and as much current study of the New Testament shows. However, if one stipulates that one cannot in principle accept what transcends natural and human powers as occurring in history or worthy of credence, then this is an instance not of critical intelligence but one of absolutizing the methods of the physical or human sciences as the access to truth.

III. Comparison with Other Views of Salvation

We have explicitly or implicitly compared the view of salvation we defended in this chapter with some other Christian interpretations. Here we wish briefly to compare it with views of some world religions. In the next chapter we shall recall something of the presence of revelation in these other religions, and we rely on that here. We are not concerned to show that in other religions there may well be human mediators of salvation. We take that for granted because, as we showed in our previous volume, "to save" is an analogous word that was used in different ways in the Hebrew Scripture,[42] and there were human agents who mediated the salvation God gave his people in differing circumstances (e.g., Moses, David, prophets, wisdom teachers). Something more than liberation from simple earthly straits and ignorance was mediated through these men and women. We have no problem acknowledging that God could use Gautama, Confucius, Mohammed, and others in analogous ways. The limitations in vision and life of Hebrew mediators of God's saving activity for his people does not preclude them from being such mediators; no more can this be used against such mediators in other religions.

We must take these human agents within the historical situation of their time and place and simply ask whether they led others to a more profound life and knowledge as it related them to divinity. If so we must acknowledge, it seems to me, that God was working through them, though not working through everything they said and did. This in no way involves a questioning of the uniqueness of the saving act of

[42]Farrelly, *Belief in God*, 367–8.

Jesus Christ.[43] If, from the fullness of our Christian belief, we assert that grace was given to people of the first covenant in view of the merits of Christ, then we can say this for all in the world who received God's grace. Vatican II acknowledged that "the Holy Spirit was at work in the world before Christ was glorified" (*AG* 4; see *LG* 16). We restrict ourselves here to pointing out that the salvation mediated broadly by Asian religions is related to a primordial revelation, that this is not sufficient for what these cultures face in our time, and that the apocalyptic salvation offered by Jesus Christ accepts such primordial revelation but enables us to focus on a wholistic salvation that integrates history and the whole of the human family.

Before this, however, we should face a widespread Jewish denial that Jesus could be the Messiah, because, as Martin Buber wrote, "the bloody body of our people" is proof that the world is still unredeemed.[44] Jesus did not effect an order of peace and justice based on obedience to God's will and so could not be taken as the Messiah. This objection deserves an extended answer that we cannot give here, but perhaps the following remarks will be pertinent.

We have shown that Jesus did seek to renew his people in a way that accorded with the messianic prophecies of the Hebrew Scripture, but as he came to an awareness that the Jewish leaders would reject him, he spoke of the salvation he would offer in more apocalyptic terms. Thus for the early Church the moment of the salvation mediated by Jesus was preeminently to be at his parousia, though they recognized that there were already partial anticipations of this salva-

---

[43]See, for example, Russell Aldwinckle, "Salvation and Saviors," *Jesus—A Savior or the Savior? Religious Pluralism in Christian Perspective* (Macon, Ga.: Mercer University Press, 1982) 121–48; David Rausch and Carl Voss, *World Religions: Our Quest for Meaning* (Minneapolis: Fortress Press, 1989); "Theological Colloquium, Pune, India, August, 1993," *Pro Dialogo* (1994/1) Bulletin 85–6.

[44]See Aldwinckle, *Jesus,* 39, where he refers to M. Buber, *Two Types of Faith* (New York: Macmillan, 1961). For positive Jewish, Muslim, and Hindu interpretations of Jesus, see Angelo Amato, "The Unique Mediation of Christ as Lord and Saviour," *Pro Dialogo,* 15–40. John Pawlikowski reviews some post-Holocaust Jewish reflections on God in "Toward a Theology for Religious Diversity: Perspectives from the Christian-Jewish Dialogue," *Journal of Ecumenical Studies* 26 (1989) 138–53. Largely agreeing with Emil Fackenheim, Irving Greenberg, and Arthur Cohen, he notes that "the role of the human community in keeping history free of further eruptions of radical evil akin to Nazism is strongly enhanced, as all three scholars have correctly insisted. . . . The human role in the process of salvation has been upgraded significantly. Humanity finds itself facing the realization that 'future' is no longer something God will guarantee. Survival, whether for the People Israel or for humanity at large, is now more than ever a human proposition." I agree that the only valid interpretation of God's providence must accept this; see Farrelly, "Providence," cited in note 12 above.

tion among those who believed in him. Thus the Church is the sacrament of salvation. Rejections of Jesus are not unique to the leaders of the Jews at the time of Jesus; they have continued through history and have brought untold sufferings on multitudes of innocent people. One central part of our Christian faith is that these innocent people enter quickly into a share of the apocalyptic kingdom of Christ in a definitive way through their death. All their tears are wiped away, and they enter into the joy of the Lord. The oppression that they suffered paradoxically hastened their entrance into this joy of the fullness of the kingdom of God.

In responding to the question of what the relevance of our interpretation of salvation is to world religions, we can first recall that in our previous volume we suggested that there were two prominent ways of escaping the sacred in our time. One way is characteristic of those who accept modern historical consciousness; the other, of those who do not accept this.[45] Many who do accept modern historical consciousness look on their lives from a restrictedly naturalistic viewpoint, in the sense that in practice they consider only human goals, resources, and knowledge as relevant to their activity. This activity is governed by a pragmatism that rejects the sacredness of the person and the moral order and the limits to human interests these call for.

Obviously, people and institutions dominated by such a viewpoint reject salvation in the Christian sense and seek it only from their own efforts. History shows that in the process they create more fragmentation in society. They are, in fact, destroying even the kind of innerwordly salvation that many of them proclaim to be dedicated to. Some Western leaders are abdicating moral leadership for the world by policies that are excessively marked by pragmatism. And by the way in which they identify democratic, industrial, and technological styles of life with this irreligion, they provoke fundamentalisms.[46] Many people of the developing countries of the world are grasping more clearly that it is some religious rather than political or cultural leaders of the West whose words and actions have moral authority.

There are those who accept the sacred as it is found in the past of their traditional societies and cultures but resist accepting new manifestations of the sacred associated with modern historical conscious-

---

[45]See Farrelly, *Belief in God,* 346–7.

[46]Gilles Kepel, *The Revenge of God: The Resurgence of Islam, Christianity, and Judaism in the Modern World* (University Park, Pa.: Penn State Press, 1994).

ness. In our earlier volume we reflected on how God does manifest something of himself and does offer means of salvation through the sacred present, for example, in Hinduism and Buddhism. This can be seen more easily, we claimed, if our understanding of God is more Trinitarian than Christocentric. Part of Hinduism's sense of the sacred has affinity with actions ascribed by traditional Christian theology to the ministry of the Holy Spirit, namely an immanent dynamism toward unity with God. Part of Buddhism's sense of the sacred as Nirvana has affinity with the way the First Person of the Trinity is said to evoke (or spirate) the response of the Holy Spirit, namely as the Good, and to be this Good for all human beings; Jesus said, "No one is good but God alone" (Mark 10:18). As valid and important as these mediations of God's revelation and salvation are, they are associated with the primordial and with nature and are not sufficient for the moral demands implicit in our world of rapid historical change and interrelationships among many peoples.

For example, a prominent philosopher in India, Margaret Chatterjee, writes of the traditional Indian worldview:

> At its best such a world view can affirm both the dignity of man and the dignity of nature. It still needs reinforcing by a sense of the indispensable link between man and society, and a sense of history. But the basic backdrop remains, an indissoluble co-partnership between man and the elements which nurture him, a co-partnership built into the ancient concept of *rta* (cosmic order), and a pervasive creativity for which both man and the cosmos consisting of all living things provide mutually reinforcing paradigms.[47]

Buddhism takes as a primal experience the transitoriness of all things on which people set their hearts in this life before enlightenment and relates the Ultimate dialectically to this as Nirvana. It offers a salvation that is therefore related to the plight of the individual caught in *samsara,* or the endless cycle of rebirths, but not to a society that needs to help people create a wholistic world that includes peoples of many cultures. In the China of antiquity, too, "the Chinese were certainly interested in the question of origins and in the signifi-

---

[47]Margaret Chatterjee, "Man and Nature in the Indian Context," *Man and Nature: The Chinese Tradition and the Future,* ed. Tang Yi-Jie, Li Zhen, and George McLean (Washington, D.C.: The Council for Research in Values and Philosophy, 1989) 98–9.

cance of some original model of individual and social harmony found in the distant past," though "[t]here is something of a counterpoint between a Taoist nostalgia for the cosmogonical behavior of the 'noble savage' that depends on ultimate origins and a Confucian advocacy of a progressivist doctrine of 'sacred history' that classically goes back to the first appearance of a civil order."[48] What one Western philosopher who has taught for many years in Taiwan writes is true of much of Asia:

> Industrialization and the process of modernization have within decades changed the face of this country. The many rapid changes in the socio-economic field have become a challenge to the traditional value system which has led to a rather widespread disorientation in matters of morals. A new value order is not yet in sight. This period of transition from a formerly well established order, which lasted unquestioned for hundreds of years, to a new order of which the contours are not yet clearly visible, affects all members of society in general and adult students in particular.[49]

In our previous volume, we did seek to show foundations for a moral order that emerged from and integrated a genuine modern historical consciousness,[50] and we sought to show that God ordered the human individual and society toward change that promotes human welfare. But this is not sufficient. Earlier traditional interpretations of the moral order were integrated with a religious understanding of the world and humanity that gave reason for observing the moral order. Through such observance one would be saved. The Christian understanding of salvation, as we have shown, is that Jesus Christ will give the kingdom to those who respond with faith to God's initiative to bring about a relation of belief, trust, and love of him and a wholistic human order that even now instantiates in part the values of the kingdom. There is reason to observe this moral order, because God

---

[48]Norman Girardot, "Behaving Cosmogonically in Early Taoism," *Cosmogony and Ethical Order: New Studies in Comparative Ethics,* ed. Robin Lovin and Frank Reynolds (Chicago: University of Chicago Press, 1985) 72, 78.

[49]Arnold Sprenger, "Higher Moral Education in Taiwan," *Chinese Foundations for Moral Education and Character Development,* ed. Tran Van Doan, Vicent Shen, and George McLean (Washington, D.C.: The Council for Research in Values and Philosophy, 1991) 176.

[50]See Farrelly, *Belief in God,* 179–214, 299–312; idem, "The Person and the Human Good," *God's Work,* 77–160.

holds us accountable, and the future of this order will be effected by God counter to every human effort to subvert it. This Christian understanding does not simply deny earlier understandings, as it does not deny earlier Jewish understandings. Also, something in these earlier understandings points to a future mediator of salvation, for example, Maitreya Buddha and Muhammad's belief that Jesus would come again, and thus show these religions open to growth. In the next chapter, where we treat the question of Christian revelation, we shall return briefly to this subject.

8

Christian Revelation and Faith

In this chapter we propose a constructive foundational theology of Christian revelation and faith, that is, one that is particularly appropriate to some central difficulties in our time. What we write here presupposes everything we have written to this point. It presupposes our understanding of the problematic of revelation and faith in our time. We saw in chapter 1 of this volume and in our earlier volume the Christian understanding of revelation and faith in Vatican II's articulation of this theme in *Dei verbum,* an analysis that was largely supported by the World Council of Churches' Faith and Order Commission statement. This is somewhat different from, for example, Thomas Aquinas' view of revelation and faith. He explained God revealing largely on the model of a teacher and the human person believing on the model of a student. His central problem was the relation between natural and supernatural knowledge, faith and reason.

The major difficulties today with revelation and faith are related to a conflict between a Christian identity as articulated by Vatican II and also by the World Council of Churches' Faith and Order Commission, and an identity of people with a modern historical consciousness that is largely naturalistic. As related to our theme here, many modern men and women find the Church's teaching on Christian revelation and faith to be counter to their sense of self as autonomous adults at a particular point in history who guide themselves by all the human knowledge available to them, whatever its provenance, that supports their fulfillment and liberation and that of the community with which they identify. Their viewpoint has special difficulty with giving to what happened in Israel two thousand years ago a superior weight to all other knowledge and declaring all other human knowledge and world religions subordinate to it. Giving such preeminence to Christian revelation and faith is found to be opposed to openness to what is new in our changing world and important for our constructing our individual and community lives.

We find the context for our treatment of revelation and faith in the conversion experiences of such people as Thomas Merton, C.S. Lewis, and others whom we recalled in volume one. In the present chapter we are building on what we have seen in volume one and therefore on people's having already received God's revelation and having found reason to believe in God to some extent. The question now is the further and historical revelation that comes through Jesus Christ and that calls for a further conversion and a Christian identity as a disciple of Jesus Christ. This in part builds on what people have already received and in part may appear to contradict what they have already accepted, as we found also in Peter's coming to Christian faith. Our first volume primarily addressed people who do not believe in God and those Christians who believe but without accepting modern historical consciousness; our present volume primarily addresses those—and that includes many of us believers—who believe in Christ but subordinate this belief to other messages and interests that come from within them and their culture, or who believe in Christ without accepting modern historical consciousness.

We have found that Scripture does support Vatican II's and other Christian Churches' teaching on revelation and faith as fully Christian. That does not relieve us of the need to address the problems that come from current views that have as much difficulty with Scripture as with the Churches' teaching. How can we explain Christian revelation and faith to people of our time and place when this seems in part opposed to their conception of their own fulfillment and the knowledge on which they base their identity? In dealing with this question, we are not giving here a narrative theology as in our earlier treatment of Peter's faith, though we depend on that and are faithful to it. Rather, we are analyzing what revelation and faith are. We do so through the use, analogical though it is, of the understanding of God, the human person and community, and their interaction, which we proposed and defended in our first volume, as well as the interrelation of the Christian mysteries.

In our treatment of revelation and faith in Scripture, we found Peter to be a paradigmatic figure. Through inclusion within his own people he had an identity previous to his encounter with Jesus; through this encounter he was called to go beyond this identity to one that enabled him to be a leader in the community of the age to come. We find in Peter a process of faith in which there is a dialogical moment, a dialectical moment, and then the distinctive Christian faith— all interpreted as a response to God's providential action toward him through Christ and the Spirit. Initially he had only a half-vision of who Jesus was, but then, through Jesus' death, resurrection, and the coming of the Holy Spirit, he had a full Christian faith.

Something analogous happens to men and women who are converted to Christian and Catholic faith in our time, as we saw in volume one of this work. As in Scripture we saw something of the continuity and difference between revelation and faith in Peter's pre-Christian Jewish life and then Christian life, so we can show something of the meaning and foundations of Christian revelation and faith today by relating it to what we saw in volume one concerning a not-yet Christian revelation and faith available to men and women in our time and a modern human identity that accepts this. What can a human being today, as we examined this in the previous volume, make of Christian revelation and faith—its meaning and foundations as indicated by Scripture? What is its meaning, and is it plausible, given the self-acceptance we defended in the preceding volume, or is it opposed to a legitimate sense of self in our time? We will examine this question through analyzing (I) revelation and faith as dialogue, (II) revelation and faith through the death and resurrection of Jesus and the coming of the Spirit, and (III) revelation and faith in the context of our time.[1] We are asking whether the modern person, if he or she were to have an experience analogous to that of Peter, as we propose Thomas Merton and others in dependence on apostolic testimony and Christian tradition did have, could and should accept a response of faith analogous to his.

---

[1]There are many excellent recent theological studies of revelation and faith. Among them, see Avery Dulles, *Models of Revelation* (New York: Doubleday, 1983); Gerald O'Collins, *Fundamental Theology* (New York: Paulist Press, 1981); Aylward Shorter, *Revelation and Its Interpretation* (London: Geoffrey Chapman, 1983); Ronald Thiemann, *Revelation and Theology: The Gospel as Narrated Promise* (Notre Dame: University of Notre Dame Press, 1985); John Haught, *Mystery and Promise: A Theology of Revelation* (Collegeville: The Liturgical Press, 1993); Josef Schmitz, *La rivelazione* (Brescia: Queriniana, 1991); Wolfhart Pannenberg, "The Revelation of God," *Systematic Theology* (Grand Rapids: Eerdmans, 1991) 1:189–258; René Latourelle, "Revelation," *Dictionary of Fundamental Theology*, ed. R. Latourelle and R. Fisichella (New York: Crossroad, 1994) 905–50.

I. Revelation and Faith as Dialogue

In our narrative theology in chapter 4 we moved from Peter's faith to the revelation that was its source. Here we shall analyze first God's revelation and then human faith as its response. We are not trying here to prove that this faith and revelation exist; we seek to explain this revelation, which Scripture affirms and we have defended, and to show that it is worthy of acceptance by contemporary men and women.

1. God's Revelation

Peter in his time and we in our time believe in Jesus Christ on the basis of God's historical revelation. We can understand something of God's revelation through Jesus Christ by analyzing it as we saw it affirmed in the New Testament, as a divine act of communication, with its message, and with its medium.

a. A divine act of communication. Christian revelation and, indeed, earlier revelation is an *act of God.* God is, as we defended in our earlier volume, a transcendent personal being who brings the world and human beings into being from his free and loving desire to share his goodness and being with them, who has given testimonies to himself through conscience and the evolving physical world, and who is profoundly affected by what happens to those he loves. Many peoples testify to the deity's impact upon their lives through their myths, which reflect diverse ways in which God gives himself to be experienced and the limits and distortions of human interpretations. God's ultimate purpose in his engagement with his creation is personal, that is, to bring human beings into communion with him and establish a human community in such union.

Once we accept that God is fully personal and thus free, it becomes plausible that his initial communications through, for example, conscience and the cosmos, are just that—communications that he may well follow up by further revelations in the process of history. Thus it is not surprising that he would convey further messages to human beings than what he conveyed primordially; revelations in the process of history are not surprising for such a personal and engaged God. To say that revelation is an act of God is to say that its initiative is wholly his. Counter to some modernists who identify revelation with an experience of the divine that emerges from within the human, we are saying that it is a free, deliberate, and loving act by God, who has loved us first. Only this does justice to what Scripture, whether Jewish or Christian, tells us.

Revelation is a special kind of divine act, namely one of *communication*. "To reveal" says something different from "to save"; while the latter means to liberate someone from a death-dealing situation, the former means to unveil what was previously veiled, to make at least partially known what was previously unknown. Thus Scripture refers to God as speaking to humans: "In times past God spoke in partial and various ways to our ancestors through the prophets; in these last days, he spoke to us through a son" (Heb 1:1-2). This ascription to God of a progressive self-revelation to his people in and through history is made on the basis of Israel's and the early Church's experience. God is said to communicate by speaking, but we must not take this in a univocal sense. As we saw in Scripture, in his historical revelation God speaks through events as well as human words, a subject we will return to below.

As modern study of language makes clear, in "speaking" there are several elements we should note.[2] In speaking to a human being or community, God personally encounters or addresses these others—is present to them. In speaking to them or us, God also expresses himself, because communication, and particularly personal communication, is self-implicating (an illocutionary act). He shows us his attitude of love toward us, which is the source of his communicating with us and offering us his kingdom and is present and expressed in his communication. In speaking to us God communicates a message, which we will analyze further below. God conveys both an informative message (a locutionary act) and something other than simply a message, such as a call to us, a promise, a command (a perlocutionary act, or an act with a performative character). Thus God's speaking to us is not simply a communication from the divine mind to a human mind, or simply the giving of a message; it is a fully personal act to a fully personal subject. The liturgy, as we shall see, offers us a better model to understand revelation than does the model of a teacher. The kind of knowledge given by God's historical revelation is not

---

[2]See, for example, Edward Schillebeeckx and Bas van Iersel, eds., *Revelation and Experience,* Concilium 113 (New York: Crossroad, 1979); Jean Ladrière, "Meaning and Truth in Theology," *Proceedings of the Catholic Theological Society of America* 42 (1987) 1–15; M. Cristina Carnicella, "Communication," *DFT* 185–90.

primarily objective information but, as we will show below, knowledge of God's offer to us of salvation and thus of God who offers it.

The *motive* for this revelation is God's love for us—his desire to free us from darkness and to bring us into communion with himself and with one another—his desire to save us. This communication comes from his wisdom; the more we know it the more we know how suitable his way of communicating is for us while we are still on the way so that it can preserve our freedom, so that his own transcendence does not crush our liberty, so that our response of faith is a genuinely free surrender to him—a liberation from self rather than a constricted self-dependence that prevents us from being liberated from our own limits and illusions. We will develop this theme further when we treat the response of faith. His speaking to us, as shown in the narrative history of the Jewish and Christian Scripture, is not for God's need but rather for our benefit; nor is it an arbitrary act of divine authority, as it has at times been pictured.

b. Revelation's message. What is the *message* that is revealed? Here we are speaking, as we do throughout this section, primarily of that message to Peter and the apostles, and indeed to the larger Israel of that time. We are not speaking exclusively of this, because what we have to say applies also to the whole history from Abraham to the present, mediated, as Christian revelation is, to us by apostolic testimony and Christian tradition. We are speaking of the whole of God's historical revelation reflected in Scripture. What was revealed was what the focus of Jesus' ministry indicated, namely God's offer of salvation through him. This is what Peter's response of faith, "You are the Christ," signified. *The* answer to his people's anxieties and sense of powerlessness against the forces that controlled their destiny was what was revealed to Peter. And thus it was the answer to Peter's own deepest concerns, since he identified with his people. What was revealed was God's eschatological salvation, that definitive saving intervention by God for his people that had been the hope of Israel and the promise of God through the prophets. We examined this in the third chapter. Transposing that to our own time, as we did in the seventh chapter, this is a promise of a future of permanent communion with God and with one another in a kingdom of justice, love, and truth, one that overcomes all the obstacles within and outside of us that stand in the way of such a future for ourselves and for others. It is the deepest answer to the concerns of men and women of our time of historical consciousness, whose future is threatened by forces that tend to destroy such hope. Only God has the power to bring such a future about, and the promise of the kingdom is the promise that he will indeed bring it about and will not be thwarted in his determination to do so.

This revelation is also, perhaps indirectly more than directly, a revelation of God's love and of who Jesus is as related to this kingdom. Jesus' works that, as we shall see below, mediate the revelation of God's offer of salvation show a disposition and presence of gratuitous love for the needy, the powerless, and the marginalized. They also show a divine power operating to release people from powers that keep them in bondage. This revelation similarly shows that it is Jesus who is the prime agent by whom this kingdom will come about; Peter expresses this by stating that Jesus is the Christ, his culture's main expression of the one through whom God's kingdom would come.

Thus too the object of this revelation is God's vision for the future, his plan for his people and the way through which he will save them. This plan is historically contingent; it could not be deduced from what preceded it. God's love is given freely to reach a particular people—and through them the larger world—and it is offered according to God's design and plan, a plan hidden in previous ages, not a human design. Further, the object of this revelation was a call to Peter and others to share this kingdom with Jesus and to share in bringing it about; the revelation was a call to discipleship, or communion with Jesus, in friendship and mission and not simply information. Thus too, it is a revelation of what it means to be human in history as it actually is.

What was revealed was not simply an unknown fact or an answer to human problems; it was *mystery.* Jesus told his apostles, "The mystery of the kingdom of God has been granted to you" (Mark 11).[3] In our previous volume we showed how human beings are a mystery to themselves, which is gradually revealed to them; their horizon, their social environment, their very humanity, is revealed in the process of life in deeper and deeper dimensions, to the point where

---

[3]See Beda Rigaux and Pierre Grelot, "Mystery," *Dictionary of Biblical Theology,* rev. ed., ed. Xavier Leon-Dufour (New York: Seabury, 1973) 374–7; Haught, *Mystery and Promise,* 43–60; J. J. Bacik, *Apologetics and the Eclipse of Mystery: Mystagogy According to Karl Rahner* (Notre Dame: University of Notre Dame Press, 1980).

the relation to God is central. Similarly, the evolving physical world evokes a wonder that it is at all, and for those open to it, it manifests God as operating in it. In our age of historical consciousness, our individual and social history is a mystery, the source and outcome of which we can never fully understand.

A mystery in this sense is a reality that encompasses us, that science does not master, that is personal more than simply intellectual, that we live and can open ourselves to but never encompass. Mystery is not something that begins to be revealed to us through Jesus Christ. What is revealed through him is presented as the mystery of mysteries that subsumes all others. This mystery of the kingdom orients us not (as many myths do) to the primordial so much as to the transformed future, as hoped for as coming to us as God's gift, yet as a communion with him to which we are invited and in the power of which we are asked to help bring this future about. The kingdom is both a future reality and yet sacramentally and dynamically present through Jesus.

c. The mediation of revelation. We should now ask *how* Jesus revealed this, or *what mediated revelation.* How was this mystery conveyed to Peter and the other believers? We saw in our earlier volume how God's testimonies through conscience and the evolving cosmos manifest him or reveal something of him to human beings through symbols, human experience, and a creative imagination by which the one coming to believe envisages the self within the newly revealed relationship. We saw how the traditions of a particular culture can mediate some revelation of divine mystery and human relation to it. And we saw how a new call from God can be revealed by the need of the common good in changing circumstances. Thus "signs of the times" as well as new insights into the physical world as evolving show a kind of continuing revelation from God. We are investigating here the historical revelation by which Jesus revealed to Peter and the apostles; however, most of what we say applies as well to earlier revelation made to Israel and to this revelation as it comes to us today. We shall examine this by showing that this revelation comes through historical mediators, through external deeds and words that have an essential relationship to one another, and through an internal influence of God on the believer.

First, Judeo-Christian revelation is a historical revelation; it is *mediated by persons chosen by God* to give his message. Moses, the prophets, and Jesus himself were thus chosen. Jesus' baptism reflects such a commission for his ministry (e.g., Luke 3:21-22); after his baptism, Jesus reads to the people of Nazareth, "The Spirit of the Lord is upon me, because he has anointed me to bring glad tidings to the poor" (Luke 4:18). God's revelation through these prophets and Jesus, more than a prophet (Matt 12:41), is thus mediated by people, actions, and words of a particular time and place in history, and so through tradition by which their words and deeds are handed down to us.

Judeo-Christian revelation is, as we said above, a free and loving unveiling of God's attitude toward us and his offer of salvation to us. It is most appropriate that it come to us through witnesses chosen by God to give testimony to the reality of his love and promise. If one thinks it should come to each individually by a religious experience without such mediators, the Judeo-Christian proclamation is that it has, in fact, come to us through these chosen witnesses by God's free and wise design. We will show that there is a religious experience also involved here, but not one dissociated from the facticity of history. The love of God for human beings is most appropriately made known by a concrete historical figure who knows, shares, and expresses this love. God's love and plan for our salvation is a contingent reality that we receive as a totally unmerited gift, not a "universal truth" like that of science or philosophy. And such a reality can be conveyed to us only by one to whom it has been made known and who can give testimony to it.

The philosophers of the Enlightenment felt that the mature person should free himself from tradition and lead himself by his own experience and judgment. They took the knowledge of the physical sciences as models of human knowledge. But as we recalled above in chapter 2, there has been much philosophical work done in our century to show that the knowledge necessary for our forging our human identity depends on our integrating ourselves into a tradition. This knowledge, which has to do with who we are, what models of human living we should accept as worthy of us, how we should relate to the human community of which we are a part, comes to us through the language we are brought up in, the figures of our tradition who are presented to us as models, the literature and arts of our society, and the political events and documents that are at the origin of our society.

Hans-Georg Gadamer has investigated at length what makes this kind of knowledge, as distinct from the knowledge of the physical sciences, possible.[4] As Gadamer writes, "Long before we understand ourselves in retrospect we understand ourselves as a matter of course in the family, society and state in which we live. . . . Hence the individual's prejudgments much more than his judgments are the historical reality of his Being."[5] It comes to us as a heritage; it is not beneath our dignity to accept knowledge concerning human living that comes from a long tested experience, as it is not beneath our dignity to accept the superior knowledge that a doctor has.

Second, this revelation is mediated *symbolically by the person of Jesus and his words and deeds having an internal unity.* What we say here applies largely as well to earlier mediators of revelation in the Judeo-Christian tradition, though we are developing this theme particularly in reference to Jesus. In chapter 2 we saw that the writers of the Gospels wished us the readers (and earlier, the hearers) to see Jesus' actions and words *as* coming from God; only thus are they really seen as God's revelation. The evangelists did feel a degree of freedom to use their creative imaginations to bring out the implications and meaning of Jesus' words and deeds. But the primary creative imagination at work was God's, who through Jesus acted and spoke in such a way that the relationship he offered to human beings might be evident through these words and deeds as through symbols. This characteristic of Christian revelation once more shows us its external and historical mediation, so important to recall because of how central this is and also because different forms of Gnosticism, ancient and modern, resist this in favor of the primacy of people's own internal "religious experience" or estimates of what brings human beings forward.

We have seen that Jesus revealed the kingdom by parables, wisdom sayings and the like, and by his works. For example, when the disciples of John the Baptist asked Jesus whether he was the one who was to come, he told them to report to John what they see: "[T]he blind regain their sight, the lame walk, lepers are cleansed, the deaf hear, the dead are raised, and the poor have the good news proclaimed to them" (Matt 11:5). Jesus' proclamation of the kingdom

---

[4]See H.-G. Gadamer, *Truth and Method* (New York: Crossroad, 1975); Theodore Kisiel, "The Happening of Tradition: The Hermeneutics of Gadamer and Heidegger," *Hermeneutics and Praxis,* ed. Robert Hollinger (Notre Dame: University of Notre Dame Press, 1985) 3–31; George McLean, "Hermeneutics and Heritage," *Man and Nature: The Chinese Tradition and the Future,* ed. Tang Yi-Jie, Li Zhen, and George McLean (Washington, D.C.: The Council for Research in Values and Philosophy, 1989) 57–70.

[5]Gadamer, *Truth and Method,* cited by Kisiel in "Happening of Tradition," 7.

announced it by deeds that showed the reality of God's saving intention and presence and by words that clarified what these actions meant. An event is not really a historical event by its sheer facticity; it is so only if it is interpreted. As Josef Schmitz writes:

> The word of the prophet therefore unveils the situation as an event coming from God and oriented to God in whom the prophet is conscious that the prophetic word has been given to him. The specific nature of historical revelation consists therefore in the fact that God manifests to man through historical events something decisive and that he creates meaning by what is within these events. The historical events are comparable to symbols that allude to a meaning revealed in them and born contemporaneously with them. Historical revelation presents a symbolic structure. But the allusion made to the more profound meaning of the happening, the "understanding," is not conceived as a content simply added by the mind.[6]

The very happening of the events or deeds mediates Judeo-Christian revelation. What is revealed to us through Jesus is not primarily a speculative truth but God's offer of a relationship. Thus the very happening or act and not only the revealing word mediates this communication. In a symbolic act such as the act by which a young man proposes to a young woman and gives her an engagement ring, the very act is intrinsic to the symbol. Beyond words, the act shows the disposition of the one revealing his love for the other. Such symbolic communication conveys both a message content and the attitude of the one who is communicating, both logos and desire. In this attitude the revealer is present to the one to whom he is revealing in a way that words themselves do not sufficiently convey.

Through the symbol what is conveyed to the other is, as we shall repeat below when we reflect on faith, a participatory knowledge in the revealer's disposition and not only an objective knowledge. This has in the one who receives it a transforming impact on the person and not simply on the person's knowledge. There is thus a sacramental character to Christian revelation most appropriate to what is revealed, because what is revealed is the reality of God's saving gift and presence or relationship that he offers us and calls us to, and not simply

---

[6]Schmitz, *La rivelazione,* 107.

the message about this. This shows once more why such revelation occurs through contingent historical acts, because love is only conveyed by such free contingent acts; it is not conveyed by the form of knowledge that philosophers of the Enlightenment esteemed as universal.

This interpretation of Christian revelation differs from the interpretation of those who interpret it either as simply an extension of the revelation conveyed by the cosmos or self or as having its origin in a simply human experience that is symbolized. Paul Ricoeur's analysis of symbols at times may give the impression that he interprets Christian symbols as not having an origin other than cosmic experiences or experiences of the self. This is found in others as well.[7] Ricoeur deliberately restricts himself to the perspective and limits of a philosopher in examining Christian symbols, and as a philosopher he is deeply influenced by Heidegger's rejection of "onto-theo-logy," a position that restricts what he is able to acknowledge in Scripture.

Some theologians have ascribed Christian revelation to "common human experience" that is structured by the human subject to give rise to the Christian symbols. Neither is this faithful to Scripture; it is an over-assimilation of Christian revelation to contemporary naturalism. And some theologians have reduced Christian revelation to the general sense of God's love for us but have considered the New Testament so ideologically skewed that what is more specific there is subject to what is revealed by signs of the time in our own age and our evaluation of what brings us forward. This approach reflects great suspicion in regard to Scripture and tradition but very little in regard to what is within us that resists God's offer of love and salva-

---

[7]See, for example, Paul Ricoeur, "Poétique et symbolique," *Initiation à la pratique de la théologie,* bk. 1, *Introduction,* ed. Bernard Lauret and Francois Refoulé (Paris: Cerf, 1982) 37–61; Thomas Fawcett, *The Symbolic Language of Religion* (Minneapolis: Augsburg Publishing House, 1971) especially 168–85. I have written on the symbolic character of revelation and its origin in a review article on Louis Dupré, *The Other Dimension: A Search for the Meaning of Religious Attitudes* (New York: Doubleday, 1972), in *American Ecclesiastical Review* 167 (1973) 284–7. In this case it seemed that the interpretation of the origin of symbols was too much influenced by Ernst Cassirer and Susanne Langer. I contested Langdon Gilkey's interpretation of Christian symbols in "Christian Interpretation of History: A Dialogue," in M. John Farrelly, *God's Work in a Changing World* (1985; reissued, Washington, D.C., The Council for Research in Values and Philosophy, 1994) 34–48, especially 37–39, and contested a theology too much influenced by Heidegger's philosophy in my review of Lauret and Refoulé, *Initiation,* bk. 1, in *TS* 44 (1983) 705–7. My treatment of Christian revelation and faith is analogous to my earlier study. See M. John Farrelly, *Belief in God in Our Time* (Collegeville: The Liturgical Press, 1992) 216–20, 230–4. For an interpretation of Christian revelation counter to ours, see Gordon Kaufman, *In Face of Mystery* (Cambridge, Mass.: Harvard University Press, 1993); William Placher's critical review in *Christian Century* (May 19–26, 1993) 557–61.

tion. What is legitimate in this approach can be addressed, many of us are convinced, by a hermeneutics that accepts contemporary experience as giving us a new perspective on Christian revelation without seeking to control it.

It is, of course, not only by his words and deeds that Jesus reveals symbolically but by his very person. It is enormously appropriate that God reveal to us through a person, because revelation is destined to invite us into a personal relation and communion with God. God and his disposition toward us can be symbolized best not by the cosmos or by an interior sense of conscience but by a person, since God is personal; a specifically religious relation is one that involves both subjectivity and objectivity, as we showed in our previous volume. The words, deeds, care, gestures, initiatives, by which Jesus reveals are those of a person. It is by the very presence of Jesus and his words and deeds as testimony to God's attitude and message that Christian revelation is conveyed. And by his person Jesus not only reveals God's design and person to us but the human response to God to which we are called as believers or disciples. He reveals to us not only God's identity but our identity.

Third, what mediates this revelation is not simply the external, historical dimensions we have been recalling but an *interior influence* on the person. All the hearers of Jesus experienced the external dimensions of his ministry, but many passages show God's revelation through Jesus to have a further dimension. For example, Jesus tells Peter after his confession, "Flesh and blood has not revealed this to you, but my heavenly Father" (Matt 16:17). And according to John, Jesus identifies coming to him with faith and adds, "No one can come to me unless the Father who sent me draw him. . . . Everyone who listens to my Father and learns from him comes to me" (John 6:44-45). In the interior influence that is an essential element of revelation, then, we find, as we did in our examination of the external mediation of revelation, both logos and desire, because there is both an interior illumination and an interior drawing offered to the person invited to believe.

We can say that interiorly there is conveyed a preconceptual influence and a nonconceptual influence. The preconceptual is the impact given to all the senses and imagination and leads to a concept, as it did for Peter, who said "You are the Christ." The interior illumination allowed Peter to discern this, for he was taught by the Father. But there was a nonconceptual influence also, related to the external attitude shown by Jesus and even the emotional currents of love that came from Jesus' actions. This does not lead initially to a concept, but through the interior "drawing" it leads to the response of acceptance that faith is. Some Catholics accept the necessity of this interior drawing for belief but do not think it was interior or essential to revelation itself; it is for them the grace that enables one to respond to revelation by faith. However, this view is associated with the interpretation of the content of revelation as an intellectual message. If, as we have argued above, what is revealed is personal knowledge of God and Jesus and a relationship that is offered, then the actual drawing is interior to revelation, because a personal relationship is conveyed externally by symbolic acts that involve both the agent's logos and desire as well as by the interior influence that continues both the one and the other.

This interior gift is essentially related to what is mediated externally. This influence was ascribed to the Holy Spirit in the early Church, and thus John includes in Jesus' last discourse the statement: "The Advocate, the Holy Spirit that the Father will send in my name—she will teach you everything and remind you of all that I told you" (John 14:26, my translation). The interior illumination and drawing that comes from God is not in tension with what Jesus mediated by his words and deeds but enables the believer to penetrate these words and deeds in order to see and accept their meaning at an ever-deepening level. This is what we find the evangelists testifying to as they compose their Gospels, because these Gospels show the early Church's growing understanding of the revelation given through Jesus. Christians believe that the early Church's interpretations of Jesus' words, deeds and life, death and resurrection, are intrinsic to the meaning of his historical ministry because the Spirit was operative in this development of the Church.

2. The Human Response of Faith

Here we ask what the human being offers in response to God's revelation. To answer this theologians have depended on their models of the human being. Similarly, we depend on our understanding of the human person developed in the preceding volume. We understand the human being somewhat differently from Thomas, because he tended to relate the person to revelation on the model of the student's relation to the teacher. For example, he saw revelation as descending from God to us, and our knowledge of God through his effects as ascending from us to God. However, this may overdraw the distinction, because faith includes discovery, and our knowledge of God through the cosmos and conscience includes discernments of God's testimonies to himself. Similarly, we take a somewhat different model from that of the early Rahner, who interpreted the individual person existentially, somewhat apart from the society of which he or she is a part.

We have interpreted the individual person as a cultural being within a particular historical context of time and space. With the help of Erikson and others we saw something of how an individual grows through the interaction between the growing person and his or her enlarging social environment, an environment that is of a particular culture and historical period. This model seems more helpful in interpreting Peter's coming to faith in Jesus than that of a student or existential individual, because Peter was a person who came from and was embedded in a particular culture with its hopes and presuppositions, some of which made it easier for him to discern who Jesus was and some of which made it more difficult. This model also is more appropriate for understanding the process of coming to faith in our own time. People today who are faced with Christian revelation are people of a particular culture that has its hopes and fears, its presuppositions, its messages, its cultural leaders. Some of these favor the person's response to Jesus and some are obstacles to the discernment of who Jesus is.

This is a very different situation from that envisaged by the philosophers of the Enlightenment, and the acknowledgment of this today has led some to think that reason itself is so modified by a particular culture that it is relativistic. While Heidegger, Gadamer, and others have shown the inadequacy of the Enlightenment interpretation of human knowledge, particularly as this is found in knowledge significant for human identity, they have not escaped relativism. It is true that in the formation of a human identity, and that is what the response to revelation is, there is no escape to the position of a neutral observer or a universal knowledge unaffected by one's own or one's community interests.[8] We showed in our previous volume that one could

[8]See Paul Giurlanda, *Faith and Knowledge: A Critical Enquiry* (Lanham, Md.: University Press of America, 1987) 93: "To summarize: what we have seen so far is that Gadamer's enterprise in *Truth and Method* is an appeal to an ancient tradition stemming from Aristotle and continuing up until modern times in the tradition of rhetoric and in humanistic studies. This ancient tradition to which Gadamer appeals, the tradition we are calling the *phronesis* tradition, rests on a very different concept of understanding than that which prevails in positivistic philosophies of science.

acknowledge this and find that it does not undercut the possibility and necessity of metaphysical knowledge of being. It is from the background of this understanding of the human person that we shall examine faith as a part of a dialogue, as dependent upon a modification under grace of one's subjectivity, and as in accord with critical reason.

a. Faith as response in dialogue. Revelation is indeed God's act, but Judeo-Christian revelation is a dialogue between God and the human person and community. In reference to this we will show faith (1) as correlative to God's revelation and (2) as what the believer offers in this dialogue.

(1) Faith has been interpreted in many different contexts because of particular problems the theologian or the Church was facing. It has been interpreted in reaction to those who thought that one could be saved by works, in reaction to those who experienced a conflict between reason and faith, in reaction to those who gave their religious experience or reason a too-determining role as criterion for what was to be believed, in reaction to those who were authoritarian in proclaiming the faith, and in reaction to other views that were considered unbalanced on this theme. We have seen some of these interpretations in chapter 6 of this volume and chapters 2 and 4 of the preceding volume. What is necessary in our time is a search for an integrative interpretation of faith that does justice to these diverse concerns. I have proposed that one way to do this is to look to the faith of Peter, which is presented as paradigmatic for us in the Gospels. We are here specifically speaking of the first phase of his faith response, but what we say of it is largely true of the distinctively Christian stage of his faith response, as we shall later indicate. Our interpretation of faith is correlative to our interpretation of revelation. We propose that it is an understanding of faith as a *personal knowledge* of God through Jesus Christ that overcomes many of the mutually opposed interpretations of Christian faith that we have seen.

Specifically, it depends on a communitarian, participatory, fiduciary (to use the Polanyian word) notion of what it means to *know.*" On *phronesis,* or practical wisdom or prudence, see Aristotle, *Nichomachean Ethics,* bk. 6, chs. 5, 11. We argued in our earlier volume that the acceptance of the situated character of practical wisdom does not result in "nonfoundationalism" because there is metaphysical knowledge and a constitutive human good in the context of which such practical wisdom operates. See Thomas Guarino, "Between Foundationalism and Nihilism: Is *Phronesis* the *Via Media* for Theology?" *TS* 54 (1993) 37–54; James Ross, "Rational Reliance," *JAAR* 62 (1994) 769–98.

Peter's initial faith in Jesus was, as we indicated when we were treating Scripture, both faith *that* Jesus was the Christ and a commitment of discipleship to Jesus, or faith *in* Jesus. Thus too, the believer's faith in Jesus is fiducia, or trust, and it is an intellectual judgment that finds its expression in a proposition stating a truth about Jesus. It is a whole human personal response to Jesus—a personal knowledge of Jesus and so of God's design and presence. It is participative knowledge in that it is not simply objective or neutral; rather, the believer gets the insight he or she does through being engaged by Jesus—through the mediation of apostolic testimony, Christian tradition, and the Spirit—and responding in kind. He or she wants to have a part with Jesus in his kingdom.

We saw that God's revelation was by symbolic mediation through Jesus' testimony by word and deed that had a logos character to it, or message, and was an act expressing God's and Jesus' desire for the salvation of those whom he addressed. And the interior means by which God's revelation was communicated similarly was both illuminating and drawing. Correlatively, the believer's faith is a response to this whole personal communication that God makes to him or her through Jesus and the Spirit. It is not primarily a response to an internal experience nor to objective evidence neutrally evaluated but a response to a person by a person. It is, as we showed in our study of Scripture, both a gift—and so not a human achievement—and a free act. It is based both on God's authority and on experience, as Peter's faith was based on his historical experience of Jesus, whose loving and authorized offer of salvation and love was expressed in his deeds of healing and his words of wisdom. The believer's submission to authority is no problem for one who knows one's own need, because this authority is one of God's loving, bending down to lift up the insignificant of the world and sinners to give them a share in God's kingdom and communion with Jesus.

(2) In a dialogue both parties have something to offer. We see this specifically in the first stage of Peter's coming to faith in Jesus. Jesus *asked* his apostles, "But who do you say that I am?" (Matt 16:15). God revealed through Jesus who he was, but not in a way that disallowed a human contribution to this revelation; rather, he invited the human contribution. He wanted this to be a discovery on the part of his followers. Jesus' revelation to one who believes is not the first he or she receives; we all are a part of communities that have been privileged with God's care and revelation in the past, and we share the

beliefs and the hopes and concerns of our cultures. Jesus wants himself to be believed and hoped in, in a way that is in continuity with earlier beliefs and hopes that have their origin in God and human experience under God.

For Peter, as for us, there were various figures in tradition under which the hopes for their future and the mediators of this hope were expected. Peter took one of these, a more popular image, and responded on behalf of the other apostles: "You are the Messiah" (Matt 16:16). There were many limitations to Peter's belief and hopes here, but Jesus commended him and proclaimed that this belief came from God's revelation. There was ambiguity in Jesus' life and words, but Peter had pierced the mystery and accepted its unknown practical implications to some extent, and he expressed it in his faith response—his confession that Jesus was the Christ and his profession of discipleship. Revelation is a processive reality in God's dispensation; thus Jesus adapts himself to those whose belief is to develop by steps. By acknowledging Jesus as Messiah, Peter did give him a more central place in the mediation of God's revelation and kingdom than if he had simply considered him another prophet. Though an intermediate position between the Jewish religion at the time and Christianity, it was an important step. Through Peter's faith the new people of God had a beginning; Peter and those for whom he spoke had begun to bridge the space between God's earlier revelation and call and his new and definitive revelation and call.

This dimension of faith and of God's dispensation evoking faith has important implications for the problems of *inculturation* that face the Church in our time.[9] Not infrequently the Church has had such a fear that people would misinterpret the Christian message that it has skipped this stage of revelation in its proclamation and catechesis. The result has been at times that it has alienated a whole culture, as when it rejected Confucian rituals as incompatible with Christianity, only to declare them compatible a couple of centuries later. And at times the result has been to instill the Christian message only as a second-level knowledge in a people, unrelated to their earlier beliefs and culture.

---

[9]On this problem, see, for example, Aylward Shorter, *Toward a Theology of Inculturation* (Maryknoll, N.Y.: Orbis Books, 1988); Robert Schreiter, "Faith and Cultures: Challenges to a World Church," *TS* 50 (1989) 744–60; David Tracy, "On Naming the Present," Concilium 1 (1990) 66–85; "Inculturation and Catholicity," the theme of *Proceedings of the Catholic Theological Society of America* (1990).

Thus Christianity has continued with them but as an overlay to a deeper and previous belief that continues to be practiced, perhaps hiddenly, and that distorts the Christian overlay, made more superficial by its unrelatedness to the earlier culture. This has happened in many places in Latin America, when the Spanish feared to express the Christian message in a way related to the people's earlier culture out of fear of contaminating the message, and so presented it in Spanish categories, names, and even language. Such failures of Christian proclamation have come also from an overidentification of the Christian message, with a European culture. This approach was repudiated by Vatican II (see *GS* 53–63) and by Pope Paul VI, who wrote:

> What matters is to evangelize man's culture and cultures (not in a purely decorative way as it were by applying a thin veneer, but in a vital way, in depth and right to their very roots). . . . The Gospel, and therefore evangelization . . . cannot avoid borrowing the elements of human culture or cultures. . . . [T]hey are capable of permeating them all without becoming subject to any one of them. The split between the Gospel and culture is without a doubt the drama of our time, just as it was of other times (*EN* 20).

Events since the writing of this text (1975) have shown how difficult the dialogue between the Church and cultures is. It is a major if not the major difficulty that faces both the Church and cultures.

b. Faith, grace, and subjectivity. A further question about faith is how one comes to the change or conversion that Christian faith is. Much modern Catholic Neoscholastic theology stressed that one first makes a judgment of credibility, that is, that this message does come from God's revelation, by natural knowledge, and one then reasonably believes. Catholics were very afraid of Protestant subjectivism and so stressed the objective bases for faith, at times to the extent of falling into an objectivism. We ask here how coming to faith depends upon a change of subjectivity, and below we will treat the question of the place of critical reason in a person's coming to believe.

In analyzing faith, we found that it was both belief *that* and commitment to discipleship, or belief *in* Jesus. This faith involves accepting a new structure for the self and a new mediation of one's relation to God and one's hope. When we examined the stages of personal development in the last volume with the help of Erikson, we saw that a new stage of personal development was evoked, because "the encounter with some living fellow creature serves as a catalyst that enables the person to transform himself and shape his own self."[10] This is a better context for examining what leads one to faith than a predominantly intellectual study of the relation of faith and reason, because Christian faith is specifically personal knowledge of Jesus.

Such faith emerges from the whole human person's encounter with God's offer of salvation and revelation. As we see in Peter and modern converts, the person *experiences* a lack in life, both individual and communal, that he or she cannot fulfill. This makes the person open to the offer of a love, a healing, an enablement, an acceptance, a hope, a salvation that is proferred. The person experiences this offer through *symbols* expressive of the attitude and message of Jesus and so of God, which strike the individual's *creative imagination.* That is, it strikes the whole person, both as one who desires and as one who knows, in an integral way. And it evokes from the person a creative use of the imagination, whereby the individual projects himself or herself into what an engagement of acceptance would mean for him or her. It is in this context that the individual seeks to *discern* the logos and appeal addressed to him or her by this symbolic communication, in part by the help of what he or she already accepts as having been revealed by God. Is God present through this address or not? As we said above, the individual has received not only the external historical communication but an interior illumination and drawing by God that touches the person's affectivity.

What this means can be expressed in different ways. Thomas Aquinas speaks of an *instinctus fidei:* "The light of faith makes us see the things believed in. As by other virtues one sees what is appropriate to him by that virtue, so through the virtue of faith the human mind is inclined to assent to those things that agree with right faith and not to others."[11] The individual through a particular habit has a connaturality with a kind of action, attitude, and knowledge that accords with that habit. For example, the chaste person has an experiential knowledge, or "connatural knowledge," in a particular circumstance that calls for the exercise of this virtue of how he or she

---

[10]D. Yankelovich and W. Barrett, *Ego and Instinct: The Psychoanalytic View of Human Nature— Revised* (New York: Random House, 1970) 152. Our study of faith in what follows is in accord with my *Belief in God,* "Critical Grounding of Faith: An Epistemological Question," 216–34.

[11]*ST* II–II, 1, 4, ad 3.

should act, even before analyzing the moral principles involved and their application.

Similarly, the person of faith has, through the light of faith, an inclination to believe what is appropriate to that faith. This happens not only when the person is already established in faith but as he or she is on the way to faith. Thomas writes: "The one who believes has sufficient motive for believing. For he is inclined to believe by the authority of the divine teaching confirmed by miracles and, what is greater, the interior appeal of God inviting him *(interiori instinctu Dei invitantis)."*[12] This interior appeal translated into an inclination or instinct of faith is a grace necessary for one coming to believe. It has an illumining influence on the mind as well as an inclining influence on the will, enabling the person to discern the signs or symbols for what they really are. Such a one does not need endless signs for him or her to accept God's revelation. For the acceptance of God's genuine revelation, what is first of all necessary is such subjective receptivity. This can be expressed also by saying that "the subjectivity of the receiver of revelation is co-constituted by God himself."[13] One's subjectivity is changed and raised so that one can conspire with God in his loving revelation. This is reflected in Scripture, as when Paul says: "The Spirit itself bears witness with our spirit that we are children of God"; hence we cry *"Abba,* Father!" (Rom 8:16, 15).

Some Catholic theologians do not see this inner appeal and *instinctus fidei* as intrinsic to revelation; however, if we understand revelation as communicating personal knowledge rather than simply intellectual knowledge, then we can see it as intrinsic to revelation, because personal knowledge is conveyed by the whole person and received by the whole person, mind and affectivity. We may add that far from such faith being an enemy of human maturity, it is the condition of human maturity. Maturity depends upon our openness to personal relations and responsiveness to the other, a fortiori our openness to a personal relation offered us by the Other, who is God. The

[12]*ST* II–II, 2, 9, ad 3. Is this *instinctus fidei* the habit of faith or, in the case of one on the way to faith, an operating or active grace? Perhaps this question would be put in a better context if we recall that someone like Peter already had faith when he encountered Jesus. See T. C. O'Brien's notes in Thomas Aquinas, "Faith," *Summa theologiae* (New York: McGraw-Hill, 1974) 31:98–9, 166–7. Also see Pierre Rousselot, *The Eyes of Faith* and *Answer to Two Attacks* (New York: Fordham University Press, 1990). These were originally published in 1910 and 1914 and are here translated and explained by Joseph Donceel, John McDermott, and Avery Dulles.

[13]Schmitz, *La rivelazione,* 130.

Enlightenment interpretation of the human person as autonomous reason is a reduction of the human person and his or her maturity.

c. Faith and critical reason. What is the place of *critical reason* in one's coming to faith? There is a history to this question. In response to the Enlightenment many Catholic theologians largely accepted the Enlightenment interpretation of reason and constructed apologetics on this basis. Thus they thought that if a person would approach the question of Christian faith in a genuinely neutral way, they could show him from objective arguments such as miracles that this faith was worthy of human acceptance. When this was undercut, for example by the historical-critical method in the study of the Gospels, some theologians disclaimed the earlier approach and based faith simply on praxis, such as hope in promises offered by Christian revelation of the interior light of faith.

However, both the earlier reaction to the Enlightenment attack on Christian faith and the more recent disavowal of the place of critical reason in the question of how one comes to Christian faith have falsely supposed that neutrality is the prime requisite for a critical evaluation of Christian revelation. The falsity of this as it regards human knowledge of what is of significance for personal identity has been shown by such philosophers as Heidegger, Gadamer, and Polanyi. We have shown in our earlier volume that what is of central importance in evaluating what promotes our human welfare is a genuine desire for that welfare in its deeper dimensions, that there are criteria for what the human good is, that there is much in us and around us that is an obstacle to our accepting the costs of seeking these deeper dimensions, and that metaphysical knowledge is possible and is indeed the condition for the possibility of scientific knowledge.

It is relevant to recall that the use of the historical-critical method was frequently infected by a naturalism and that those who used it frequently did not take the Gospels for the form of writing that they are. It was recognized that the authors were deeply involved in promoting a particular message, and they were thus not neutral observers of the events of Jesus' life. Their portrayal of the life of Jesus was a work of imagination.

However, as recent literary criticism has shown and as we recalled in our second chapter, this use of imagination by the evangelists was very appropriate to the genre of proclamation and is in accord with their substantial veracity about Jesus' historical words and deeds.

The evangelists sought to enable their readers to see Jesus' deeds and words *as* God's offer of salvation and revelation. The central creative imagination at work in what the Gospels proclaim was that of Jesus himself, and God through Jesus. The evangelists exercised their own creative imaginations in service of and fidelity to this foundational imagination reflected in Jesus' symbolic activity. They presented the message not as neutral historical observers but as proclaimers of the message. Specifically, miracles were central to Jesus' ministry. But they should be seen as signs or symbols of the presence of God's salvation more than extrinsic proofs of God's vindication of Jesus' ministry. So Peter's faith had grounds in what Jesus said and did and was not based on wishful thinking. And our faith that is based on the apostolic testimony as well as on the interior witness of the Holy Spirit, as we shall recall more below, has grounds in what Jesus said and did and is not based on wishful thinking.

In *conclusion,* we can note several false dichotomies that this approach to revelation and faith allows us to overcome. This helps us to overcome the opposition between faith as based on authority and faith as based on religious experience. Since Christian revelation is mediated by both external and internal testimony, faith is based on both authority and religious experience, though not a religious experience unrelated to historical words and deeds of Jesus. This helps us, as many theologians have noted since Vatican II, overcome the opposition between an objectivism and a subjectivism; for while faith does depend on the interior testimony of the Holy Spirit, there are objective grounds for Christian belief in the historical words and deeds of Jesus that are accessible to us if the Gospels are correctly understood as the kind of documents they are.

Our faith depends on our raising our minds and hearts to desire the good that Jesus offers us, and this we cannot do without the help of the Holy Spirit, but this is not a substitute for the objective grounds for faith; rather, it is what enables us to discern them as God's presence and revelation. All of this is relevant to the question of certainty in faith, for this depends on the firmness of one's adherence to the good offered. And it is relevant to the question of the knowledge of the fact of revelation, because this knowledge is as dependent upon human conversion as it is upon intellectual signs.

II. Revelation and Faith Through
the Death and Resurrection of Jesus

We have been examining revelation as dialogical and the response of faith to God through this revelation. Now we examine this revelation through the death and resurrection of Jesus and the response to this. We treat Christian revelation as a process. Some theologians do not put it in this context, and as a result they treat it as dialogical without doing justice to its dialectical character, or they treat it as dialectical but do not do justice to its dialogical character or to God's earlier revelations. In viewing Christian revelation as a process, we gain a perspective that can interrelate these stages, because it is the same God who first reveals something about himself through Jesus and then reveals something even more mysterious that subsumes into a new paradigm but does not discount the earlier revelation. Of course the death and resurrection of Jesus are dimensions of one Christian mystery. What the evangelists wrote of his death they wrote from the perspective of his resurrection. The crucifixion's meaning is not present without the resurrection, and the resurrection is the resurrection of the crucified Jesus. But they are also distinct events and should be looked on as distinct events. We are only treating these events in relation to our question of the nature of Christian revelation and faith and even doing this in only an introductory fashion.

1. Revelation and Faith Through the Death of Jesus

We treat this question through reflecting *(a)* on Jesus' prediction of his suffering and death and *(b)* on his passion and death itself.

a. Jesus' prediction of his death. We saw in chapter 3 that there is strong reason to accept as substantially accurate the Synoptics' account of Jesus' predictions of his passion and death. After Jesus had commended Peter and his apostles' belief in him as Messiah, he began to predict that the Son of Man would suffer at the hands of the elders, the chief priests, and the scribes and be put to death and rise. Peter responds by rejecting such a destiny for the Messiah, and Jesus answers him: "Get behind me, Satan. You are an obstacle to me. You are thinking not as God does, but as human beings do" (Matt 16:23; see Mark 8:33; Luke softens Mark's portrait of Peter, see Luke 9:20-21). Counter to Jesus' earlier commendation of Peter, here he rebukes him. We can ask whether this is a real revelation and then look to Peter's response. This has implications for Christian revelation and faith for all times, as it relates to Church communities in particular cultures and to individuals.

Is there a real revelation present here? We have to say that there is. It is mediated by Jesus; he proclaims it or makes it known to his disciples; his authority is as present here as it is in his other messages about the kingdom; he rebukes a rejection of this prediction as being opposed to God's thoughts; and he holds Peter responsible for not accepting this message. In one sense it is not a full revelation, because it is not accepted. But the whole objective dimension of revelation must be acknowledged to be here, because otherwise Peter would not be responsible for rejecting it; what was lacking was the subjective dimension of revelation, namely its acceptance. This revelation on the part of Jesus came after a dialogical stage in which Jesus *asked* the apostles who they say Jesus is.

Here he does not ask; he *tells* them what sort of Messiah he is. And he does not proclaim this by both deeds and words immediately, but by words alone. This is a deeper dimension of his personal mystery and God's plan of salvation that he reveals; it transcends what the apostles have already assented to and seems to contradict what they have accepted. Jesus corrects the disciples' inadequate understanding of himself and God's plan. God's revelation continues, and one cannot excuse one's nonacceptance of later revelations by one's acceptance of an earlier revelation.

Peter's response is not faith but refusal of faith. As Jesus' commendation of his earlier profession stressed that Peter's insight had come not from flesh and blood but from the Father, so here Jesus' reprimand showed that Peter's resistance came not from the Father but from human thoughts. Human subjectivity is as present here as it was in Peter's earlier faith profession. But here it is an obstacle to belief, whereas earlier it was open to belief. What his subjectivity revealed here was not God's revelation but Peter's own resistance to God's full message and salvation through Jesus and his own incapacity on his own to surrender to Jesus as disciple. Jesus' new revelation seemed to Peter to contradict his hopes and his concept of what the Messiah was, and Peter allowed his human criteria to control his response rather than allow his criteria to be controlled by Jesus' message.

Peter had not found in his culture a preunderstanding for such a message; in fact, this message shocked and shattered his preunderstanding. It was discontinuous with his human hopes and human concepts, even those that he had drawn from God's earlier revelation. We know that in the Old Testament there were figures like Job whose understanding of God drawn from revelation was shocked by evils that came upon them, and they had to struggle to be open to such a new revelation—to accept it without understanding (see, e.g., Ps 73:22). The results of Peter's resistance were his later flight and denial when Jesus was crucified. This has obvious implications for all Christians. We are all capable of erecting what comes from our concepts and our views of what will bring us forward into criteria of what God can be revealing through Jesus Christ, and thus setting ourselves up as seeking to control God rather than to surrender to him. We can interpret unwelcome aspects of Christ's message as evidence that it is not from Christ rather than as evidence of who we are and what we must be saved from.

b. Jesus' passion and death as revelation. Jesus' passion and death were themselves revelation. This has been strongly emphasized by Barth, Moltmann, Jüngel, and by von Balthasar, Kasper, and other Catholic theologians such as Dermot Lane.[14] This is indeed paradoxical—that something of God should be revealed in the weakness, the emptying, the vulnerability of Jesus, who experiences the silence of his Father and abandonment by him as well as by his disciples. At times aspects of this revelation have been given too little emphasis in Catholic theology. It is largely through the insistence of some Protestant theologians that Catholics have come to see the need to incorporate this into their understanding of God's revelation. That the crucifixion of Jesus was a revelation was not seen by his disciples initially but only from the perspective of the resurrection. There are, however, indications that Jesus had before his death presented it as a revelation. If there is any basis for his institution of the Eucharist at the Last Supper, this is the case.

What is revealed by the crucifixion of Jesus? We will present several aspects of this revelation. *First,* it reveals the degree of Jesus'

---

[14]See e.g., Jürgen Moltmann, *The Crucified God* (New York: Harper & Row, 1974); Eberhard Jüngel, *God as the Mystery of the World: On the Foundation of the Theology of the Crucified One in the Dispute Between Theism and Atheism* (Grand Rapids: Eerdmans, 1983); see also my comments on this book in *TS* 45 (1984) 166–8; Hans Urs von Balthasar, *Mysterium Paschale,* trans. Aidan Nichols (Grand Rapids: Eerdmans, 1993); Walter Kasper, *The God of Jesus Christ* (New York: Crossroad, 1984) 189–97; Dermot Lane, *Christ at the Centre* (New York: Paulist Press, 1991) 53–79.

love of the Father and love for his disciples. As von Balthasar writes: "On the Cross, the Son's glory breaks through, inasmuch as it is then that he goes to the (divine) extreme in his loving, and in the revelation of that love."[15] Jesus looks on his going to death as preference for the Father's will to his own (Matt 26:39), and thus as a sign of his love for his Father: "The world must know that I love the Father and that I do just as the Father has commanded me" (John 14:31); thus his acceptance of death is itself part of his glorification (John 17:4-5). Jesus emptied himself, humbled himself, "becoming obedient to death, even death on a cross" (Phil 2:9). God himself did not refuse obedience. Jesus' acceptance of death is similarly a sign of love for his disciples: "No one has greater love than this, to lay down one's life for one's friends. You are my friends" (John 15:13-14). As Paul tells the Corinthians, "for your sake he became poor although he was rich, so that by his poverty you might become rich" (2 Cor 8:9).

Second, the crucifixion of Jesus shows us the Father's love for us: "For God so loved the world that he gave his only Son . . . that the world might be saved through him" (John 3:16-17). And Paul writes: "He who did not spare his own Son but handed him over for us all, how will he not also give us everything else along with him?" (Rom 8:32). This is not to say that God took the initiative to sacrifice his own Son, though unfortunately that is the way this has frequently been interpreted; rather, in the circumstances of the Jews' rejection of Jesus, he did not hesitate to accept the consequences and costs to him of their free actions and make this very rejection the means of our salvation. This shows also that not only Jesus suffers but the Father suffers; what cost would it be for him if he did not suffer at the pain his Son endured? Traditional theology did not accept this, but recent theologians have gotten beyond the excessive influence of Greek philosophy and have widely begun to accept it.[16] Thus it also reveals something of God himself, of the trinitarian relations between Father, Son, and Holy Spirit, though an articulation of this is more appropriately treated in the study of the Trinity.

Third, the crucifixion reveals what sin is. It is the rejection of such a love. Von Balthasar writes concerning Jesus, scourged and crowned with thorns and spat upon, whom Pilate presented to the people with the words "Behold, the man!": "Here now is the only valid and obligatory

[15]von Balthasar, *Mysterium Paschale,* 29.

[16]See books cited above; see also Farrelly, *Belief in God,* 326–31.

image of what the sin of the world is like for the heart of God, made visible in 'the' man. In the image of the complete Kenosis, there shines 'the light of the knowledge of the glory of God in the face of Jesus Christ' (2 Cor 4:6)."[17] And it shows God's attitude toward sin. Von Balthasar quotes E. Riggenbach: "God cannot love moral evil, he can only hate it. Of its very nature, it stands in complete opposition to God's essence. It is the counter-image of his holy love. There is no right love without wrath, for wrath is the reverse side of love. God could not truly love the good unless he hated evil and shunned it."[18] Jesus bore the evil of sin: "For our sake he [God] made him to be sin who did not know sin, so that we might become the righteousness of God in him" (2 Cor 5:21). Jesus experienced being a curse (Gal 3:13) and being abandoned by God (Mark 16:34). Thus the crucifixion also reveals the present condition of salvation; it does not occur through simply an evolution of humanity but in the midst of a radical opposition to God's love and purposes in the world and in our "flesh." And so it reveals something of the life to which Jesus calls his disciples (John 15:20).

In conclusion, we can see through this how the crucified Christ was "a stumbling block to Jews and foolishness to Gentiles," and yet for those who believe "the power of God and the wisdom of God. For the foolishness of God is wiser than human wisdom, and the weakness of God is stronger than human strength" (1 Cor 1:23-25). God's acceptance of such weakness and foolishness is the most profound sign of his love for us and, indeed, of who he is. And the ambiguity of such a revelation leaves us free to accept or not accept it. This revelation has evoked in many a repentance for sin and a change of life. It does not discount earlier and other signs of who he is and what his attitude is toward us, and it should not be used by theologians to discount God's earlier revelations. It calls us to subsume these into the paradigm of God revealed by the cross of Christ.

2. Revelation and Faith Through the Resurrection of Christ and the Coming of the Holy Spirit

What is the revelation and faith that comes through the appearances of the resurrected Jesus and the coming of the Holy Spirit? We

---

[17]von Balthasar, *Mysterium Paschale,* 118–9.

[18]Ibid., 138–9.

treated this question in chapters 4 and 5, and we are not repeating the story or history here; we are dealing with it basically in terms other than story, though we shall refer to this history dimension. Here we are primarily asking how Christian revelation and faith are seen in terms of the understanding of God, of the human person and community, and of their interaction, which we articulated in volume one. We shall reflect briefly on this as revelation, as belief, and as proclaimed by the disciples in the early Church.[19]

a. God's revelation through the resurrected Jesus and the Spirit. God, who earlier had revealed through the testimonies to himself given by conscience and the cosmos and through traditions of particular peoples, through the history of Israel, and through the ministry of Jesus and his death, now continues and still further fulfills his revelatory process through the appearances of the resurrected Jesus and the gift of the Spirit. This personal God who cares for all human beings in his love and in his design for the salvation of all peoples reveals his plan of salvation and himself in a way transcendent to all earlier revelations. This is the definitive stage of the process of Christian revelation. Though it was implicit in the ministry of Jesus it cannot be reduced to that ministry, and it brings the disciples to the distinctively Christian dimension of faith. It is a further act on God's part. It is wholly God's initiative, because it is God who has raised Jesus from the dead. Through this God made something known: "God has made him Lord and Messiah" (Acts 2:26; see Gal 1:12, 15).

The medium through which God made this known was his symbolic act and words. It was made known by the appearances of the resurrected Jesus and by the gift of the Holy Spirit. It is through God's creative imagination that by these means he expressed his revelation here. As earlier God had revealed through both external words and deeds of Jesus and internal illumination of those called to faith, so too here his revelation, which conveys logos and his desire, comes through the appearances of the resurrected Jesus and the coming of the Spirit. As James Dunn expressed it in a passage we quoted earlier:

[19]For some treatments on revelation occurring through the resurrection of Jesus, see in addition to books referred to earlier, e.g., Gerald O'Collins, *Jesus Risen* (New York: Paulist Press, 1987); Brian McDermott, "The Resurrection of Jesus," *Word Become Flesh: Dimensions of Christology* (Collegeville: The Liturgical Press, 1993) 105–51; Wolfhart Pannenberg, *Jesus—God and Man* (Philadelphia: Westminster Press, 1968).

> After Jesus' death the earliest Christian community sprang directly from a sequence of epochal experiences of two distinct sorts—experiences in which Jesus appeared to individuals and groups to be recognized as the one who had already experienced the eschatological resurrection from the dead, and experiences of religious ecstasy and enthusiasm recognized as the manifestation of the eschatological Spirit. . . .
>
> *Above all, the distinctive essence of Christian experience lies in the relation between Jesus and the Spirit.*[20]

It is only through both that God's distinctive revelation occurs. This is intimated in Acts in Luke's own way by his account of the apostles' asking Jesus before his ascension and the coming of the Spirit: "Lord, are you at this time going to restore the kingdom to Israel?" (Acts 1:6), thus showing they had not grasped the implications of the resurrection. The distinctively Christian revelation is a new and deeper personal knowledge of Jesus, and it depends essentially on the Spirit's gift. As Paul writes: "No one can say, 'Jesus is Lord,' except by the holy Spirit" (1 Cor 12:3), and "no one knows what pertains to God except the Spirit of God" (1 Cor 2:11). And externally, it is through both the appearances and words that this revelation is conveyed. It is not only by brute fact but by interpreted fact, interpreted by Jesus' words and those of Scripture, for example, the words of the psalms and of Daniel in the apocalyptic tradition. The resurrection was expected to occur at the end of time, and here was Jesus sharing in that risen and transformed state. He had referred to one who was to come as the Son of Man. Perhaps now for the first time did the apostles understand and accept that he was the one who, as the Danielic Son of Man, was going to mediate the apocalyptic kingdom and not only the Messiah who would mediate the messianic kingdom. It was by historical fact or deed that God revealed this, at least in the sense that the risen Jesus appeared to them in a particular time and space, though it was an incursion of the age to come into this age.

What was the message, then, that God revealed through this medium? God, who had earlier revealed dimensions of himself and of how he was the goal of the human person and community and the savior of his people, now revealed in a definitive way what this salvation was and the promise that it would be offered to those who be-

[20]James Dunn, *Jesus and the Spirit* (Philadelphia: Westminster Press, 1975) 357, 358 (his italics).

lieve and would not be thwarted by any opposition, even death itself. He brought to fulfillment earlier intimations of what God had in store for human beings by giving us a proleptic experience of what this future would be and a promise of this future.[21]

Thus God revealed that counter to all the dashed hopes of the apostles he would still establish his kingdom, what this would be, and that Jesus was vindicated and would be the mediator of this kingdom. God's love for his Son and his saving power is shown through the resurrection of Jesus and the coming of the Spirit—a love and power no force can withstand. The kingdom is primarily that which the apocalyptic tradition and Jesus' proclamation to this effect had earlier foretold, for it is this that is made known both through the resurrection that was understood to be a central element of the age to come and the giving of the Spirit, also a characteristic gift of the new age.

The anticipated resurrection gave some revelatory experience of what this transformed existence in a new world would be—what the final fulfillment and liberation of history would be. It would be a social salvation, a union with God and with one another under the leadership of Jesus. For Jesus is vindicated by the resurrection, and he is revealed to be the mediator of the apocalyptic kingdom—the judge and savior, *Lord* in the proper sense, not only a human figure but one who shared divine agency as judge and savior.[22] God *will* bring this about. And the apostles are *commissioned* to be stewards, ambassadors, proclaimers of the offer of the kingdom to those who believe. This revelation was meant for the whole world. All this is revealed as a *mystery,* that is, not as something to be grasped, as another human fact of knowledge is, but only through that participatory knowledge that faith is.

Thus this revelation shows something about God himself—his love, his saving power, his intention, and his offer through Jesus Christ and the Spirit. This shows too that the salvation God offers us comes from the future—a salvation to be achieved when Jesus comes again, and (as the apostles quickly realized) as being given *in part* already. The age to come is already having an impact upon the present age. It is thus the revelation too, through establishing it, of the new

---

[21]See Pannenberg, *Jesus—God and Man,* 157 and passim; Jürgen Moltmann, "The Resurrection and the Future of Jesus Christ," *Theology of Hope* (New York: Harper & Row, 1967) 139–229.

[22]See, for example, Pheme Perkins, "Christology and the Resurrection," *Christology in Dialogue,* ed. Robert Berkey and Sarah Edwards (Cleveland: The Pilgrim Press, 1993) 173–81.

people of God—the people of the new age—the inheritors of this kingdom, those who believe in Jesus Christ.

b. The response of faith among the first disciples. What was the faith response of the first disciples to this definitive revelation by God through Jesus Christ and the Holy Spirit? We have seen something of earlier or less definitive faith responses to God's stages of revelation. Here we can speak briefly of the object of this faith, and its basis. *What* the first disciples believed was what God declared, namely that Jesus was both Messiah and Lord, and God's gift of the kingdom came through him, as we expressed above. Thus they had a more profound personal knowledge of Jesus than they had had previously and a more profound trust in him and commitment to him, or discipleship. They penetrated God's saving design and who Jesus was in a definitively Christian manner by their faith response. This faith was also a conversion by which they turned away from their earlier inadequate belief, which had been shattered, and an acceptance of the costs of discipleship, costs they continued to bear.

How did this come about? It came through the appearances of the risen Jesus to them and their reception of the Holy Spirit. We can look upon the appearances as both God's symbolic act that mediated revelation and as evidence or grounds for belief. The experience of the appearances give them an experience of God's symbolic act by which he expressed his message and his love, and also appealed to their desire for truth and the good, or fulfillment and liberation. With the gift of the Spirit their subjectivity was co-constituted by God, so that they could indwell what was revealed, their imagination be profoundly touched, their affectivity powerfully enlivened and raised. They could then give priority to Jesus as Lord and to the apocalyptic kingdom over their previous acceptance of Jesus as Messiah and the kingdom as messianic. Whereas previously they had accepted only a part of the divine design and revelation, now they were empowered to accept it integrally and wholistically, not denying what they had previously accepted but subsuming that within this definitive revelation.

The appearances can also be looked upon as *grounds* for their belief. They did not believe without reason. It would simply be bias without basis and counter to what the apostles claim for historians of our time to think them untouched by the need of critical reason. The change in the apostles from a shattered belief to a new and unshakable belief was not magical; counter to much modern naturalistic explanation of the emergence of their belief, it was due to these appearances. The appearances were evidence for them, or grounds for them, that God *did* reveal what he declared, namely that Jesus was Messiah and Lord.

It is true that the apostles were in a privileged position when compared with those who were called to believe through their testimony. The evangelists recognized this, though paradoxically they also recounted Christ's words: "Blessed are those who have not seen and have believed" (John 20:29). Counter to what some people influenced by a democratic view think, namely that all should be in the same situation as regards the bases for faith, their special position and responsibilities as apostles (and this includes a number of women) show this to be appropriate. However, their growth in this definitive Christian faith made great room for their continued discovery, because the enormous implications of this revelation were not initially spelled out. They had to risk articulation of these implications for belief and action in their own words and decisions, though under the influence of the Spirit, whom Jesus sent to teach them and remind them of what he had said (John 14:26). As we see from the varied theologies of the apostolic age, the revelation did not deaden but rather stimulated their creative imaginations.

c. How did the apostles mediate this revelation to others? We have examined this previously through a study of Acts 2, but it is important for us to reflect on it briefly once more because there is much that is similar between the way we now receive Christian revelation and the way the hearers of the apostolic preaching received it. The apostles conveyed God's revelation through external mediation analogous to that of Jesus and to which the internal gift of the Holy Spirit was added. And the people received it through sharing in the religious experience of the apostles, through the grounds of faith that they were given, and through openness to conversion.

The apostles and others proclaimed what they believed, and they witnessed to how Jesus had conveyed this to them. They witnessed through their words but also by their deeds, because they witnessed by their lives, which they put at the risk of being ostracized and outlawed because of their witness. They witnessed by their deeds of caring, their healings, their care for the poor. Thus as Jesus had conveyed God's revelation by symbolic words and deeds, so too did those who proclaimed the message in the apostolic age. The spirit in which the apostles proclaimed the good news is beautifully made their own by the fathers of Vatican II, who borrowed from John to quote in the prologue to *Dei verbum:*

> What was from the beginning, what we have heard, what we have seen with our eyes, what we looked upon and touched with our hands concerns the Word of life—for the life was made visible; we have seen it and testify to it and proclaim to you the eternal life that was with the Father and was made visible to us—what we have seen and heard we proclaim now to you, so that you too may have fellowship with us; for our fellowship is with the Father and with his Son, Jesus Christ. We are writing this so that our joy may be complete (1 John 1:1-4).

The apostles appealed to a hunger in people that they knew because they had experienced it, and they had experienced Jesus to be the answer. To their proclamation there was given by God an interior illumination and drawing that came from the Holy Spirit, without which sharing in the religious experience of Jesus through the mediation of the apostles was not possible and with which the people were able to, as it were, indwell the new communion offered to them through the belief to which they were invited. The apostles appealed to the people's desire for God's word and salvation; they communicated by their whole persons and sought to convey a personal knowledge of Jesus.

The people's response was made possible by this, because through this testimony the message of salvation was offered them, and their subjectivity was co-constituted by God so that they were able to *taste* the gift they were offered. They were offered a participatory and transforming personal knowledge of Jesus. They were also offered grounds for what they were called to believe through the testimony of the apostles, so that their faith was not an abdication of intelligence. This was "dependent" revelation as distinct from the "foundational" revelation given the apostles (a theme we will return to below),[23] because it was mediated to them by the apostolic proclamation. But it did convey to those who believed a personal knowledge of Jesus analogous to that of those who had experienced Jesus

---

[23]See Gerald O'Collins, "Revelation, Past and Present," *Retrieving Fundamental Theology* (New York: Paulist Press, 1993) 87–97.

more immediately. Their belief came through conversion and it was expressed by ritual—baptism and the Eucharist, by confession with the lips (Rom 10:9-10), and by the life of discipleship. It gave them entrance into the community of the new people of God, as inheritors of the promise.

III. Further Notes on Revelation and Faith in the Context of Our Time

We wish now in conclusion to reflect briefly on some characteristics of Christian revelation and faith in the context of our time. This does not aim at completeness, because the theme of faith and revelation comes up in different parts of theology, for example, in the treatment of Christology, the Church, theological anthropology or grace, the Trinity, and eschatology. We shall reflect on the act of revelation, the comparison between the revelation that comes to us and that came to the apostles, the supernatural mystery that this revelation is, and its processive character. In this latter part we shall relate revelations found in non-Christian religions to our Christian revelation.

1. Christian Revelation, an Act of the Exalted and Earthly Christ

The distinctive act of Christian revelation, such as that which we see in Luke's account of Pentecost and Peter's proclamation that "God has made him [Jesus] both Lord and Messiah" (Acts 2:36), is an act of the exalted Christ as well as of the earthly Jesus. It is an act of Jesus who has risen from the dead and who has ascended to "the right hand of God" from where he sent his Holy Spirit upon the Church. It is a revelation not simply through the words and deeds of Jesus in his ministry, death, and resurrection appearances but through the gift of the Holy Spirit, because it is a revelation not simply of an intellectual content but of a personal knowledge of Jesus. This gift of the Spirit Jesus makes as exalted, that is, as having gone into the fullness of the kingdom. As we have said earlier, Jesus' salvation was expected to occur when he would come again, but the Church quickly realized that what he would do when he comes again he is already doing partially in the present. Similarly, we can say that the fullness of revelation was expected by the early Church to occur when Jesus would come again. But he is already revealing partially what he will reveal fully then, because the age to come is already dawning. That is, Jesus has gone into the fullness of our future, the kingdom of God, and from there he has sent his Spirit "to teach you everything and remind you of all that I told you" (John 14:26).

Christian revelation is indeed an act of God of some two thousand years ago through the Word made flesh. But it is not simply an act that occurred two thousand years ago. It is occurring now as an act of revelation or communication by Jesus Christ from the future kingdom. The Second Vatican Council did speak to this effect, for example, when it spoke of apostolic tradition poured out in the life and practice of the Church. By this same tradition "holy Scriptures themselves are more thoroughly understood and constantly actualized in the Church. Thus God, who spoke in the past, *continues to converse with the spouse of his beloved Son.* And the Holy Spirit, through whom the living voice of the Gospel rings out in the Church—and through her in the world—leads believers to the full truth, and makes the Word of God dwell in them in all its richness (cf. Col 3:16)" (*DV* 8).[24]

It is important to recall this in an age of historical consciousness, because it is at times a scandal for people today to think that they should turn back two thousand years to find the fullness of truth. People of our time are oriented toward the future and expect the fullness of truth to be found in the future. In answer to this, we must acknowledge that in part Christians have emphasized the past of revelation in an unbalanced way because they were proclaiming it to a traditional culture that looked to the past for its paradigms of life. But Christians expect the fullness of truth only in the future, when Jesus comes again, and they think that Jesus is conveying that truth in part to us now. As regards the intellectual content of this, he reveals through recalling what he told us while he walked on this earth, thus leading us to a deeper understanding of it. As regards the communication of personal knowledge of this, he does it by a present revelation through the Spirit.

2. A Comparison Between Christian Revelation as It Came to the First Disciples and as It Comes to Us

There is one sense in which Christian revelation was *immediate* to the first disciples and *mediated* to us. All knowledge of God we have

---

[24]See ibid.

in this world is mediated to us, but for the first disciples Christian revelation was mediated by the words and deeds of Jesus that they directly experienced, whereas for us it comes only through the testimony of those first disciples and particularly of the apostles. So as regards the *content* of revelation, we receive it only through the mediation of the proclamation of the early Church, first through words and deeds and then also through the writing down of this message in Scripture and continuing apostolic tradition. But there is another sense in which Christian revelation comes to us as immediately as it does to the first disciples, because this revelation as address, encounter, engaging us, inner illumination and drawing, and communication of personal knowledge of God is mediated by the Holy Spirit; and the Holy Spirit is as immediately present to us as she was to all those disciples gathered in the upper room on Pentecost. Thus we should say that Christian revelation continues after the apostolic age.[25]

As regards the content, we must say with the Church that there is no more public Christian revelation given since the apostolic age that we are called to receive. What was to come in the future was a deepening understanding of what Jesus had revealed, not a new revelation; Jesus himself was the final revelation, *the* Word of God made flesh, the completion of God's earlier revelations. Jesus did not look forward to another who would bring humankind further knowledge of God and his ways. Jesus is the perfect revelation of the Father. He tells Philip, "Whoever has seen me has seen the Father" (John 14:9). We may add, with Gerald O'Collins and others, that it seems better to say that foundational revelation was completed by the end of the apostolic age (about A.D. 100) rather than at the initial coming of the Holy Spirit after the resurrection. Though the *external events* through which Christian revelation was conveyed were completed by then (see *DV* 4), the Church was "built upon the foundation of the apostles and prophets, with Christ Jesus himself as the capstone" (Eph 2:20). As the apostolic preaching contained in a special way in the canonical writings of the New Testament is normative for the later Church (*DV* 8), the interpretations of the deeds and words of Jesus found in these books are also part of the Church's foundational revelation, and

---

[25]As Avery Dulles points out, this is in accord with the use of the word "revelation" during the patristic and medieval periods. See Dulles, "Faith and Revelation," *Systematic Theology: Roman Catholic Perspectives,* ed. Francis Schüssler Fiorenza and John P. Galvin (Minneapolis: Fortress Press, 1991) 1:101–4.

so it is best to say that this revelation was completed during the apostolic age rather than earlier.

While the specifically Christian revelation was completed in the above sense in the apostolic age, other revelations continue to be made to us, and they affect the way we interpret Christian revelation. Modern physical sciences have given us insights into the physical world that we can ascribe to God and call his revelations, and these affect the way we interpret Christian revelation's message about creation. We can say something analogous about the insights given to us by the modern human sciences such as psychology, anthropology, and history. And again we can say something similar to this about the insights given us by world religions of Asia. Perhaps Pope John XXIII's and Vatican II's use of the term "signs of the times" reflects this, and so our interpretation of the Christian revelation is appropriately historically conditioned. In our first volume we sought to integrate some of these insights into our interpretation of the Christian understanding of God, the human person, and their interrelation. At times the Church has resisted an incorporation of these new revelations into an understanding of the Christian mystery. Fundamentalism continues to resist such incorporation.

3. Christian Revelation as a Supernatural Mystery

The Church speaks of Christian revelation as a supernatural mystery, as when in Vatican I it taught that "it pleased his [God's] wisdom and goodness to reveal himself and the eternal decrees of his will to the human race by another and supernatural way."[26] As we mentioned earlier in speaking of the message Jesus revealed, the word "mystery" here does not mean some additional fact to our human knowledge, such as the number of galaxies there are. It is rather God's loving, free, and unpredictable offer of salvation to us and thus too something of who God is (Eph 1:9; 3:4, 9), conveyed to us as personal knowledge of God in faith. It is appropriately called supernatural, because this gift that is revealed, and God as the giver, is totally beyond our human rights, capacities, and exigencies as creatures. It is supernatural not only in its content or message but in the way this revelation is offered to us, namely through the Word made flesh and through the Holy Spirit. Indeed, it is God's own self-gift to us.

[26]DS 3004.

Two bases for modern objection to the call to believe a supernatural mystery are the following. *First,* it may appear to some to be an arbitrary demand that we accept as an irrational proposition. However, while this objection may be in accord with an Enlightenment view of reason, such an interpretation of reason is itself historically conditioned. "Reason" is part of us as persons, and one is not a full or liberated person if one is not able to open oneself up to another person, and above all to the Other who is the personal God. We cannot live as persons unless we can open ourselves to what another person reveals to us, to a personal mystery that initially was veiled and then was unveiled *(a-lētheia)* to us, even though this may challenge our earlier presuppositions. We need to allow ourselves to be open to what does not fall within our present criteria rather than to consider "reason" as it is presently formed within us as static and irreformable.[27] Even science has to allow itself to be open to new paradigms. God, who revealed to us through intimations of conscience and the wonders of the physical world, can freely grace us with further revelations of his way of saving us and his own love and being. As we have shown previously, he can give us basis for accepting such further revelations as coming from him.

Second, some people have interpreted a "supernatural" revelation as a new layer of reality added somewhat arbitrarily to our own nature and thus as somewhat irrelevant to our human desire. We acknowledge that God's gift has been presented in theology and catechesis at times in a way that would justify such an interpretation. In part this has been due to the way Neoplatonism has influenced the context in which theology interrelated the Christian mysteries and our humanity. This "emanationist" interpretation of creation as cascades of different levels of being that come from God has led to a viewing of grace as a new nature given to human beings rather than primarily as God's gift of personal communion with himself or, even more, God's self-gift to us. Also it has seemed to foster a return to God in a vertical way that discounts the importance of our historical future.

In this volume we have interpreted the gifts of salvation and revelation within an apocalyptic context. Revelation, like salvation, comes to us now from the future, because it comes to us from Jesus, who has gone into the fullness of the kingdom, from where he has sent his Spirit to lead us into all truth. The transcendence we are

[27]On this see Schmitz, *La rivelazione,* 209–18.

called to accept through faith is an opening to an unknown but assured and promised future, as we see in the lives of the first disciples of Jesus, who went out into the whole world to proclaim him and to transform history.

4. Revelation as Processive and Non-Christian Religions

We have seen that Christian revelation is processive. God's larger economy of revelation is similarly processive, as has been constantly affirmed from the beginning of Christianity. Vatican II affirms this also. For example, it notes that "God, who creates and conserves all things by his Word (cf. John 1:3), provides men with constant evidence of himself in created realities (cf. Rom 1:19-20)" (*DV* 3). In our earlier volume we showed how God reveals through the witness of conscience and of the physical world.

Vatican II also taught that God revealed himself to our first parents, and after their sin promised redemption (Gen 3:15), and "has never ceased to take care of the human race. For he wishes to give eternal life to all those who seek salvation by patience in well-doing (Rom 2:6-7)" (*DV* 3). Here we can recognize Hebrew and Christian Scripture's affirmation of God's revelation to Noah (Heb 11:7) and his covenant with him and all his descendants. Here too we can refer to Vatican II's quotation from Irenaeus: "From the beginning, the Son, being present to his creation, reveals the Father to all whom the Father desires, at the time and in the manner desired by the Father" (*AG* 3 n. 2, from *Adv. Haer.* IV, 6, 7).

In a number of places Vatican II acknowledges "those elements of truth and grace which are found among peoples, and which are, as it were, a secret presence of God" (*AG* 9; see *LG* 8, 16, 17; *NA* 2). The council refers explicitly to preliterate religions, to Hinduism, and to Buddhism and declares that the Church "rejects nothing of what is true and holy in these religions. She has a high regard for the manner of life and conduct, the precepts and doctrines which . . . often reflect a ray of that truth which enlightens all men" (*NA* 2). And she recognizes that the Holy Spirit is frequently at work in a people before the Church comes to them (*AG* 4; *GS* 22), because God wants all to be saved. Though the council seems to be wary of saying God has revealed himself through world religions, this seems implicit in its teaching.

In our previous volume we gave specific attention to some elements of Buddhism and Hinduism, suggesting how we can discern

God making himself known in them, particularly as the Good beyond all transient goods and the dynamic power immanent in the world and in human beings, leading humankind to union with the Ultimate.[28] We found here dimensions of revelation and religious experience that Christian tradition has associated with the Holy Spirit under the term "appropriations," that is, as having a kinship with that perfection by which the First Person spirates the Holy Spirit (the absolute goodness of the Father) and that personal characteristic that constitutes the Holy Spirit (the dynamism of personal love).

Whereas the early Church in its movement toward the West found in Hellenism a presence of the Logos, or Word, and articulated the Christian message largely in relation to that, we suggested that it is not the Word so much as the Spirit and the goodness of the First Person that spirates this dynamic response of the Spirit, which Christianity finds as a *praeparatio evangelica* in much of Asia. A preparation for the mystery of the Logos is also found in the East, but perhaps more from the way the Spirit gives access to the Word rather than from the way the Word spirates the Spirit, more from the way an experiential knowledge (e.g., sensibilities shaped by family and nature) gives rise to ethical principles than from the way ethical principles give guidance for virtue. And for many in Asia the very paucity of the "Logos" or "Word" character in their native manifestations or revelations of divinity is experienced as an emptiness that shows the great value of the gospel.

While we must acknowledge God's revelation and grace present in these traditions of world religions, it is there within the economy of God's processive revelation and as a preparation for the gospel (*AG* 3) and needs to be purified, raised to a higher level, and perfected (*AG* 9). God's revelation is present in a way more closely related to Christianity in that people with whom God entered a special covenant to prepare for the coming of the Messiah, the Jews, and, we may add, in that people who claim descent from Abraham and the blessings and revelation God gave to his progeny, the Muslims (*NA* 3, 4).

---

[28]See Farrelly, *Belief in God,* 277–99. See also David Carpenter, "Revelation in Comparative Perspective: Lessons for Interreligious Dialogue," *Journal of Ecumenical Studies* 29 (1992) 175–88. He finds a similarity between revelation in Hindu tradition and that which comes through Wisdom in Scripture. Some theologians would like to reserve the word "revelation" for what occurs through Jesus Christ, but this restriction does not seem to be in accord with Scripture or with Vatican II's assertion that Jesus Christ completed God's revelation, and its quotation from Irenaeus.

We will not enter here into dialogue with the different ways theologians relate Christianity to world religions.[29] I propose that we are agreeing with Vatican II and Scripture in the way we interrelate them. We will simply note that much in Asian religions seems to be associated with a "primordial" revelation, and that now the peoples who are largely formed by these traditions are facing a universal world and one very oriented to the future through technology and world communications. Very many people find an enormous tension between their traditions and this larger and future world they must now address. As Christianity addresses them, one element we should bear in mind is that the revelation we proclaim is primarily an eschatological and even an apocalyptic revelation that comes to us now from the future as well as from the life, death, and resurrection of Jesus Christ. It comes to us from the exalted Christ and the Holy Spirit whom he has sent. This may be part of the context by which we can relate Christian revelation to these peoples in a way that acknowledges and incorporates the great and God-given riches of their traditions while still inviting them, in Christ's name, further.[30] In the great conflicts between forms of fundamentalism and conservatism and forms of liberalism, this approach can be a mediating strategy.

Finally, the Christian revelation we have received is ordained to a full self-revelation by Father, Son, and Holy Spirit and communion with the Trinity. It is ordained to the vision and glory that is promised us. Even though the revelation we now have is eschatological, it is partial. We are told by the author of 2 Peter that we do well to attend to the message given by Christ through the apostles: "You will do well to be attentive to it, as to a lamp shining in a dark place, until day dawns and the morning star rises in your hearts" (2 Pet 2:19). Even though we now have God's definitive revelation for us wayfarers, this revelation is like a lantern at midnight. It sheds enough light so that we know where next to place our feet, but how does it compare with the dawn? It leaves a lot of darkness. This is not a triumphalist passage. St. Paul says much the same:

[29]See, e.g., Gavin D'Costa, ed., *Christian Uniqueness Reconsidered: The Myth of a Pluralistic Theology of Religions* (Maryknoll, N.Y.: Orbis Books, 1990); Peter Phan, ed., *Christianity and the Wider Ecumenism* (New York: Paragon House, 1990); David Rausch and Carl Voss, *World Religions: Our Quest for Meaning* (Minneapolis: Fortress Press, 1989); "Theological Colloquium: Pune, India, August 1993," *Pro Dialogo* (1994/1) Bulletin 85–86.

[30]I have sought to make this interrelation briefly in "Notes on Mysticism in Today's World," *Spirituality Today* 43 (1991) 104–18.

> We know partially and we prophesy partially, but when the perfect comes, the partial will pass away. When I was a child, I used to talk as a child, think as a child, reason as a child; when I became a man, I put aside childish things. At present we see indistinctly, as in a mirror, but then face to face. At present I know partially; then I shall know fully, as I am fully known (1 Cor 13:9-12).

Mirrors at that time were not as they are today; they were burnished bronze and gave only an indistinct image. Christian revelation leaves God still largely unknown. If this is the case, we should welcome other lanterns God has given us in our dark place and other mirrors, without losing confidence that Jesus Christ and the Holy Spirit have given us God's definitive revelation.

Index of Principal Authors

Index of Subjects